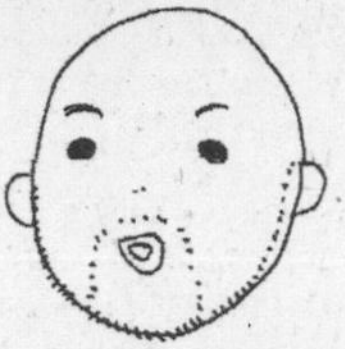

Takeshi Obata

People often tell me that my self-portrait looks too much like me or that it's scary, so I tried to draw a cute one.

—Takeshi Obata

It all began when Yumi Hotta played a pick-up game of go with her father-in-law. As she was learning how to play, Ms. Hotta thought it might be fun to create a story around the traditional board game. More confident in her storytelling abilities than her drawing skills, she submitted the beginnings of **Hikaru no Go** to **Weekly Shonen Jump**'s Story King Award. The Story King Award is an award that picks the best story, manga, character design and youth (under 15) manga submissions every year in Japan. As fate would have it, Ms. Hotta's story (originally named "***Kokonotsu no Hoshi***"), was a runner-up in the "Story" category of the Story King Award. Many years earlier, Takeshi Obata was a runner-up for the Tezuka Award, another Japanese manga contest sponsored by **Weekly Shonen Jump** and **Monthly Shonen Jump**. An editor assigned to Mr. Obata's artwork came upon Ms. Hotta's story and paired the two for a full-fledged manga about go. The rest is modern go history.

HIKARU NO GO VOL. 20
SHONEN JUMP Manga Edition

STORY BY YUMI HOTTA
ART BY TAKESHI OBATA
Supervised by YUKARI UMEZAWA (5 Dan)

Translation & English Adaptation/Naoko Amemiya
English Script Consultant/Janice Kim (3 Dan)
Touch-up Art & Lettering/Inori Fukuda Trant
Design/Julie Behn
Editor/Gary Leach

VP, Production/Alvin Lu
VP, Sales & Product Marketing/Gonzalo Ferreyra
VP, Creative/Linda Espinosa
Publisher/Hyoe Narita

Published by VIZ Media, LLC
P.O. Box 77010
San Francisco, CA 94107

10 9 8 7 6 5 4 3 2 1
First printing, August 2010

www.viz.com

THE WORLD'S
MOST POPULAR MANGA
www.shonenjump.com

Hikaru no Go

20 The Young Lions

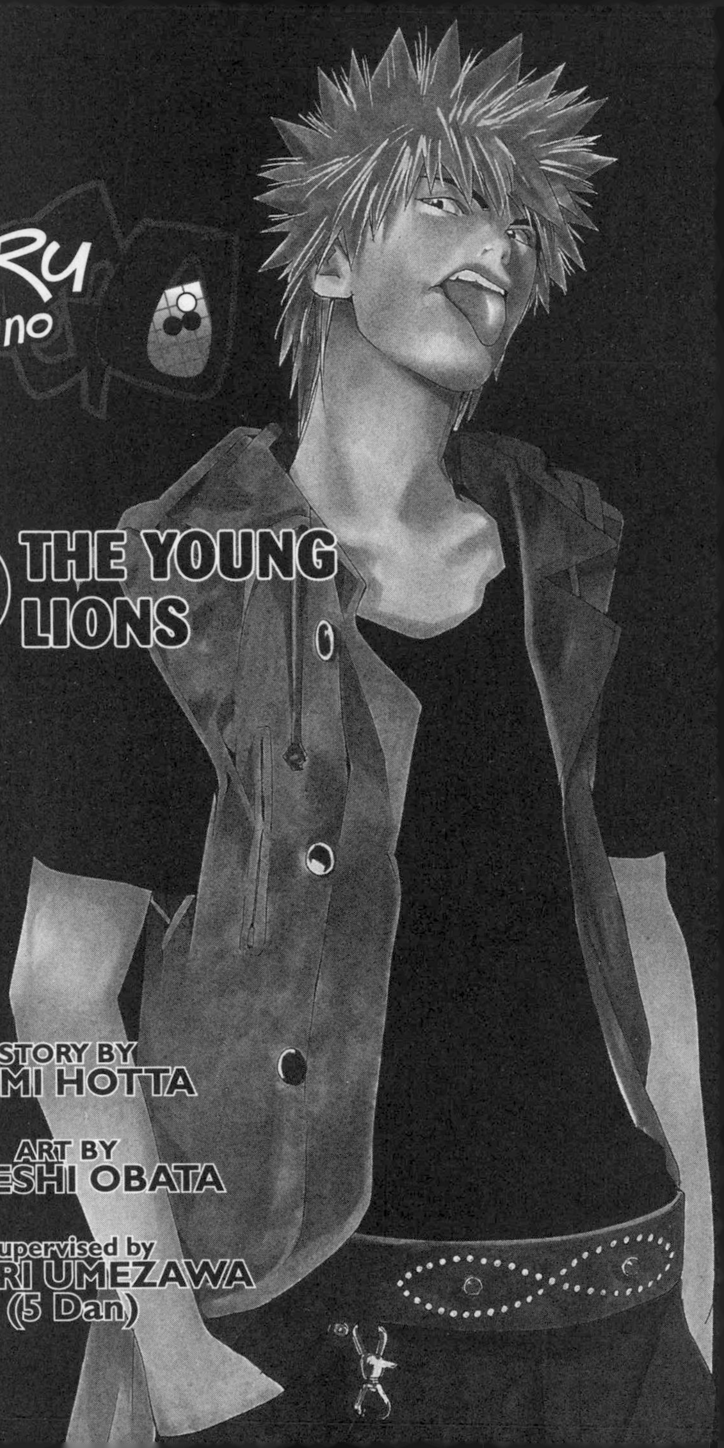

STORY BY
YUMI HOTTA

ART BY
TAKESHI OBATA

Supervised by
YUKARI UMEZAWA
(5 Dan)

CHARACTERS VOL.20

Shinichiro Isumi

Hikaru Shindo

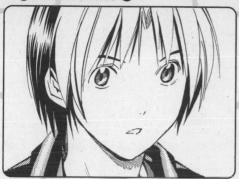

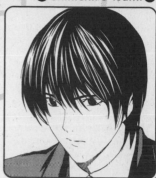

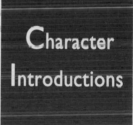

Character Introductions

Judan Ogata

Kosuke Ochi

Akira Toya

Yoshitaka Waya

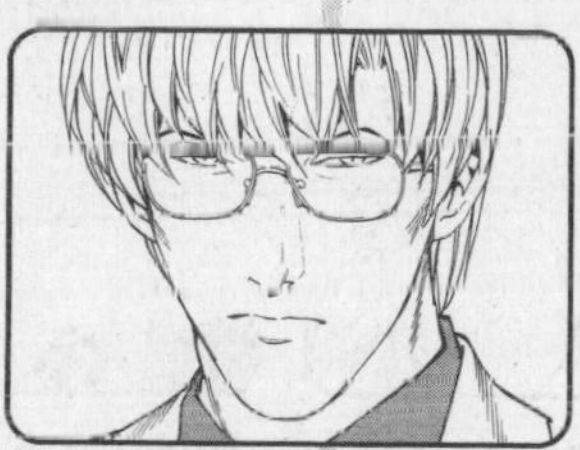

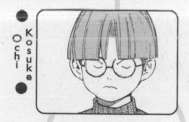

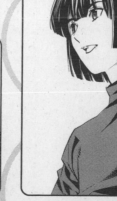

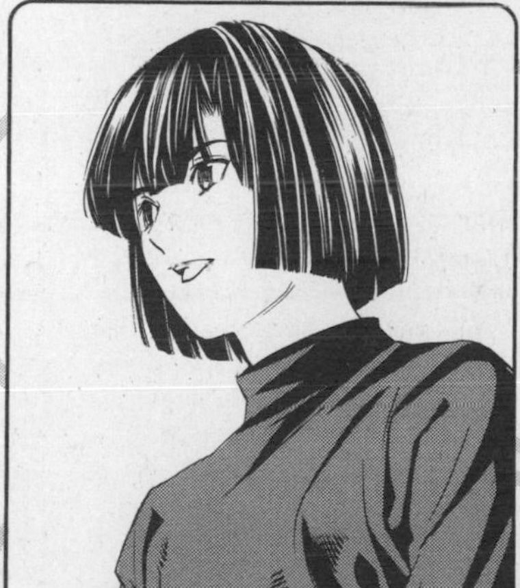

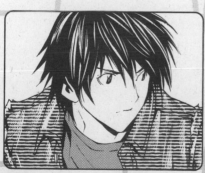

HIKARU NO GO

Story Thus Far

Hikaru Shindo discovers an old go board one day up in his grandfather's attic. The moment Hikaru touches the board, the spirit of Fujiwara-no-Sai, a genius go player from Japan's Heian Era, enters his consciousness. Sai's love of the game inspires Hikaru, as does a meeting with the child prodigy Akira Toya—son of go master Toya Meijin.

Hikaru turns pro and finally stands on the same playing field as Akira, slowly but surely improving his skills. Then he hears of an international team tournament for Japanese, Chinese, and Korean go players age 18 and under called the Hokuto Cup. Of the three places on the Japanese team, Akira has attained one, leaving two spots vacant. Hikaru puts more spirit into his training in preparation for the qualifying matches to be held in four months. In his first match against a high-ranking player, Hikaru faces Gokiso 7 dan, a man who disgraced the reputation of Hon'inbo Shusaku by passing off a fake signature as real. Hikaru defeats him with a calm, solid game of go. Then, on his way to the Japan Go Association to watch Isumi's Shinshodan match, Hikaru runs into Kadowaki, a player who passed the pro test this year along with Isumi. Having lost to Hikaru before, Kadowaki wants another chance to play him. The two sit down for a rematch. How will the game unfold…?!

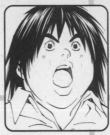
● Atsushi Kurata ●

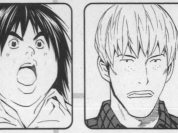
● Toshinori Honda ●

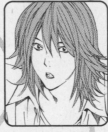
● Ko Yong Ha ●

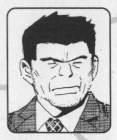
● Morishita 9 dan ●

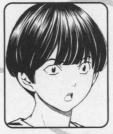
● Suyong Hong ●

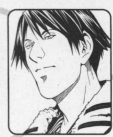
● Tatsuhiko Kadowaki ●

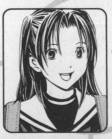
● Akari Fujisaki ●

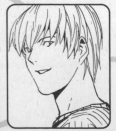
● Koji Saeki ●

CONTENTS

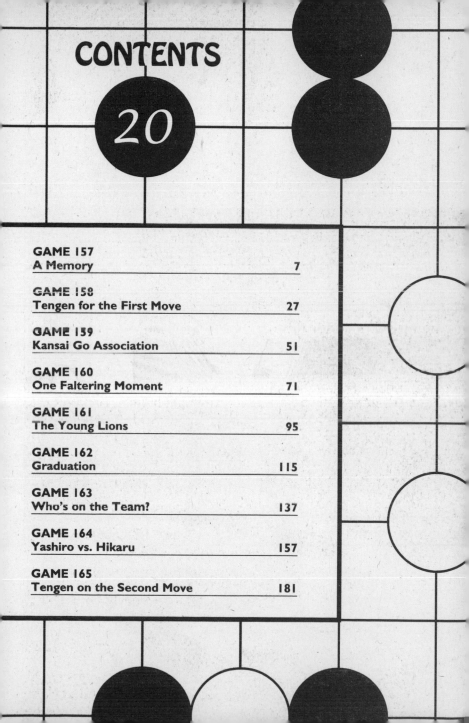

20

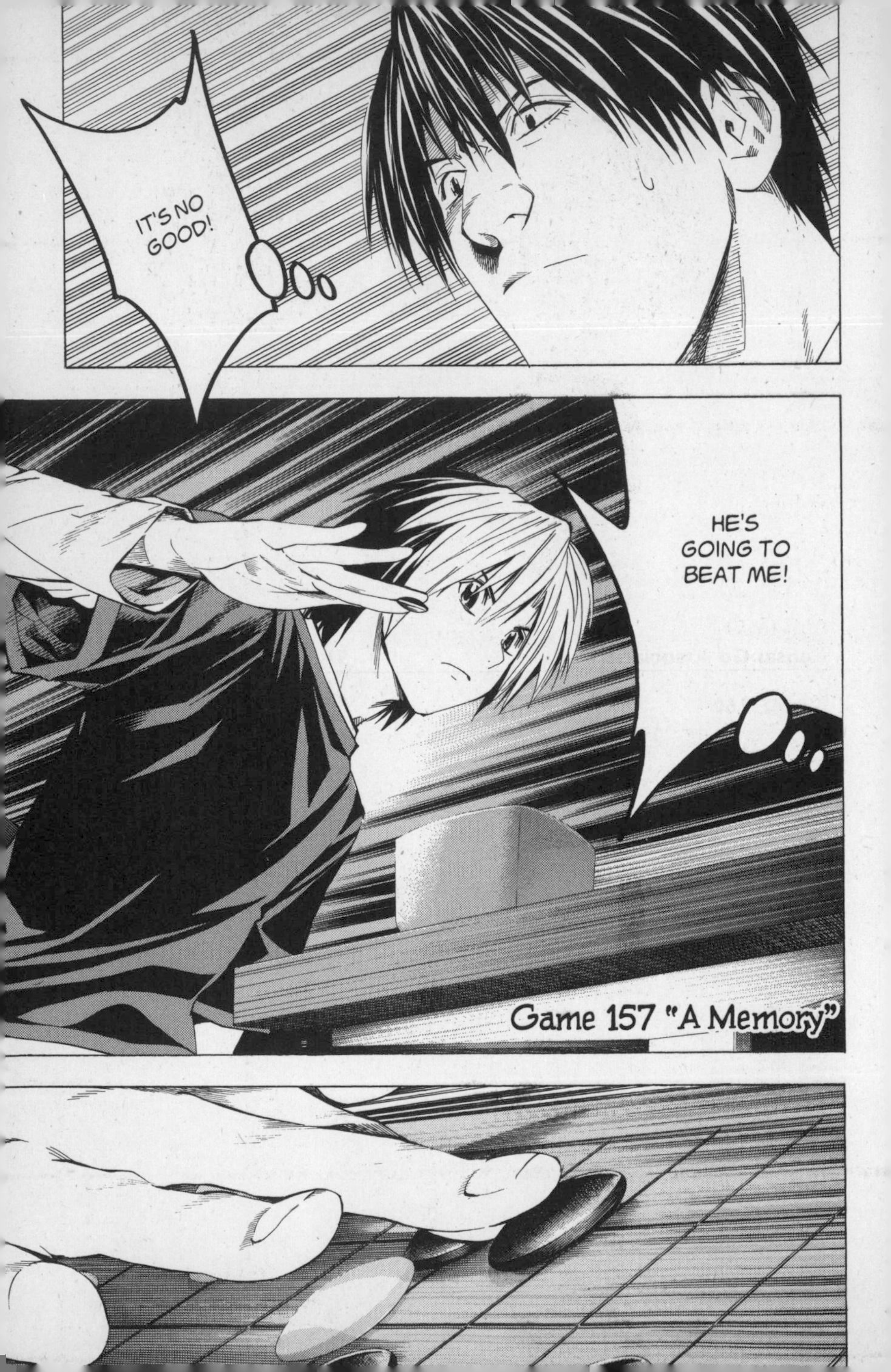
IT'S NO GOOD!
HE'S GOING TO BEAT ME!
Game 157 "A Memory"

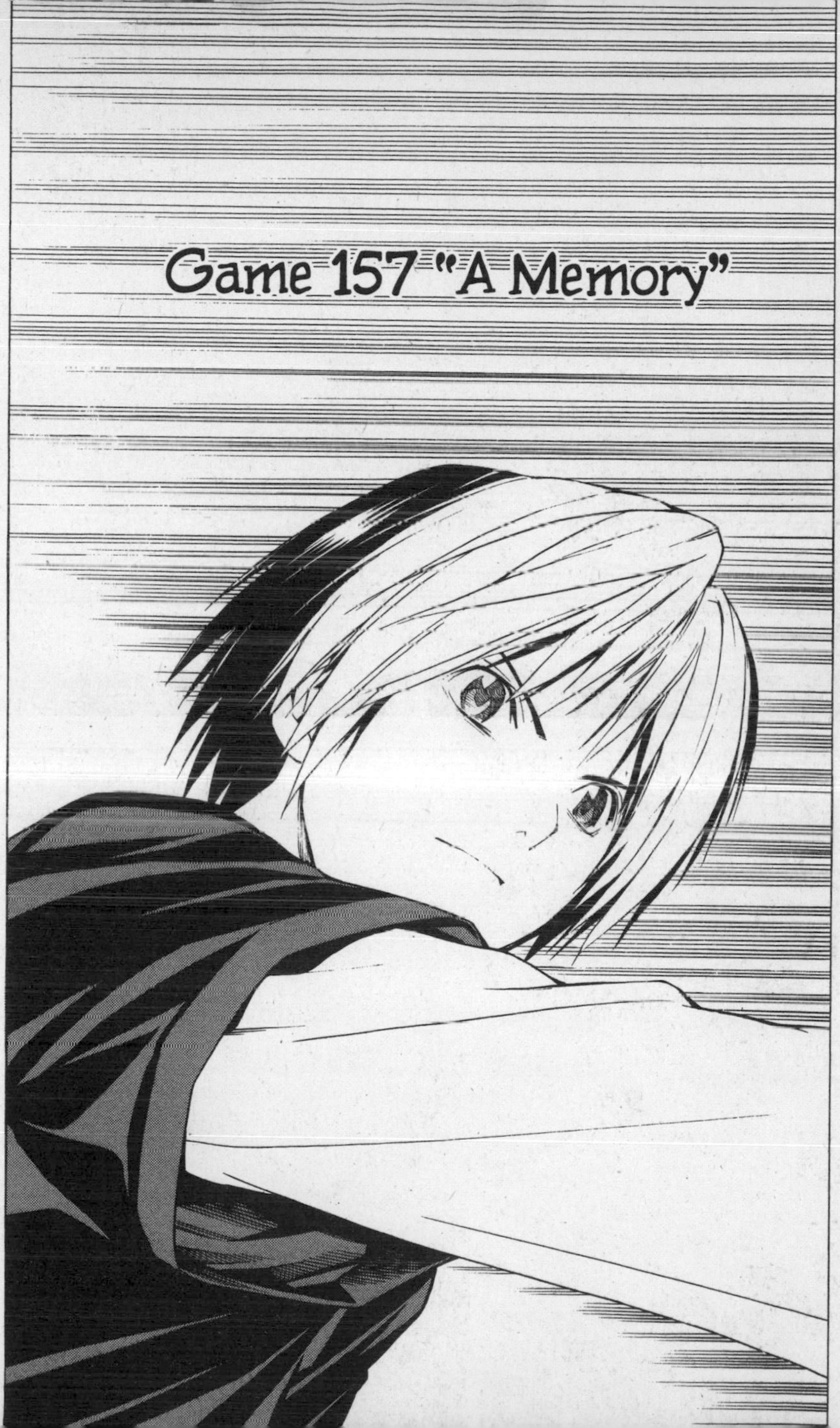
Game 157 "A Memory"

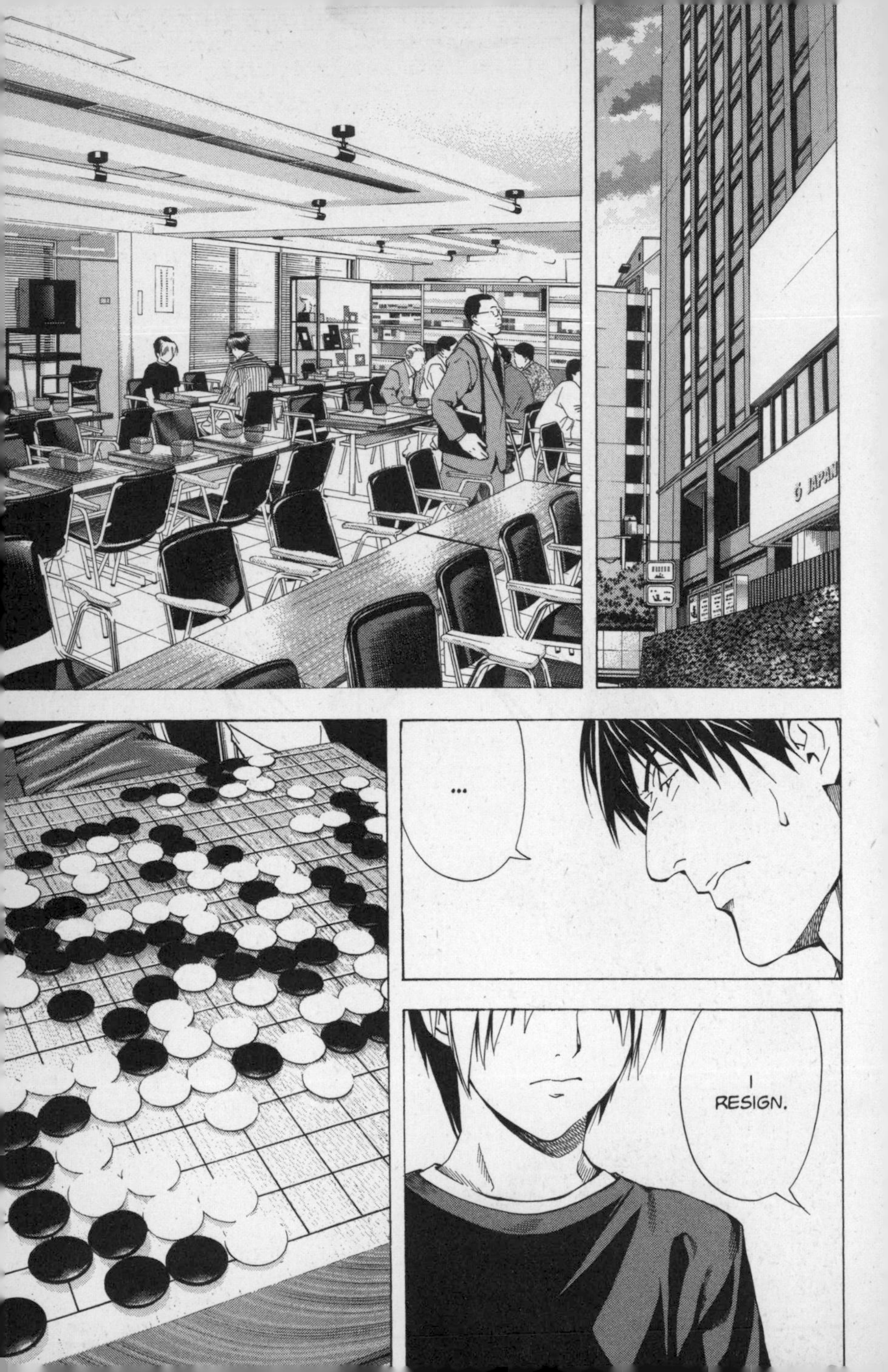
G JAPAN
...
I RESIGN.

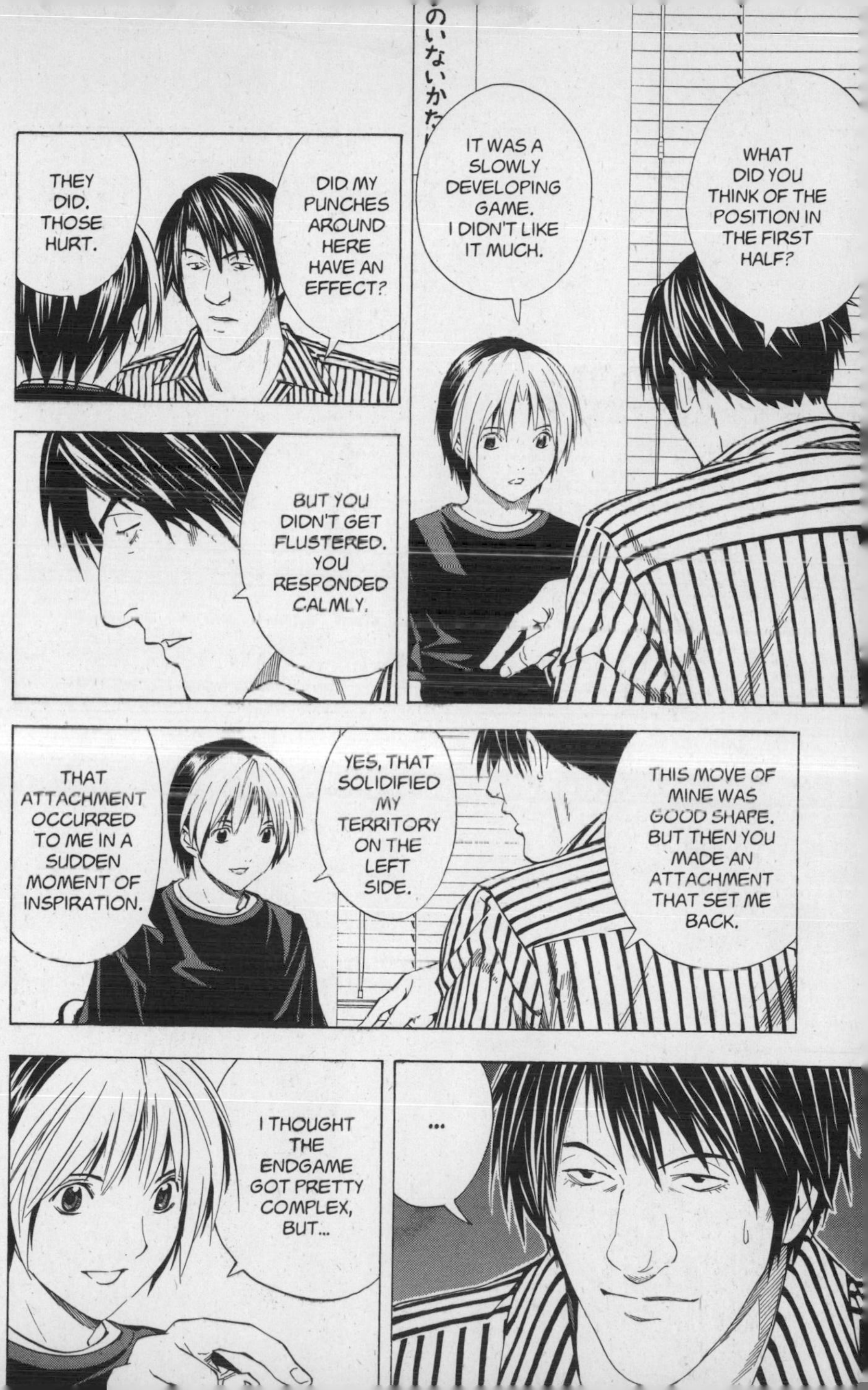
WHAT DID YOU THINK OF THE POSITION IN THE FIRST HALF?
IT WAS A SLOWLY DEVELOPING GAME. I DIDN'T LIKE IT MUCH.
DID MY PUNCHES AROUND HERE HAVE AN EFFECT?
THEY DID. THOSE HURT.
BUT YOU DIDN'T GET FLUSTERED. YOU RESPONDED CALMLY.
THIS MOVE OF MINE WAS GOOD SHAPE. BUT THEN YOU MADE AN ATTACHMENT THAT SET ME BACK.
YES, THAT SOLIDIFIED MY TERRITORY ON THE LEFT SIDE.
THAT ATTACHMENT OCCURRED TO ME IN A SUDDEN MOMENT OF INSPIRATION.
...
I THOUGHT THE ENDGAME GOT PRETTY COMPLEX, BUT...

READ THIS WAY

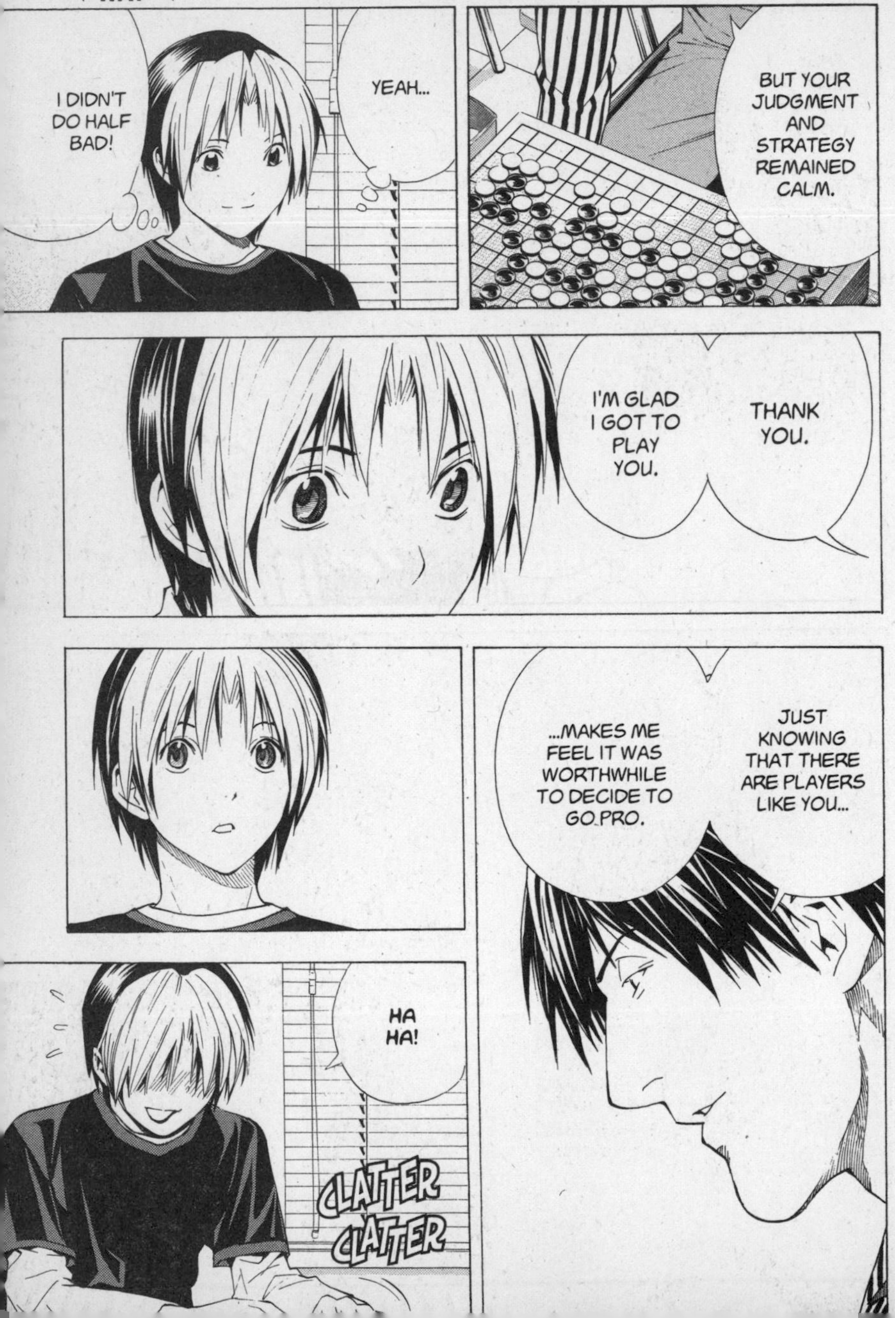
BUT YOUR JUDGMENT AND STRATEGY REMAINED CALM.
YEAH...
I DIDN'T DO HALF BAD!
THANK YOU.
I'M GLAD I GOT TO PLAY YOU.
JUST KNOWING THAT THERE ARE PLAYERS LIKE YOU...
...MAKES ME FEEL IT WAS WORTHWHILE TO DECIDE TO GO PRO.
HA HA!
CLATTER CLATTER

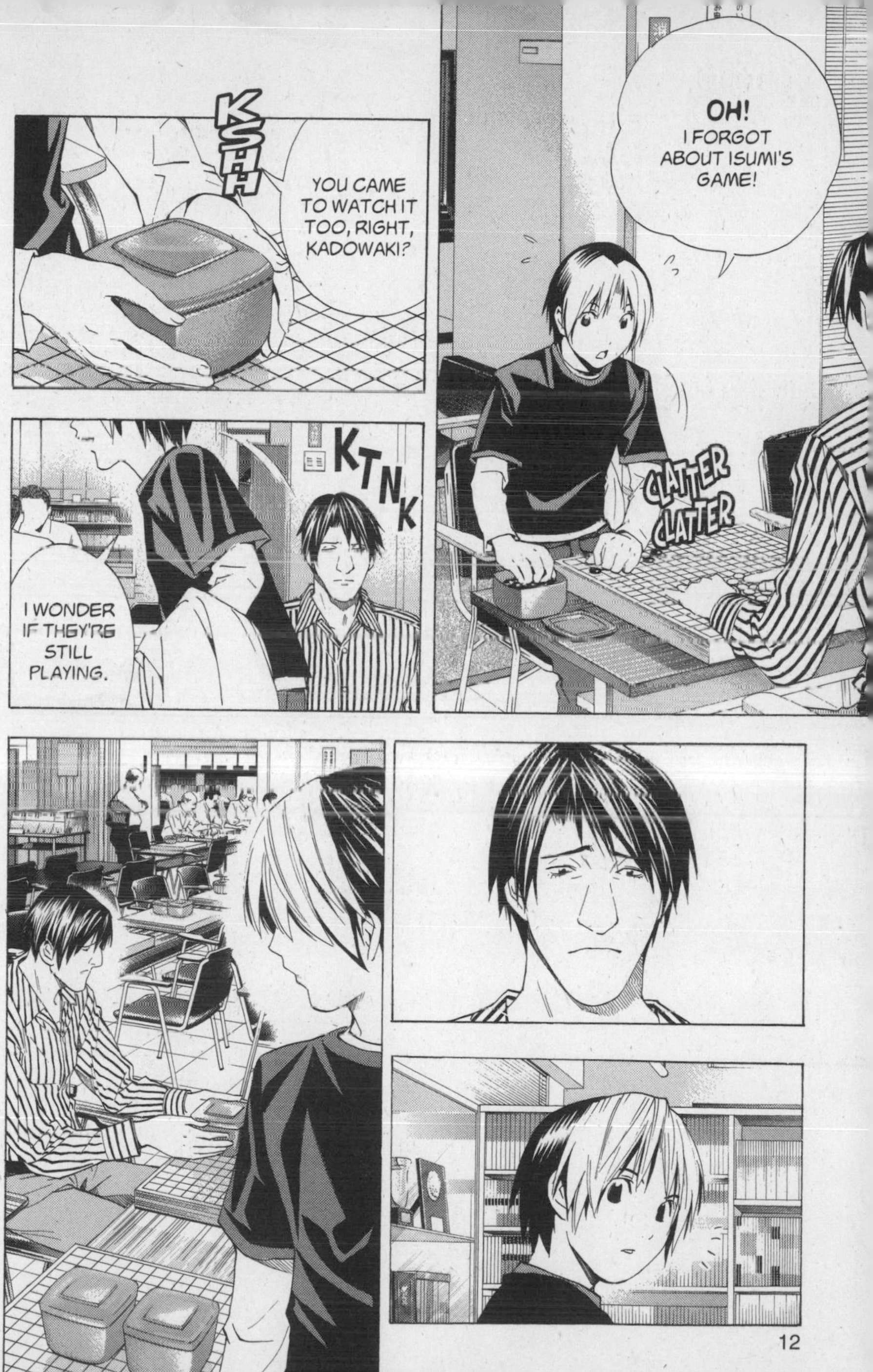
OH! I FORGOT ABOUT ISUMI'S GAME!
CLATTER CLATTER
KSHH
YOU CAME TO WATCH IT TOO, RIGHT, KADOWAKI?
KTNK
I WONDER IF THEY'RE STILL PLAYING.

READ THIS WAY

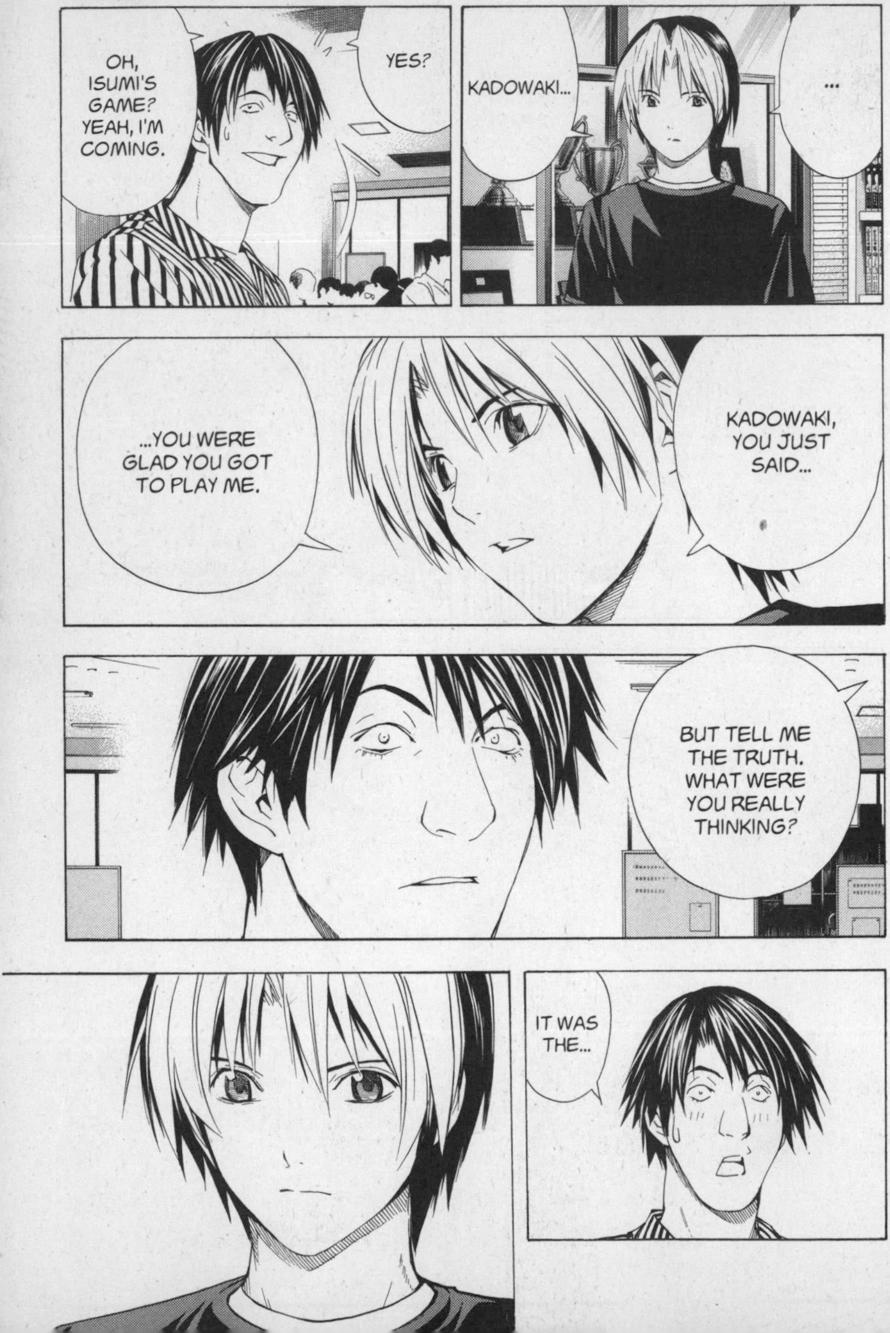
...
KADOWAKI...
YES?
OH, ISUMI'S GAME? YEAH, I'M COMING.
KADOWAKI, YOU JUST SAID...
...YOU WERE GLAD YOU GOT TO PLAY ME.
BUT TELL ME THE TRUTH. WHAT WERE YOU REALLY THINKING?
IT WAS THE...

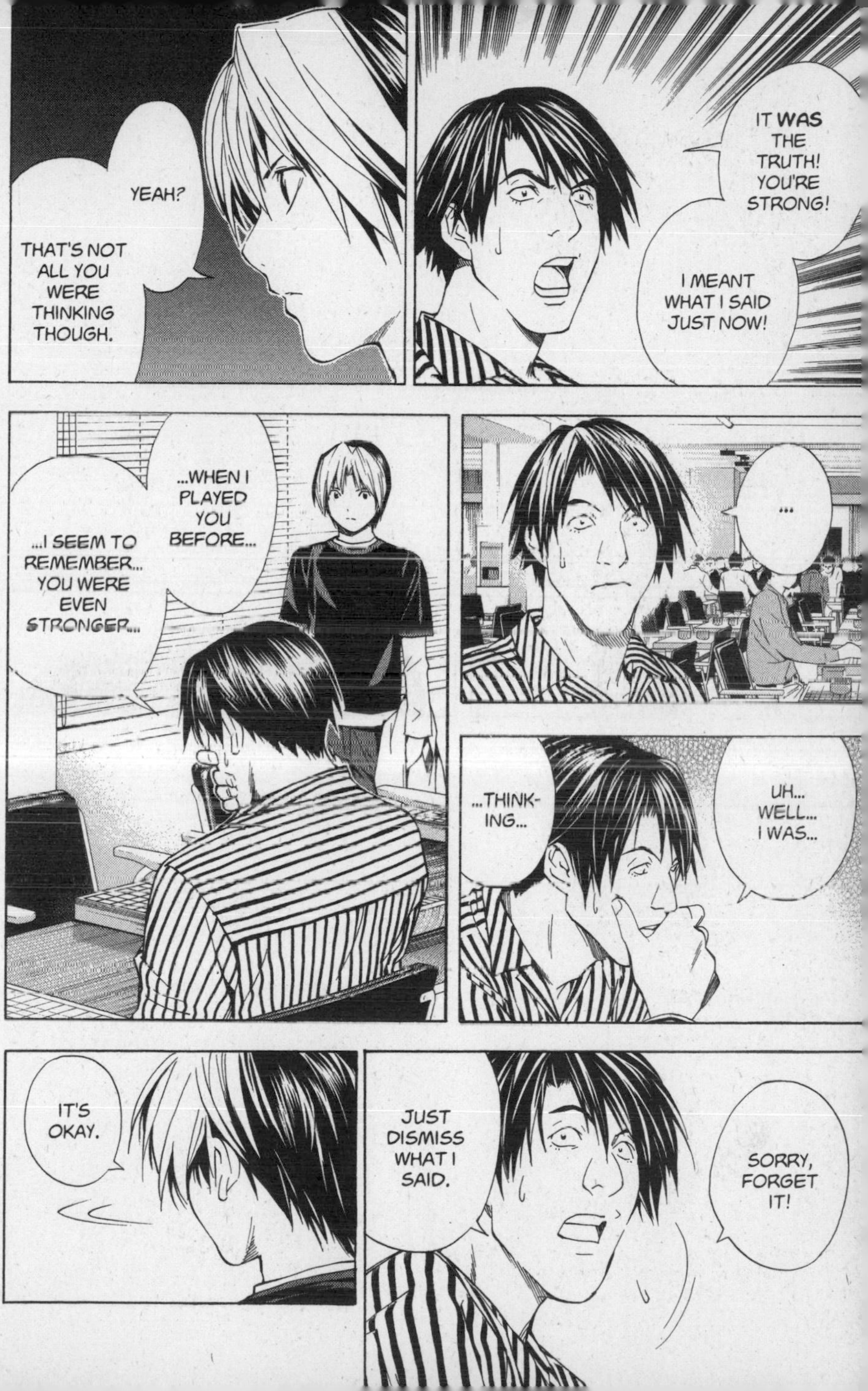
IT WAS THE TRUTH! YOU'RE STRONG!
I MEANT WHAT I SAID JUST NOW!
YEAH?
THAT'S NOT ALL YOU WERE THINKING THOUGH.
...
UH... WELL... I WAS...
...THINKING...
...WHEN I PLAYED YOU BEFORE...
...I SEEM TO REMEMBER... YOU WERE EVEN STRONGER...
SORRY, FORGET IT!
JUST DISMISS WHAT I SAID.
IT'S OKAY.

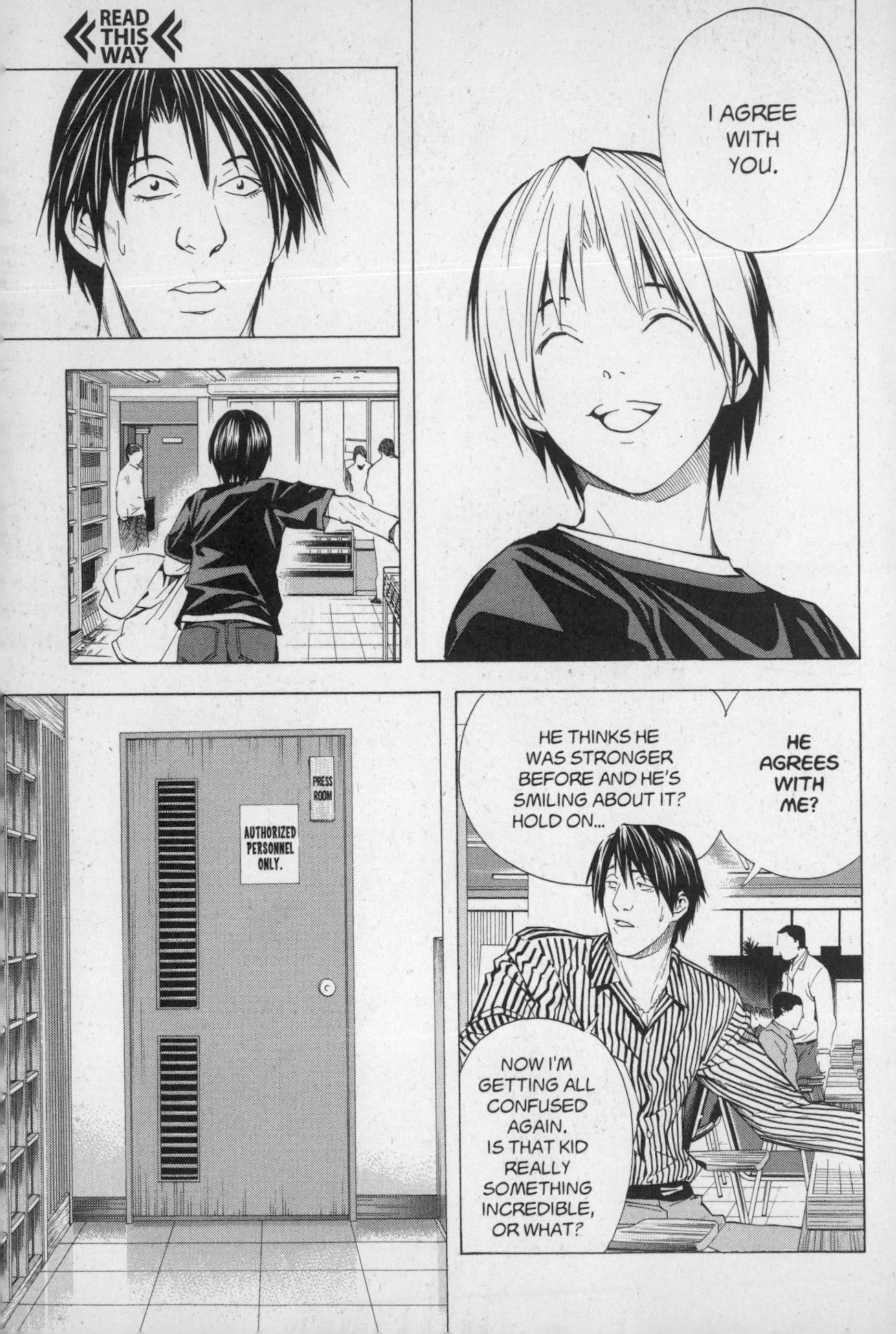
READ THIS WAY
I AGREE WITH YOU.
HE AGREES WITH ME?
HE THINKS HE WAS STRONGER BEFORE AND HE'S SMILING ABOUT IT? HOLD ON...
NOW I'M GETTING ALL CONFUSED AGAIN. IS THAT KID REALLY SOMETHING INCREDIBLE, OR WHAT?
PRESS ROOM
AUTHORIZED PERSONNEL ONLY.

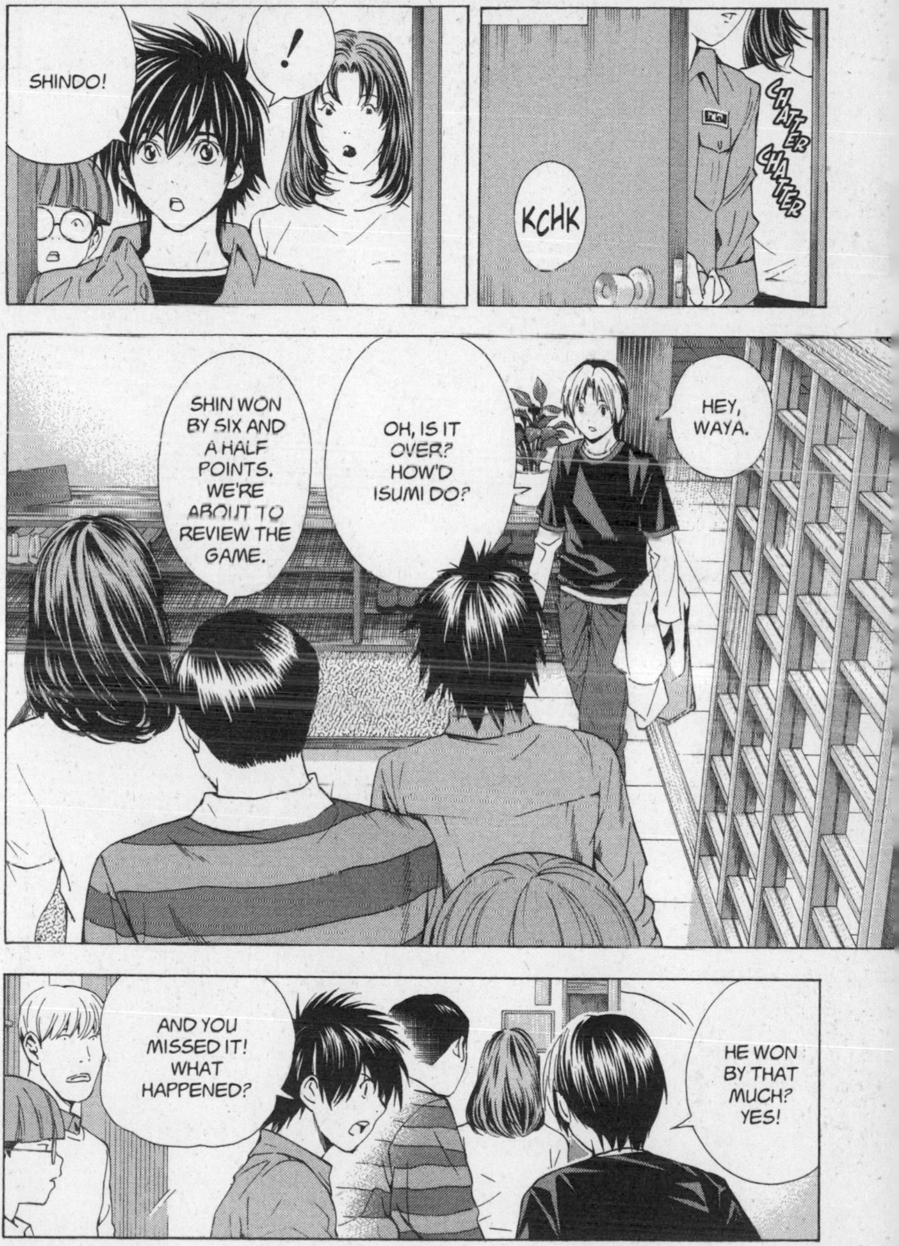
CHATTER CHATTER
KCHK
!
SHINDO!
HEY, WAYA.
OH, IS IT OVER? HOW'D ISUMI DO?
SHIN WON BY SIX AND A HALF POINTS. WE'RE ABOUT TO REVIEW THE GAME.
HE WON BY THAT MUCH? YES!
AND YOU MISSED IT! WHAT HAPPENED?

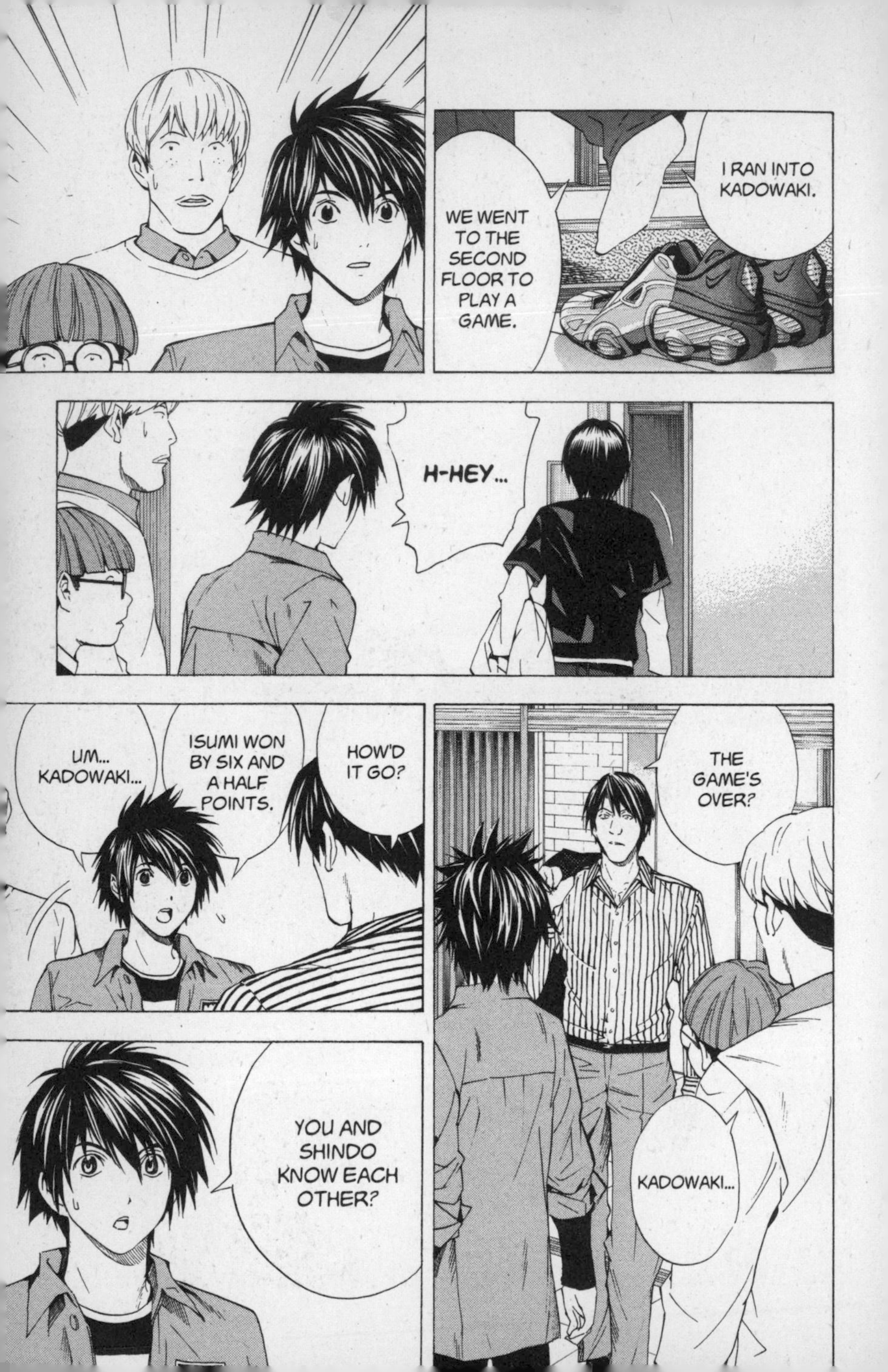
I RAN INTO KADOWAKI.
WE WENT TO THE SECOND FLOOR TO PLAY A GAME.
H-HEY...
THE GAME'S OVER?
KADOWAKI...
HOW'D IT GO?
ISUMI WON BY SIX AND A HALF POINTS.
UM... KADOWAKI...
YOU AND SHINDO KNOW EACH OTHER?

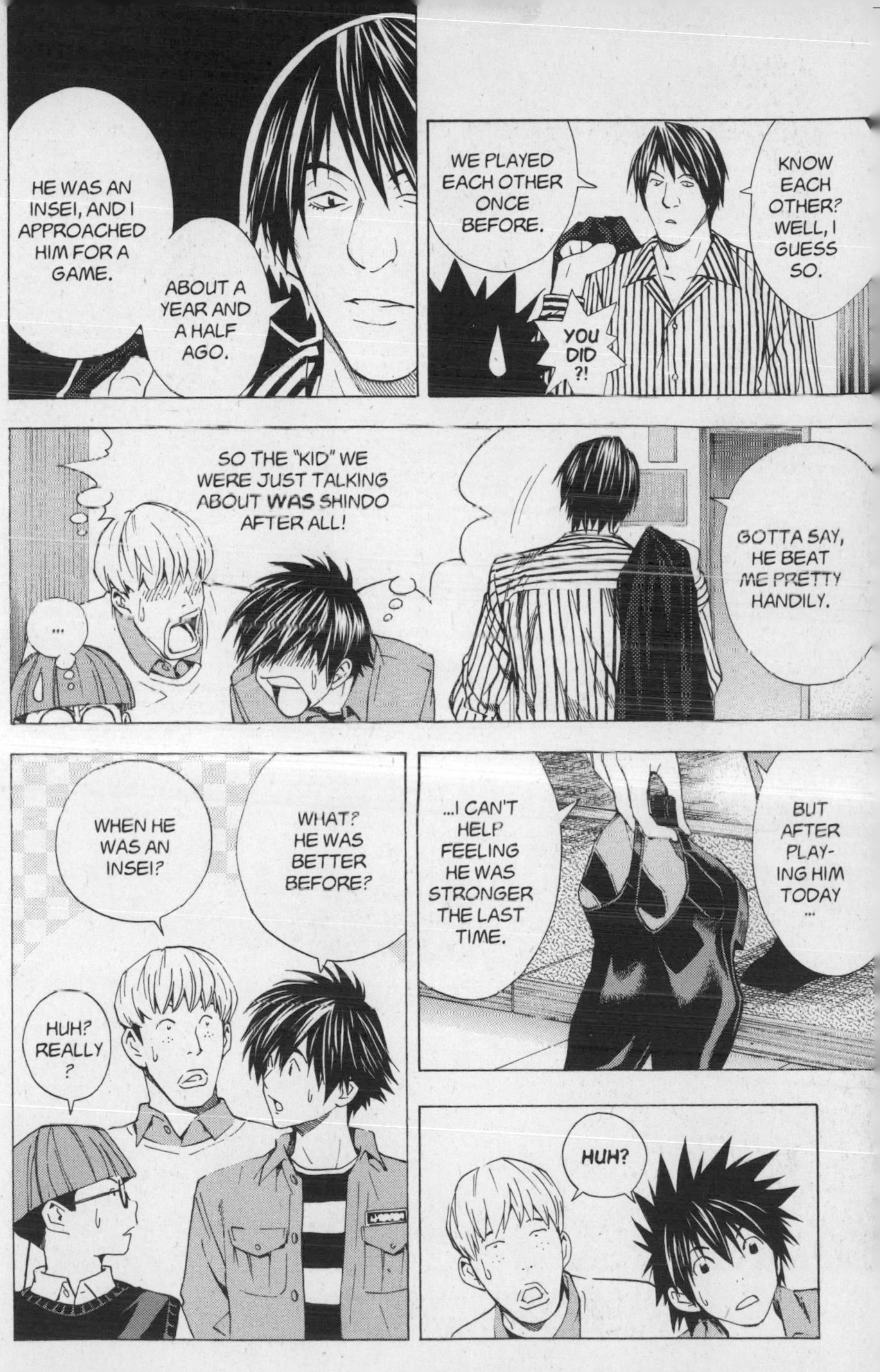
KNOW EACH OTHER? WELL, I GUESS SO.
WE PLAYED EACH OTHER ONCE BEFORE.
YOU DID ?!
HE WAS AN INSEI, AND I APPROACHED HIM FOR A GAME.
ABOUT A YEAR AND A HALF AGO.
GOTTA SAY, HE BEAT ME PRETTY HANDILY.
SO THE "KID" WE WERE JUST TALKING ABOUT WAS SHINDO AFTER ALL!
...
BUT AFTER PLAY-ING HIM TODAY ...
...I CAN'T HELP FEELING HE WAS STRONGER THE LAST TIME.
HUH?
WHAT? HE WAS BETTER BEFORE?
WHEN HE WAS AN INSEI?
HUH? REALLY ?

READ THIS WAY

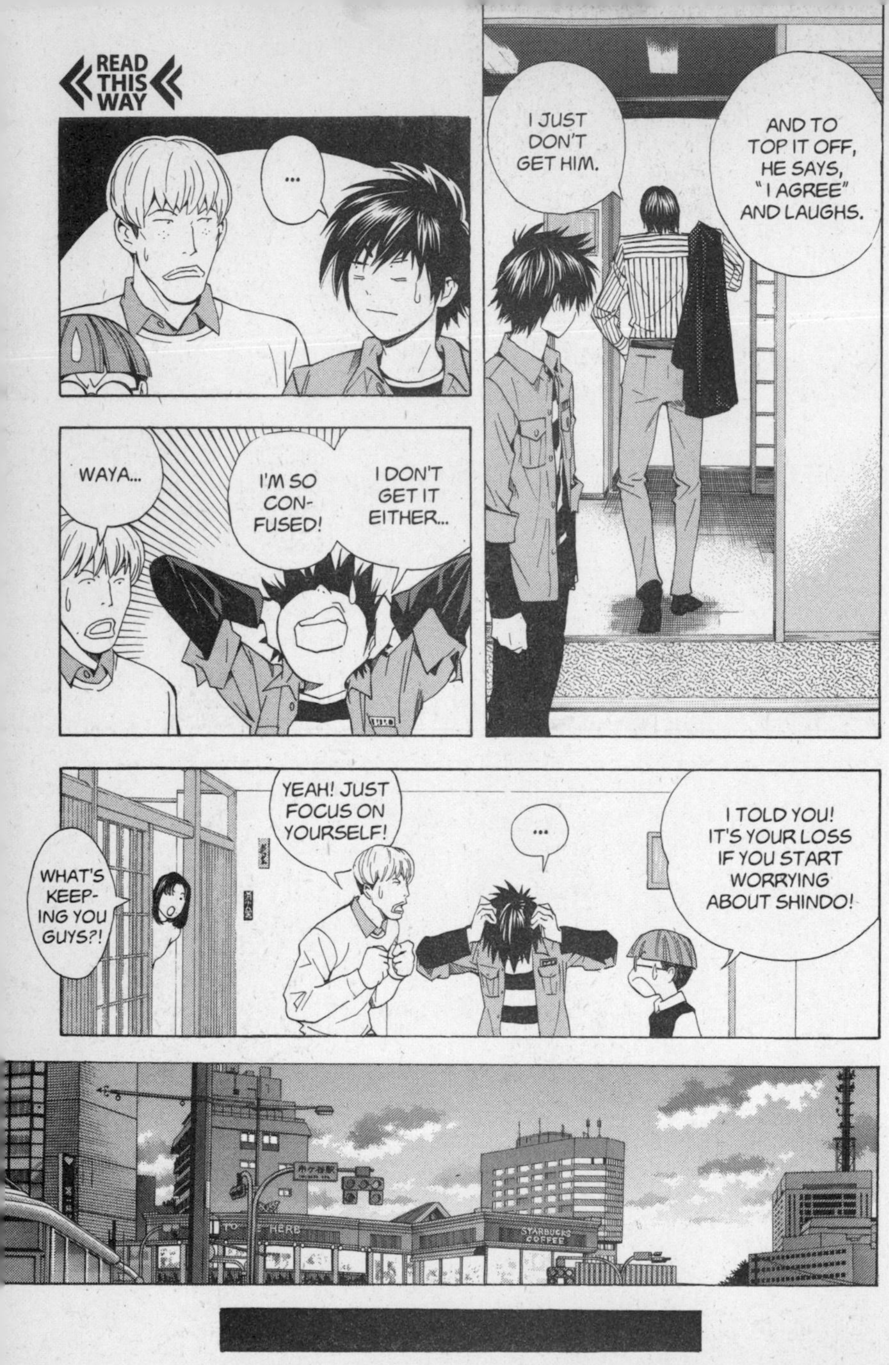
AND TO TOP IT OFF, HE SAYS, "I AGREE" AND LAUGHS.
I JUST DON'T GET HIM.
...
I DON'T GET IT EITHER...
I'M SO CON-FUSED!
WAYA...
I TOLD YOU! IT'S YOUR LOSS IF YOU START WORRYING ABOUT SHINDO!
...
YEAH! JUST FOCUS ON YOURSELF!
WHAT'S KEEP-ING YOU GUYS?!
STARBUCKS COFFEE

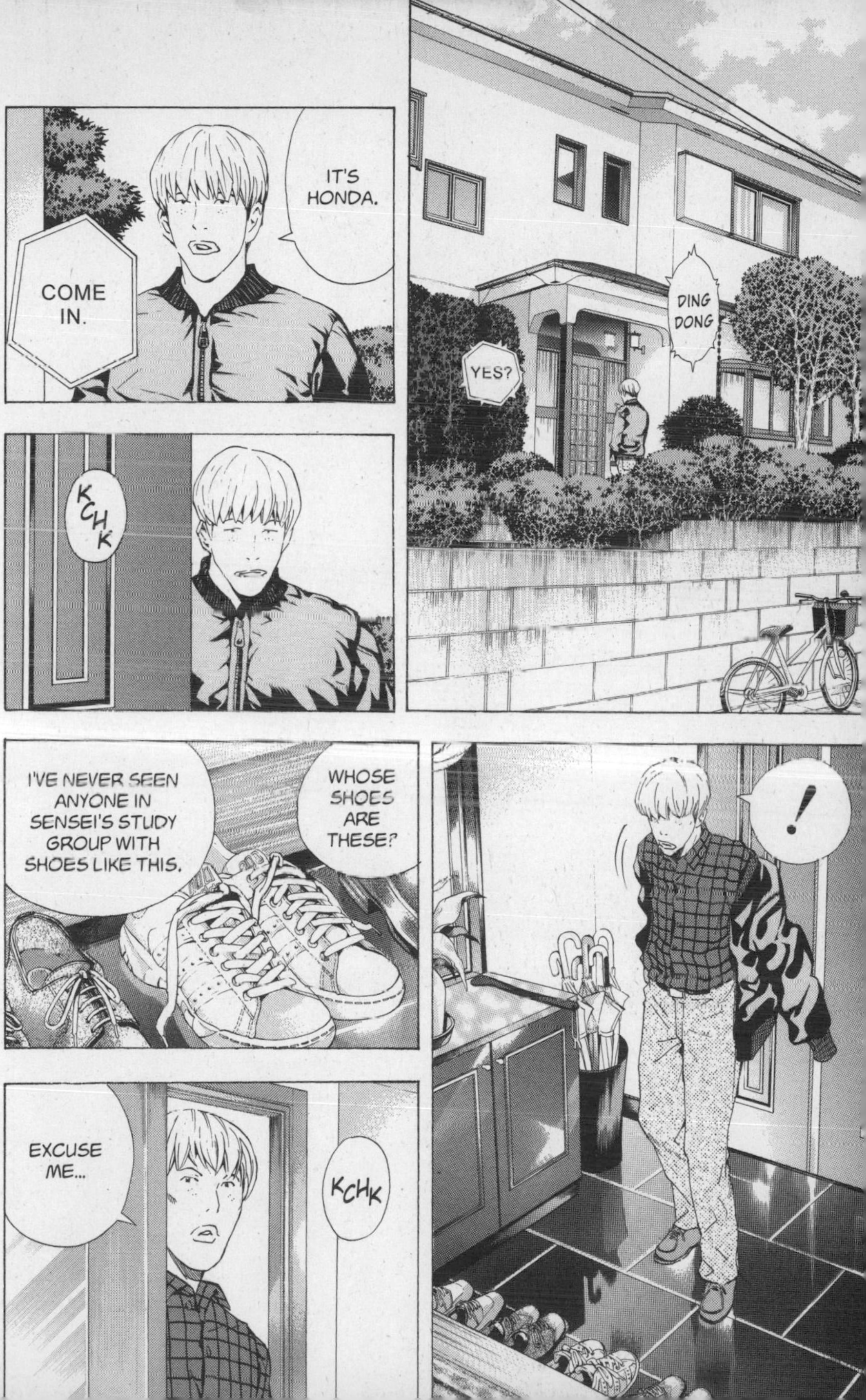
DING DONG
YES?
IT'S HONDA.
COME IN.
KCHK
!
WHOSE SHOES ARE THESE?
I'VE NEVER SEEN ANYONE IN SENSEI'S STUDY GROUP WITH SHOES LIKE THIS.
KCHK
EXCUSE ME...

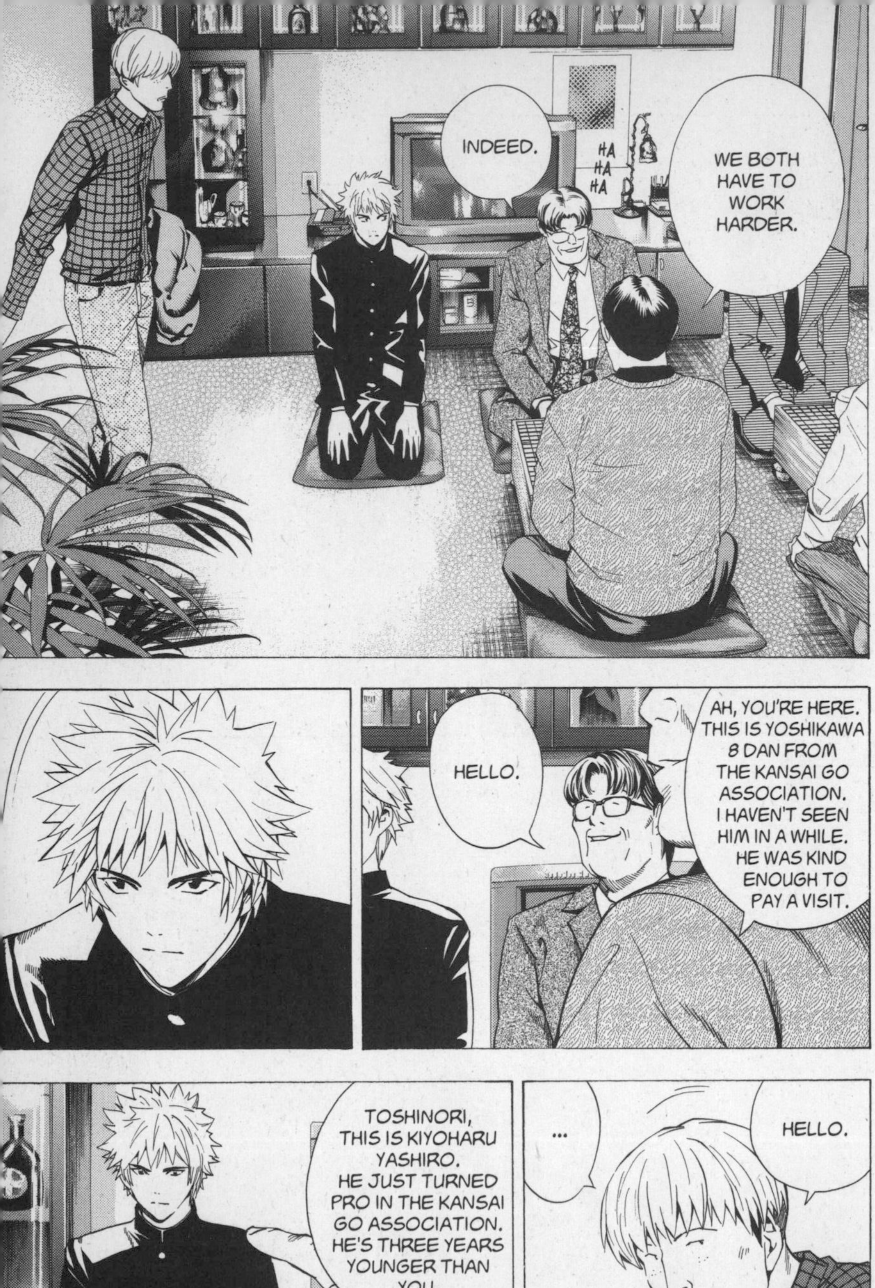
WE BOTH HAVE TO WORK HARDER.
HA HA HA
INDEED.
AH, YOU'RE HERE. THIS IS YOSHIKAWA 8 DAN FROM THE KANSAI GO ASSOCIATION. I HAVEN'T SEEN HIM IN A WHILE. HE WAS KIND ENOUGH TO PAY A VISIT.
HELLO.
HELLO.
...
TOSHINORI, THIS IS KIYOHARU YASHIRO. HE JUST TURNED PRO IN THE KANSAI GO ASSOCIATION. HE'S THREE YEARS YOUNGER THAN YOU.

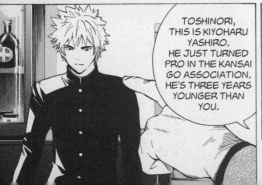

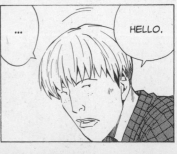

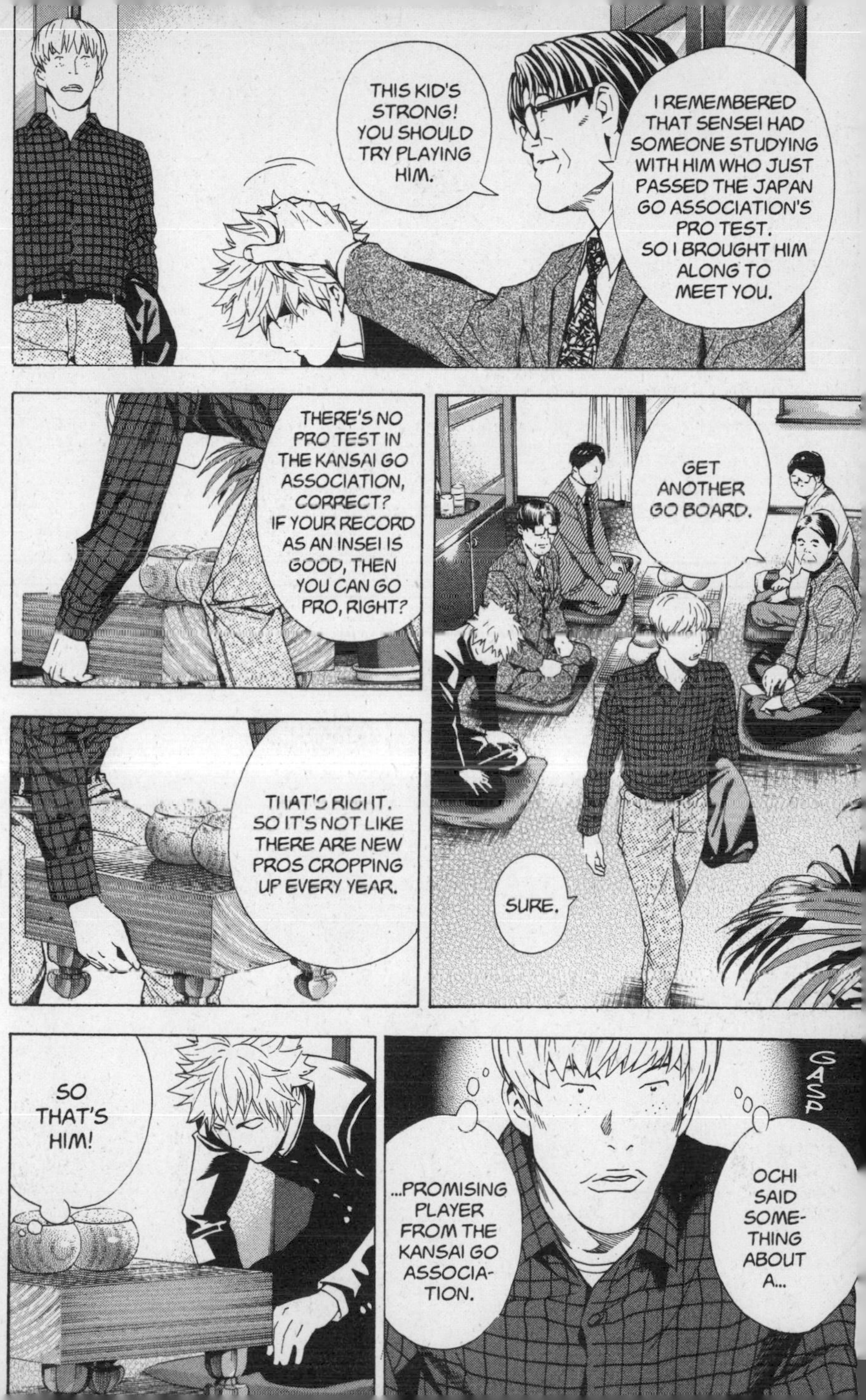
I REMEMBERED THAT SENSEI HAD SOMEONE STUDYING WITH HIM WHO JUST PASSED THE JAPAN GO ASSOCIATION'S PRO TEST. SO I BROUGHT HIM ALONG TO MEET YOU.
THIS KID'S STRONG! YOU SHOULD TRY PLAYING HIM.
GET ANOTHER GO BOARD.
SURE.
THERE'S NO PRO TEST IN THE KANSAI GO ASSOCIATION, CORRECT? IF YOUR RECORD AS AN INSEI IS GOOD, THEN YOU CAN GO PRO, RIGHT?
THAT'S RIGHT. SO IT'S NOT LIKE THERE ARE NEW PROS CROPPING UP EVERY YEAR.
GASP
OCHI SAID SOME-THING ABOUT A...
...PROMISING PLAYER FROM THE KANSAI GO ASSOCIA-TION.
SO THAT'S HIM!

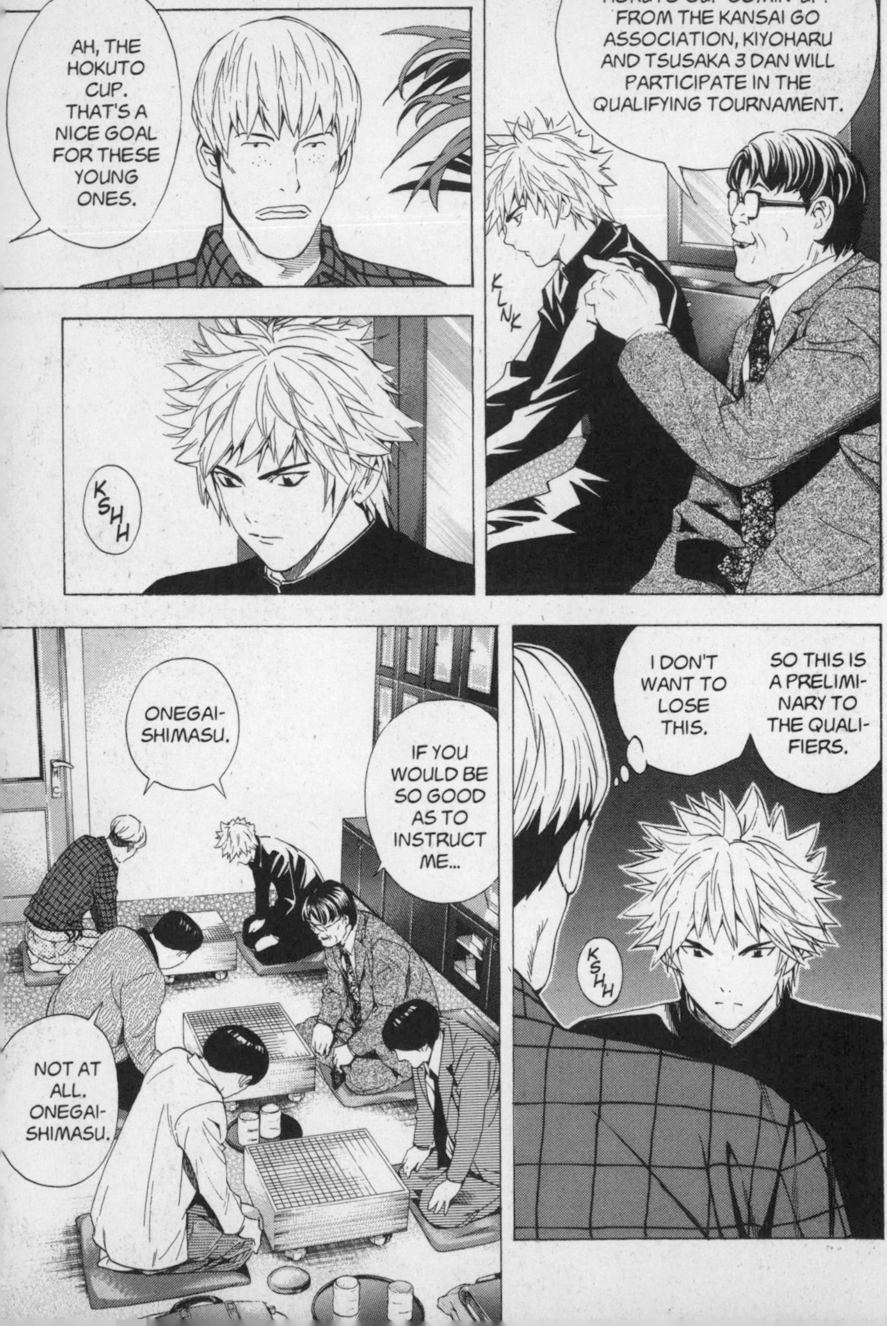
HEAR ABOUT THE HOKUTO CUP COMIN' UP? FROM THE KANSAI GO ASSOCIATION, KIYOHARU AND TSUSAKA 3 DAN WILL PARTICIPATE IN THE QUALIFYING TOURNAMENT.
KLNK
AH, THE HOKUTO CUP. THAT'S A NICE GOAL FOR THESE YOUNG ONES.
KSHH
SO THIS IS A PRELIMINARY TO THE QUALIFIERS.
I DON'T WANT TO LOSE THIS.
KSHH
ONEGAI-SHIMASU.
IF YOU WOULD BE SO GOOD AS TO INSTRUCT ME...
NOT AT ALL. ONEGAI-SHIMASU.

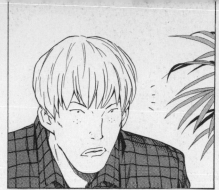
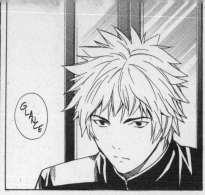

GLANCE

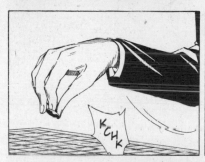

KCHK

MAYBE...
I'LL TRY
THAT
MOVE.

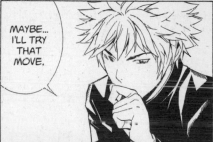

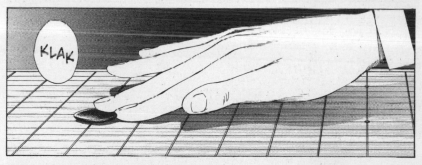

KLAK

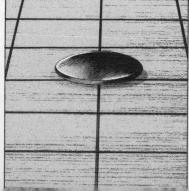

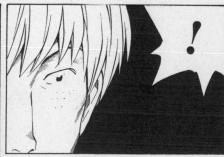

!

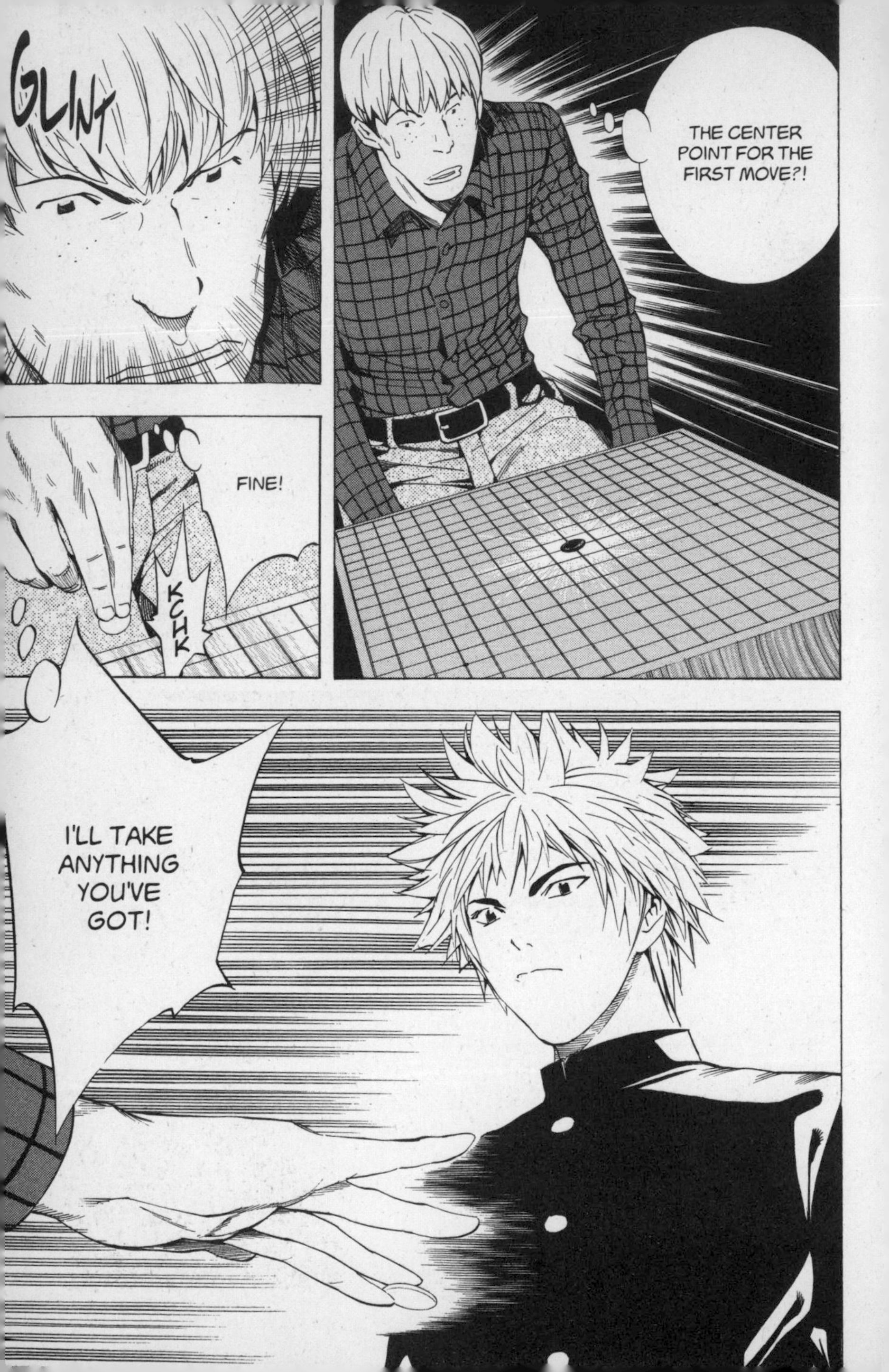
THE CENTER POINT FOR THE FIRST MOVE?!
GLINT
FINE!
KCHK
I'LL TAKE ANYTHING YOU'VE GOT!

A WORD ABOUT HIKARU NO GO

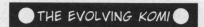

THE EVOLVING *KOMI*

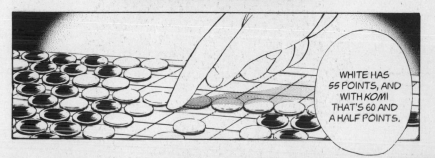

WHITE HAS 55 POINTS, AND WITH *KOMI* THAT'S 60 AND A HALF POINTS.

WHEN PLAYING *GO*, BLACK HAS THE ADVANTAGE OF PLAYING FIRST, SO THERE ARE COMPENSATION POINTS CALLED *KOMI*.

FOR A LONG TIME, JAPAN, CHINA AND KOREA ALL SET *KOMI* AT 5 AND A HALF POINTS. BUT IN SPRING OF 1998, KOREA CHANGED ITS *KOMI* TO 6 AND A HALF, AND IN SPRING OF 2002 CHINA WENT TO 7 AND A HALF. IN THE WINTER OF 2002 JAPAN MOVED TO 6 AND A HALF.

TO KEEP THINGS FROM BECOMING TOO COMPLICATED IN *HIKARU NO GO*, I'VE JUST KEPT THE PREMISE THAT *KOMI* IS 5 AND A HALF EVERYWHERE IN THE WORLD, BUT IN REALITY THE *KOMI* HAS EVOLVED AND MAY CONTINUE TO DO SO.

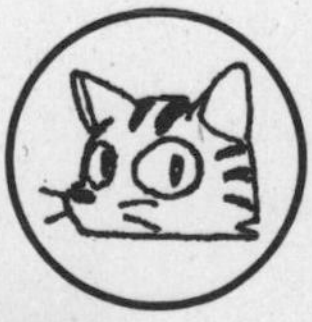

Game 158 "Tengen for the First Move"

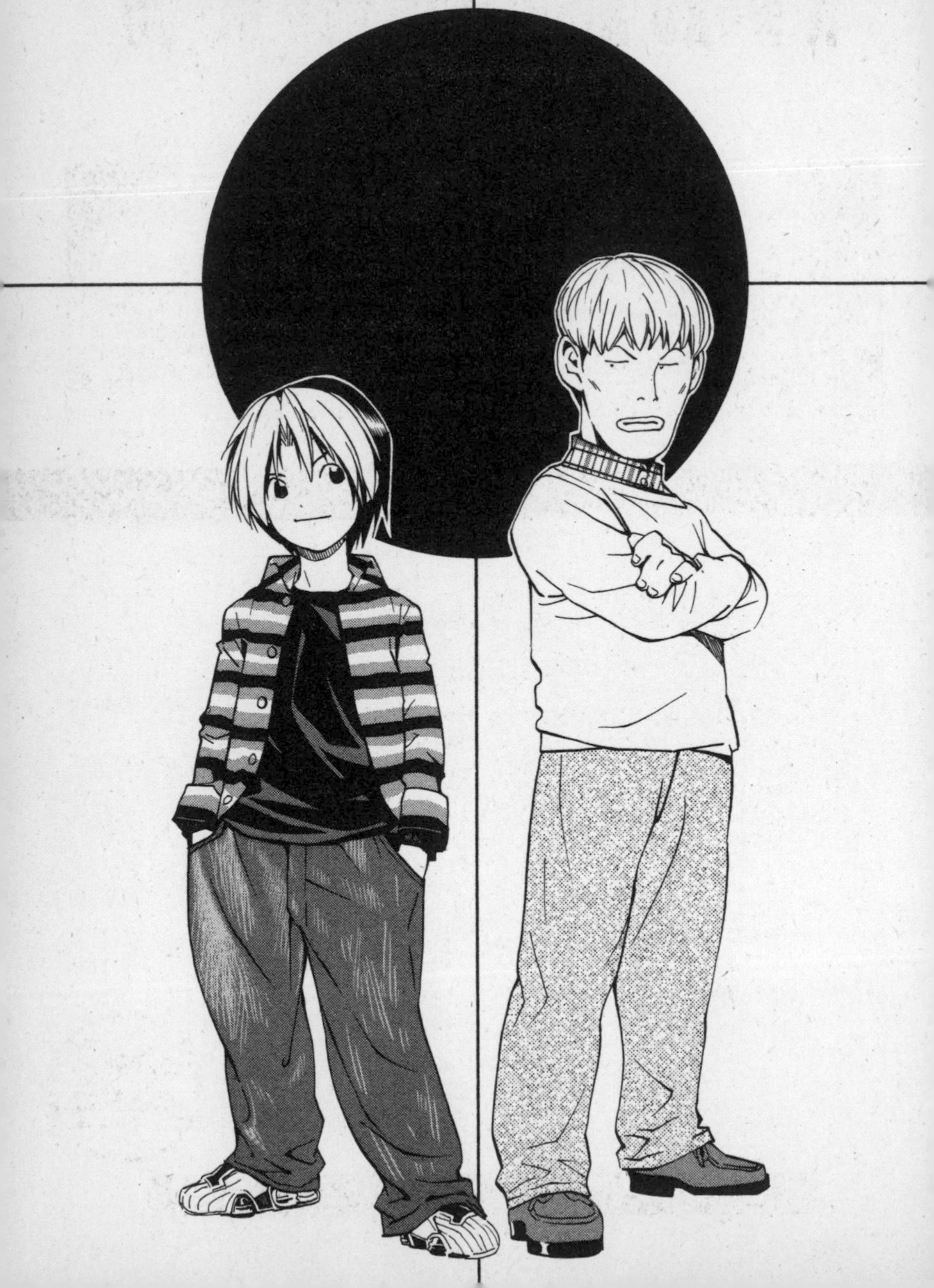

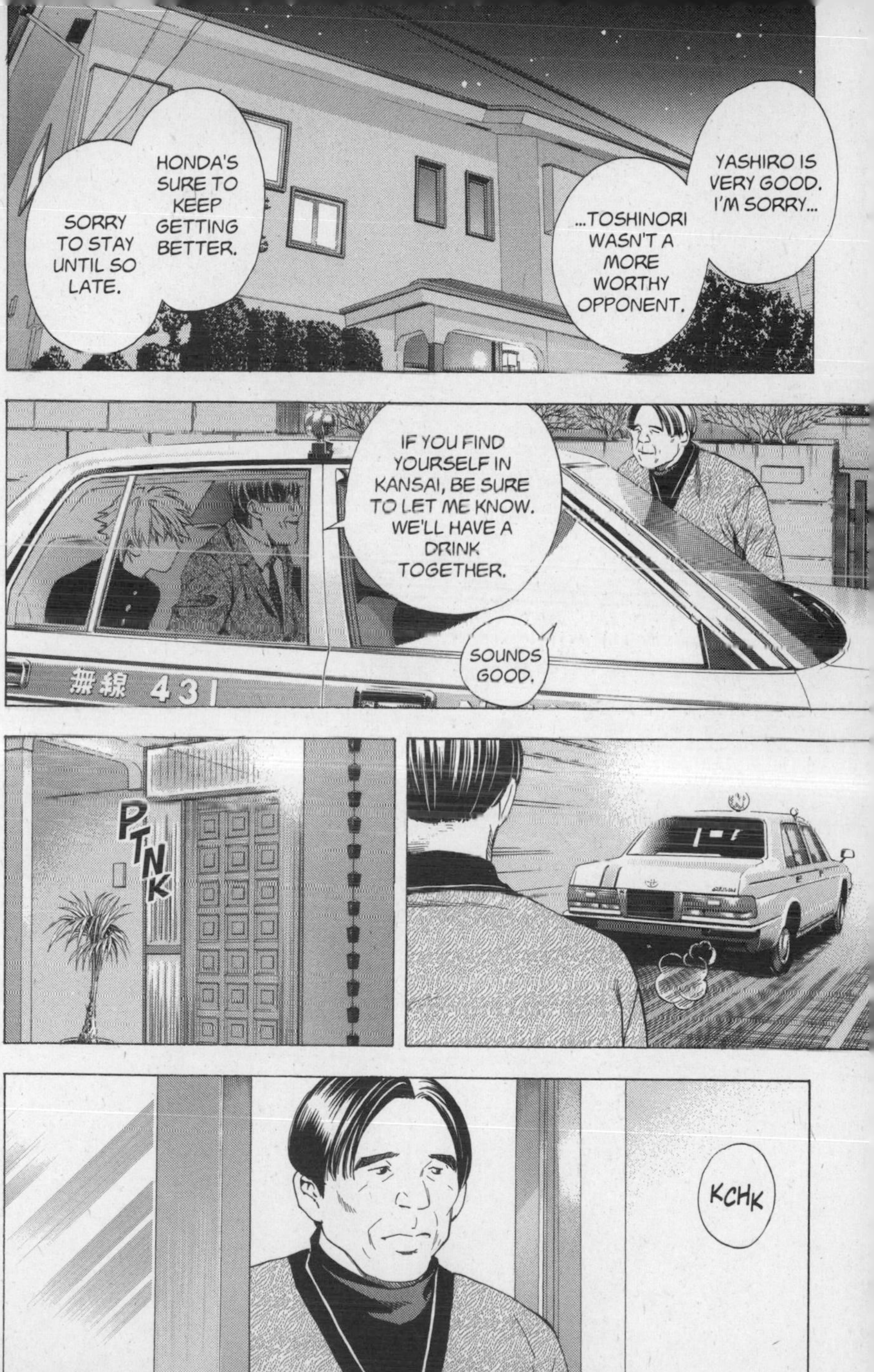
YASHIRO IS VERY GOOD. I'M SORRY...
...TOSHINORI WASN'T A MORE WORTHY OPPONENT.
HONDA'S SURE TO KEEP GETTING BETTER.
SORRY TO STAY UNTIL SO LATE.
IF YOU FIND YOURSELF IN KANSAI, BE SURE TO LET ME KNOW. WE'LL HAVE A DRINK TOGETHER.
SOUNDS GOOD.
無線 431
PTNK
KCHK

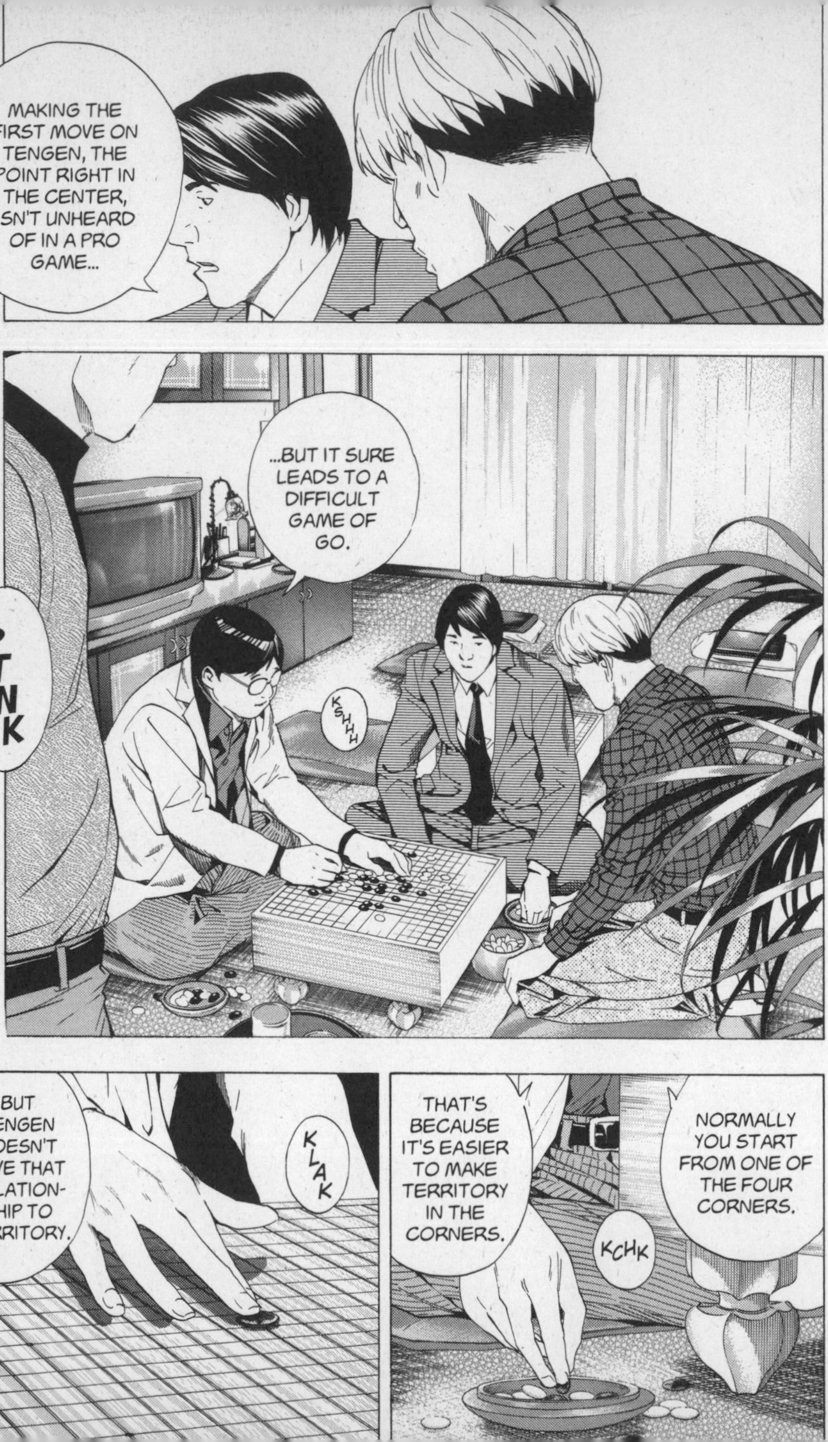
MAKING THE FIRST MOVE ON TENGEN, THE POINT RIGHT IN THE CENTER, ISN'T UNHEARD OF IN A PRO GAME...
...BUT IT SURE LEADS TO A DIFFICULT GAME OF GO.
PTNK
KSHHH
NORMALLY YOU START FROM ONE OF THE FOUR CORNERS.
THAT'S BECAUSE IT'S EASIER TO MAKE TERRITORY IN THE CORNERS.
KCHK
KLAK
BUT TENGEN DOESN'T HAVE THAT RELATION-SHIP TO TERRITORY.

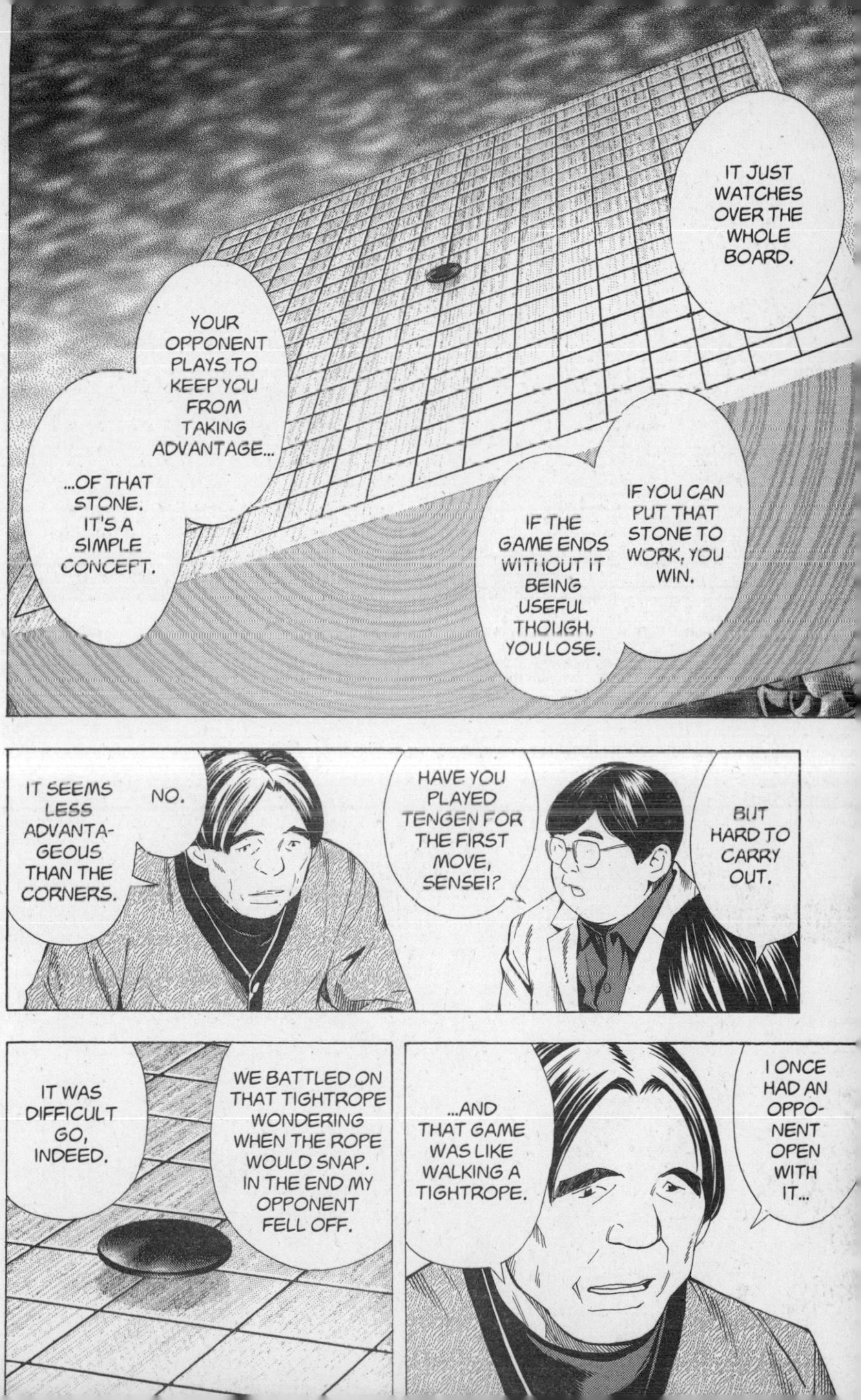
IT JUST WATCHES OVER THE WHOLE BOARD.
YOUR OPPONENT PLAYS TO KEEP YOU FROM TAKING ADVANTAGE...
...OF THAT STONE. IT'S A SIMPLE CONCEPT.
IF YOU CAN PUT THAT STONE TO WORK, YOU WIN.
IF THE GAME ENDS WITHOUT IT BEING USEFUL THOUGH, YOU LOSE.
BUT HARD TO CARRY OUT.
HAVE YOU PLAYED TENGEN FOR THE FIRST MOVE, SENSEI?
NO.
IT SEEMS LESS ADVANTA-GEOUS THAN THE CORNERS.
I ONCE HAD AN OPPO-NENT OPEN WITH IT...
...AND THAT GAME WAS LIKE WALKING A TIGHTROPE.
WE BATTLED ON THAT TIGHTROPE WONDERING WHEN THE ROPE WOULD SNAP. IN THE END MY OPPONENT FELL OFF.
IT WAS DIFFICULT GO, INDEED.

READ THIS WAY

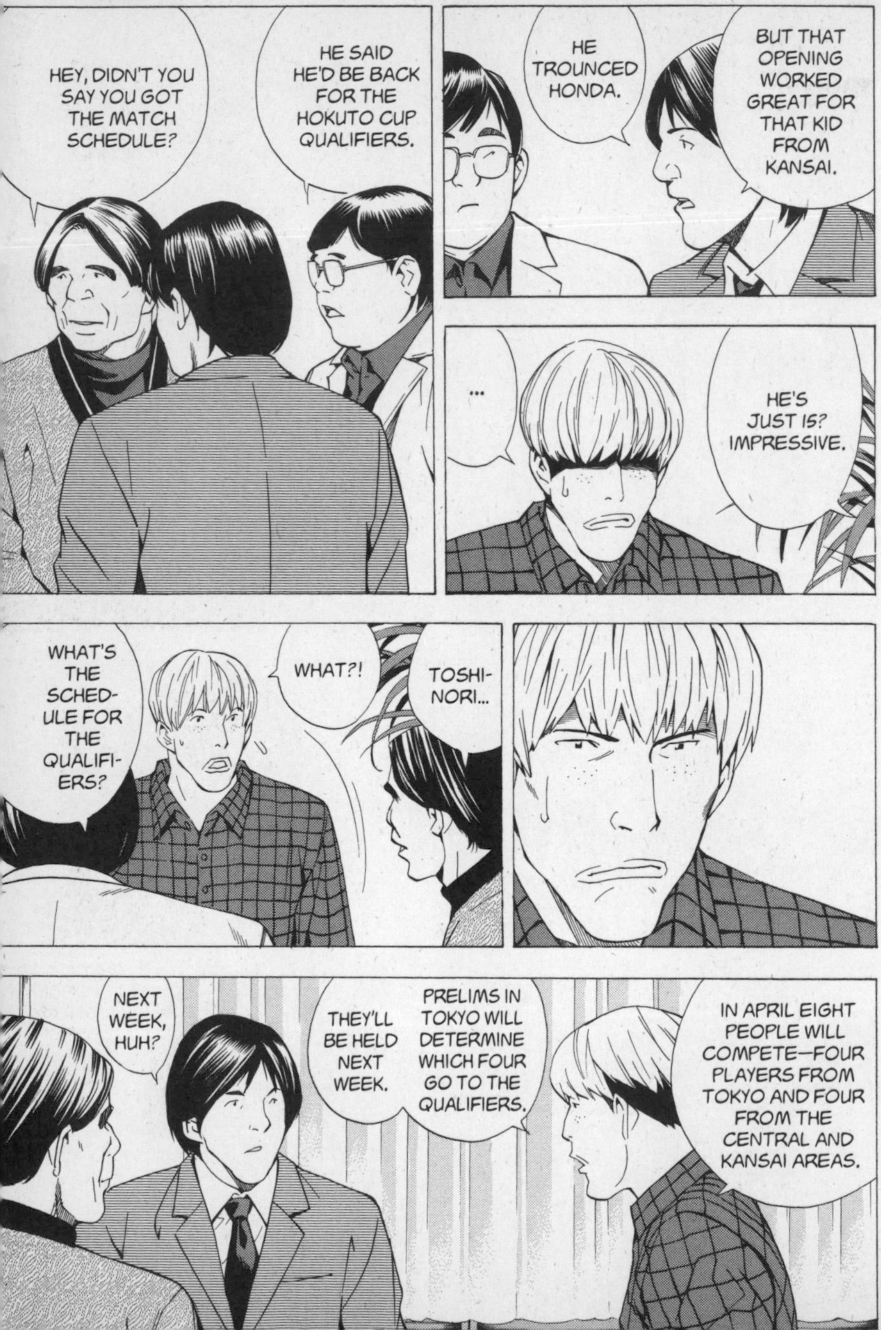
BUT THAT OPENING WORKED GREAT FOR THAT KID FROM KANSAI.
HE TROUNCED HONDA.
HE'S JUST 15? IMPRESSIVE.
...
HE SAID HE'D BE BACK FOR THE HOKUTO CUP QUALIFIERS.
HEY, DIDN'T YOU SAY YOU GOT THE MATCH SCHEDULE?
TOSHI-NORI...
WHAT?!
WHAT'S THE SCHED-ULE FOR THE QUALIFI-ERS?
IN APRIL EIGHT PEOPLE WILL COMPETE—FOUR PLAYERS FROM TOKYO AND FOUR FROM THE CENTRAL AND KANSAI AREAS.
PRELIMS IN TOKYO WILL DETERMINE WHICH FOUR GO TO THE QUALIFIERS.
THEY'LL BE HELD NEXT WEEK.
NEXT WEEK, HUH?

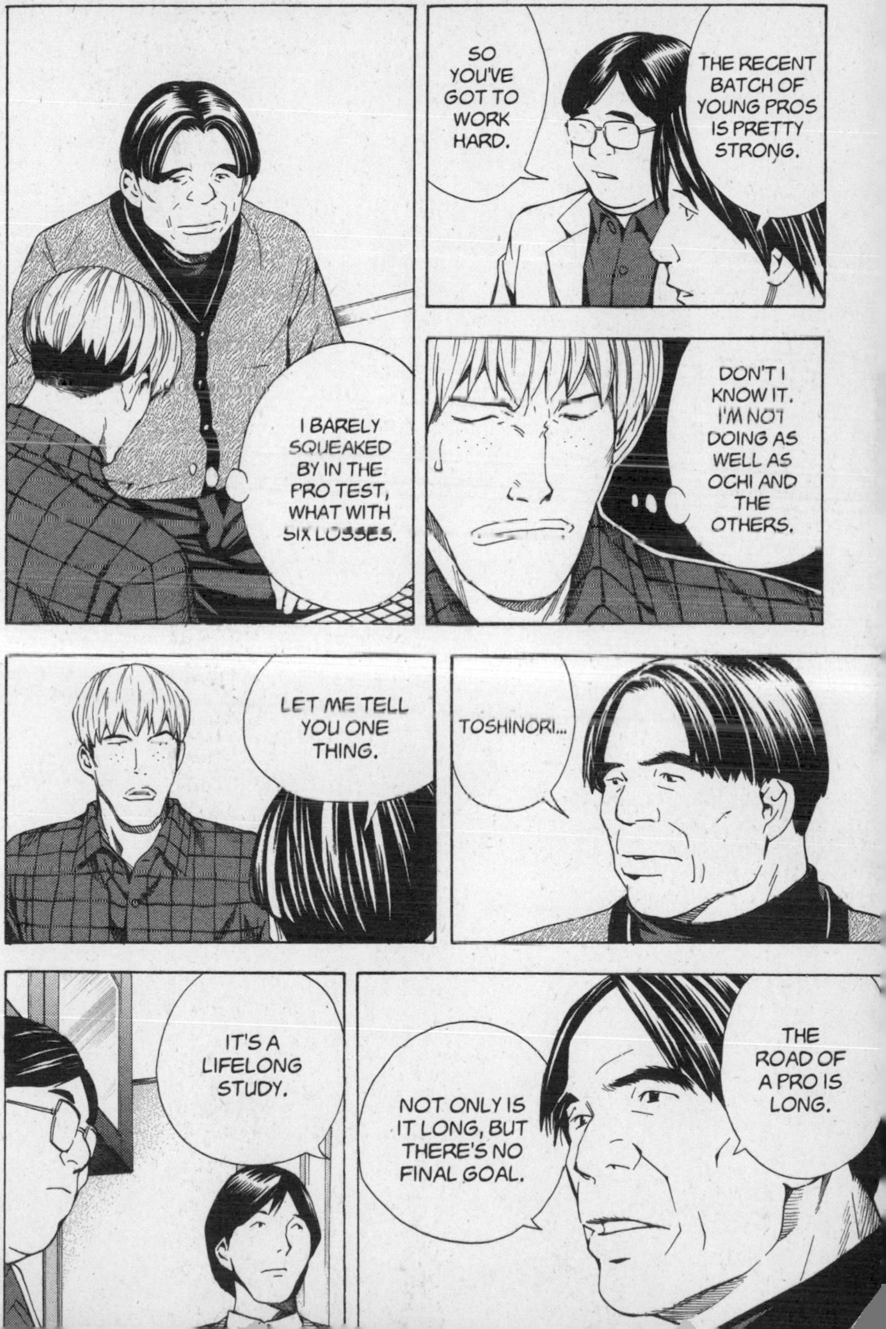
THE RECENT BATCH OF YOUNG PROS IS PRETTY STRONG.
SO YOU'VE GOT TO WORK HARD.
DON'T I KNOW IT. I'M NOT DOING AS WELL AS OCHI AND THE OTHERS.
I BARELY SQUEAKED BY IN THE PRO TEST, WHAT WITH SIX LOSSES.
TOSHINORI...
LET ME TELL YOU ONE THING.
THE ROAD OF A PRO IS LONG.
NOT ONLY IS IT LONG, BUT THERE'S NO FINAL GOAL.
IT'S A LIFELONG STUDY.

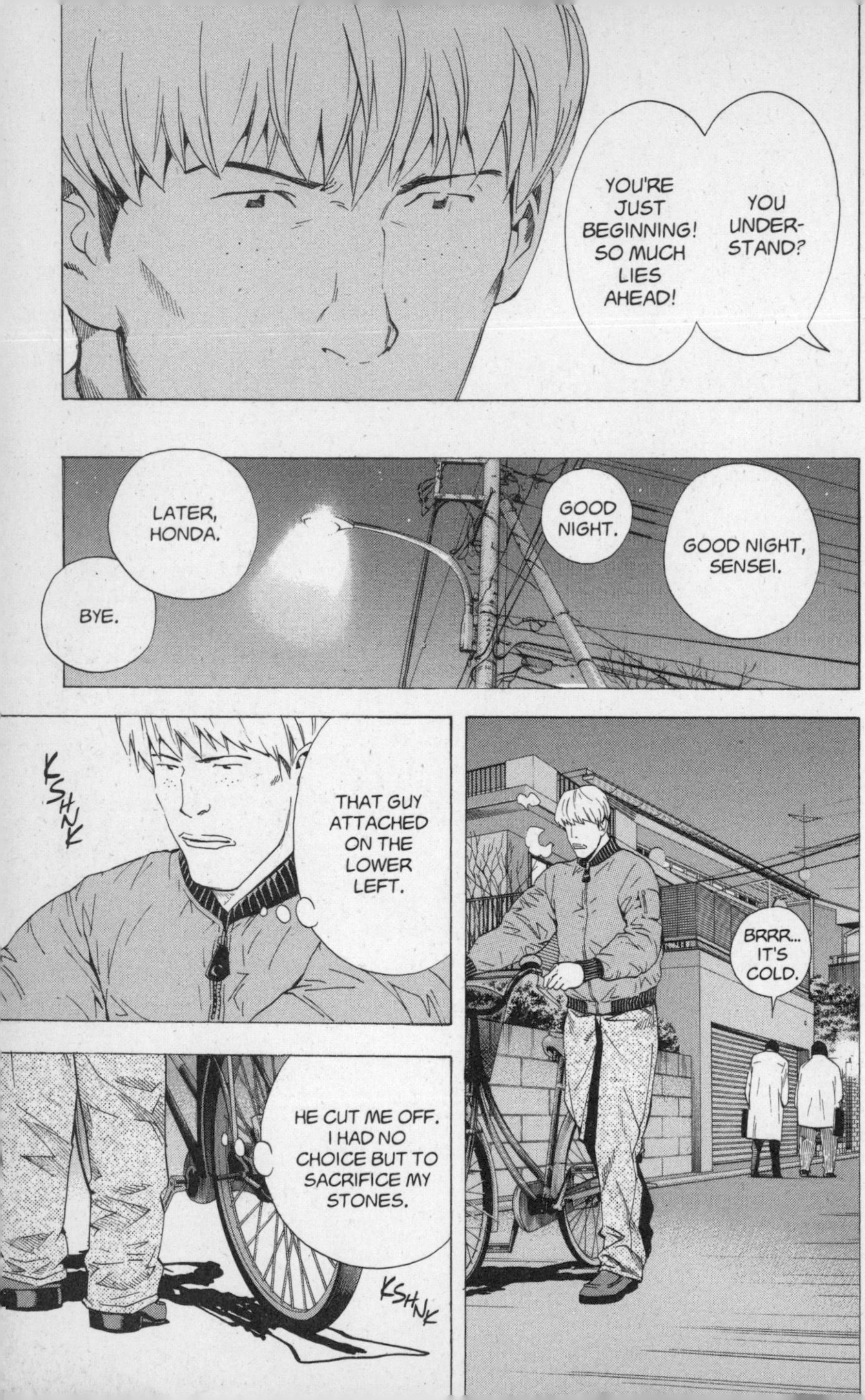
YOU UNDERSTAND?
YOU'RE JUST BEGINNING! SO MUCH LIES AHEAD!
GOOD NIGHT, SENSEI.
GOOD NIGHT.
LATER, HONDA.
BYE.
BRRR... IT'S COLD.
THAT GUY ATTACHED ON THE LOWER LEFT.
KSHNK
HE CUT ME OFF. I HAD NO CHOICE BUT TO SACRIFICE MY STONES.
KSHNK

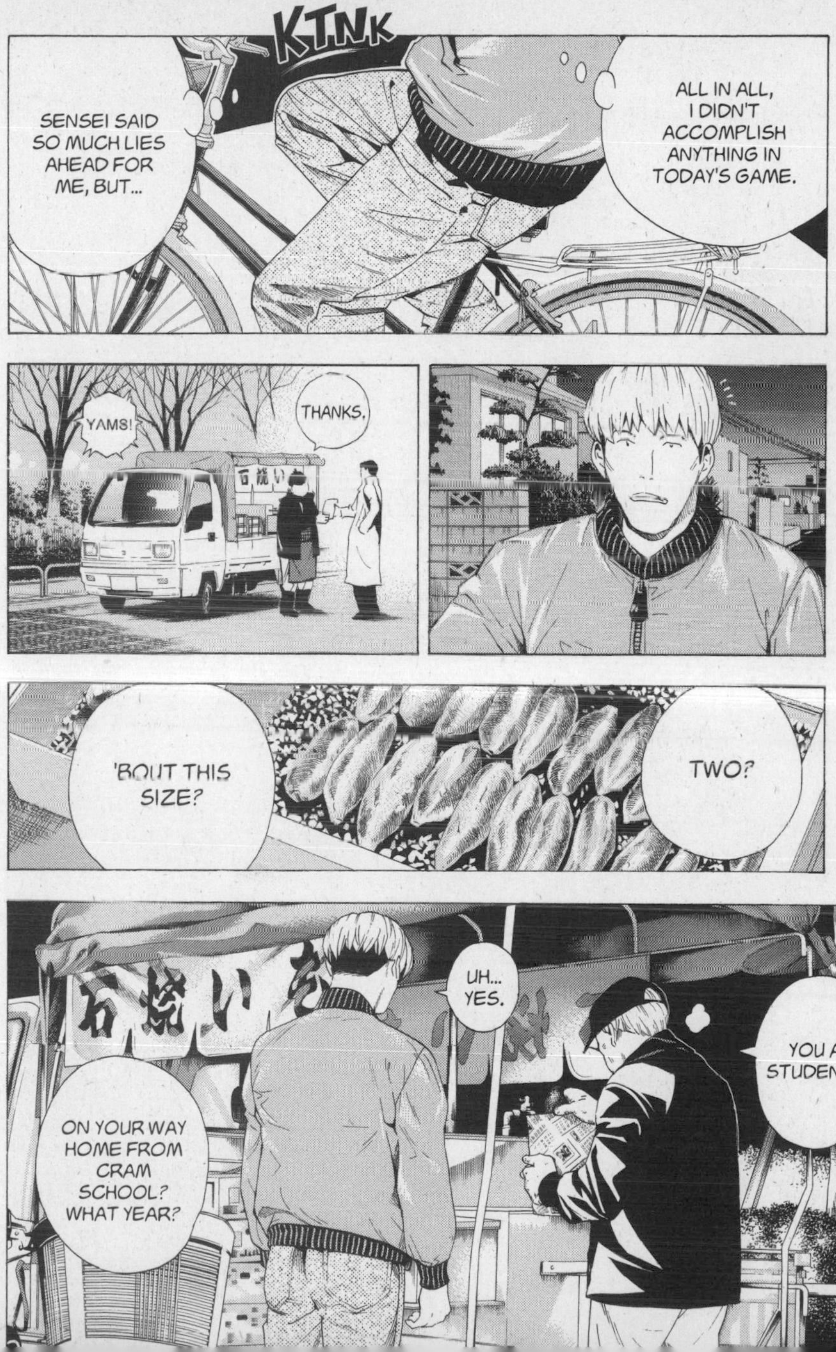
KTNK
ALL IN ALL, I DIDN'T ACCOMPLISH ANYTHING IN TODAY'S GAME.
SENSEI SAID SO MUCH LIES AHEAD FOR ME, BUT...
THANKS.
YAMS!
TWO?
'BOUT THIS SIZE?
YOU A STUDENT?
UH... YES.
ON YOUR WAY HOME FROM CRAM SCHOOL? WHAT YEAR?

READ THIS WAY

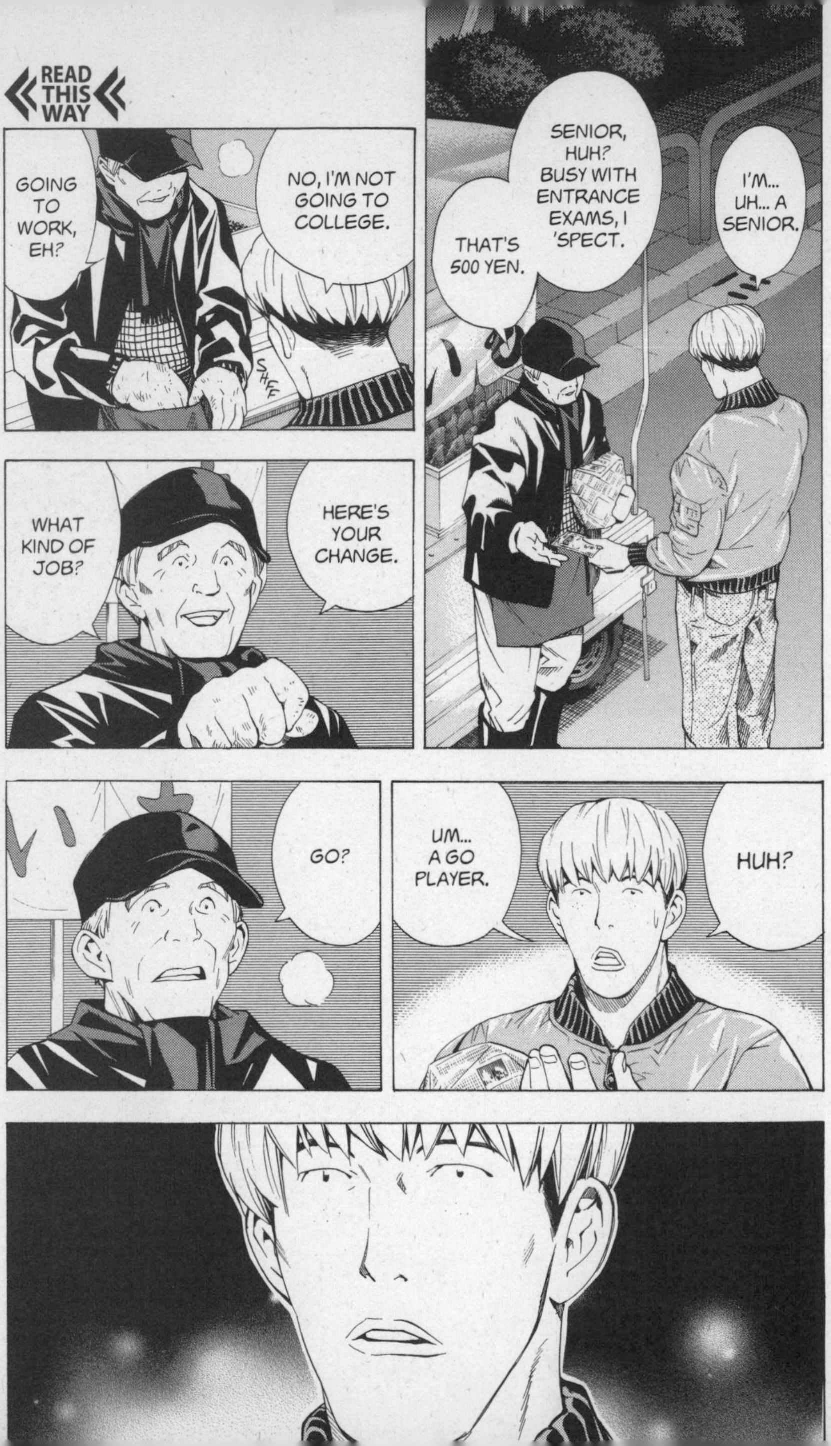
I'M... UH... A SENIOR.
SENIOR, HUH? BUSY WITH ENTRANCE EXAMS, I 'SPECT.
THAT'S 500 YEN.
NO, I'M NOT GOING TO COLLEGE.
GOING TO WORK, EH?
SHFF
HERE'S YOUR CHANGE.
WHAT KIND OF JOB?
HUH?
UM... A GO PLAYER.
GO?

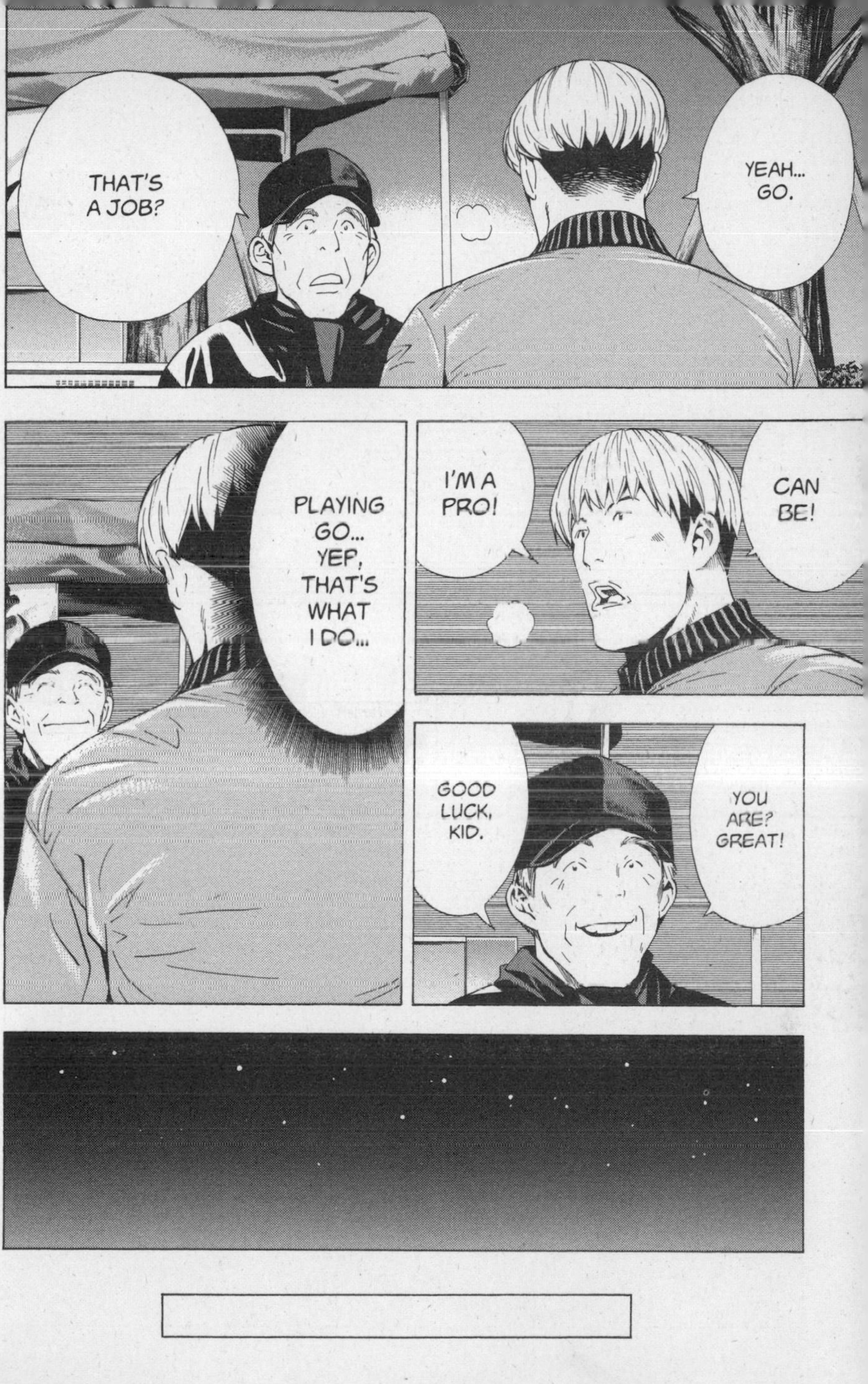
YEAH... GO.
THAT'S A JOB?
CAN BE!
I'M A PRO!
YOU ARE? GREAT!
GOOD LUCK, KID.
PLAYING GO... YEP, THAT'S WHAT I DO...

READ THIS WAY

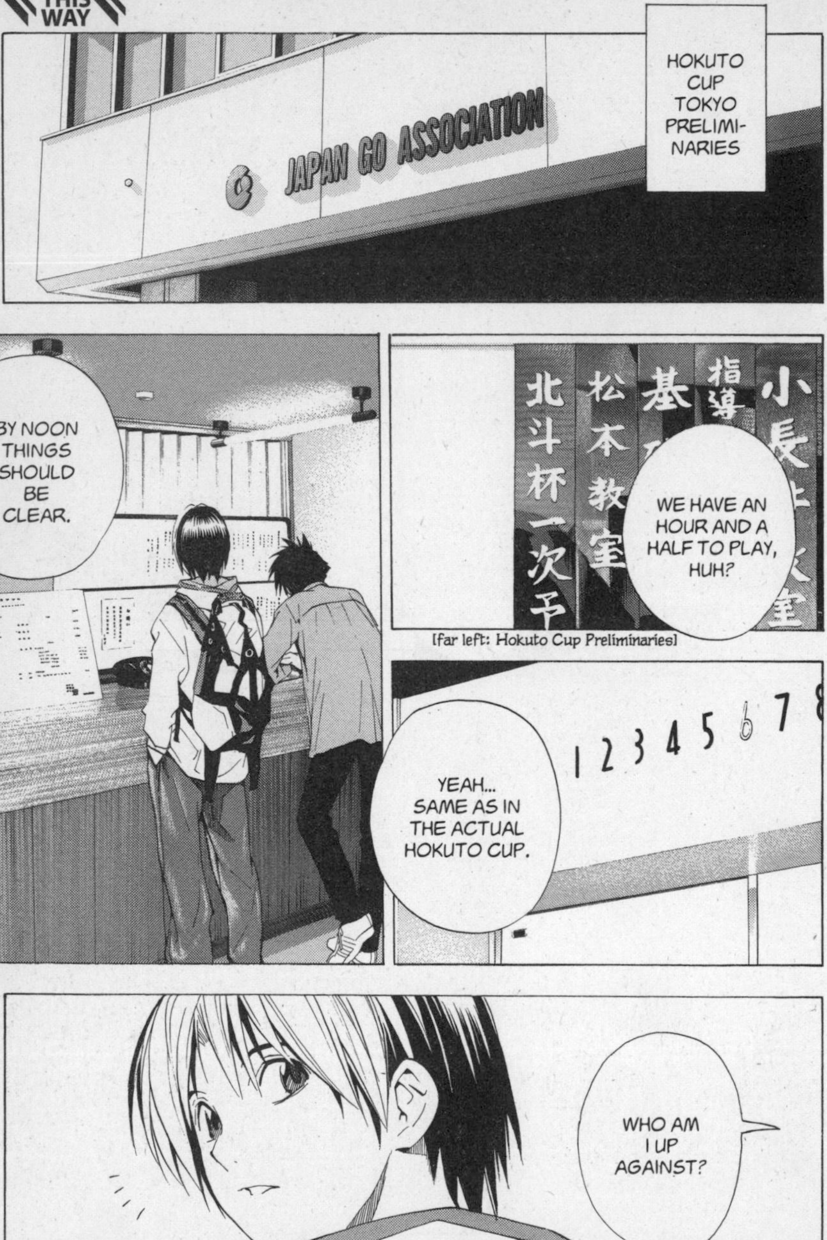
HOKUTO CUP TOKYO PRELIMINARIES
JAPAN GO ASSOCIATION
北斗杯一次予
松本教室
WE HAVE AN HOUR AND A HALF TO PLAY, HUH?
1 2 3 4 5 6 7 8
YEAH... SAME AS IN THE ACTUAL HOKUTO CUP.
BY NOON THINGS SHOULD BE CLEAR.
WHO AM I UP AGAINST?
[far left: Hokuto Cup Preliminaries]

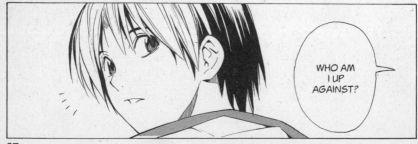

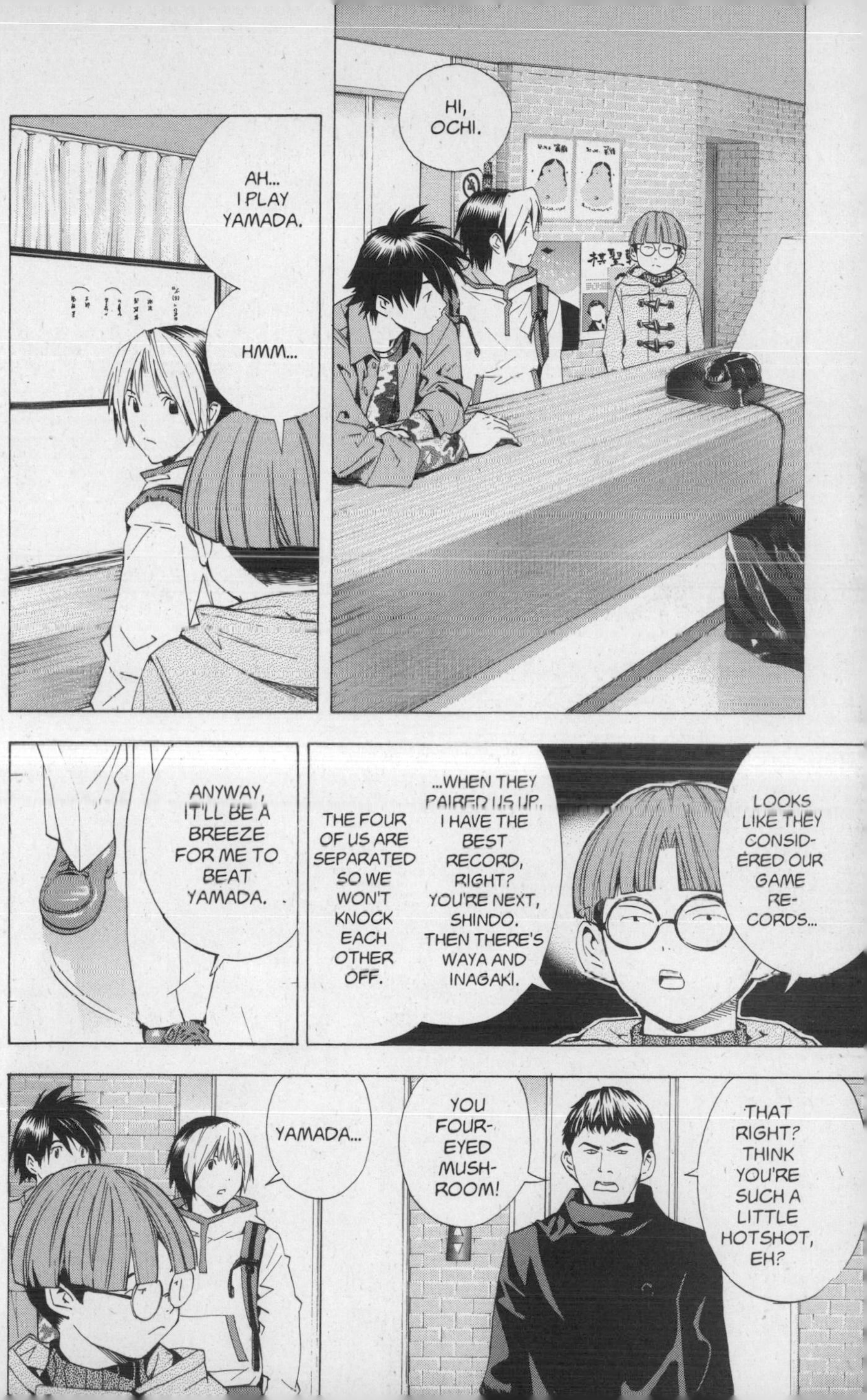
HI, OCHI.
AH... I PLAY YAMADA.
HMM...
LOOKS LIKE THEY CONSID-ERED OUR GAME RE-CORDS...
...WHEN THEY PAIRED US UP. I HAVE THE BEST RECORD, RIGHT? YOU'RE NEXT, SHINDO. THEN THERE'S WAYA AND INAGAKI.
THE FOUR OF US ARE SEPARATED SO WE WON'T KNOCK EACH OTHER OFF.
ANYWAY, IT'LL BE A BREEZE FOR ME TO BEAT YAMADA.
THAT RIGHT? THINK YOU'RE SUCH A LITTLE HOTSHOT, EH?
YOU FOUR-EYED MUSH-ROOM!
YAMADA...

READ THIS WAY

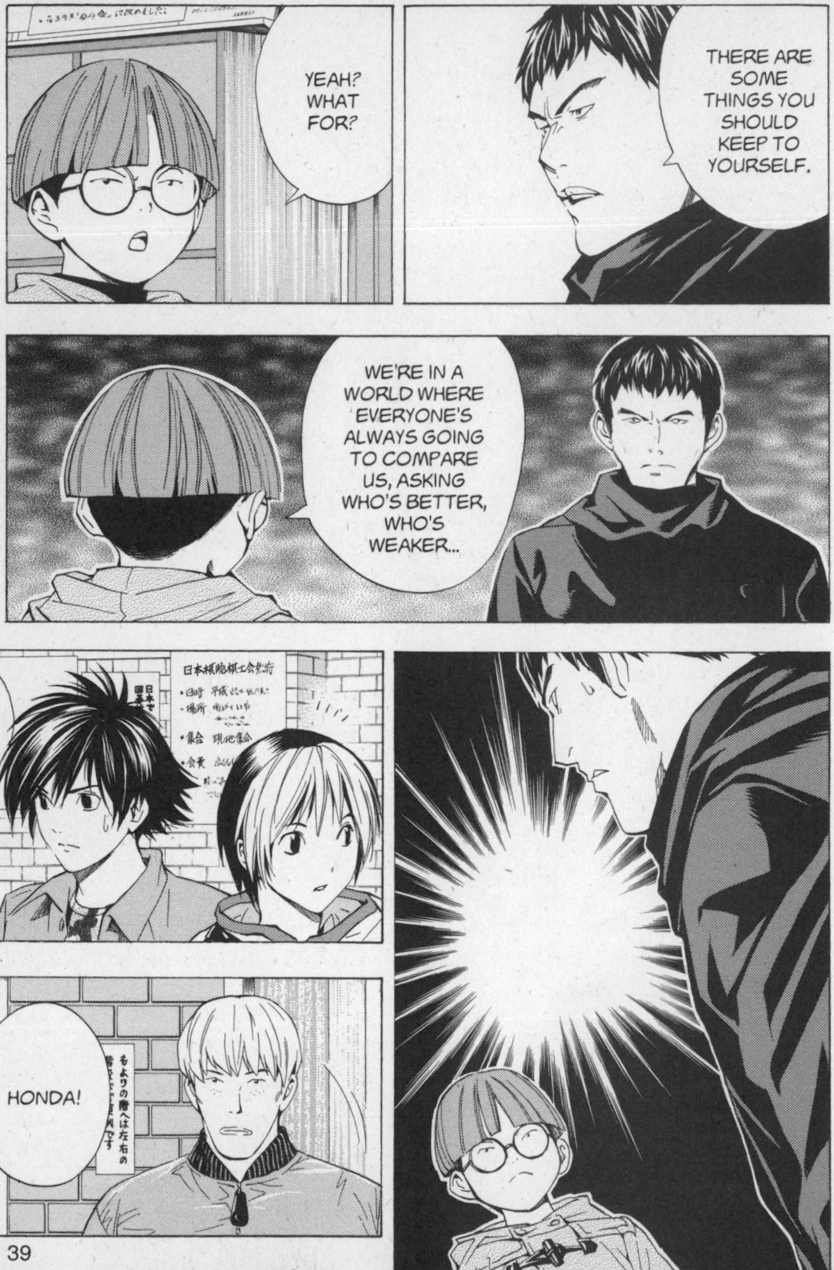
THERE ARE SOME THINGS YOU SHOULD KEEP TO YOURSELF.
YEAH? WHAT FOR?
WE'RE IN A WORLD WHERE EVERYONE'S ALWAYS GOING TO COMPARE US, ASKING WHO'S BETTER, WHO'S WEAKER...
...
HONDA!

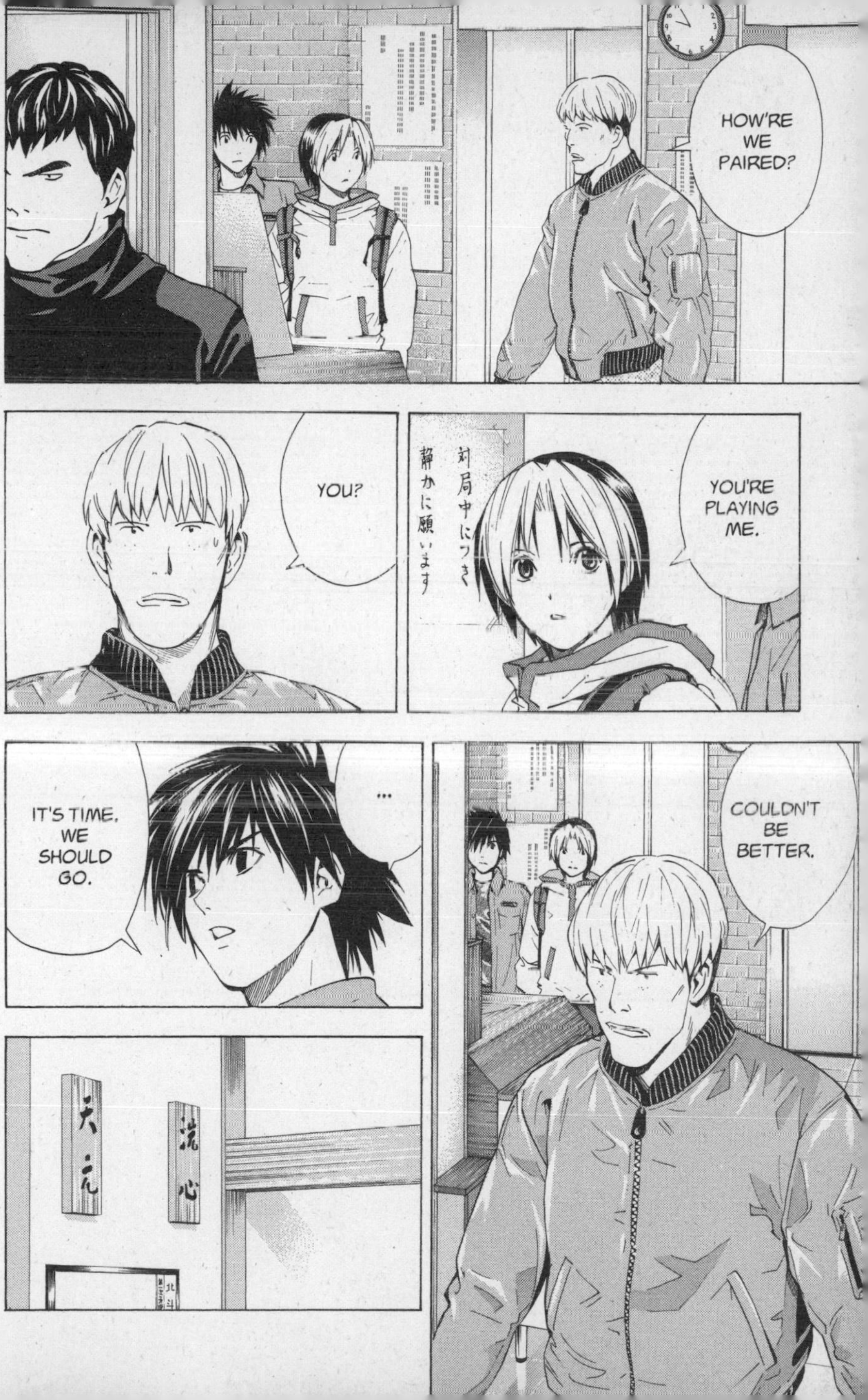
HOW'RE WE PAIRED?
対局中につき静かに願います
YOU'RE PLAYING ME.
YOU?
COULDN'T BE BETTER.
...
IT'S TIME. WE SHOULD GO.
洗心
天元

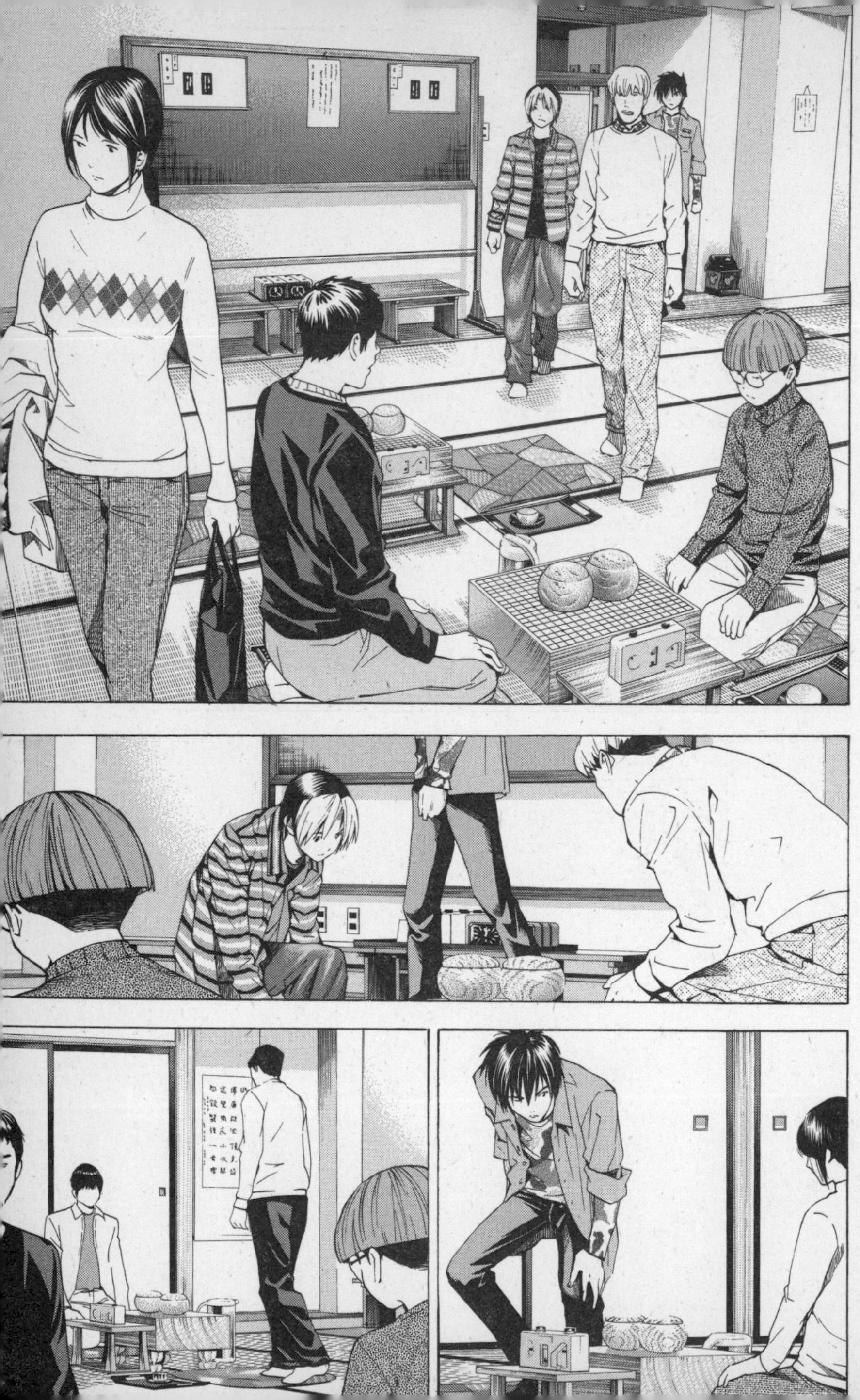

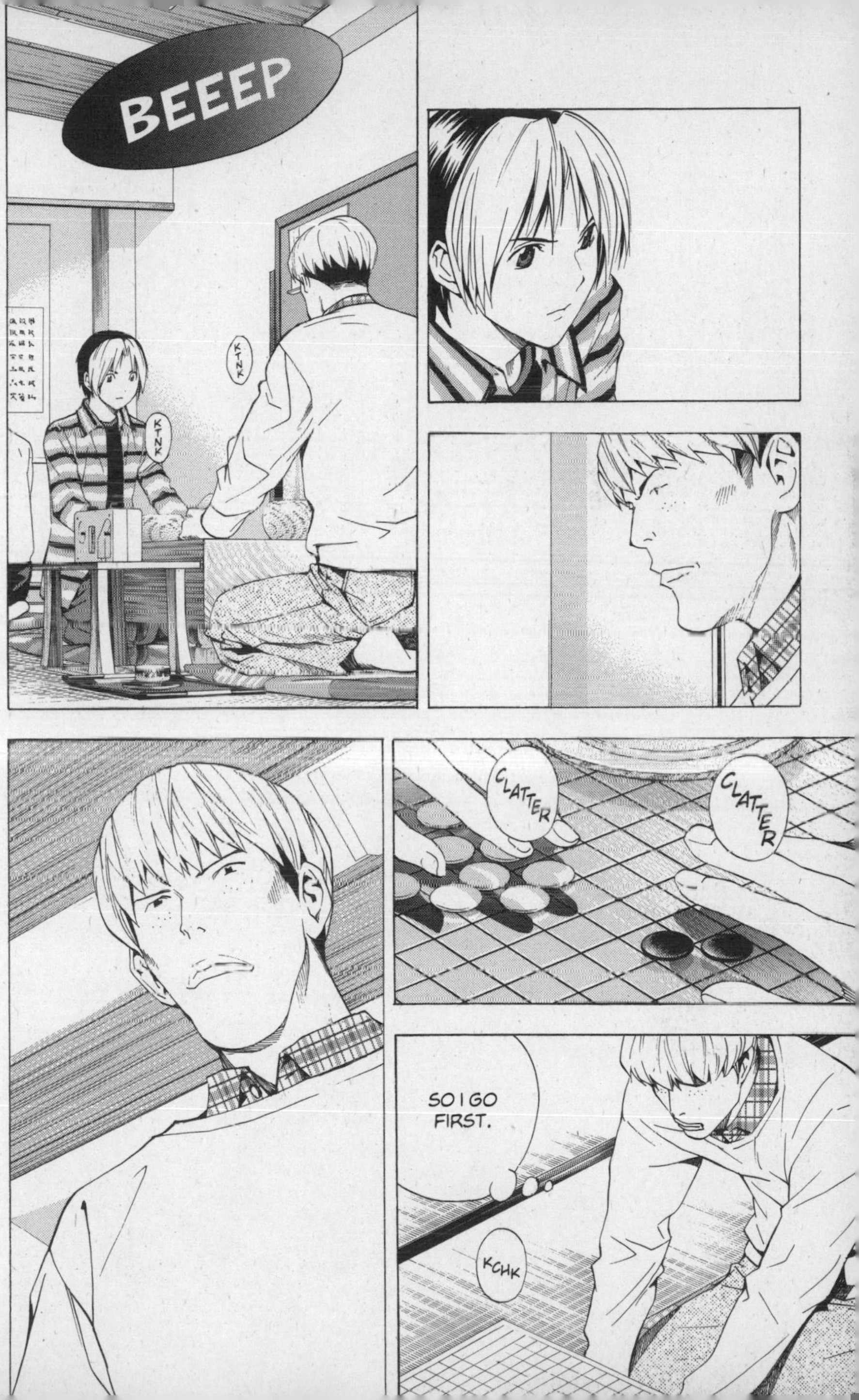
BEEEP
KTNK
KTNK
CLATTER
CLATTER
SO I GO FIRST.
KCHK

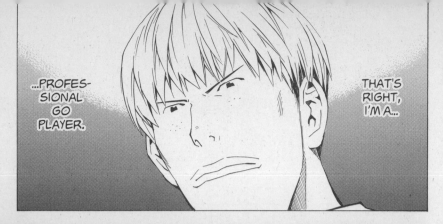

THAT'S RIGHT, I'M A...

...PROFES-SIONAL GO PLAYER.

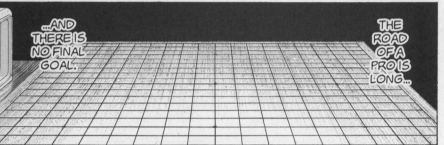

THE ROAD OF A PRO IS LONG...

...AND THERE IS NO FINAL GOAL.

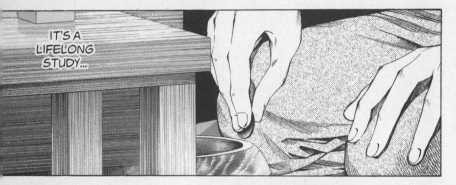

IT'S A LIFELONG STUDY...

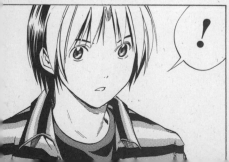

!

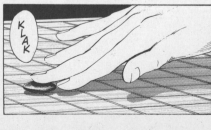

KLAK

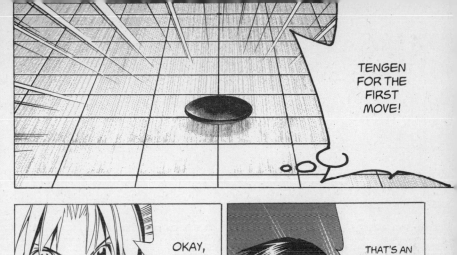

TENGEN FOR THE FIRST MOVE!

OKAY, THEN!

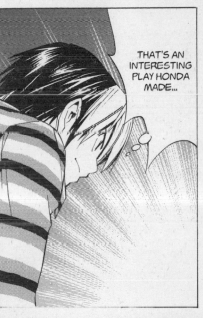

THAT'S AN INTERESTING PLAY HONDA MADE...

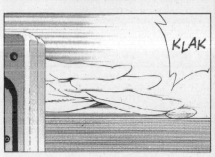

KLAK

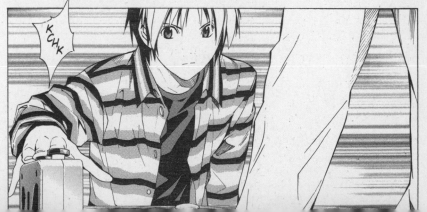

KCHK

READ THIS WAY

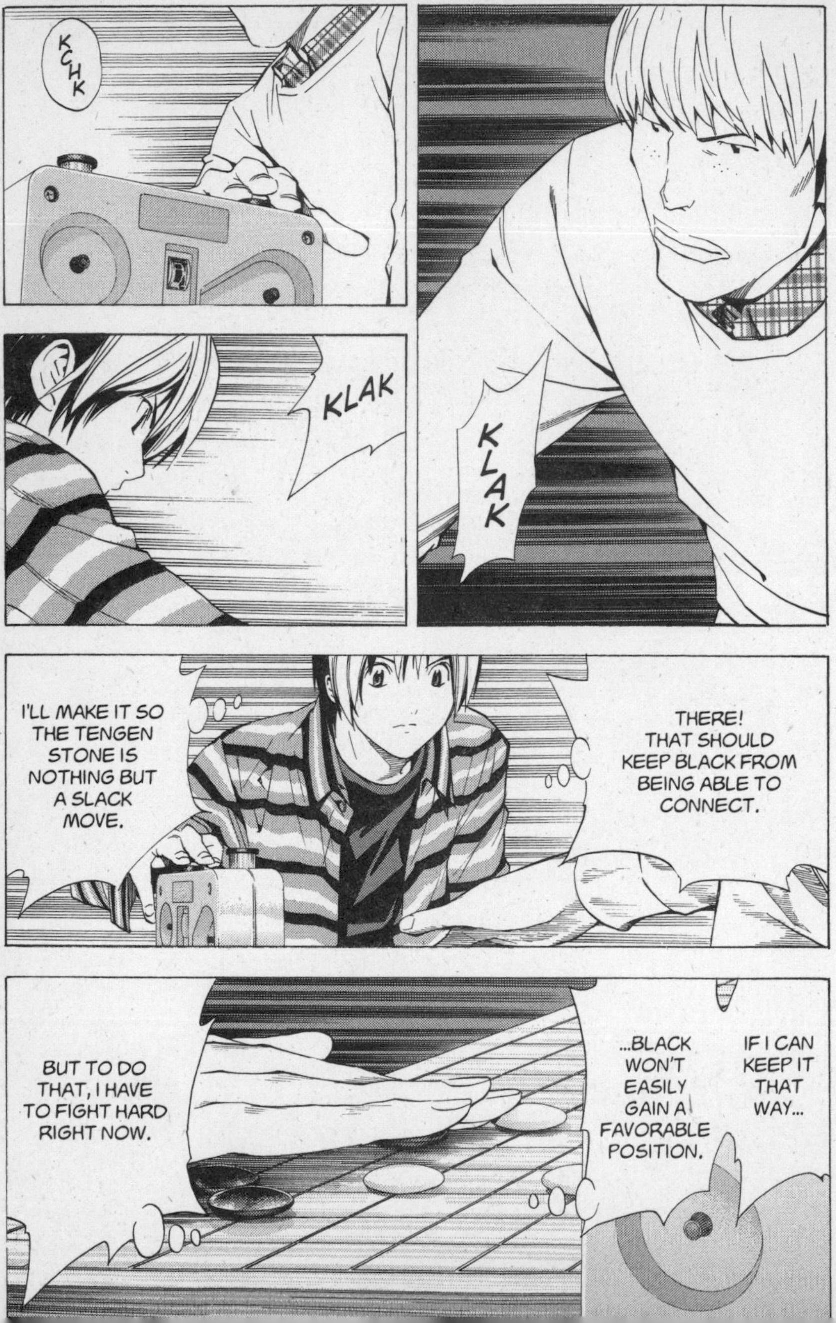
KLAK
KCHK
KLAK
THERE! THAT SHOULD KEEP BLACK FROM BEING ABLE TO CONNECT.
I'LL MAKE IT SO THE TENGEN STONE IS NOTHING BUT A SLACK MOVE.
IF I CAN KEEP IT THAT WAY...
...BLACK WON'T EASILY GAIN A FAVORABLE POSITION.
BUT TO DO THAT, I HAVE TO FIGHT HARD RIGHT NOW.

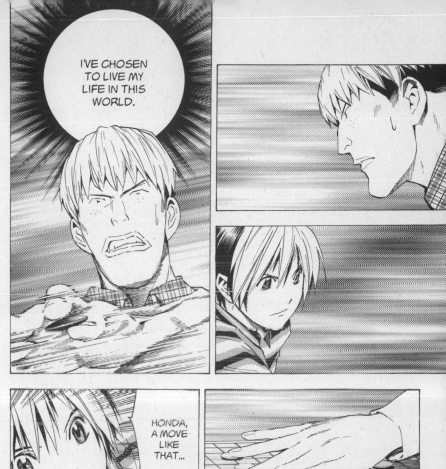

I'VE CHOSEN TO LIVE MY LIFE IN THIS WORLD.

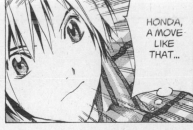

HONDA, A MOVE LIKE THAT...

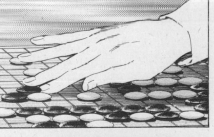

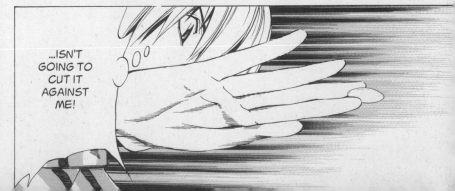

...ISN'T GOING TO CUT IT AGAINST ME!

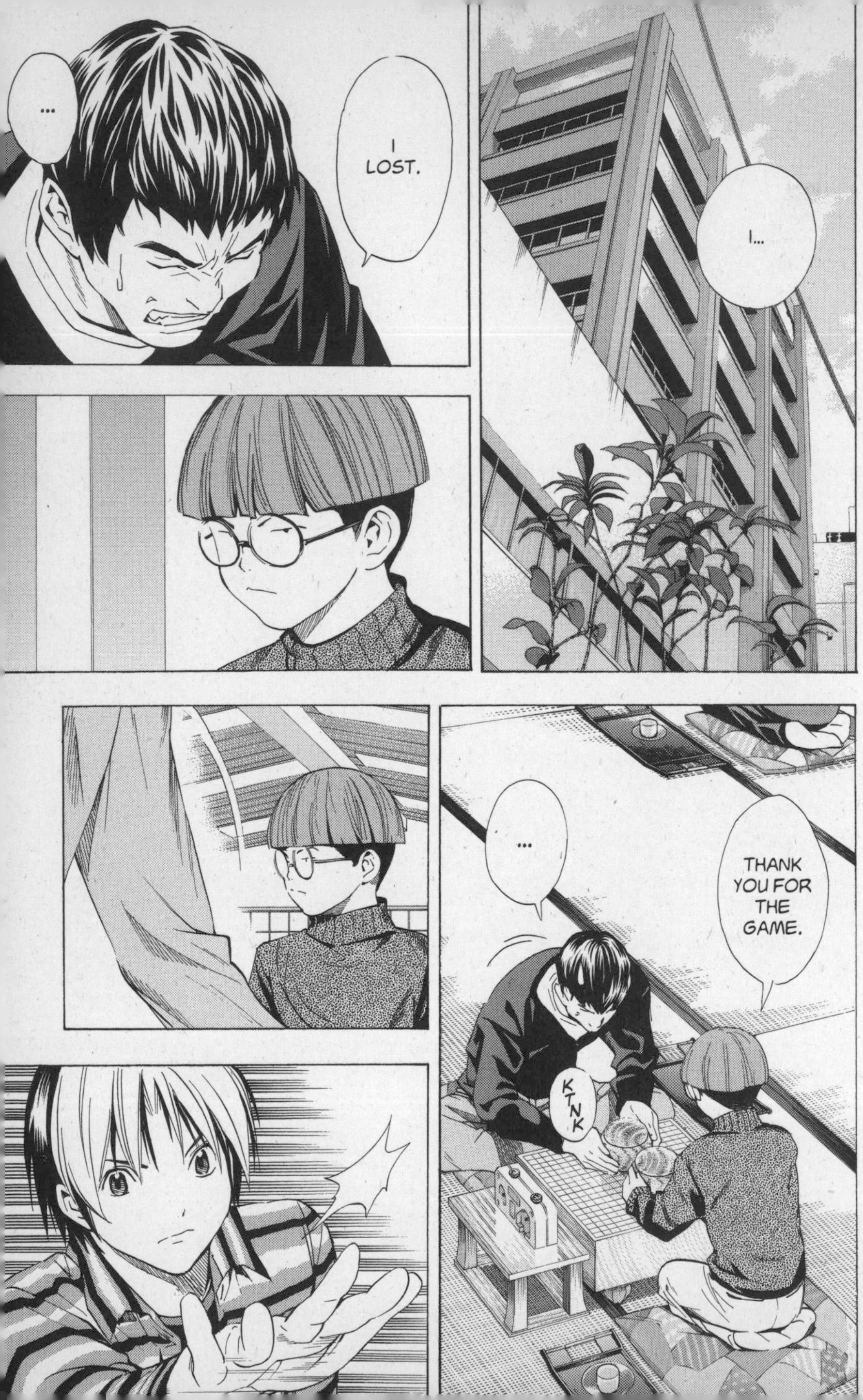
I...
I LOST.
...
THANK YOU FOR THE GAME.
...
KTNK

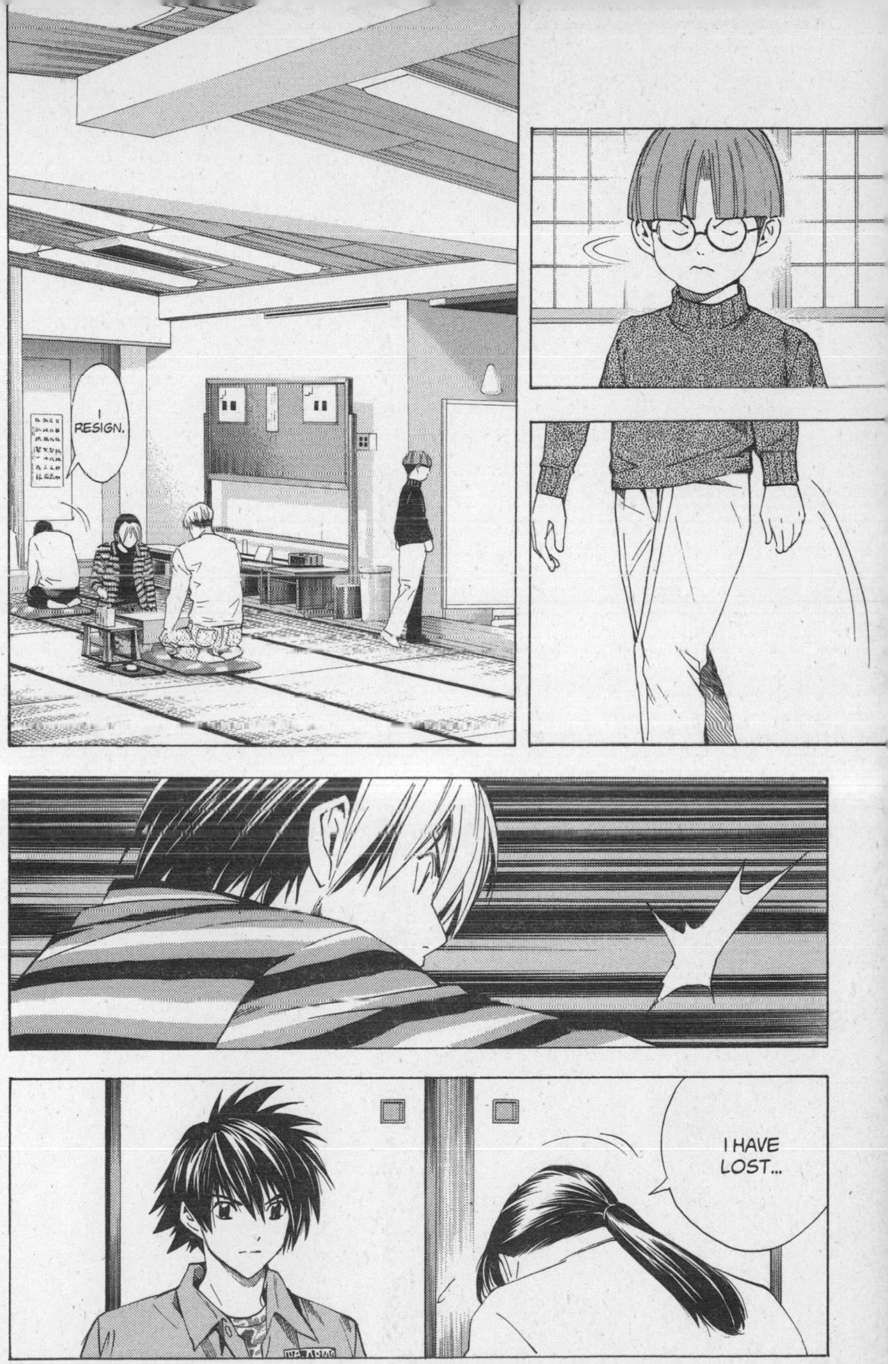
I RESIGN.
I HAVE LOST...

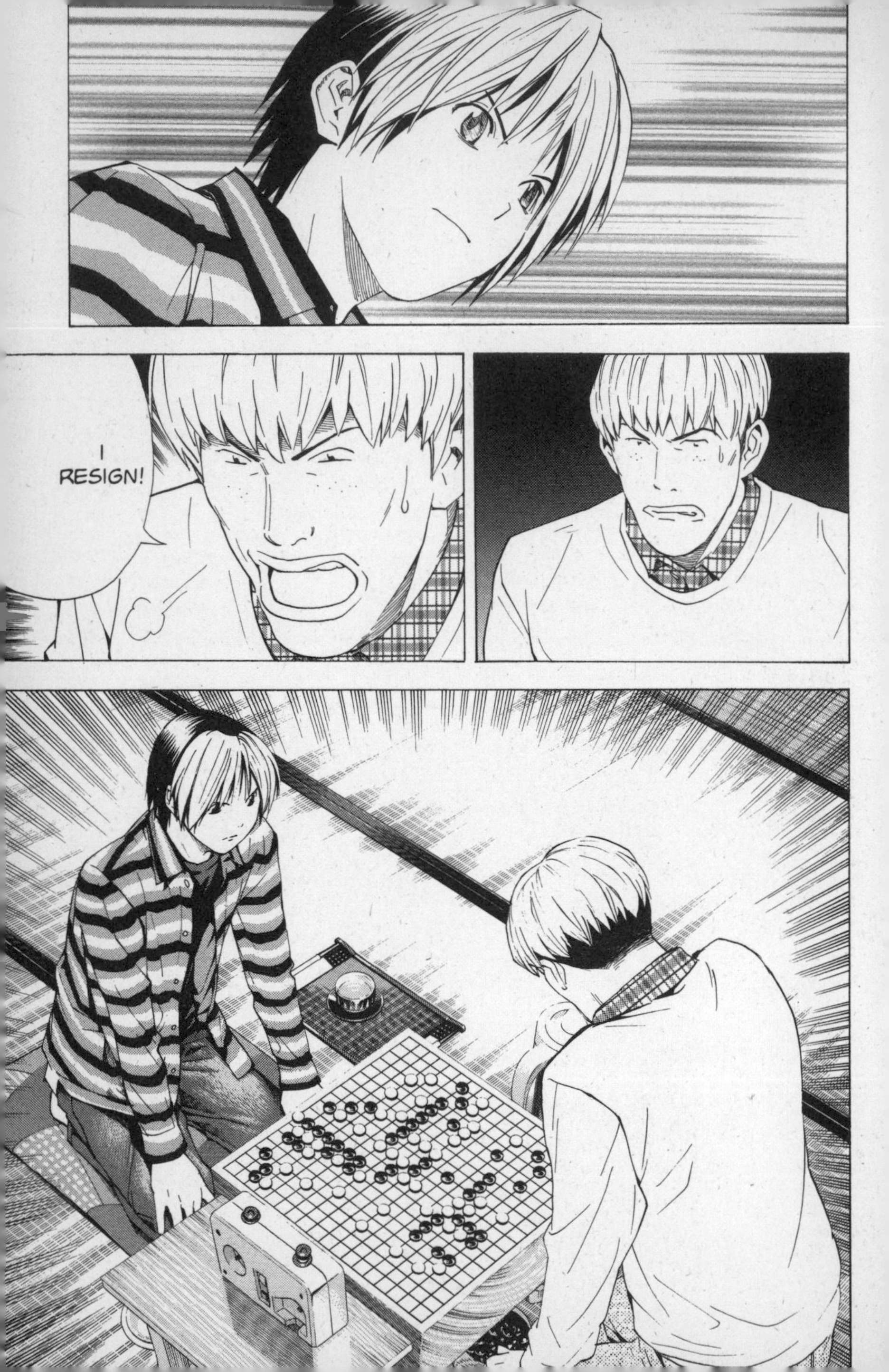
I RESIGN!

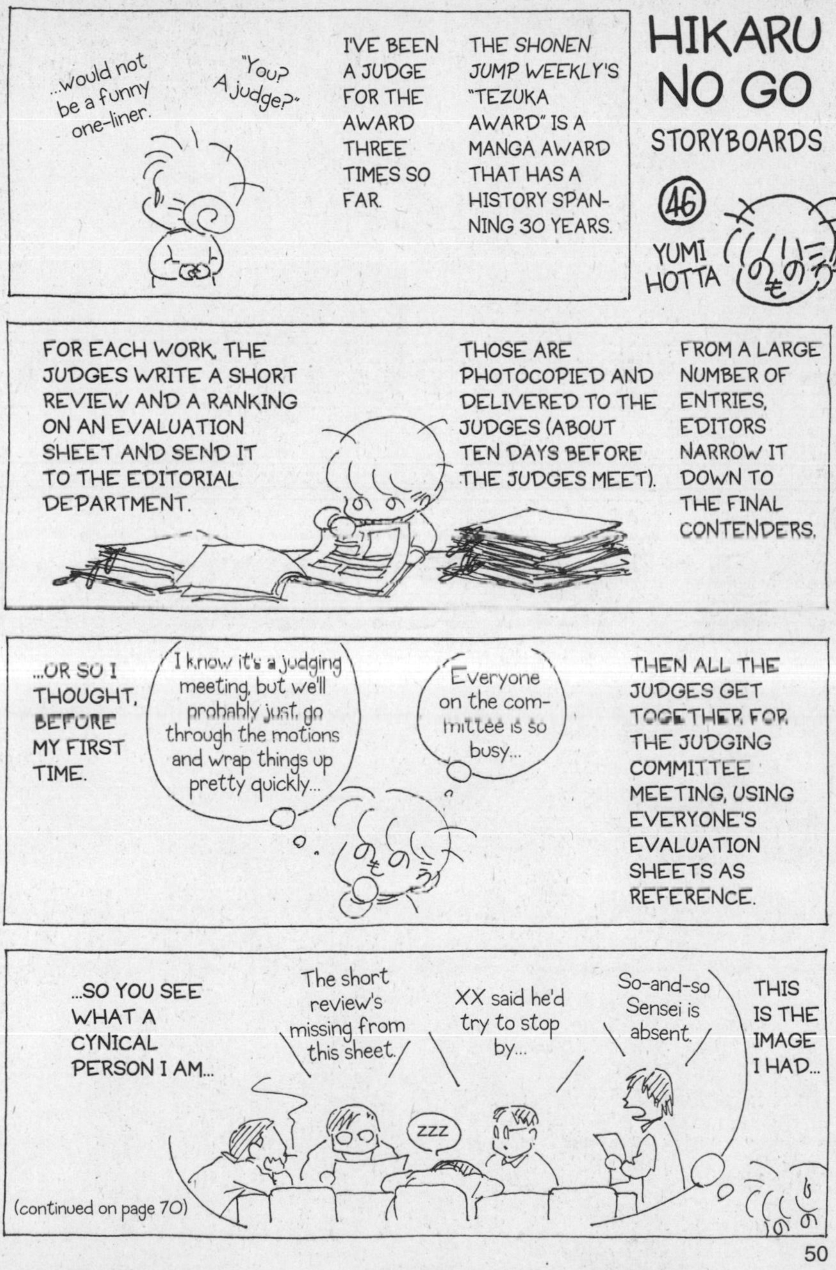
HIKARU NO GO
STORYBOARDS
46
YUMI HOTTA
THE SHONEN JUMP WEEKLY'S "TEZUKA AWARD" IS A MANGA AWARD THAT HAS A HISTORY SPANNING 30 YEARS.
I'VE BEEN A JUDGE FOR THE AWARD THREE TIMES SO FAR.
"You? A judge?"
...would not be a funny one-liner.
FROM A LARGE NUMBER OF ENTRIES, EDITORS NARROW IT DOWN TO THE FINAL CONTENDERS.
THOSE ARE PHOTOCOPIED AND DELIVERED TO THE JUDGES (ABOUT TEN DAYS BEFORE THE JUDGES MEET).
FOR EACH WORK, THE JUDGES WRITE A SHORT REVIEW AND A RANKING ON AN EVALUATION SHEET AND SEND IT TO THE EDITORIAL DEPARTMENT.
THEN ALL THE JUDGES GET TOGETHER FOR THE JUDGING COMMITTEE MEETING, USING EVERYONE'S EVALUATION SHEETS AS REFERENCE.
Everyone on the committee is so busy...
I know it's a judging meeting, but we'll probably just go through the motions and wrap things up pretty quickly...
...OR SO I THOUGHT, BEFORE MY FIRST TIME.
THIS IS THE IMAGE I HAD...
So-and-so Sensei is absent.
XX said he'd try to stop by...
ZZZ
The short review's missing from this sheet.
...SO YOU SEE WHAT A CYNICAL PERSON I AM...

(continued on page 70)

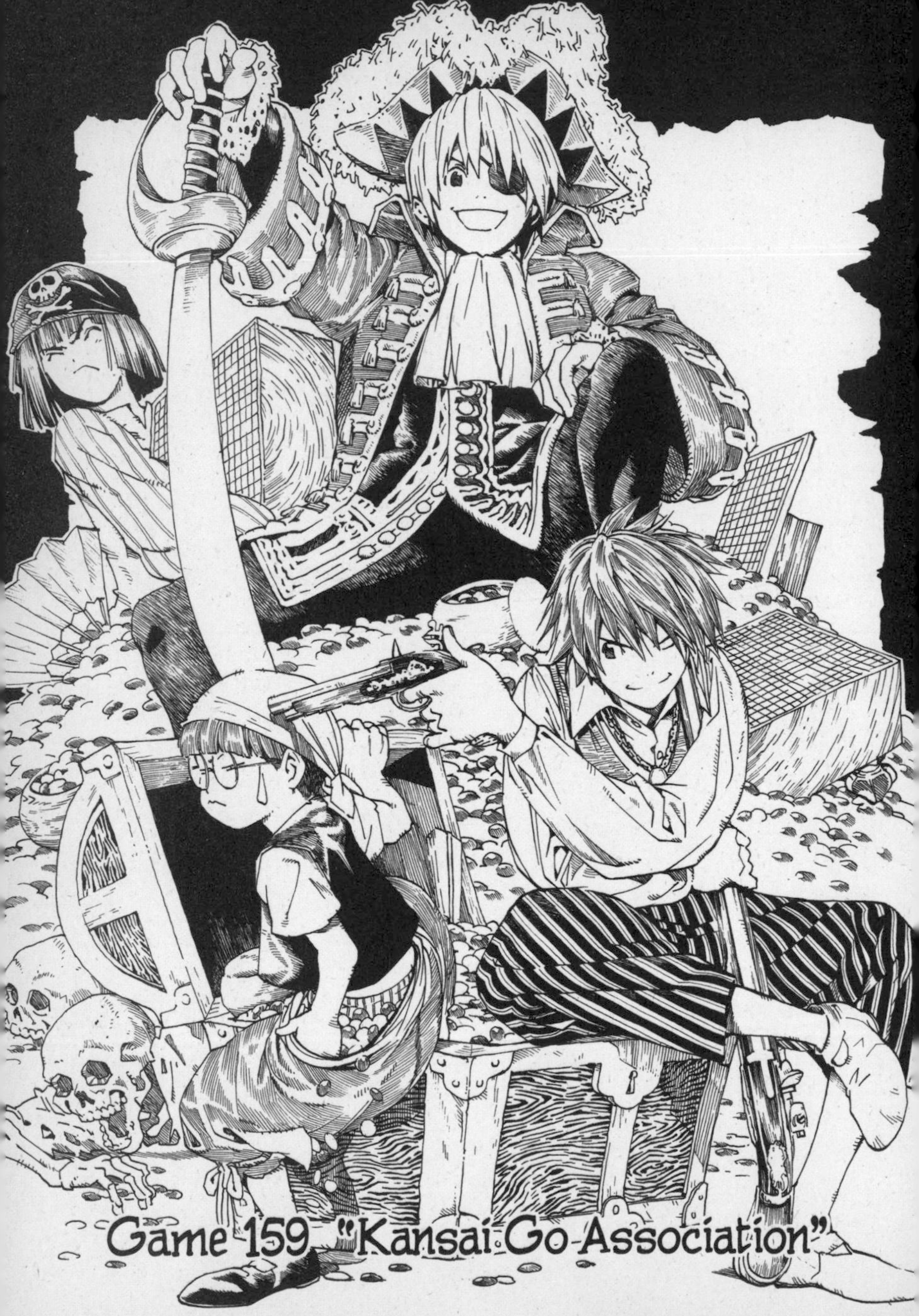

Game 159 "Kansai Go Association"

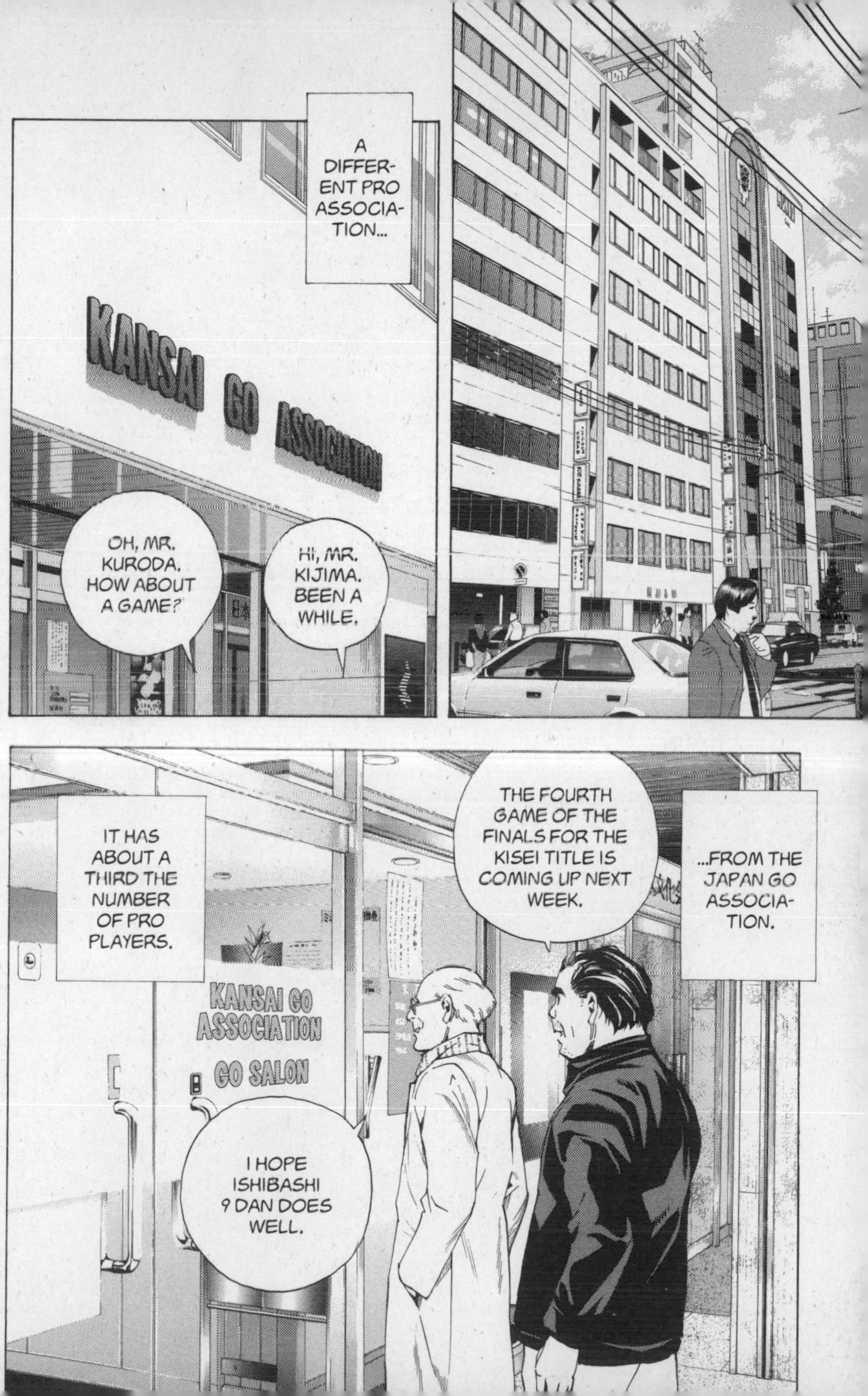
A DIFFERENT PRO ASSOCIATION...
KANSAI GO ASSOCIATION
HI, MR. KIJIMA. BEEN A WHILE.
OH, MR. KURODA. HOW ABOUT A GAME?
...FROM THE JAPAN GO ASSOCIATION.
THE FOURTH GAME OF THE FINALS FOR THE KISEI TITLE IS COMING UP NEXT WEEK.
IT HAS ABOUT A THIRD THE NUMBER OF PRO PLAYERS.
KANSAI GO ASSOCIATION
GO SALON
I HOPE ISHIBASHI 9 DAN DOES WELL.

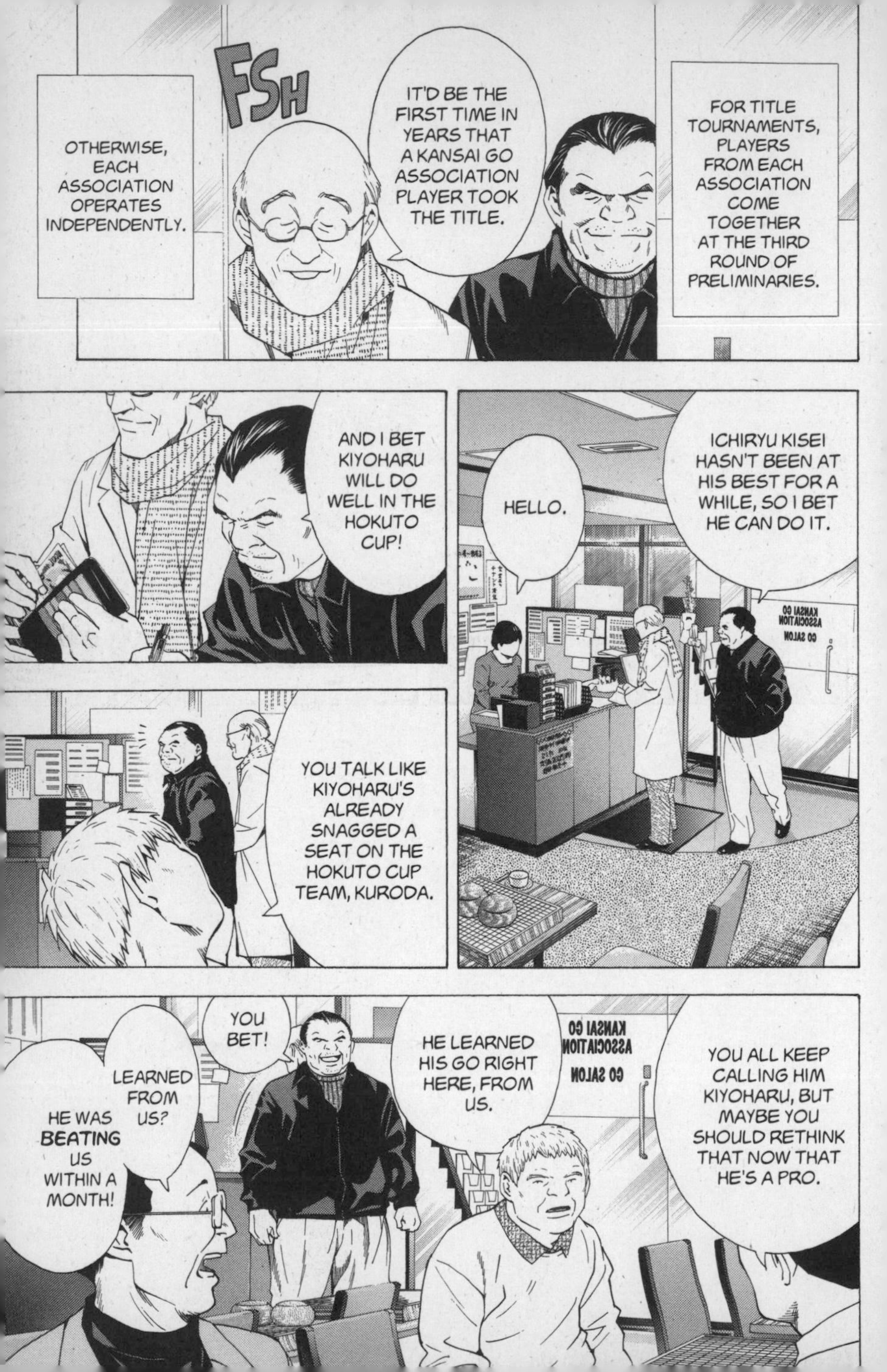
FOR TITLE TOURNAMENTS, PLAYERS FROM EACH ASSOCIATION COME TOGETHER AT THE THIRD ROUND OF PRELIMINARIES.
OTHERWISE, EACH ASSOCIATION OPERATES INDEPENDENTLY.
IT'D BE THE FIRST TIME IN YEARS THAT A KANSAI GO ASSOCIATION PLAYER TOOK THE TITLE.
FSH
ICHIRYU KISEI HASN'T BEEN AT HIS BEST FOR A WHILE, SO I BET HE CAN DO IT.
HELLO.
AND I BET KIYOHARU WILL DO WELL IN THE HOKUTO CUP!
YOU TALK LIKE KIYOHARU'S ALREADY SNAGGED A SEAT ON THE HOKUTO CUP TEAM, KURODA.
YOU ALL KEEP CALLING HIM KIYOHARU, BUT MAYBE YOU SHOULD RETHINK THAT NOW THAT HE'S A PRO.
HE LEARNED HIS GO RIGHT HERE, FROM US.
YOU BET!
LEARNED FROM US?
HE WAS **BEATING** US WITHIN A MONTH!

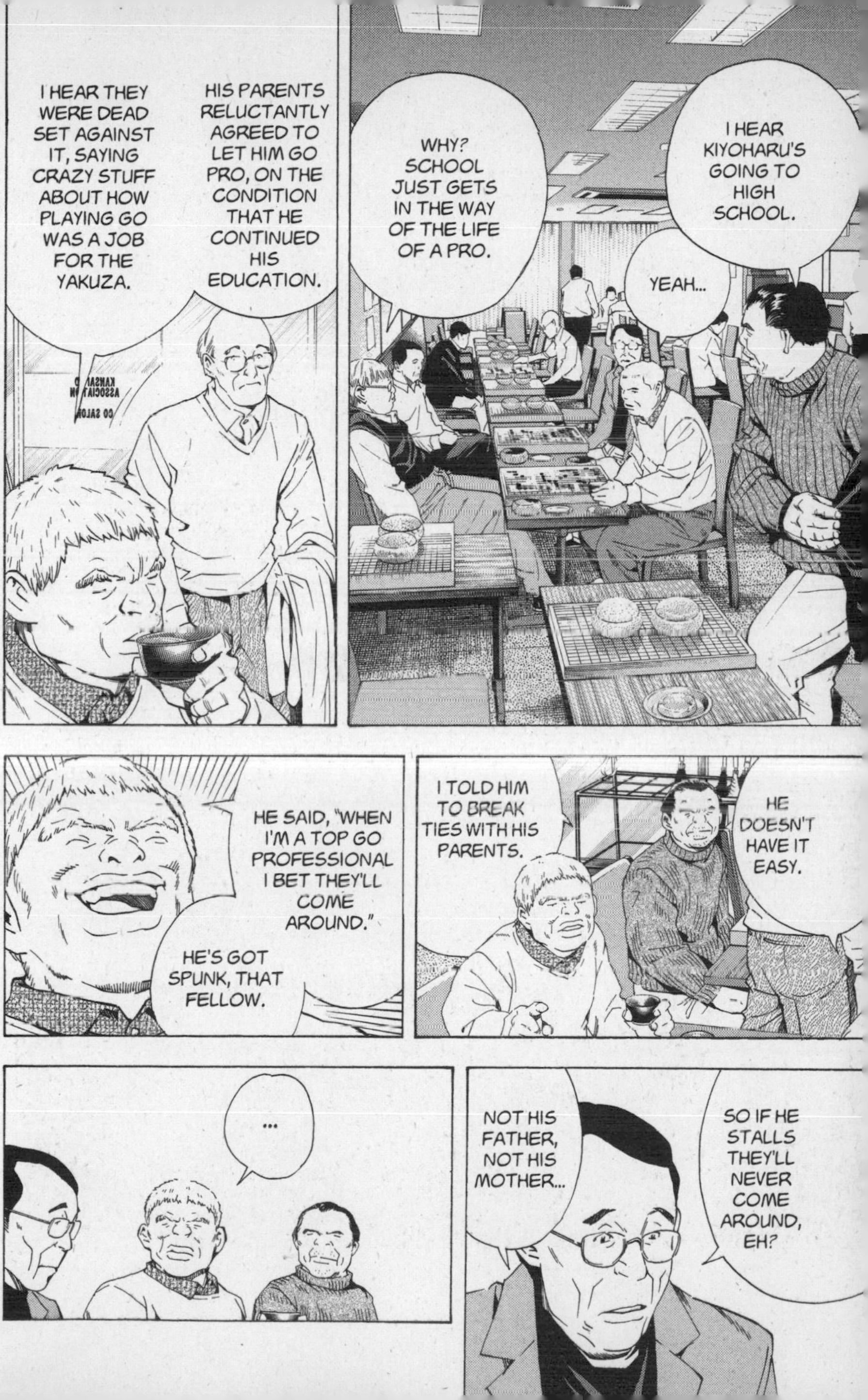
I HEAR KIYOHARU'S GOING TO HIGH SCHOOL.
WHY? SCHOOL JUST GETS IN THE WAY OF THE LIFE OF A PRO.
YEAH...
HIS PARENTS RELUCTANTLY AGREED TO LET HIM GO PRO, ON THE CONDITION THAT HE CONTINUED HIS EDUCATION.
I HEAR THEY WERE DEAD SET AGAINST IT, SAYING CRAZY STUFF ABOUT HOW PLAYING GO WAS A JOB FOR THE YAKUZA.
HE DOESN'T HAVE IT EASY.
I TOLD HIM TO BREAK TIES WITH HIS PARENTS.
HE SAID, "WHEN I'M A TOP GO PROFESSIONAL I BET THEY'LL COME AROUND."
HE'S GOT SPUNK, THAT FELLOW.
SO IF HE STALLS THEY'LL NEVER COME AROUND, EH?
NOT HIS FATHER, NOT HIS MOTHER...
...

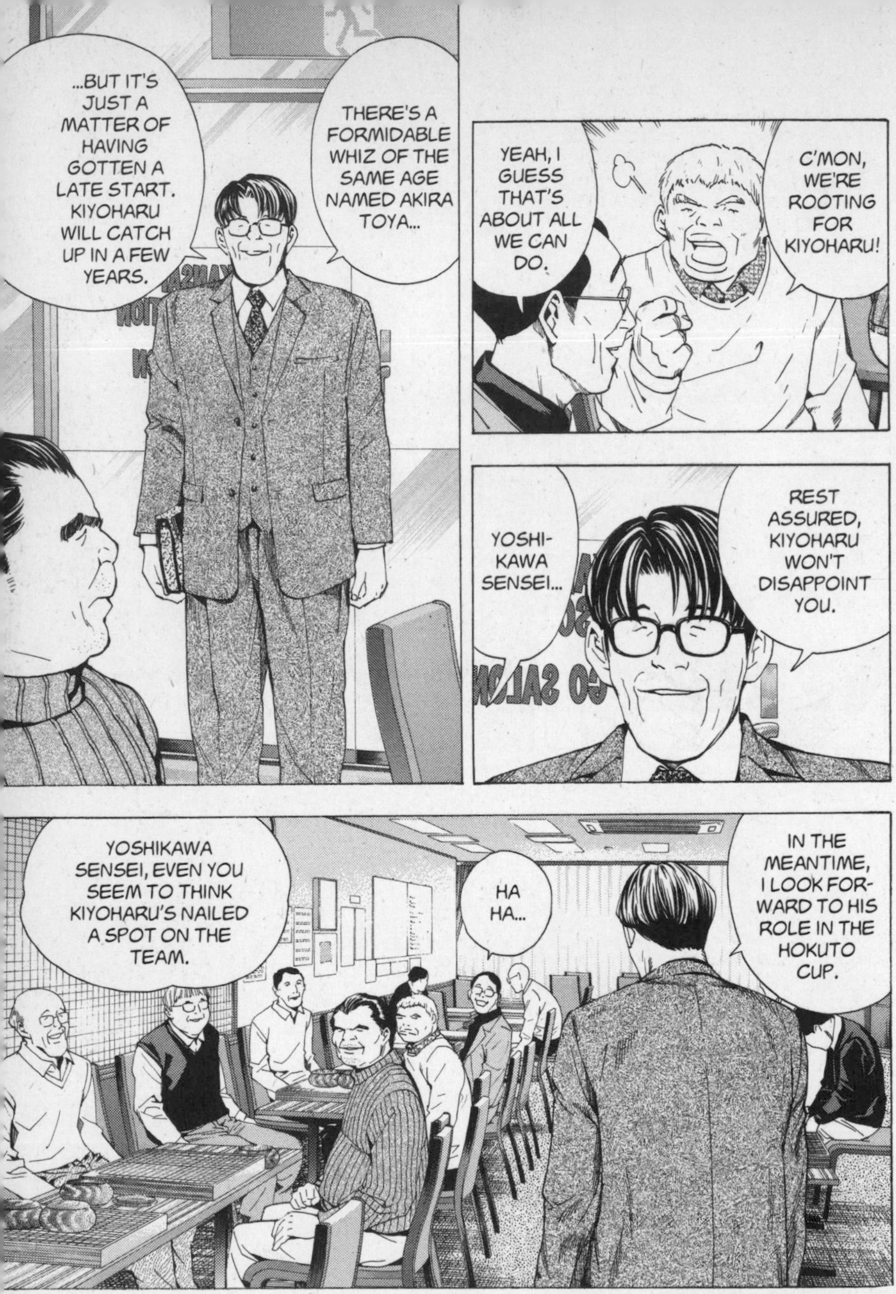
C'MON, WE'RE ROOTING FOR KIYOHARU!
YEAH, I GUESS THAT'S ABOUT ALL WE CAN DO.
REST ASSURED, KIYOHARU WON'T DISAPPOINT YOU.
YOSHI-KAWA SENSEI...
THERE'S A FORMIDABLE WHIZ OF THE SAME AGE NAMED AKIRA TOYA...
...BUT IT'S JUST A MATTER OF HAVING GOTTEN A LATE START. KIYOHARU WILL CATCH UP IN A FEW YEARS.
IN THE MEANTIME, I LOOK FOR-WARD TO HIS ROLE IN THE HOKUTO CUP.
HA HA...
YOSHIKAWA SENSEI, EVEN YOU SEEM TO THINK KIYOHARU'S NAILED A SPOT ON THE TEAM.

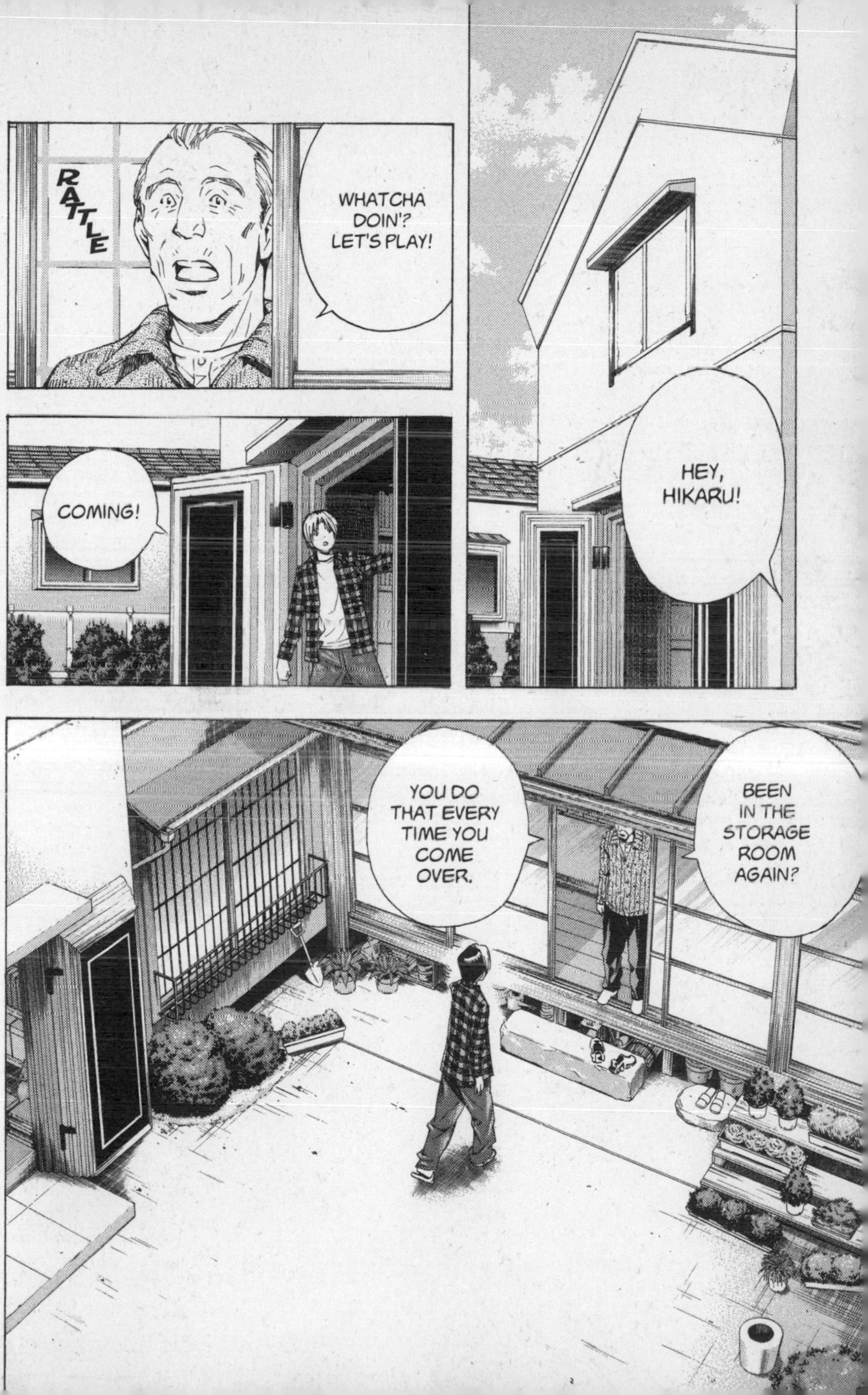
HEY, HIKARU!
RATTLE
WHATCHA DOIN'? LET'S PLAY!
COMING!
BEEN IN THE STORAGE ROOM AGAIN?
YOU DO THAT EVERY TIME YOU COME OVER.

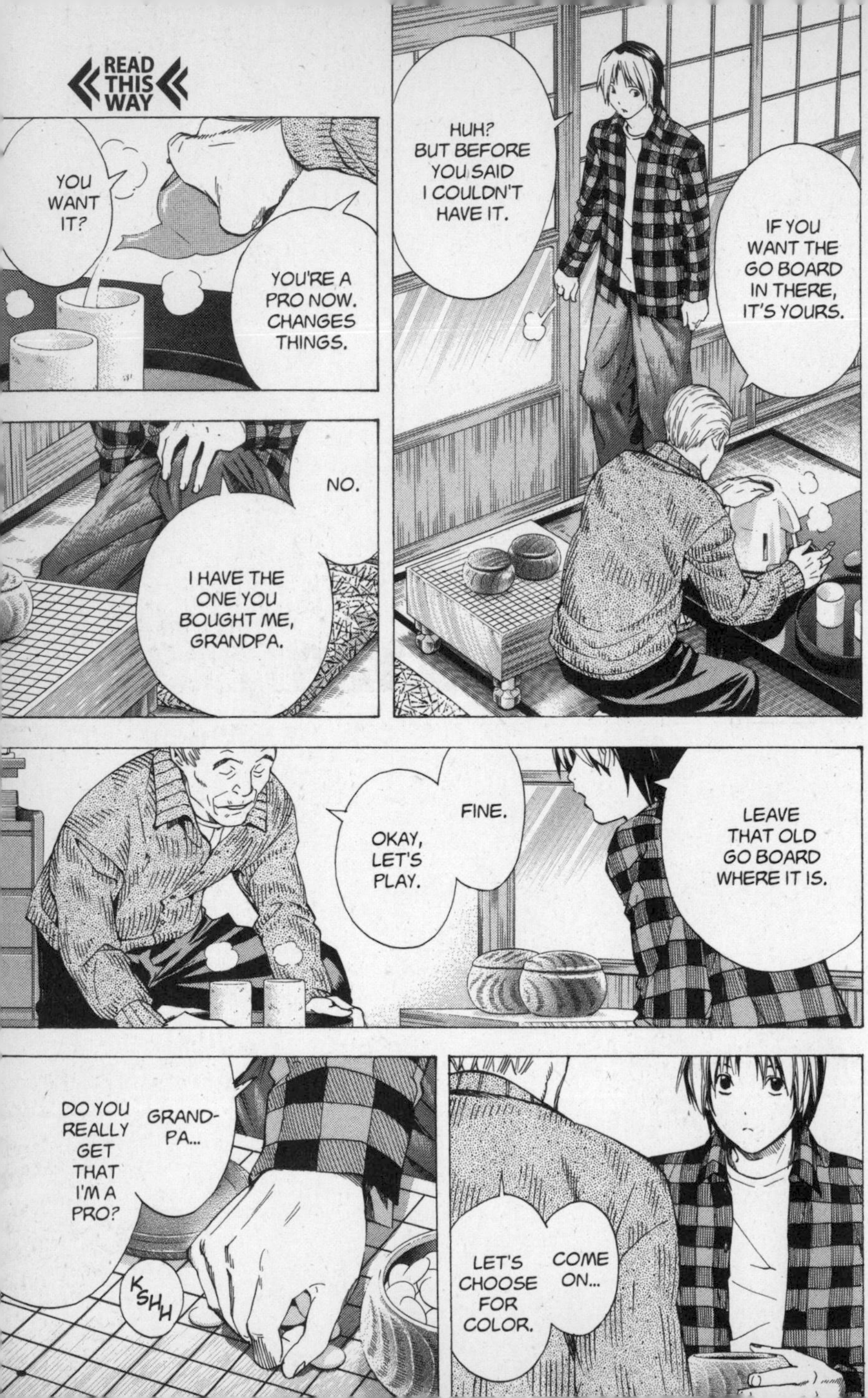
READ THIS WAY
IF YOU WANT THE GO BOARD IN THERE, IT'S YOURS.
HUH? BUT BEFORE YOU SAID I COULDN'T HAVE IT.
YOU'RE A PRO NOW. CHANGES THINGS.
YOU WANT IT?
NO.
I HAVE THE ONE YOU BOUGHT ME, GRANDPA.
LEAVE THAT OLD GO BOARD WHERE IT IS.
FINE.
OKAY, LET'S PLAY.
COME ON...
LET'S CHOOSE FOR COLOR.
GRAND-PA...
DO YOU REALLY GET THAT I'M A PRO?
KSHH

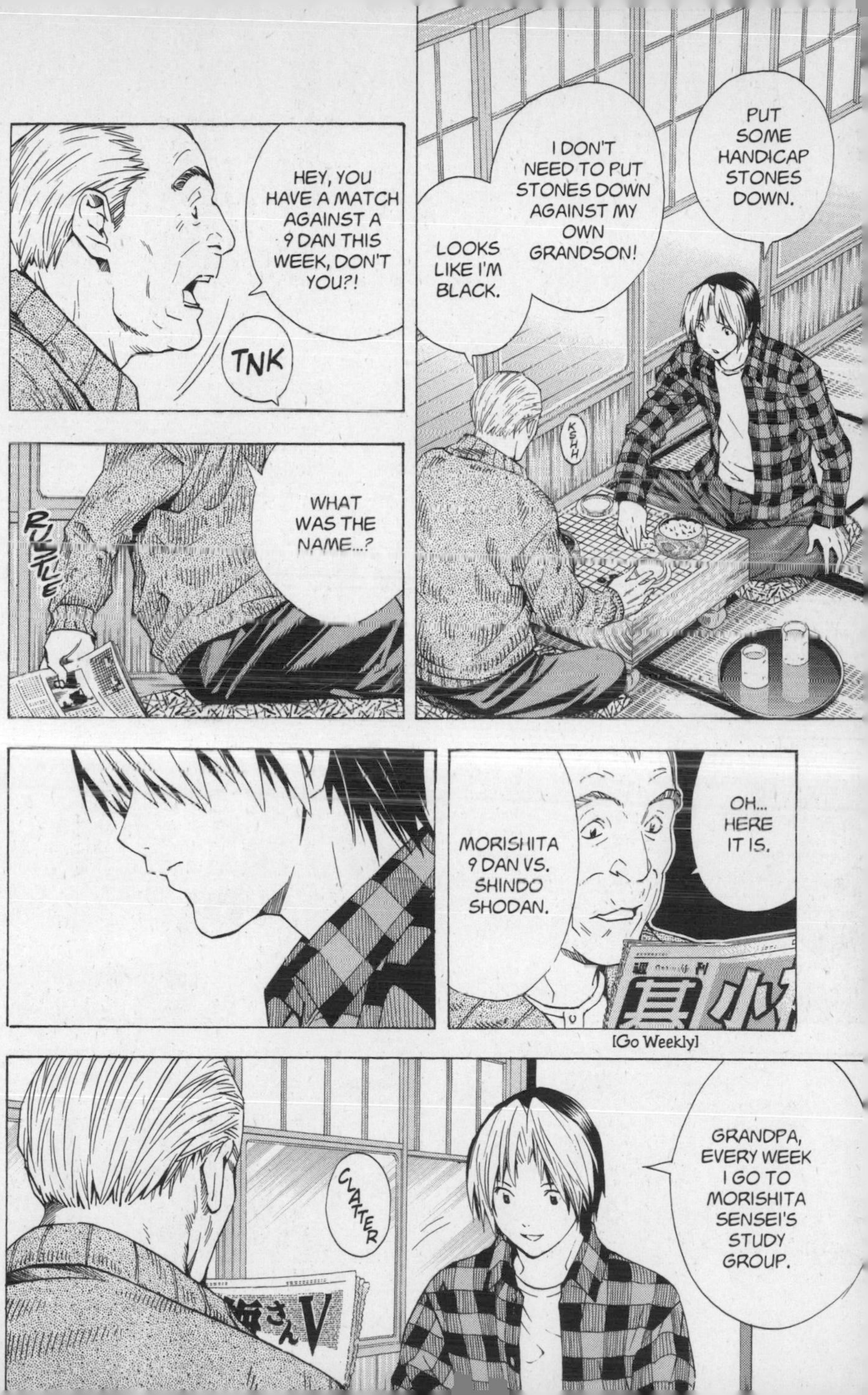
PUT SOME HANDICAP STONES DOWN.
I DON'T NEED TO PUT STONES DOWN AGAINST MY OWN GRANDSON!
LOOKS LIKE I'M BLACK.
KSHH
HEY, YOU HAVE A MATCH AGAINST A 9 DAN THIS WEEK, DON'T YOU?!
TNK
WHAT WAS THE NAME...?
RUSTLE
OH... HERE IT IS.
MORISHITA 9 DAN VS. SHINDO SHODAN.
[Go Weekly]
GRANDPA, EVERY WEEK I GO TO MORISHITA SENSEI'S STUDY GROUP.
CLATTER

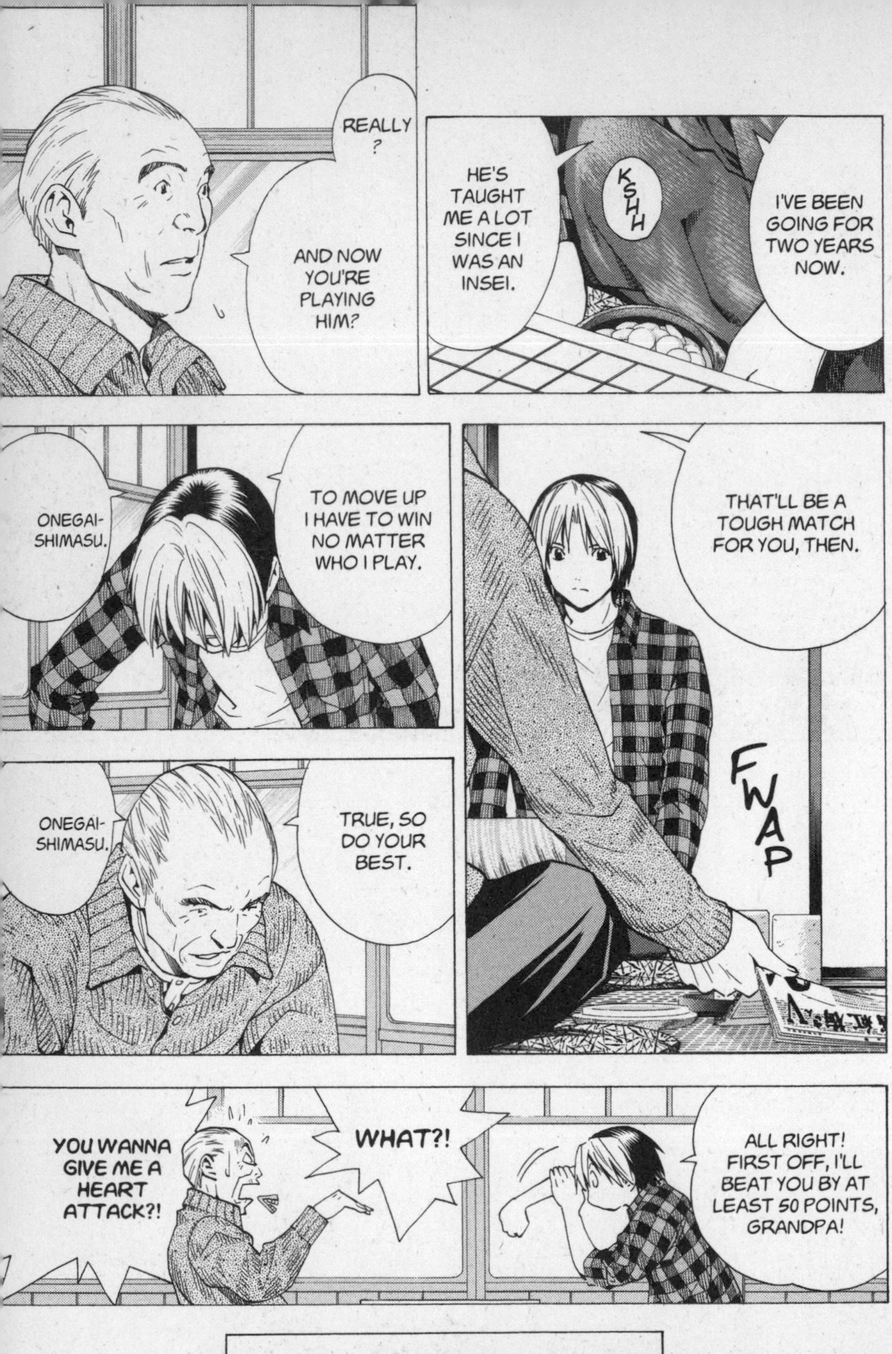

I'VE BEEN GOING FOR TWO YEARS NOW.
KSHH
HE'S TAUGHT ME A LOT SINCE I WAS AN INSEI.
REALLY?
AND NOW YOU'RE PLAYING HIM?
THAT'LL BE A TOUGH MATCH FOR YOU, THEN.
FWAP
TO MOVE UP I HAVE TO WIN NO MATTER WHO I PLAY.
ONEGAI-SHIMASU.
TRUE, SO DO YOUR BEST.
ONEGAI-SHIMASU.
ALL RIGHT! FIRST OFF, I'LL BEAT YOU BY AT LEAST 50 POINTS, GRANDPA!
WHAT?!
YOU WANNA GIVE ME A HEART ATTACK?!

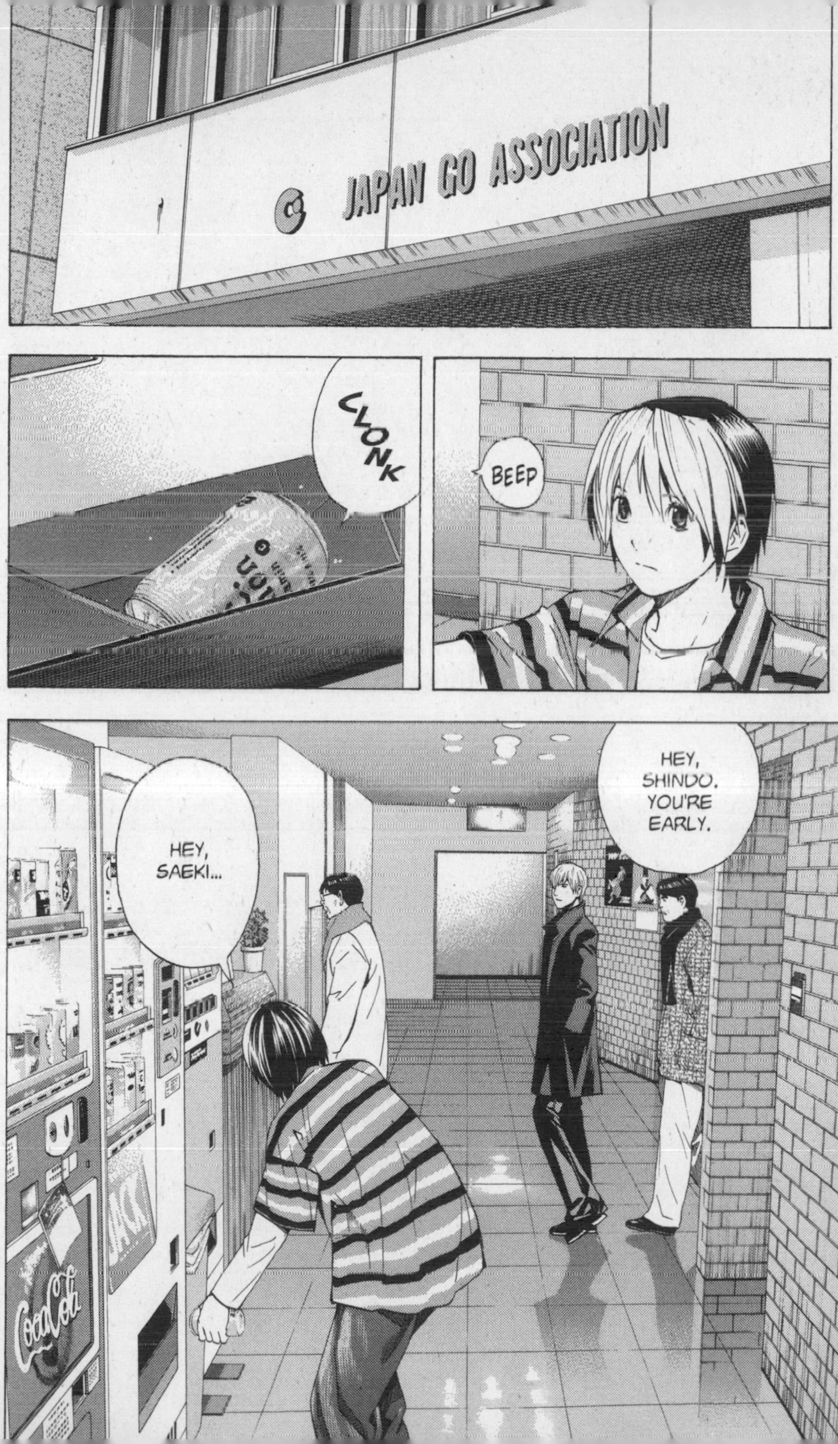
JAPAN GO ASSOCIATION
BEEP
CLONK
HEY, SHINDO. YOU'RE EARLY.
HEY, SAEKI...

READ THIS WAY

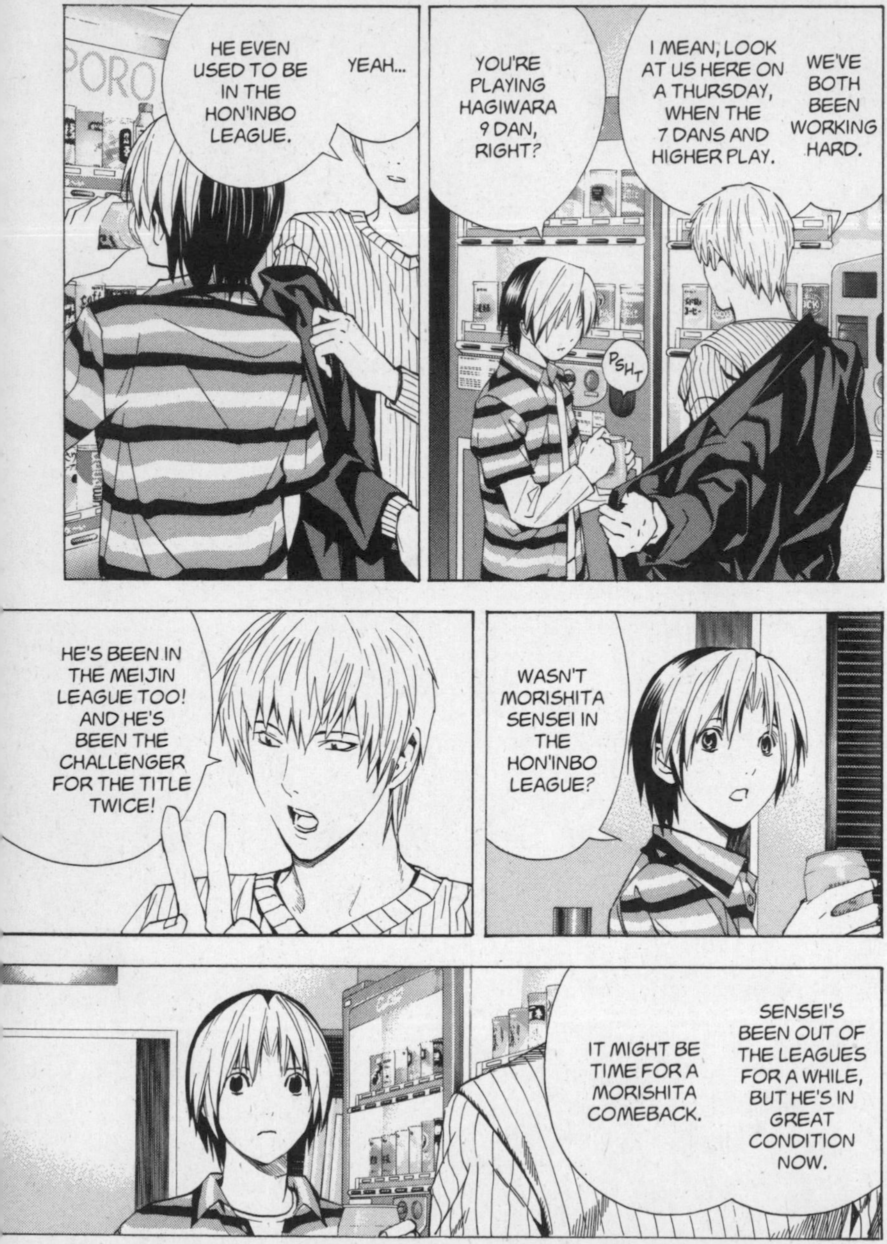
WE'VE BOTH BEEN WORKING HARD.
I MEAN, LOOK AT US HERE ON A THURSDAY, WHEN THE 7 DANS AND HIGHER PLAY.
YOU'RE PLAYING HAGIWARA 9 DAN, RIGHT?
PSHT
YEAH...
HE EVEN USED TO BE IN THE HON'INBO LEAGUE.
WASN'T MORISHITA SENSEI IN THE HON'INBO LEAGUE?
HE'S BEEN IN THE MEIJIN LEAGUE TOO! AND HE'S BEEN THE CHALLENGER FOR THE TITLE TWICE!
SENSEI'S BEEN OUT OF THE LEAGUES FOR A WHILE, BUT HE'S IN GREAT CONDITION NOW.
IT MIGHT BE TIME FOR A MORISHITA COMEBACK.

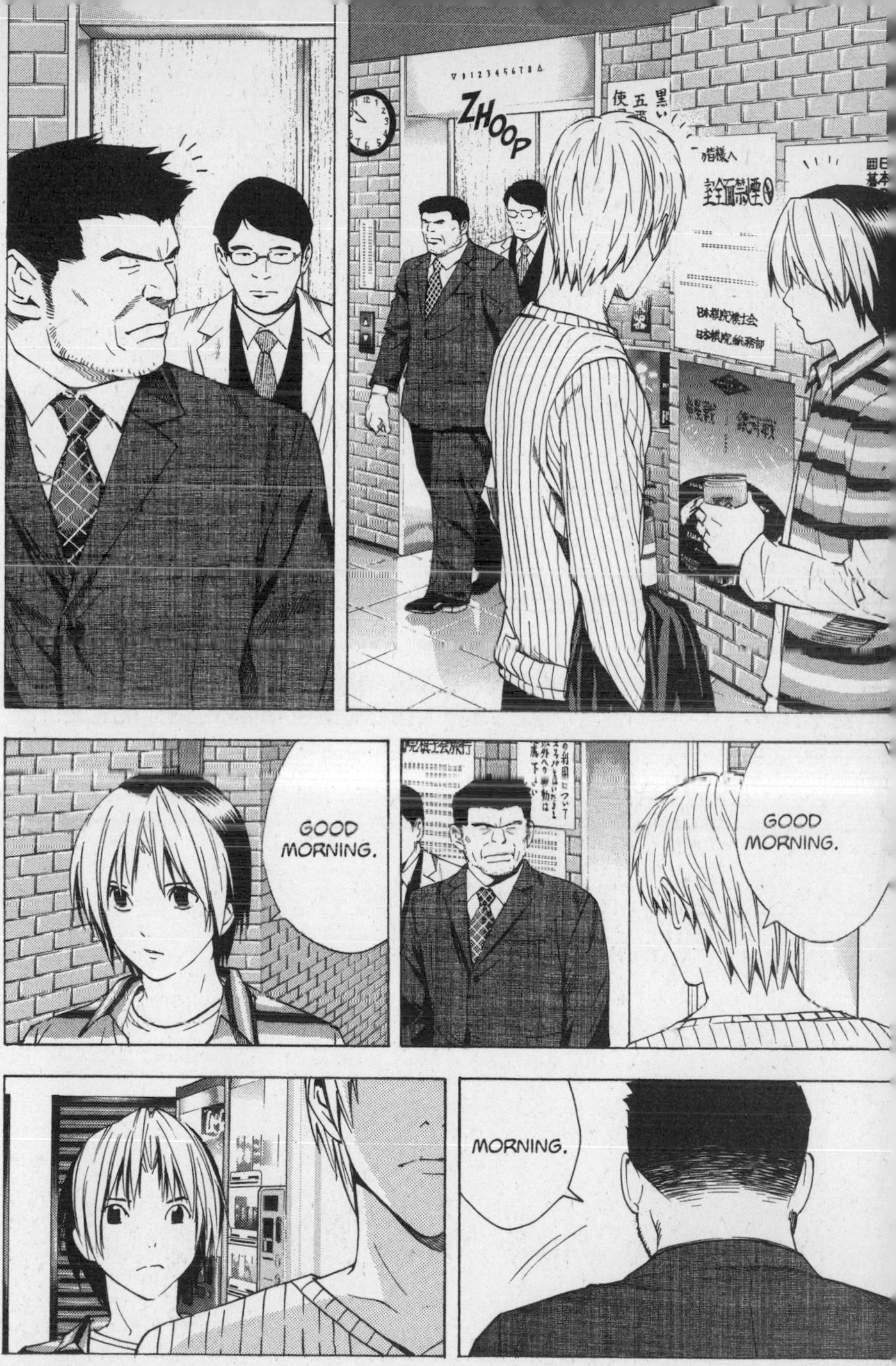
ZHOOP
GOOD MORNING.
GOOD MORNING.
MORNING.

READ THIS WAY

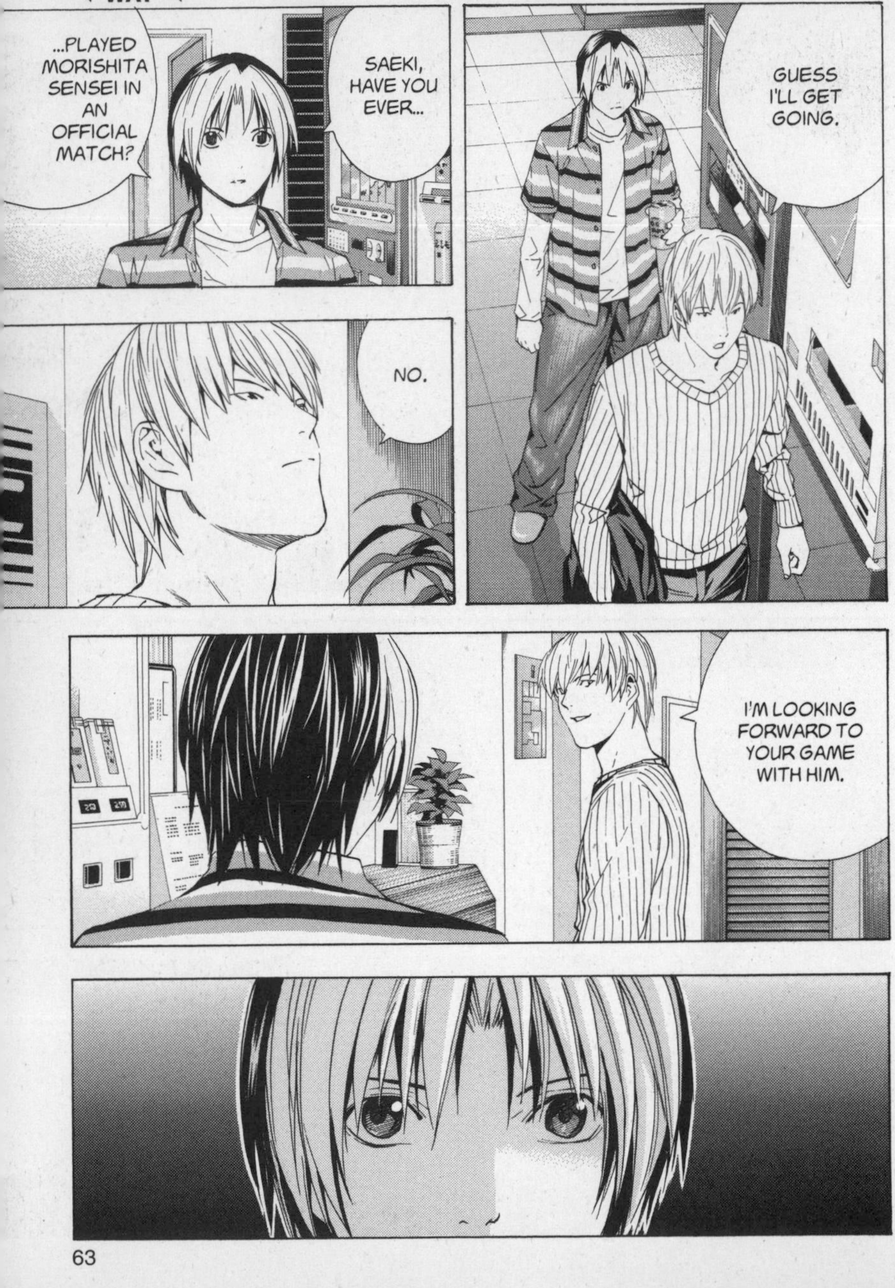
GUESS I'LL GET GOING.
SAEKI, HAVE YOU EVER...
...PLAYED MORISHITA SENSEI IN AN OFFICIAL MATCH?
NO.
I'M LOOKING FORWARD TO YOUR GAME WITH HIM.

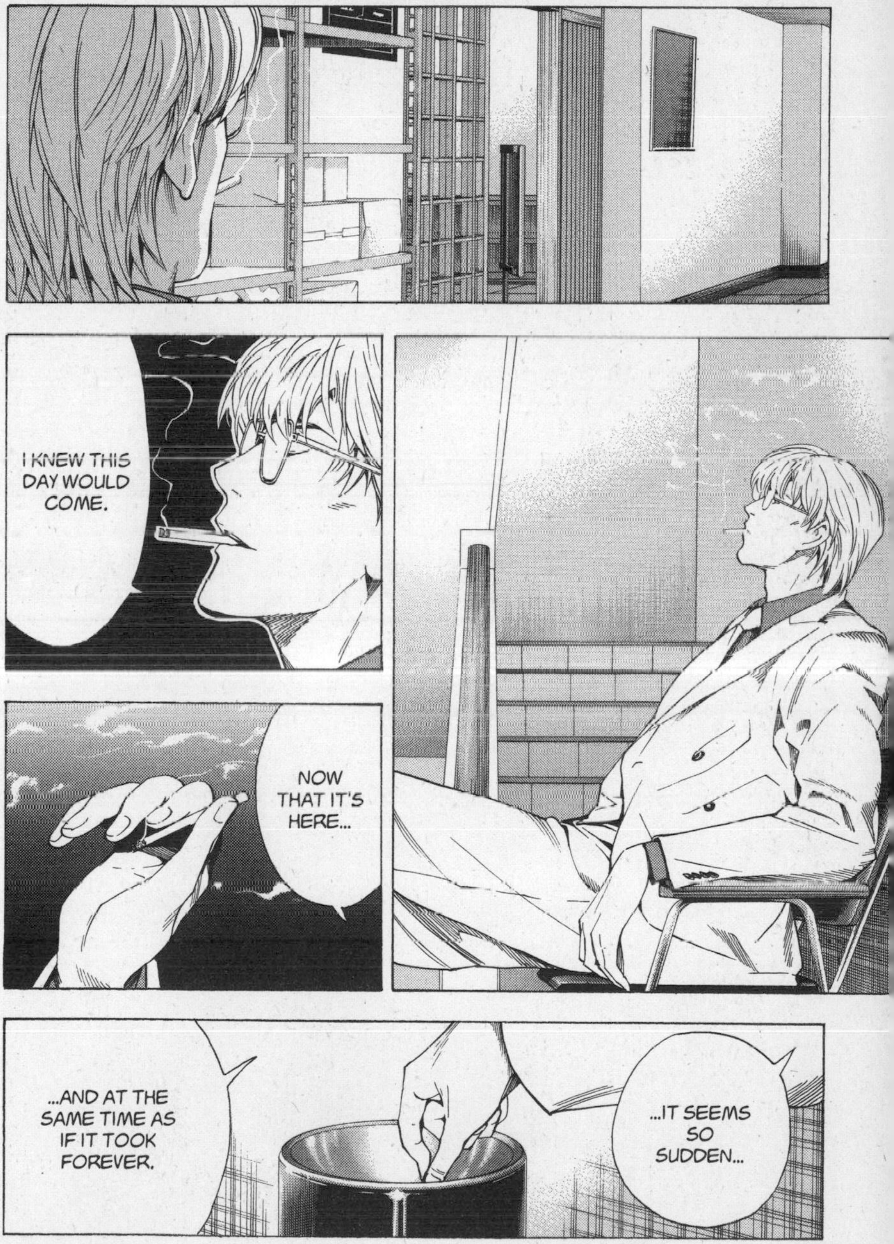
I KNEW THIS DAY WOULD COME.
NOW THAT IT'S HERE...
...IT SEEMS SO SUDDEN...
...AND AT THE SAME TIME AS IF IT TOOK FOREVER.

READ THIS WAY

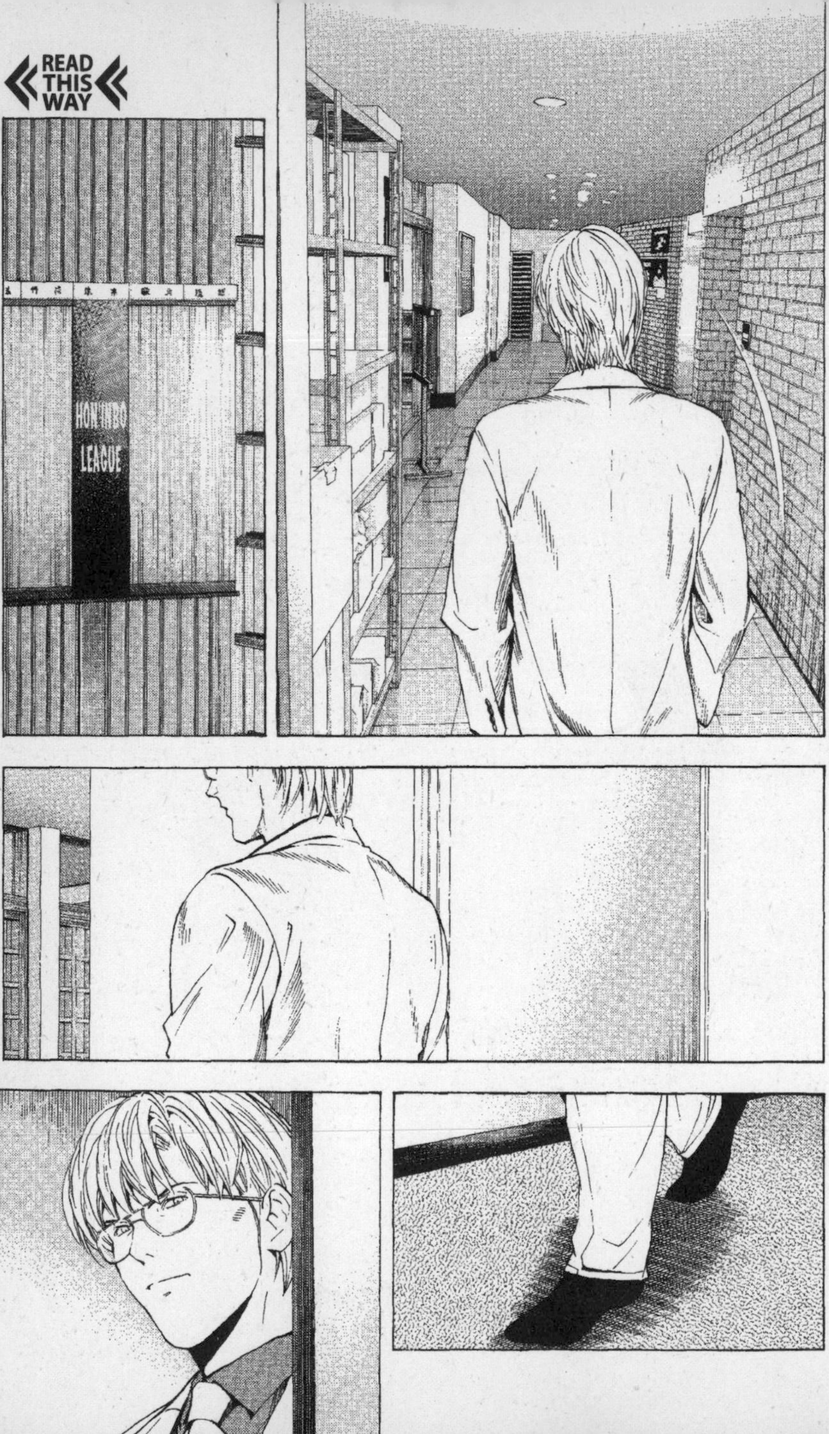
HON'INBO
LEAGUE

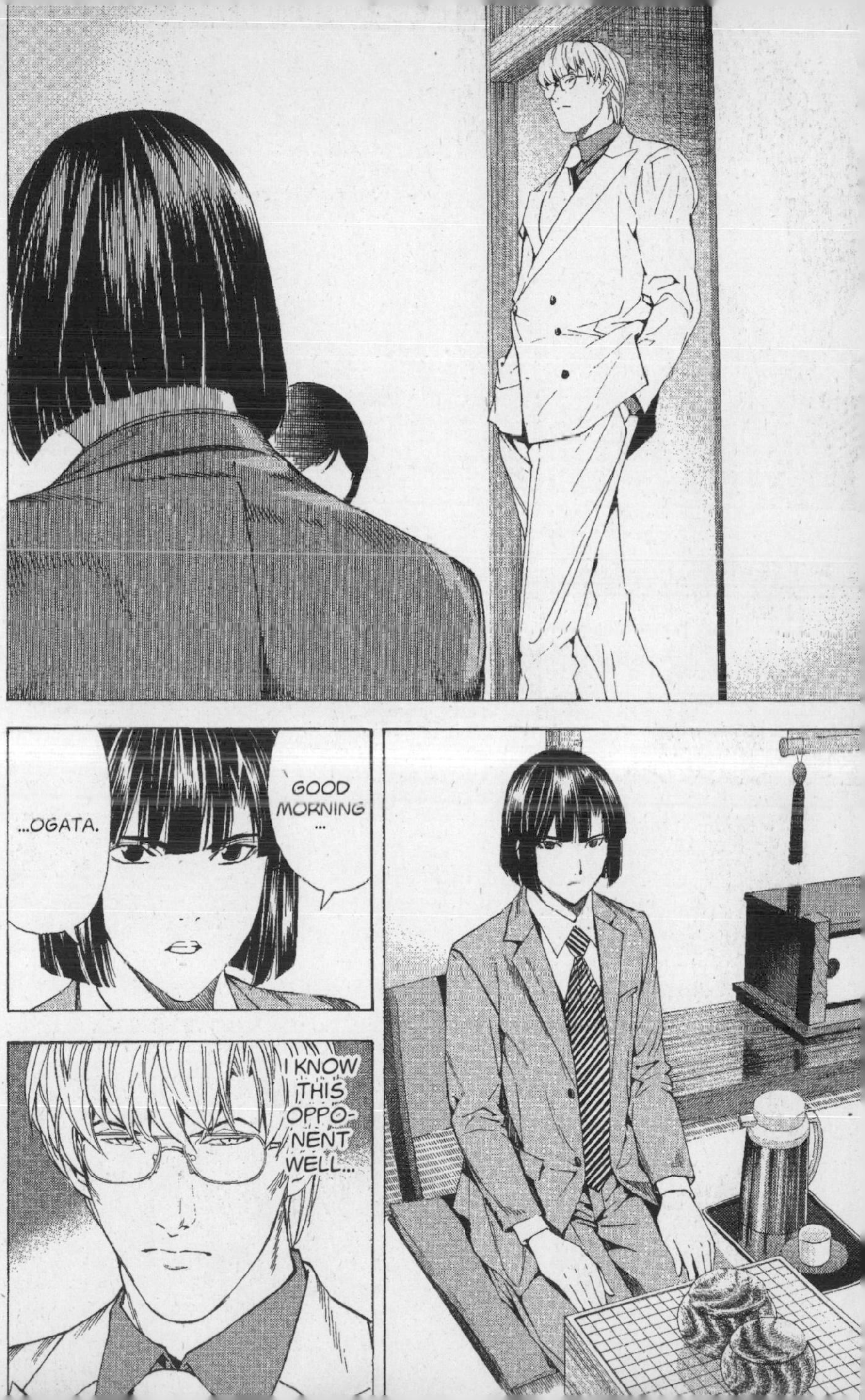
GOOD MORNING ...
...OGATA.
I KNOW THIS OPPONENT WELL...

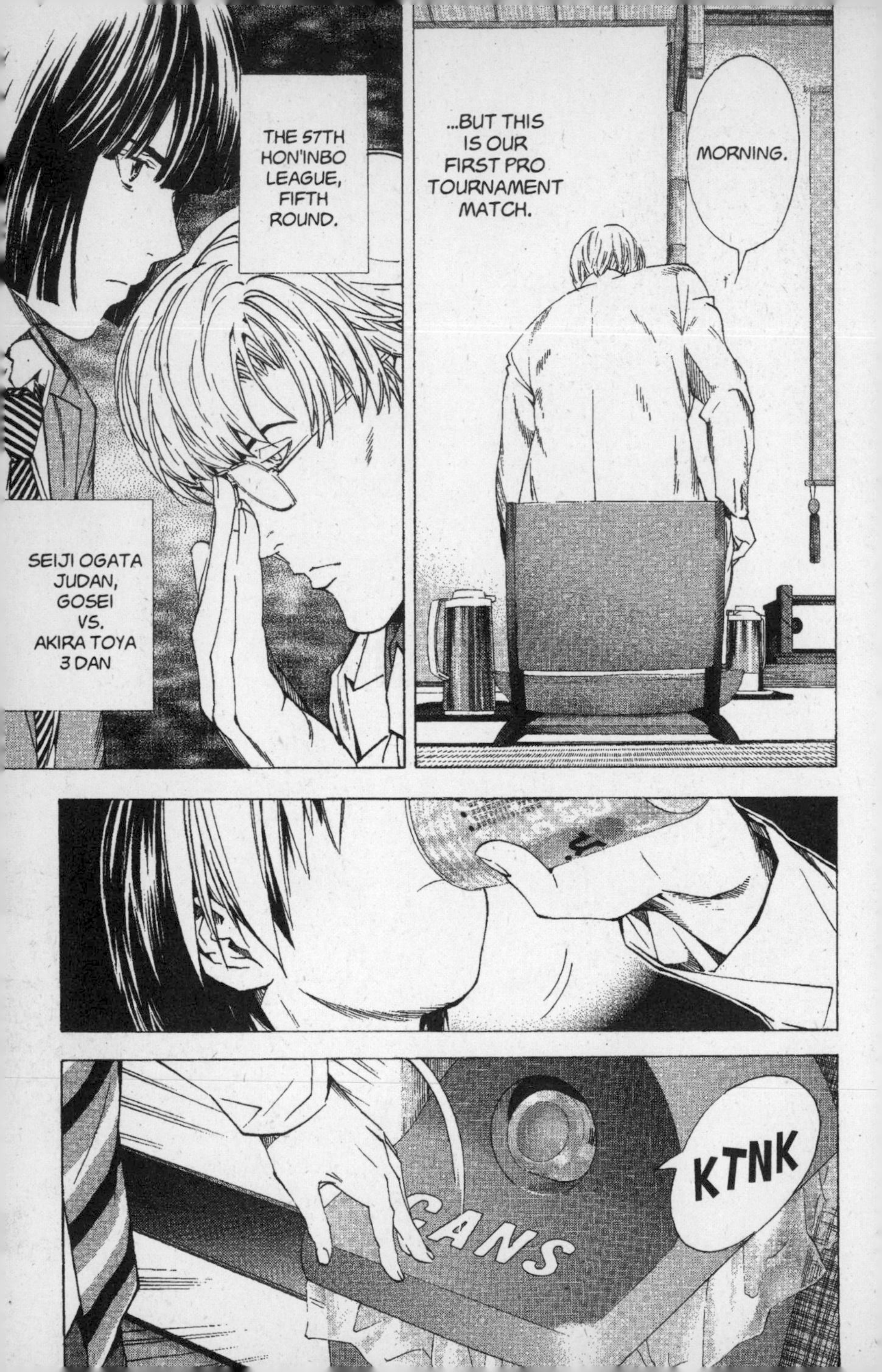
MORNING.
...BUT THIS IS OUR FIRST PRO TOURNAMENT MATCH.
THE 57TH HON'INBO LEAGUE, FIFTH ROUND.
SEIJI OGATA JUDAN, GOSEI VS. AKIRA TOYA 3 DAN
KTNK
CANS

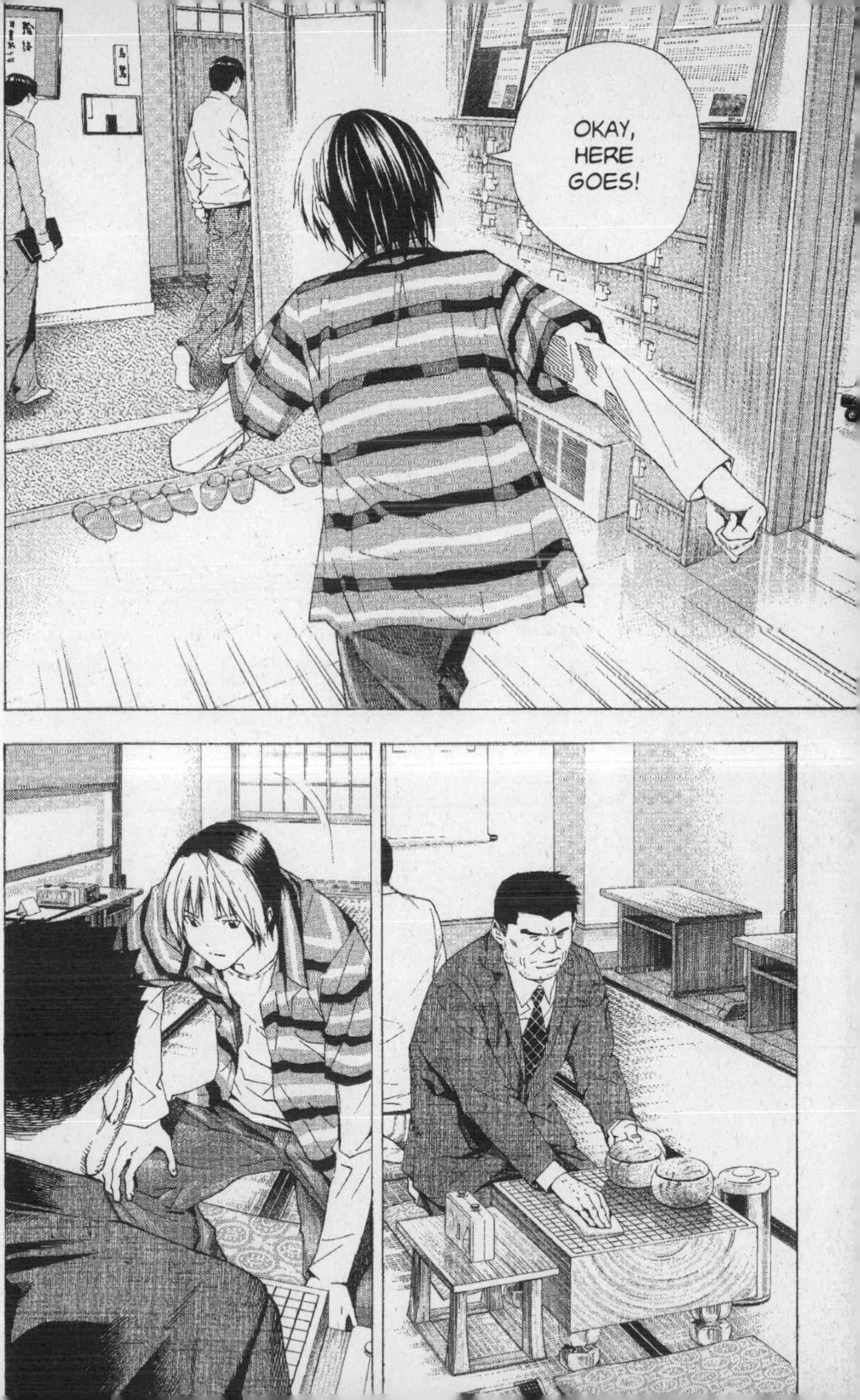
OKAY, HERE GOES!

READ THIS WAY

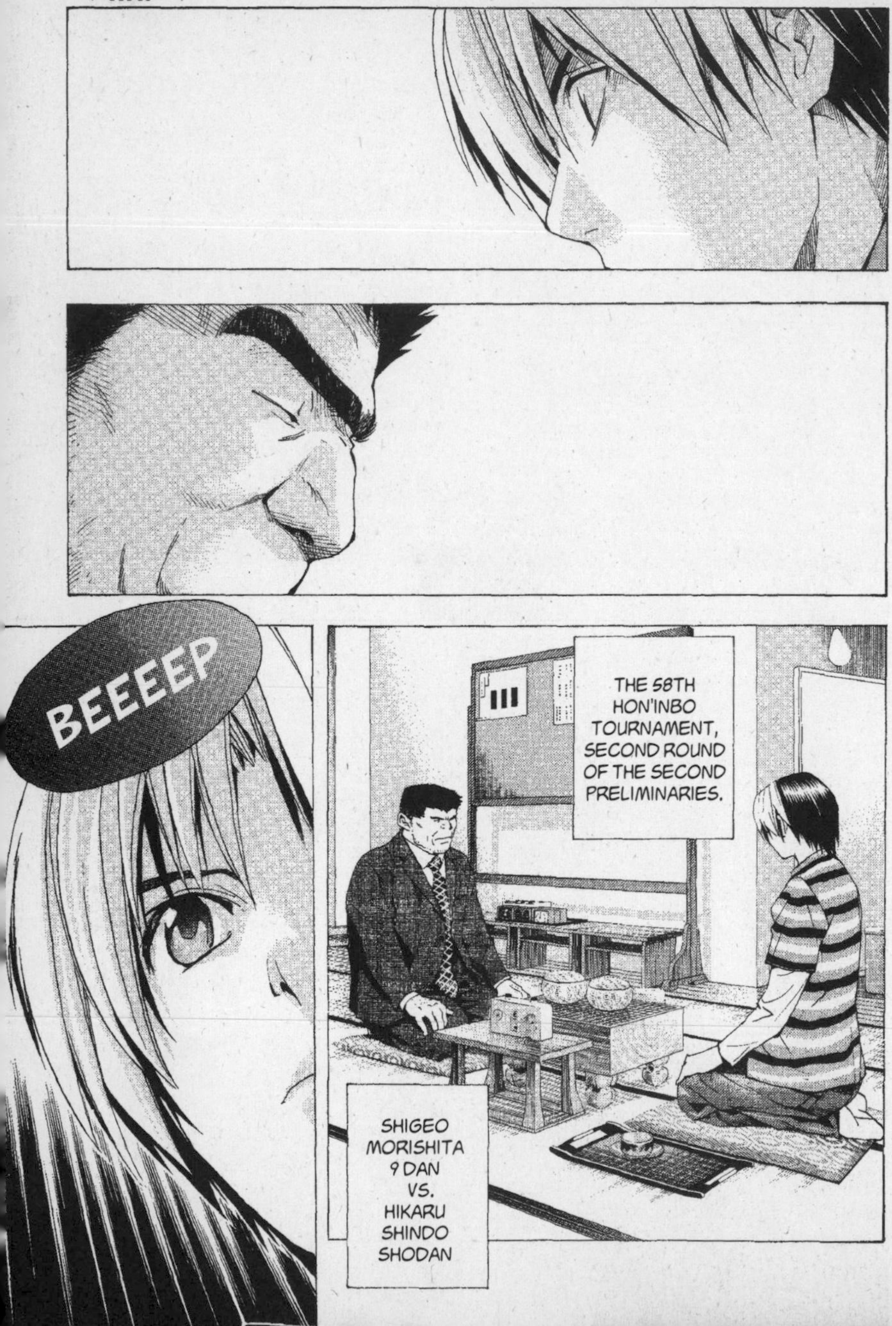
THE 58TH HON'INBO TOURNAMENT, SECOND ROUND OF THE SECOND PRELIMINARIES.
SHIGEO MORISHITA 9 DAN VS. HIKARU SHINDO SHODAN
BEEEEP

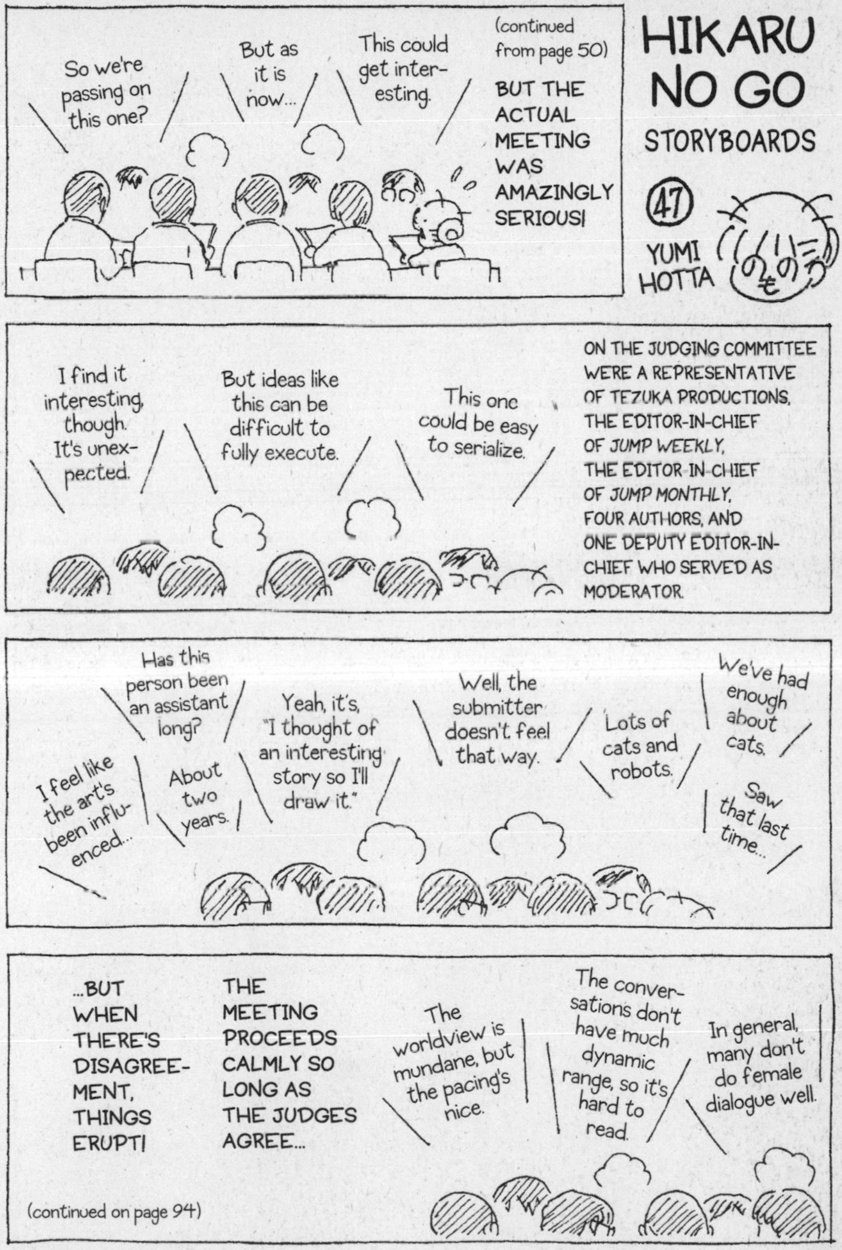
HIKARU NO GO STORYBOARDS
47
YUMI HOTTA
(continued from page 50)
BUT THE ACTUAL MEETING WAS AMAZINGLY SERIOUS!
This could get interesting.
But as it is now...
So we're passing on this one?
ON THE JUDGING COMMITTEE WERE A REPRESENTATIVE OF TEZUKA PRODUCTIONS, THE EDITOR-IN-CHIEF OF JUMP WEEKLY, THE EDITOR-IN-CHIEF OF JUMP MONTHLY, FOUR AUTHORS, AND ONE DEPUTY EDITOR-IN-CHIEF WHO SERVED AS MODERATOR.
This one could be easy to serialize.
But ideas like this can be difficult to fully execute.
I find it interesting, though. It's unexpected.
We've had enough about cats.
Saw that last time...
Lots of cats and robots.
Well, the submitter doesn't feel that way.
Has this person been an assistant long?
Yeah, it's, "I thought of an interesting story so I'll draw it."
About two years.
I feel like the art's been influenced...
In general, many don't do female dialogue well.
The conversations don't have much dynamic range, so it's hard to read.
The worldview is mundane, but the pacing's nice.
THE MEETING PROCEEDS CALMLY SO LONG AS THE JUDGES AGREE...
...BUT WHEN THERE'S DISAGREEMENT, THINGS ERUPT!
(continued on page 94)

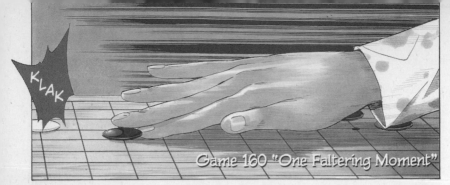

KLAK

Game 160 "One Faltering Moment"

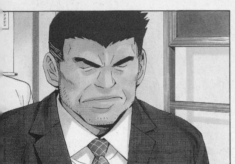

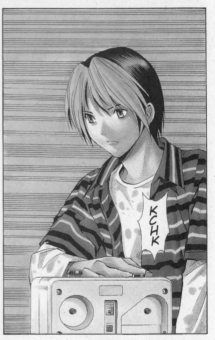

KCHK

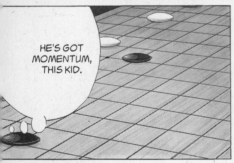

HE'S GOT MOMENTUM, THIS KID.

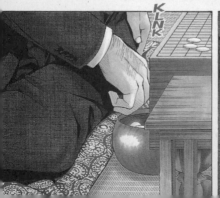

KLNK

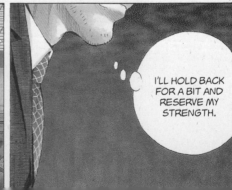

I'LL HOLD BACK FOR A BIT AND RESERVE MY STRENGTH.

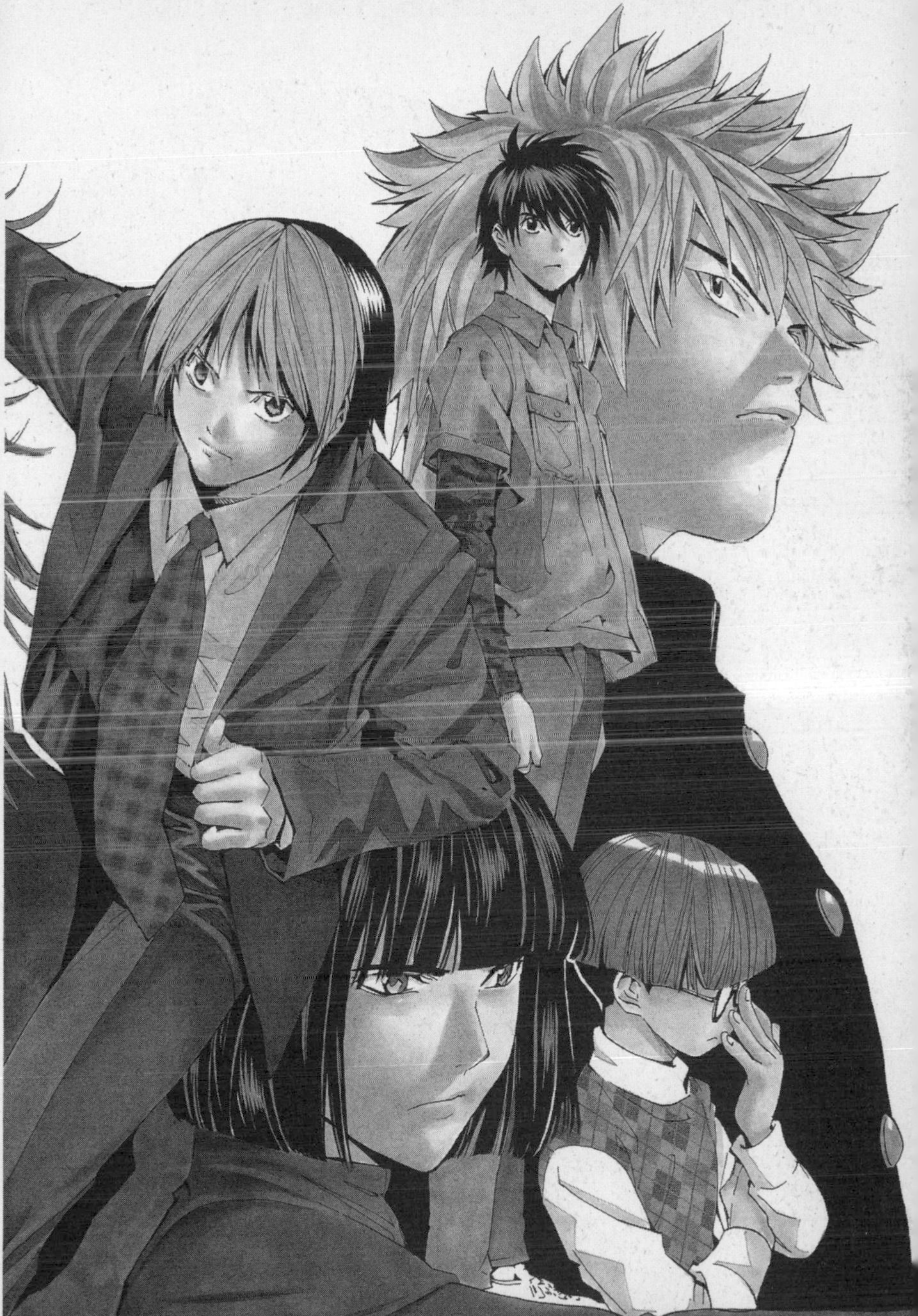

Game 160 "One Faltering Moment"

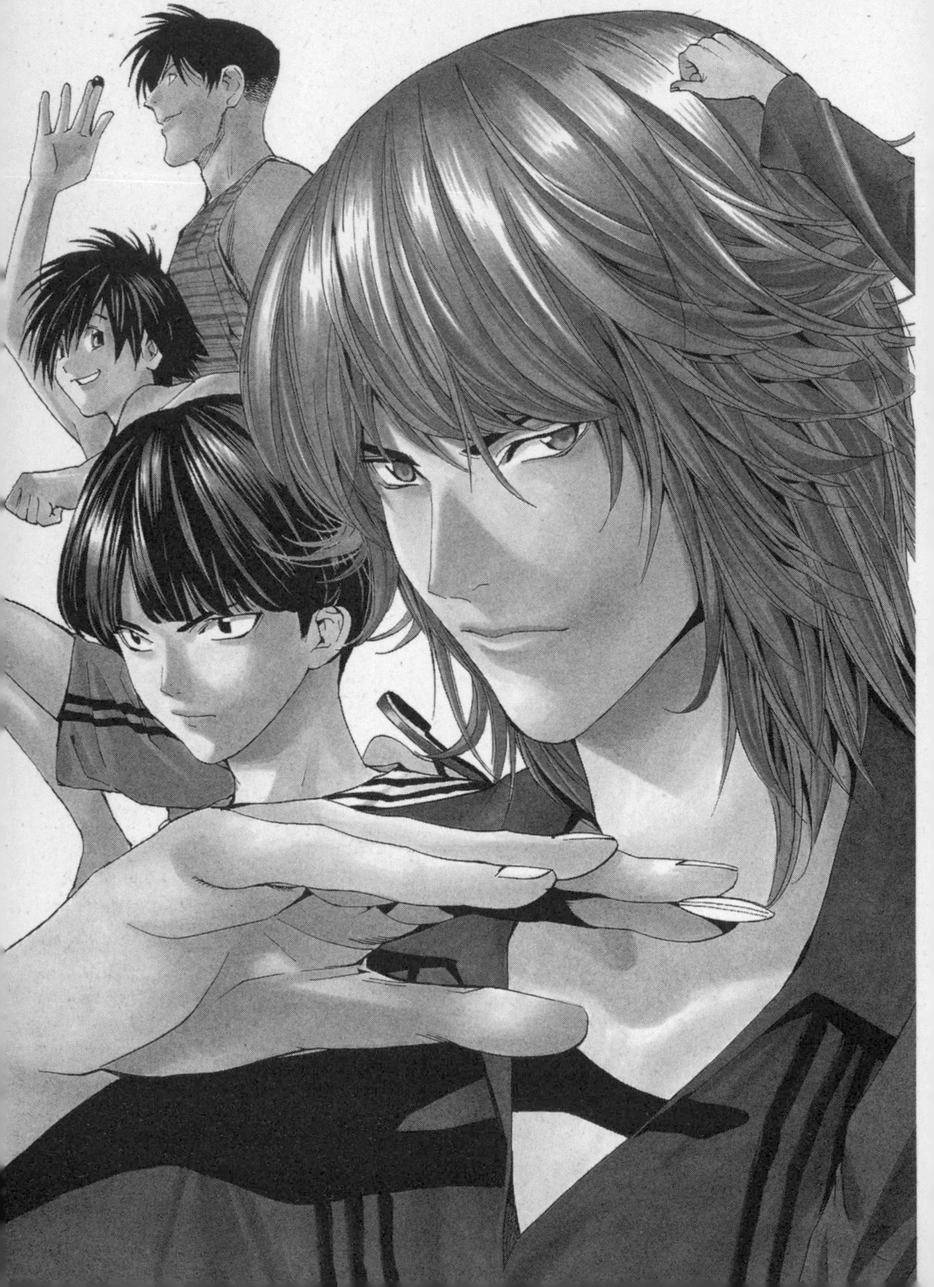

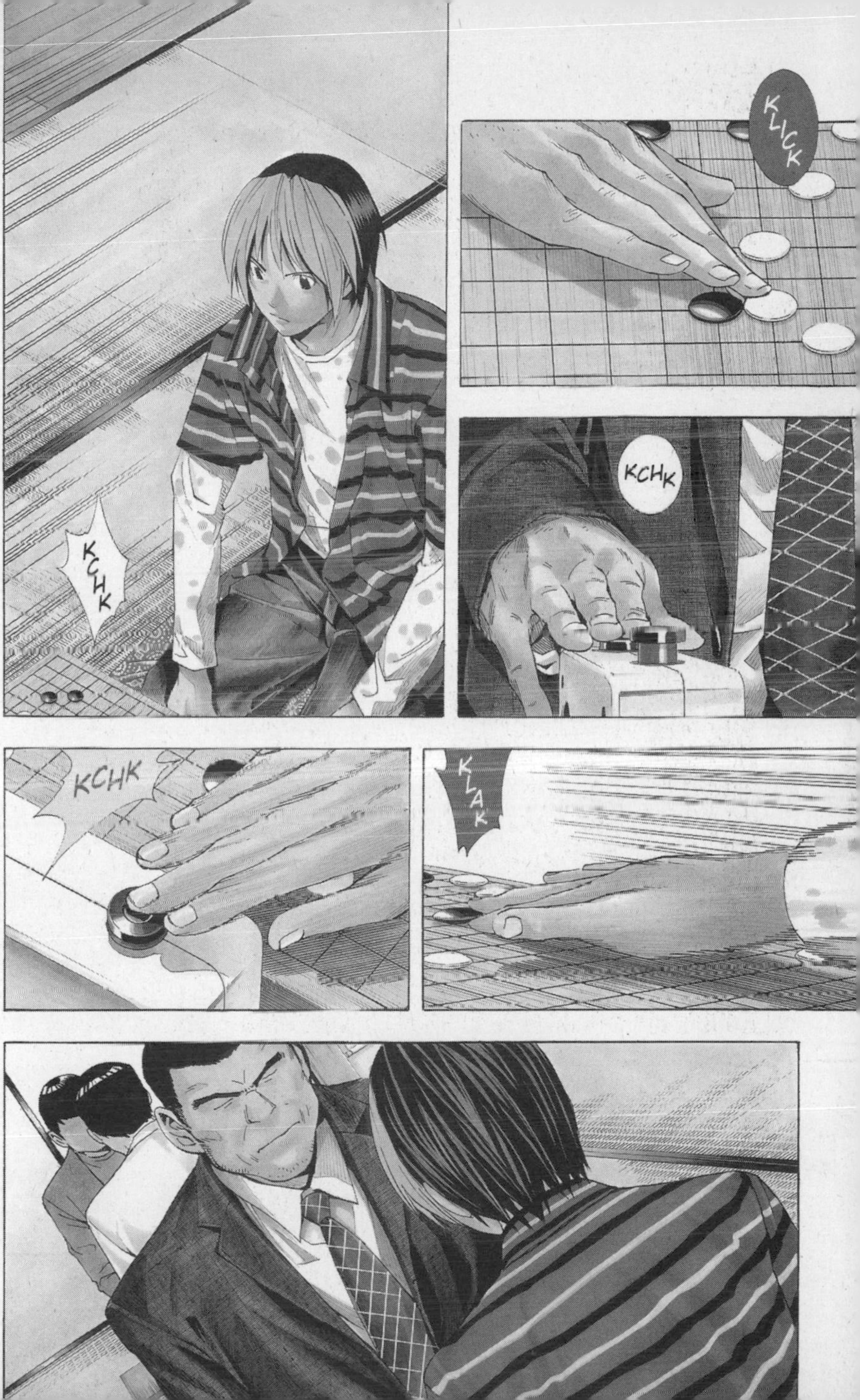
KLICK
KCHK
KCHK
KLAK
KCHK

READ THIS WAY

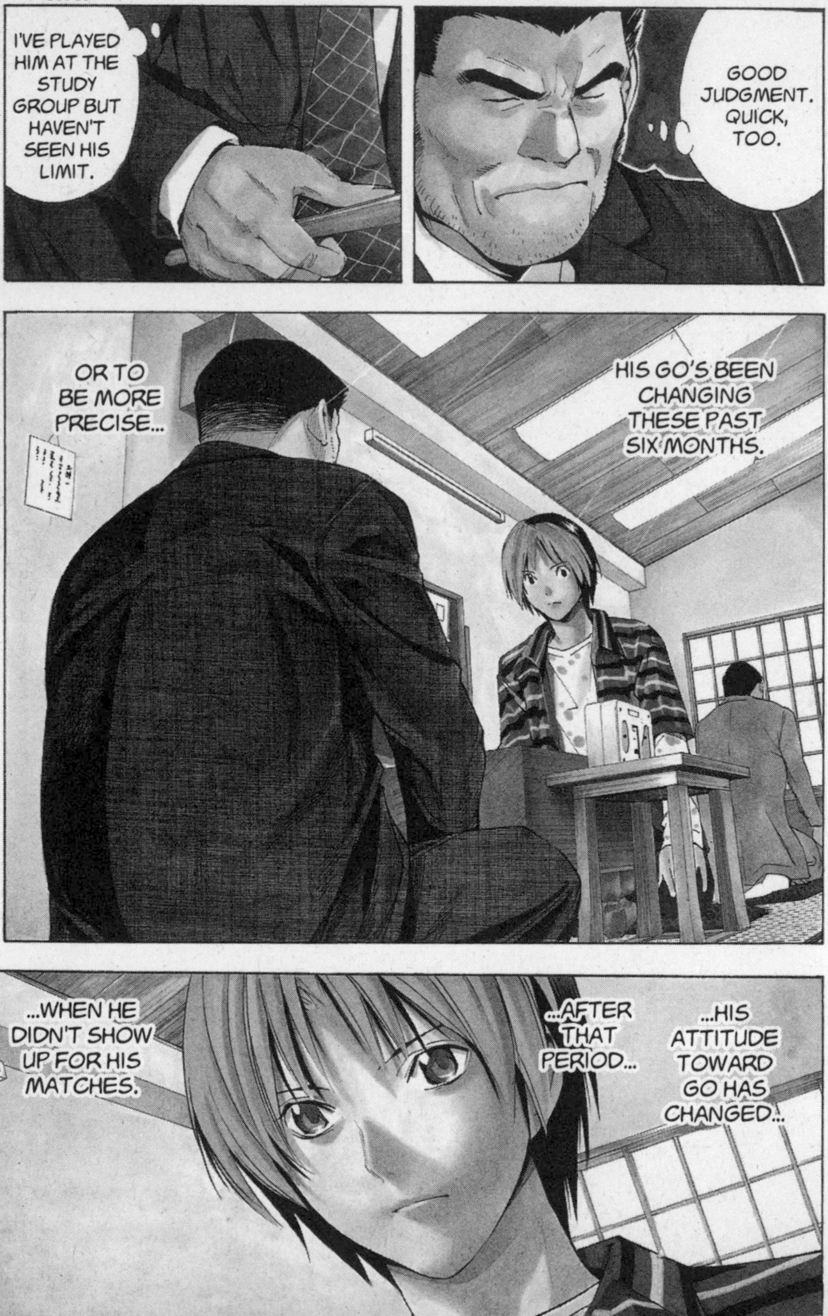
GOOD JUDGMENT. QUICK, TOO.
I'VE PLAYED HIM AT THE STUDY GROUP BUT HAVEN'T SEEN HIS LIMIT.
HIS GO'S BEEN CHANGING THESE PAST SIX MONTHS.
OR TO BE MORE PRECISE...
...HIS ATTITUDE TOWARD GO HAS CHANGED...
...AFTER THAT PERIOD...
...WHEN HE DIDN'T SHOW UP FOR HIS MATCHES.

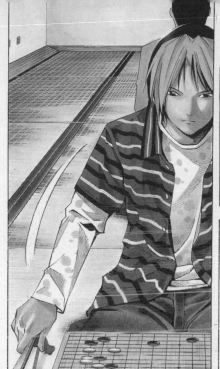
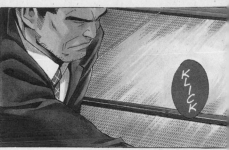

KLICK

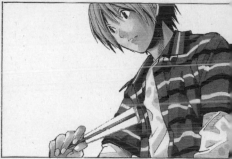

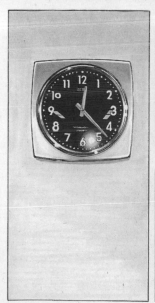

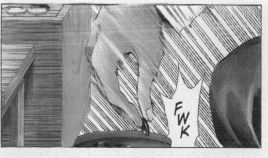

FWK

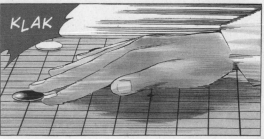

KLAK

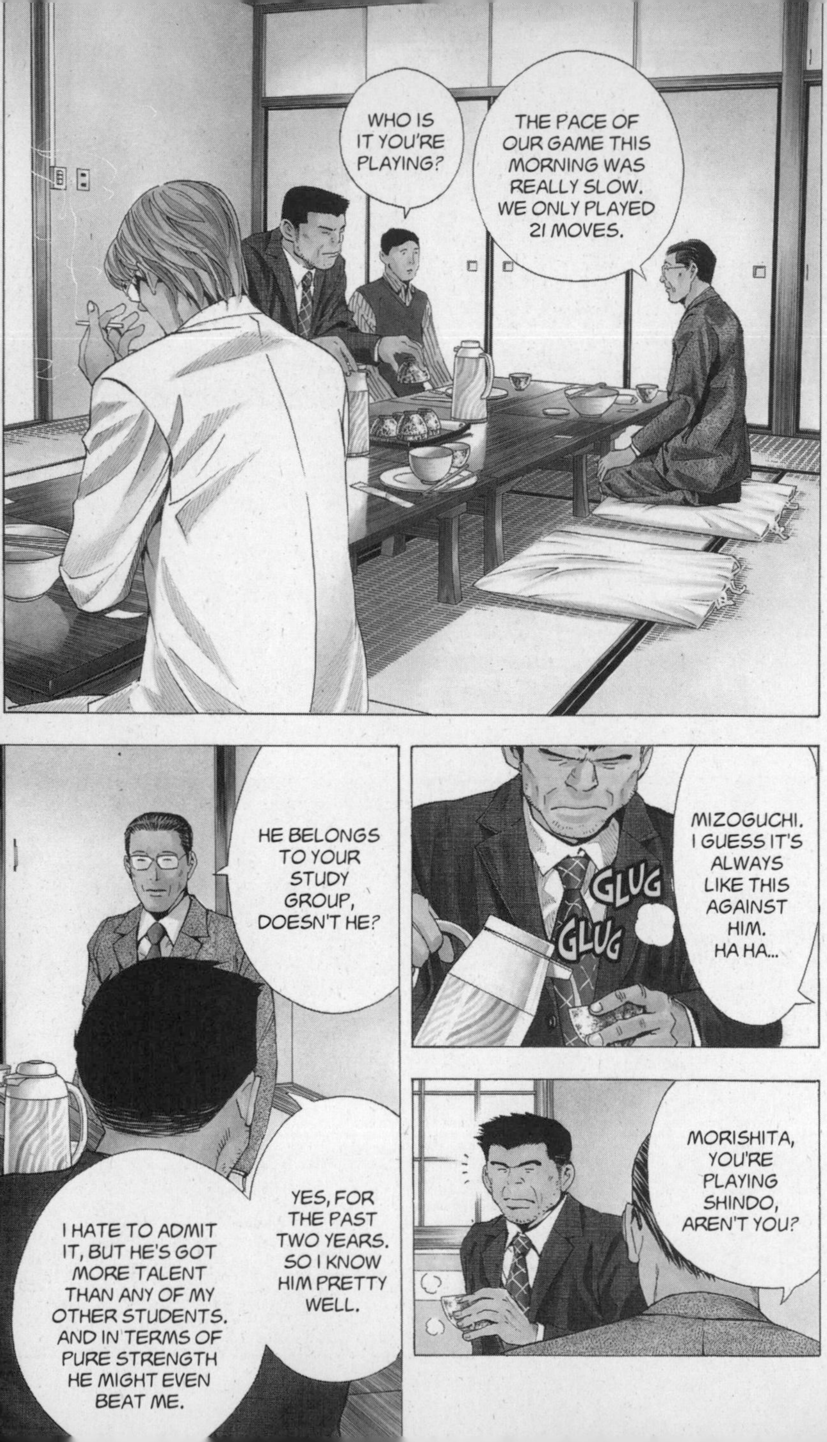
THE PACE OF OUR GAME THIS MORNING WAS REALLY SLOW. WE ONLY PLAYED 21 MOVES.
WHO IS IT YOU'RE PLAYING?
MIZOGUCHI. I GUESS IT'S ALWAYS LIKE THIS AGAINST HIM. HA HA...
GLUG
GLUG
MORISHITA, YOU'RE PLAYING SHINDO, AREN'T YOU?
HE BELONGS TO YOUR STUDY GROUP, DOESN'T HE?
YES, FOR THE PAST TWO YEARS. SO I KNOW HIM PRETTY WELL.
I HATE TO ADMIT IT, BUT HE'S GOT MORE TALENT THAN ANY OF MY OTHER STUDENTS. AND IN TERMS OF PURE STRENGTH HE MIGHT EVEN BEAT ME.

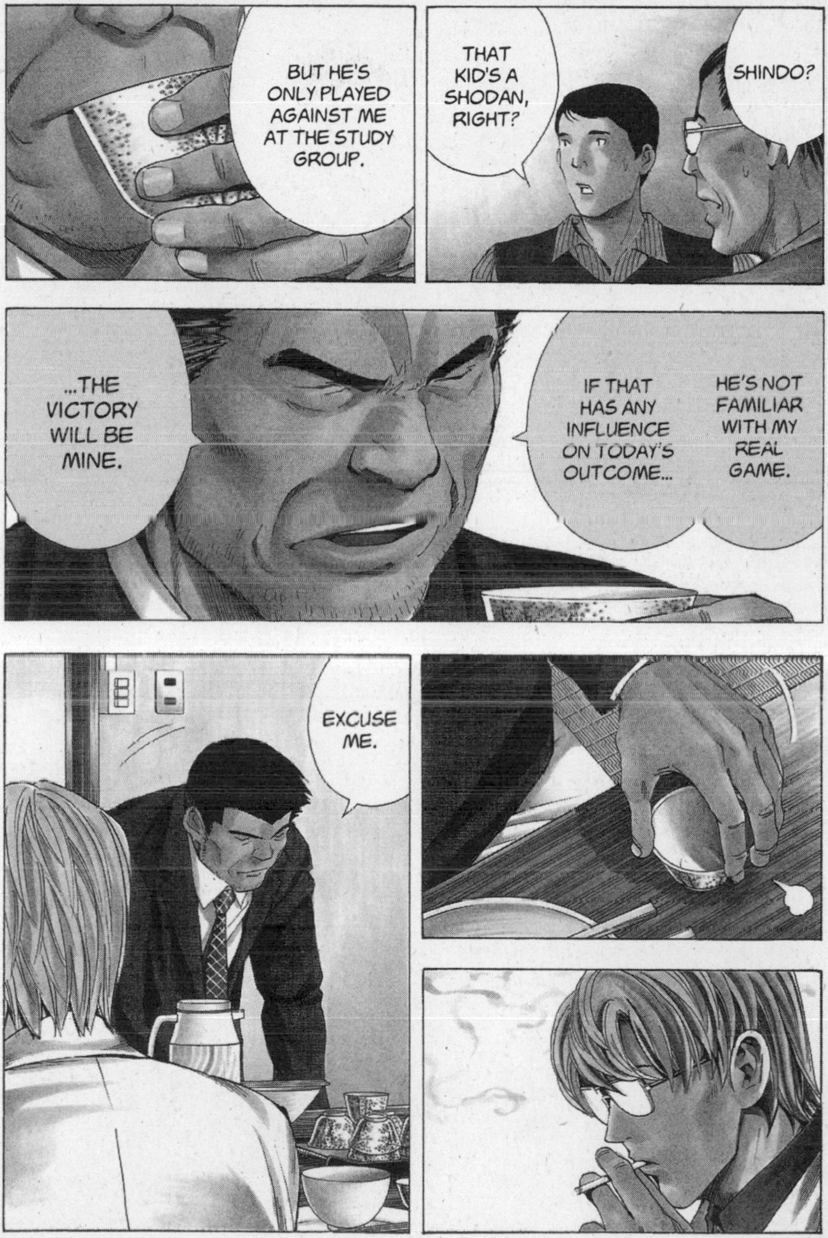
SHINDO?
THAT KID'S A SHODAN, RIGHT?
BUT HE'S ONLY PLAYED AGAINST ME AT THE STUDY GROUP.
HE'S NOT FAMILIAR WITH MY REAL GAME.
IF THAT HAS ANY INFLUENCE ON TODAY'S OUTCOME...
...THE VICTORY WILL BE MINE.
EXCUSE ME.

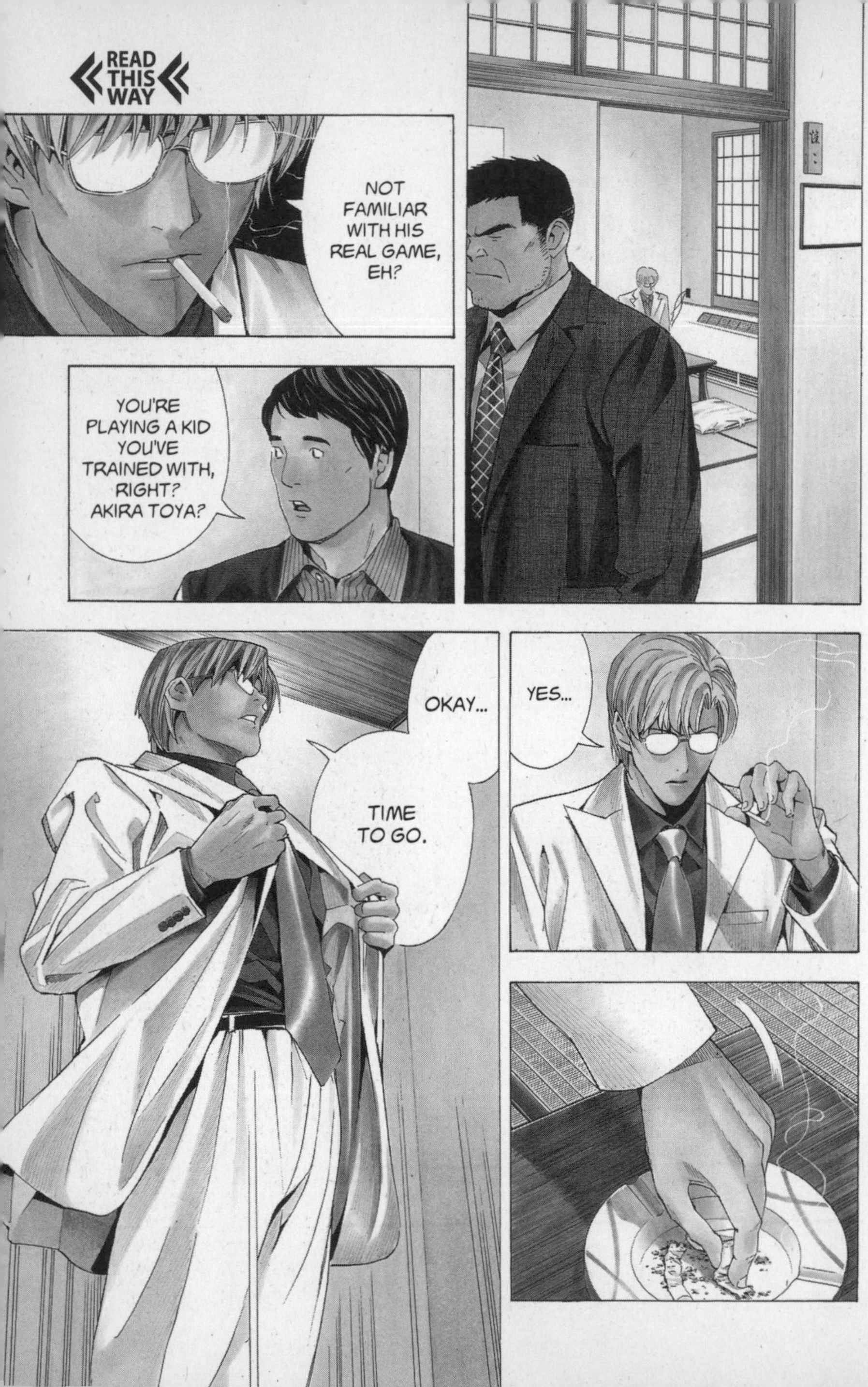
READ THIS WAY
NOT FAMILIAR WITH HIS REAL GAME, EH?
YOU'RE PLAYING A KID YOU'VE TRAINED WITH, RIGHT? AKIRA TOYA?
YES...
OKAY...
TIME TO GO.

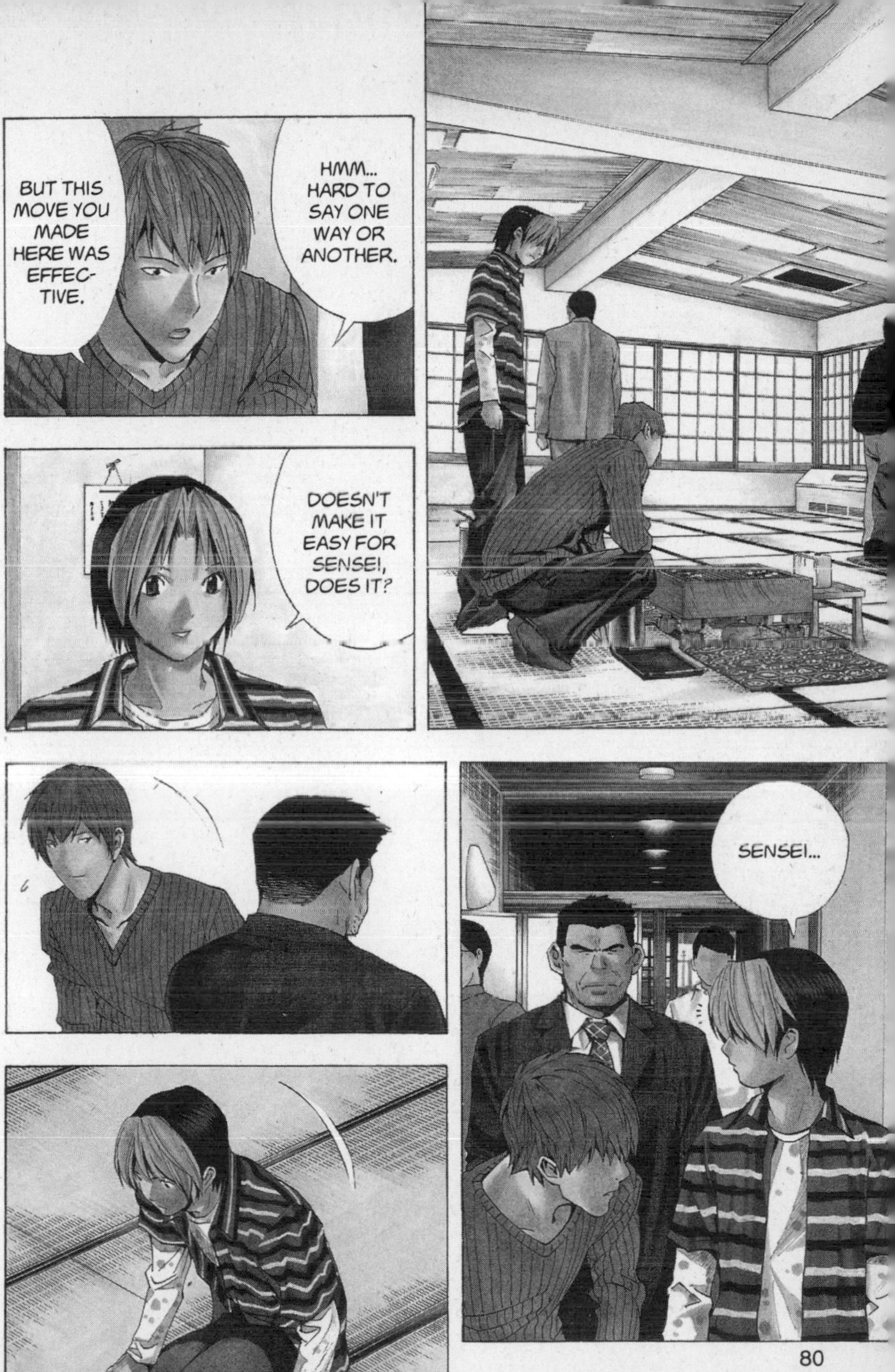
HMM... HARD TO SAY ONE WAY OR ANOTHER.
BUT THIS MOVE YOU MADE HERE WAS EFFECTIVE.
DOESN'T MAKE IT EASY FOR SENSEI, DOES IT?
SENSEI...

READ THIS WAY

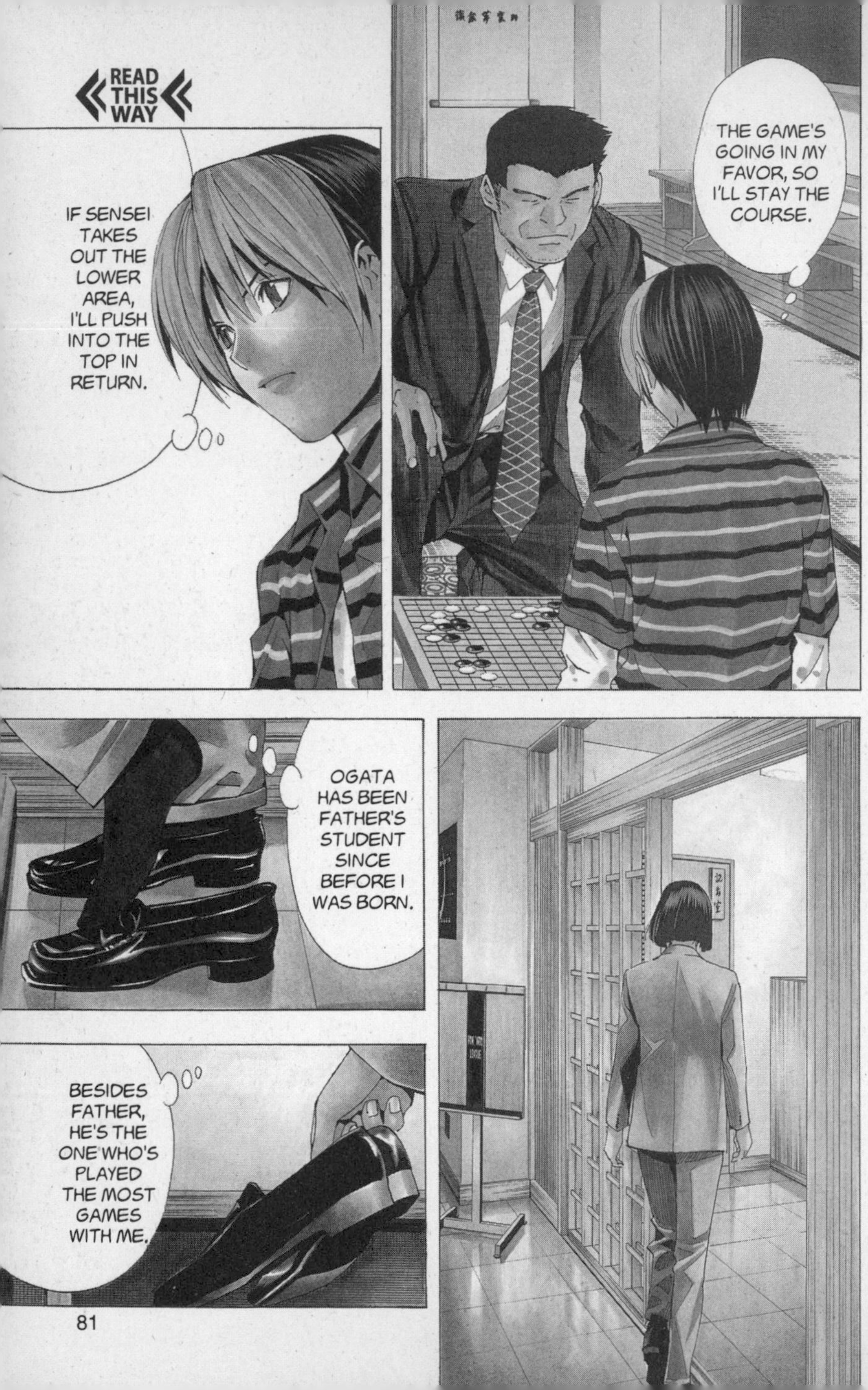

THE GAME'S GOING IN MY FAVOR, SO I'LL STAY THE COURSE.
IF SENSEI TAKES OUT THE LOWER AREA, I'LL PUSH INTO THE TOP IN RETURN.
OGATA HAS BEEN FATHER'S STUDENT SINCE BEFORE I WAS BORN.
BESIDES FATHER, HE'S THE ONE WHO'S PLAYED THE MOST GAMES WITH ME.

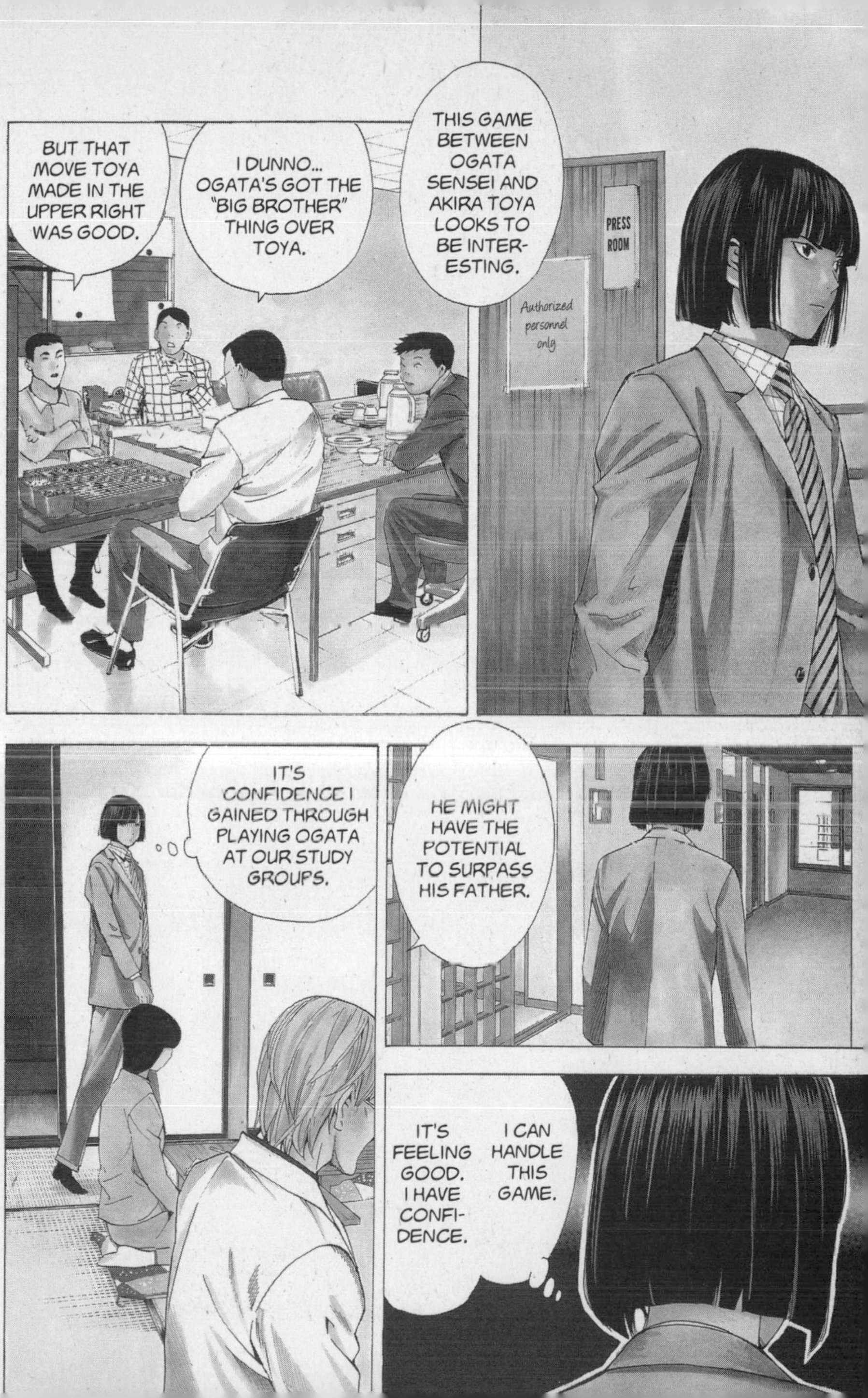
THIS GAME BETWEEN OGATA SENSEI AND AKIRA TOYA LOOKS TO BE INTER-ESTING.
PRESS ROOM
Authorized personnel only
I DUNNO... OGATA'S GOT THE "BIG BROTHER" THING OVER TOYA.
BUT THAT MOVE TOYA MADE IN THE UPPER RIGHT WAS GOOD.
HE MIGHT HAVE THE POTENTIAL TO SURPASS HIS FATHER.
I CAN HANDLE THIS GAME.
IT'S FEELING GOOD. I HAVE CONFI-DENCE.
IT'S CONFIDENCE I GAINED THROUGH PLAYING OGATA AT OUR STUDY GROUPS.

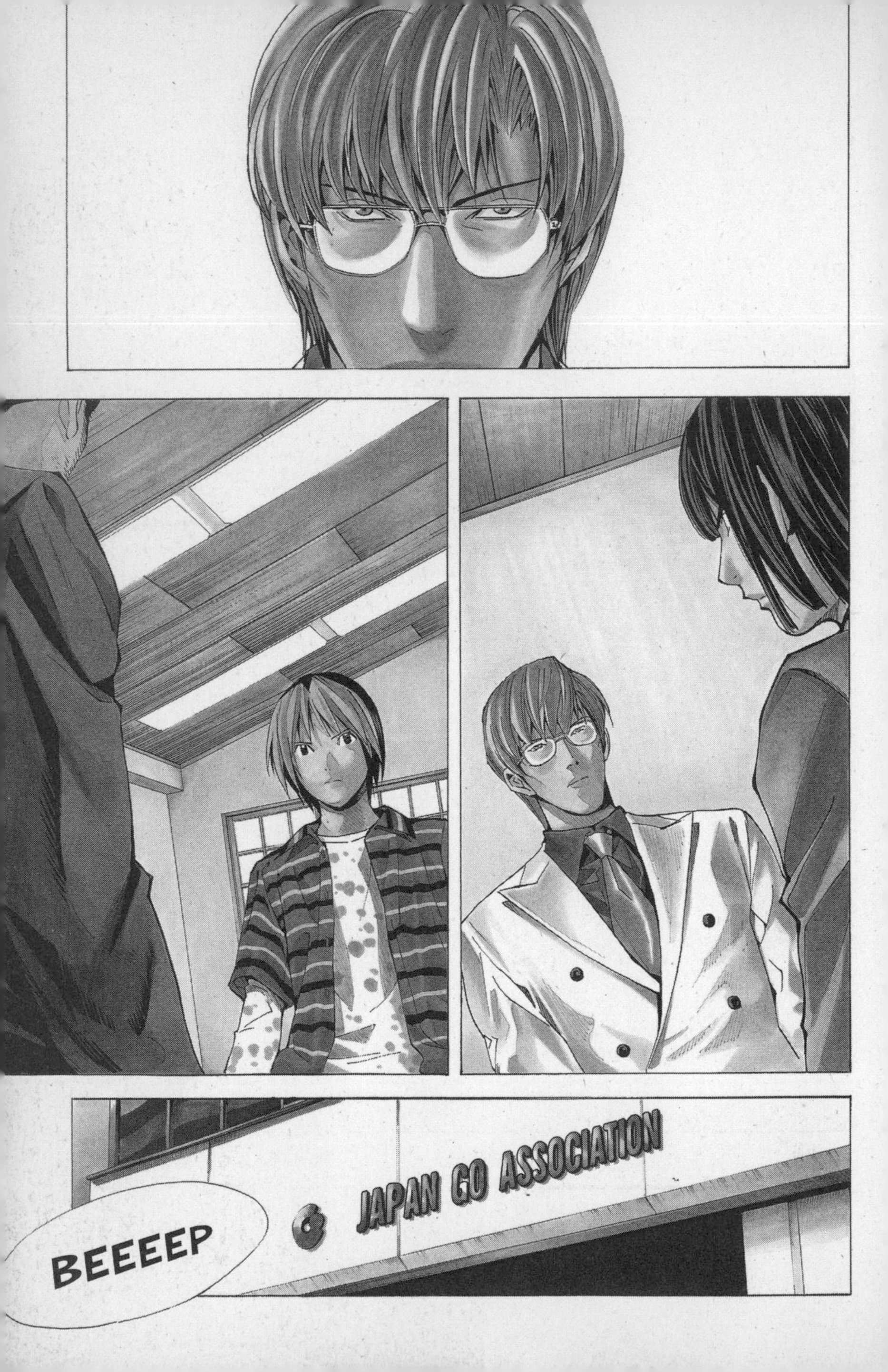

JAPAN GO ASSOCIATION
BEEEEP

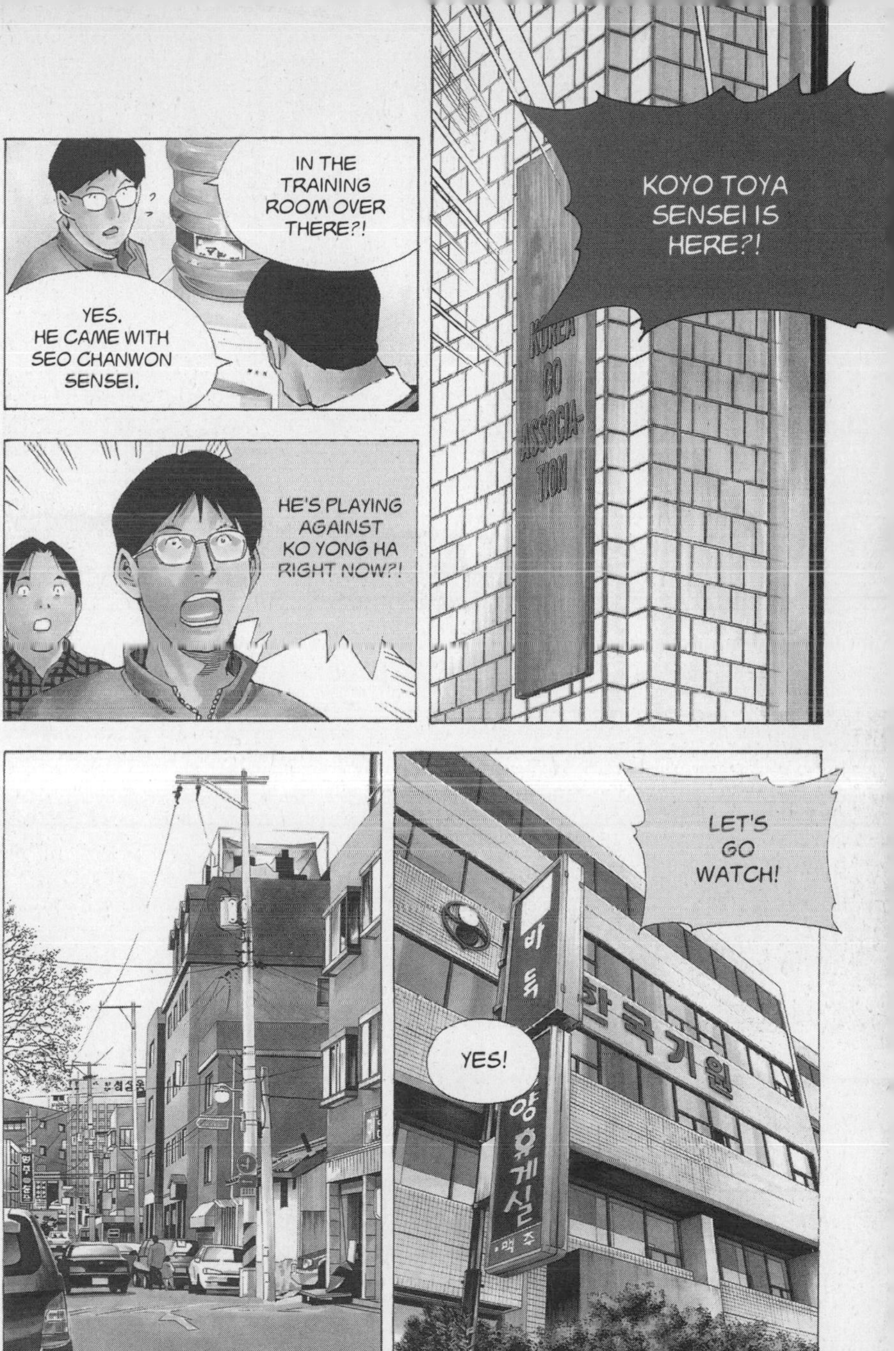
KOYO TOYA SENSEI IS HERE?!
IN THE TRAINING ROOM OVER THERE?!
YES. HE CAME WITH SEO CHANWON SENSEI.
HE'S PLAYING AGAINST KO YONG HA RIGHT NOW?!
LET'S GO WATCH!
YES!

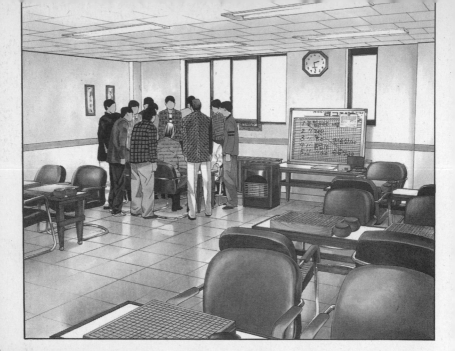

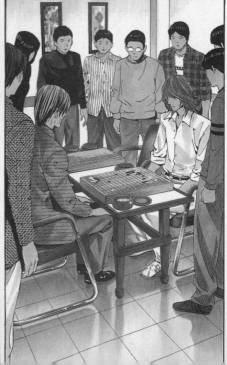

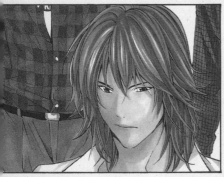

KLAK

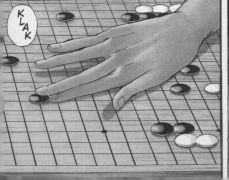

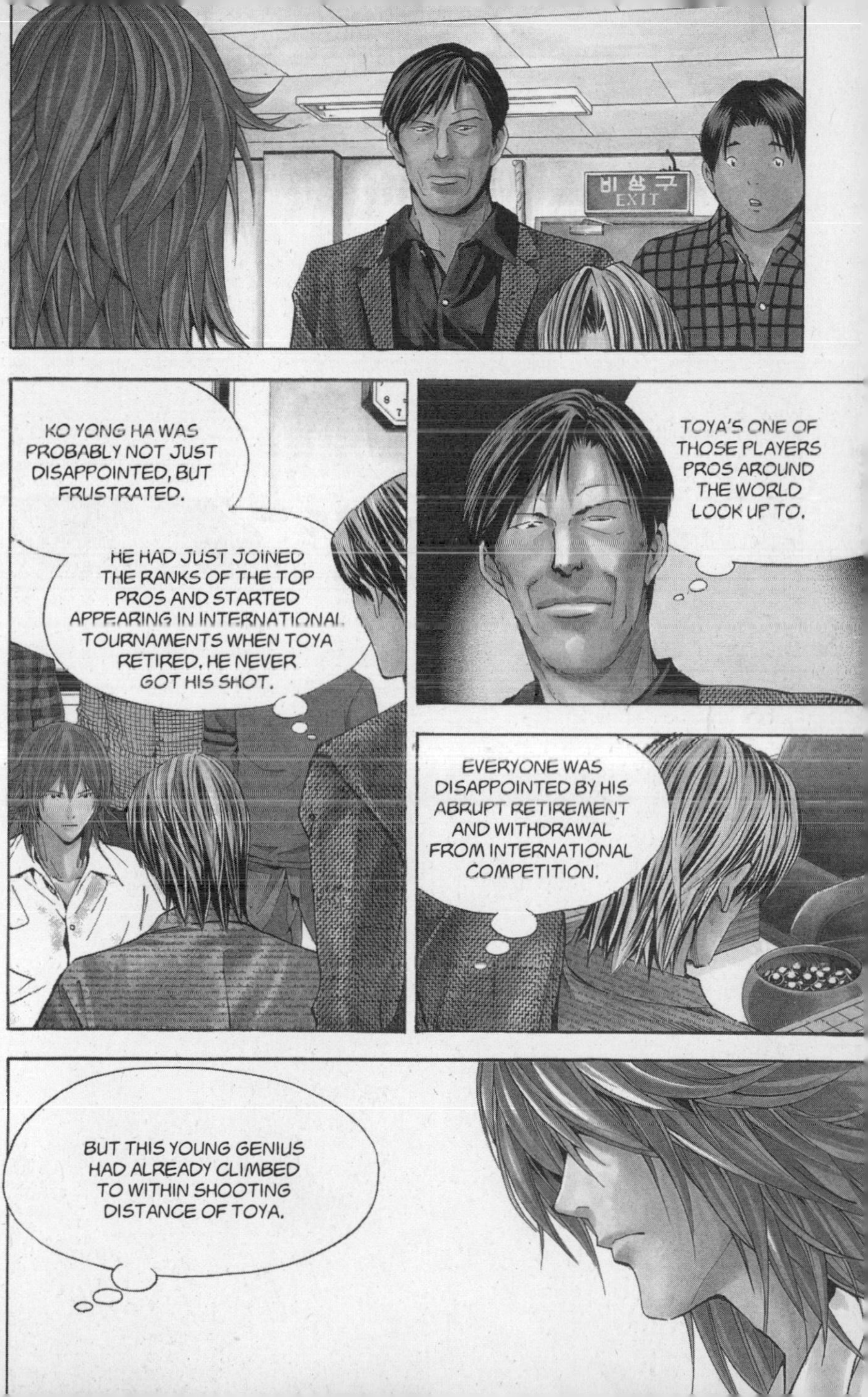
비상구
EXIT
TOYA'S ONE OF THOSE PLAYERS PROS AROUND THE WORLD LOOK UP TO.
EVERYONE WAS DISAPPOINTED BY HIS ABRUPT RETIREMENT AND WITHDRAWAL FROM INTERNATIONAL COMPETITION.
KO YONG HA WAS PROBABLY NOT JUST DISAPPOINTED, BUT FRUSTRATED.
HE HAD JUST JOINED THE RANKS OF THE TOP PROS AND STARTED APPEARING IN INTERNATIONAL TOURNAMENTS WHEN TOYA RETIRED. HE NEVER GOT HIS SHOT.
BUT THIS YOUNG GENIUS HAD ALREADY CLIMBED TO WITHIN SHOOTING DISTANCE OF TOYA.

READ THIS WAY

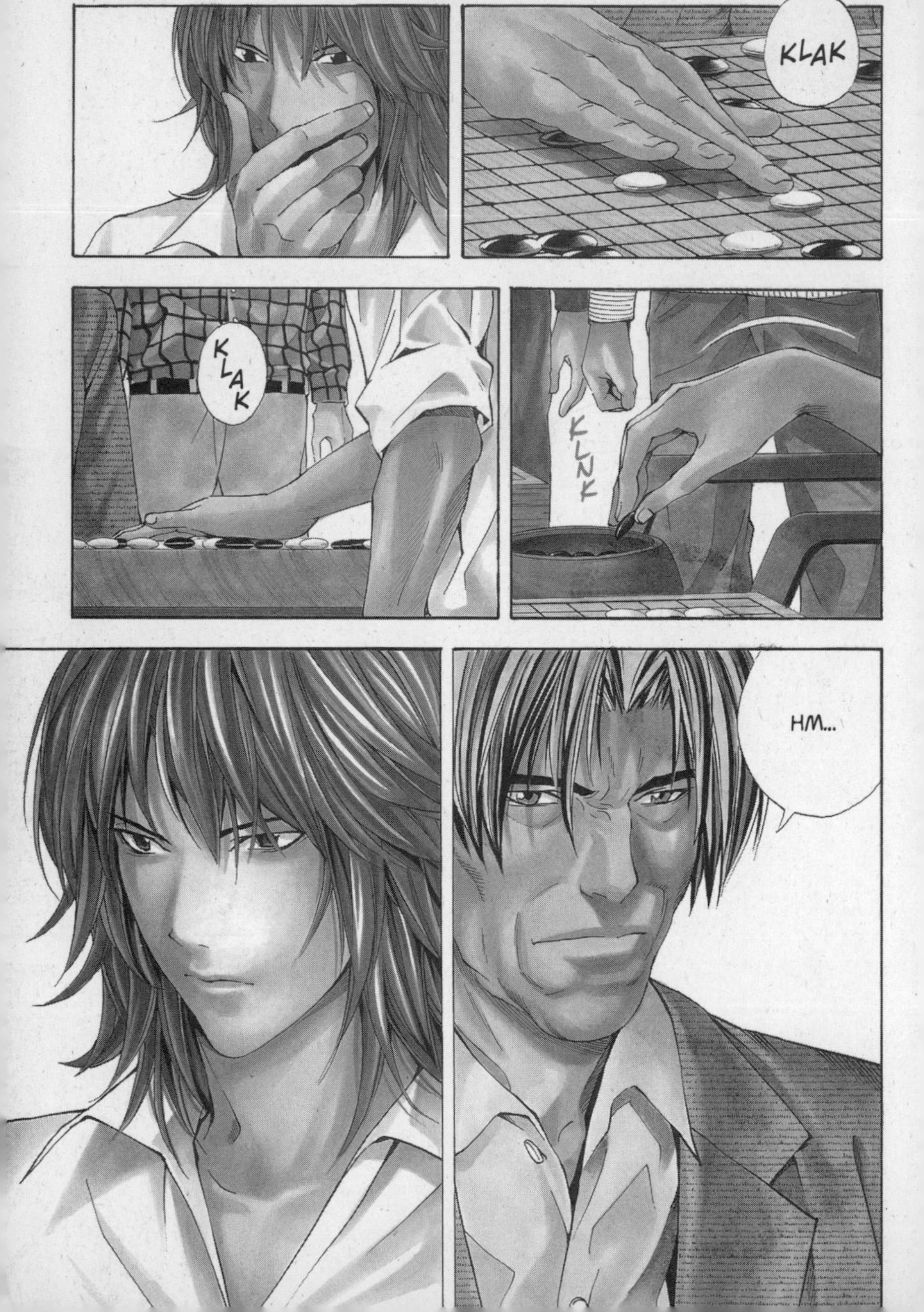
KLAK
KLNK
KLAK
HM...

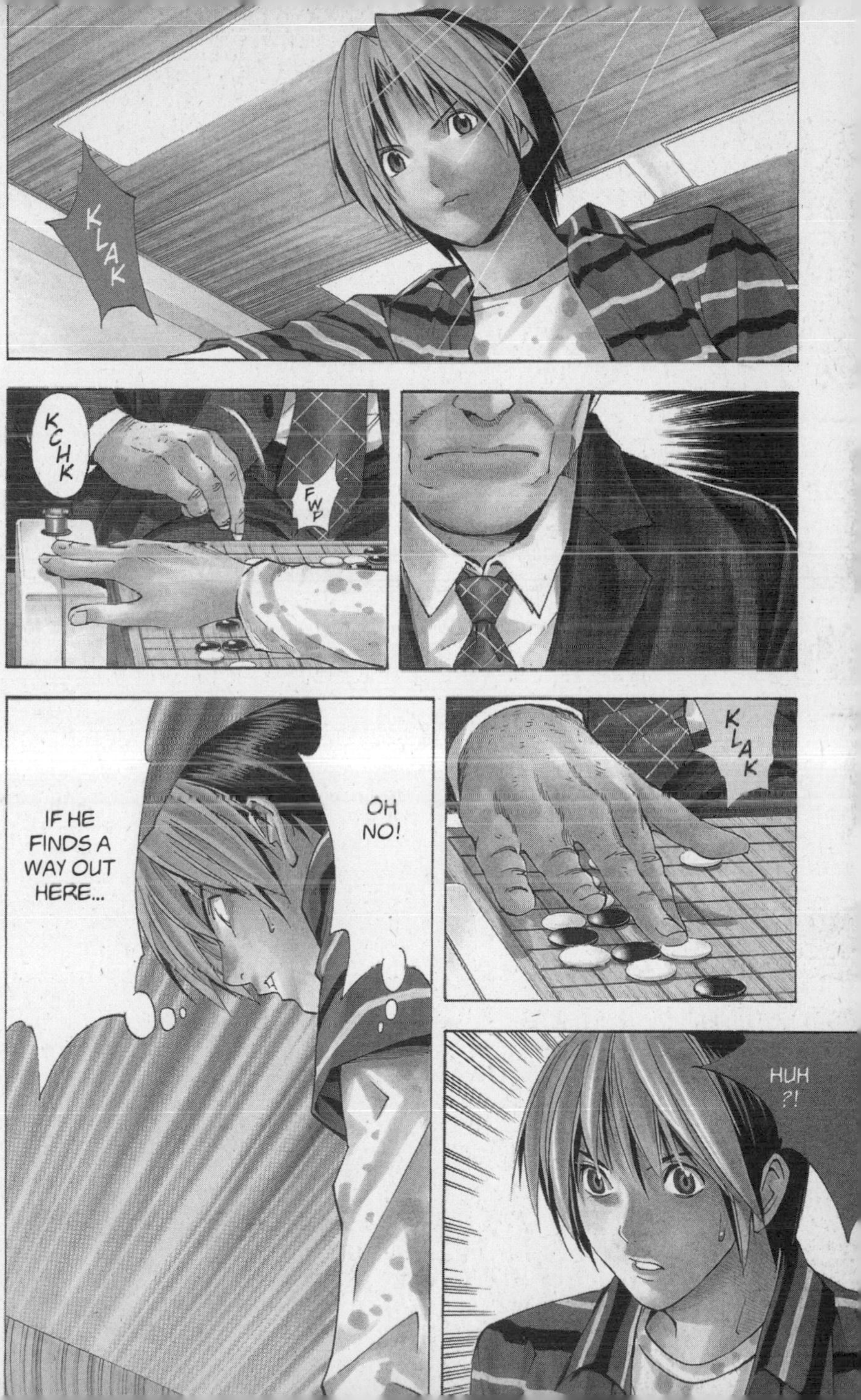
KLAK
KCHK
FWP
KLAK
HUH ?!
OH NO!
IF HE FINDS A WAY OUT HERE...

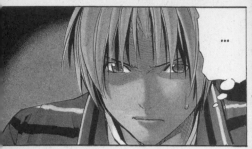

...

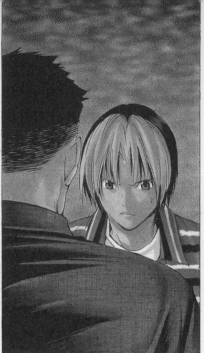

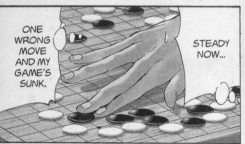

ONE WRONG MOVE AND MY GAME'S SUNK.

STEADY NOW...

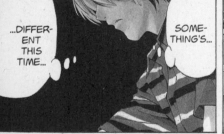

...DIFFER-ENT THIS TIME...

SOME-THING'S...

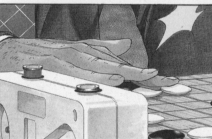

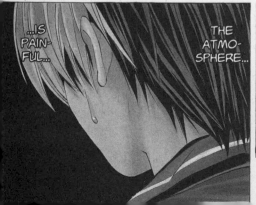

...IS PAIN-FUL...

THE ATMO-SPHERE...

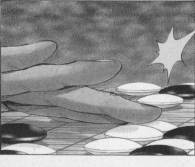

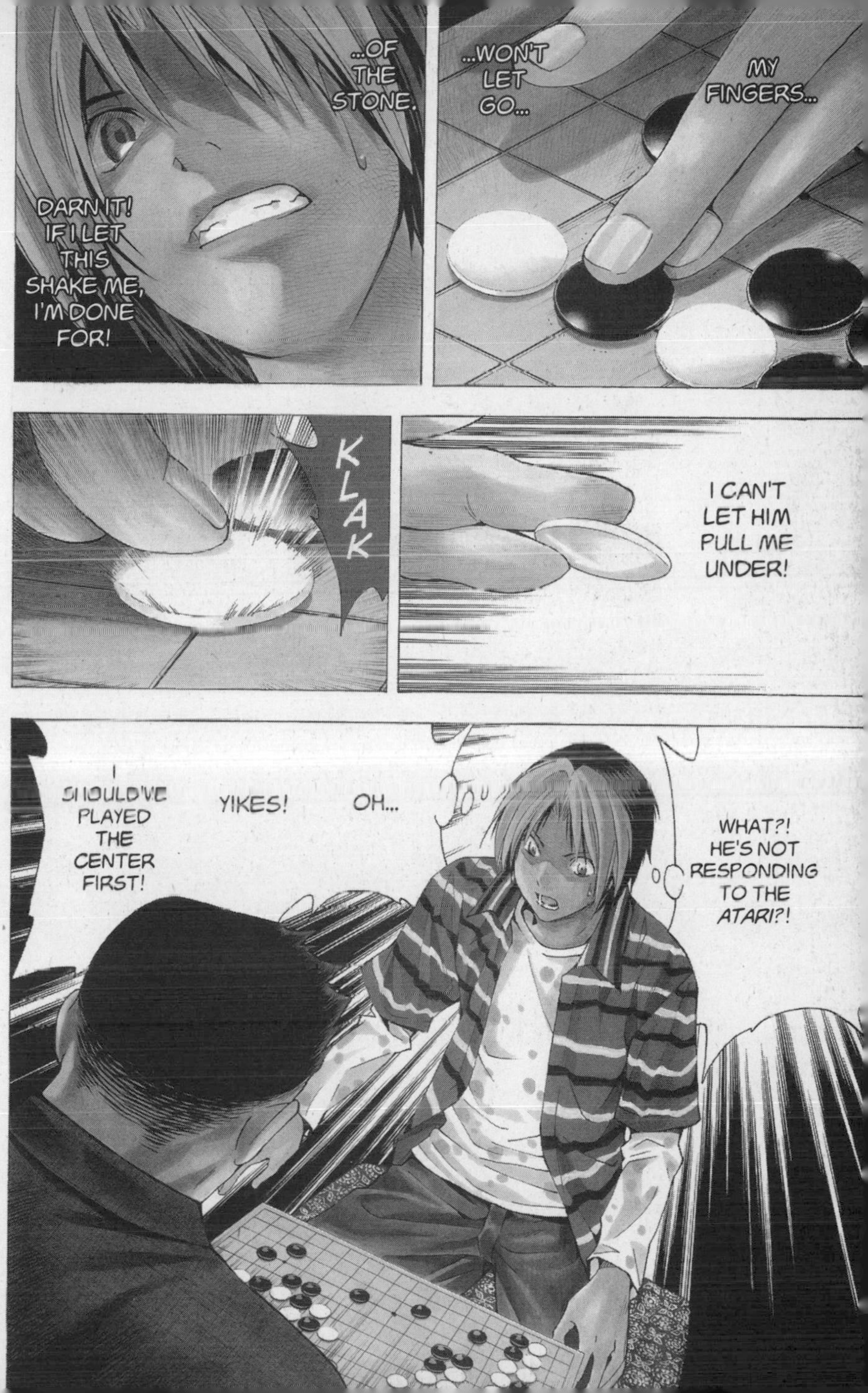
MY FINGERS...
...WON'T LET GO...
...OF THE STONE.
DARN IT! IF I LET THIS SHAKE ME, I'M DONE FOR!
I CAN'T LET HIM PULL ME UNDER!
KLAK
WHAT?! HE'S NOT RESPONDING TO THE ATARI?!
OH...
YIKES!
I SHOULD'VE PLAYED THE CENTER FIRST!

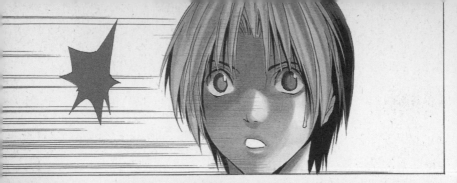

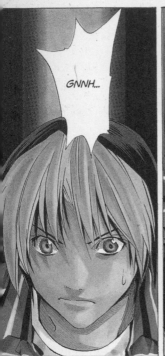

GNNH...

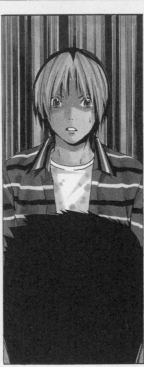

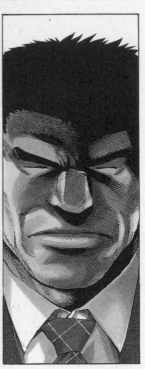

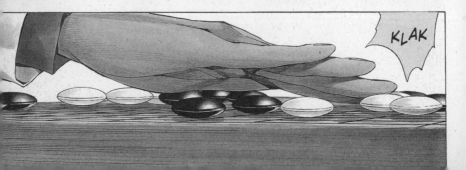

KLAK

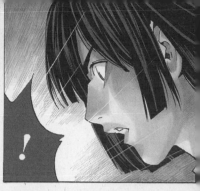

...

!

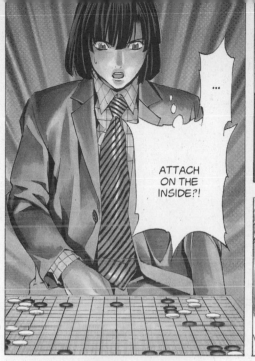

ATTACH ON THE INSIDE?!

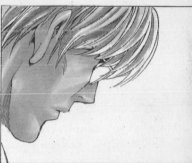

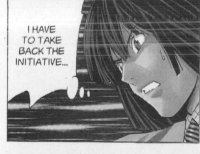

I HAVE TO TAKE BACK THE INITIATIVE...

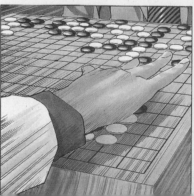

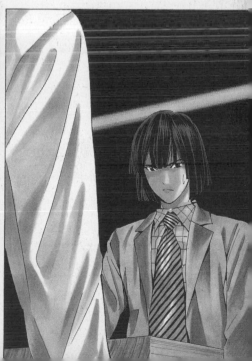

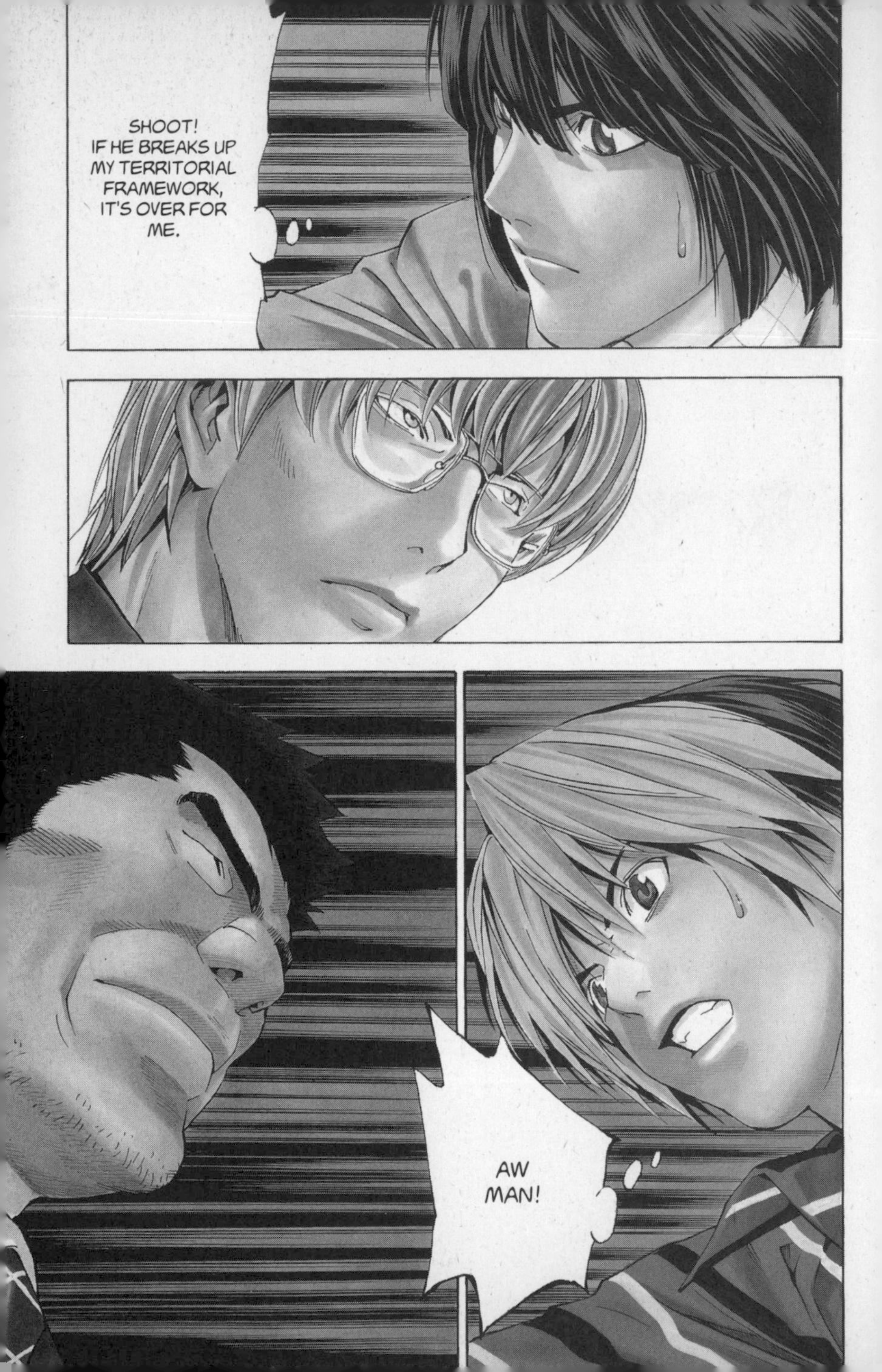
SHOOT! IF HE BREAKS UP MY TERRITORIAL FRAMEWORK, IT'S OVER FOR ME.
AW MAN!

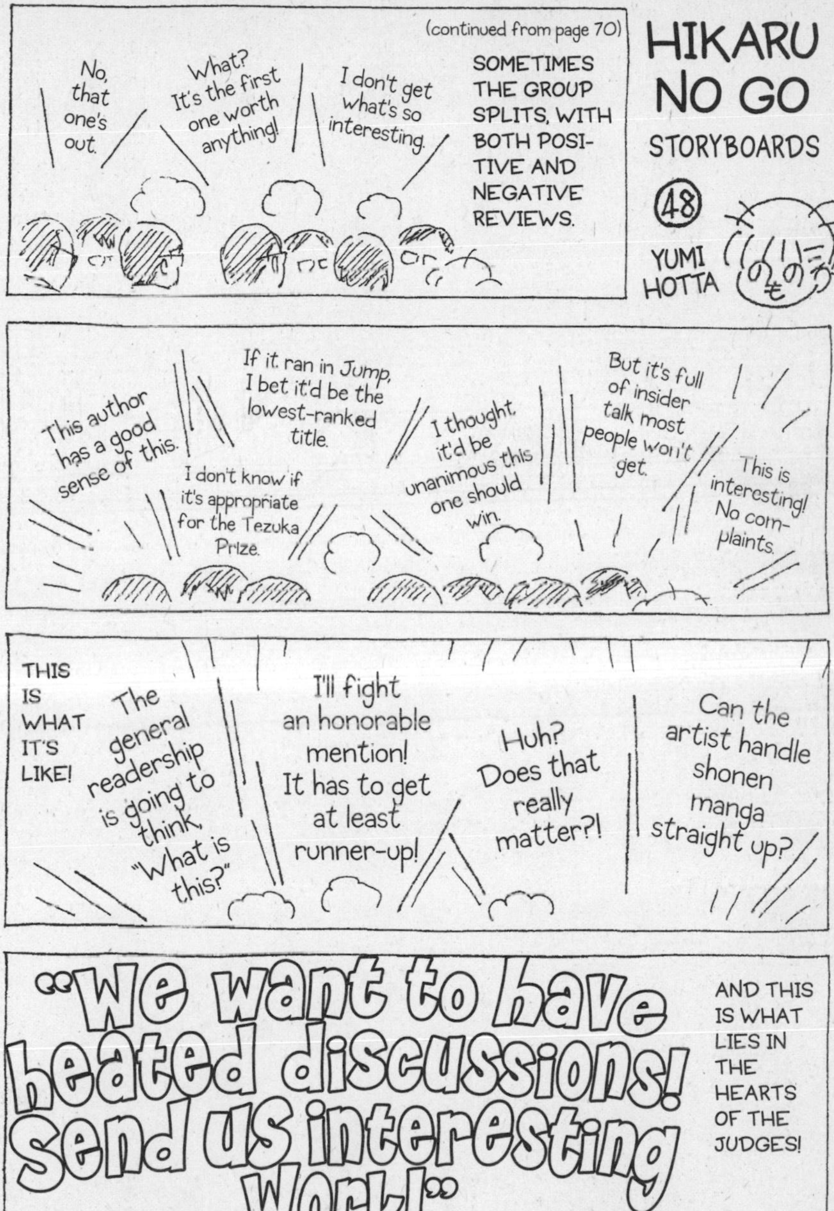
HIKARU NO GO STORYBOARDS
48
YUMI HOTTA
(continued from page 70)
SOMETIMES THE GROUP SPLITS, WITH BOTH POSITIVE AND NEGATIVE REVIEWS.
I don't get what's so interesting.
What? It's the first one worth anything!
No, that one's out.
This is interesting! No complaints.
But it's full of insider talk most people won't get.
I thought it'd be unanimous this one should win.
If it ran in Jump, I bet it'd be the lowest-ranked title.
I don't know if it's appropriate for the Tezuka Prize.
This author has a good sense of this.
Can the artist handle shonen manga straight up?
Huh? Does that really matter?!
I'll fight an honorable mention! It has to get at least runner-up!
The general readership is going to think, "What is this?"
THIS IS WHAT IT'S LIKE!
AND THIS IS WHAT LIES IN THE HEARTS OF THE JUDGES!
"We want to have heated discussions! Send us interesting work!"

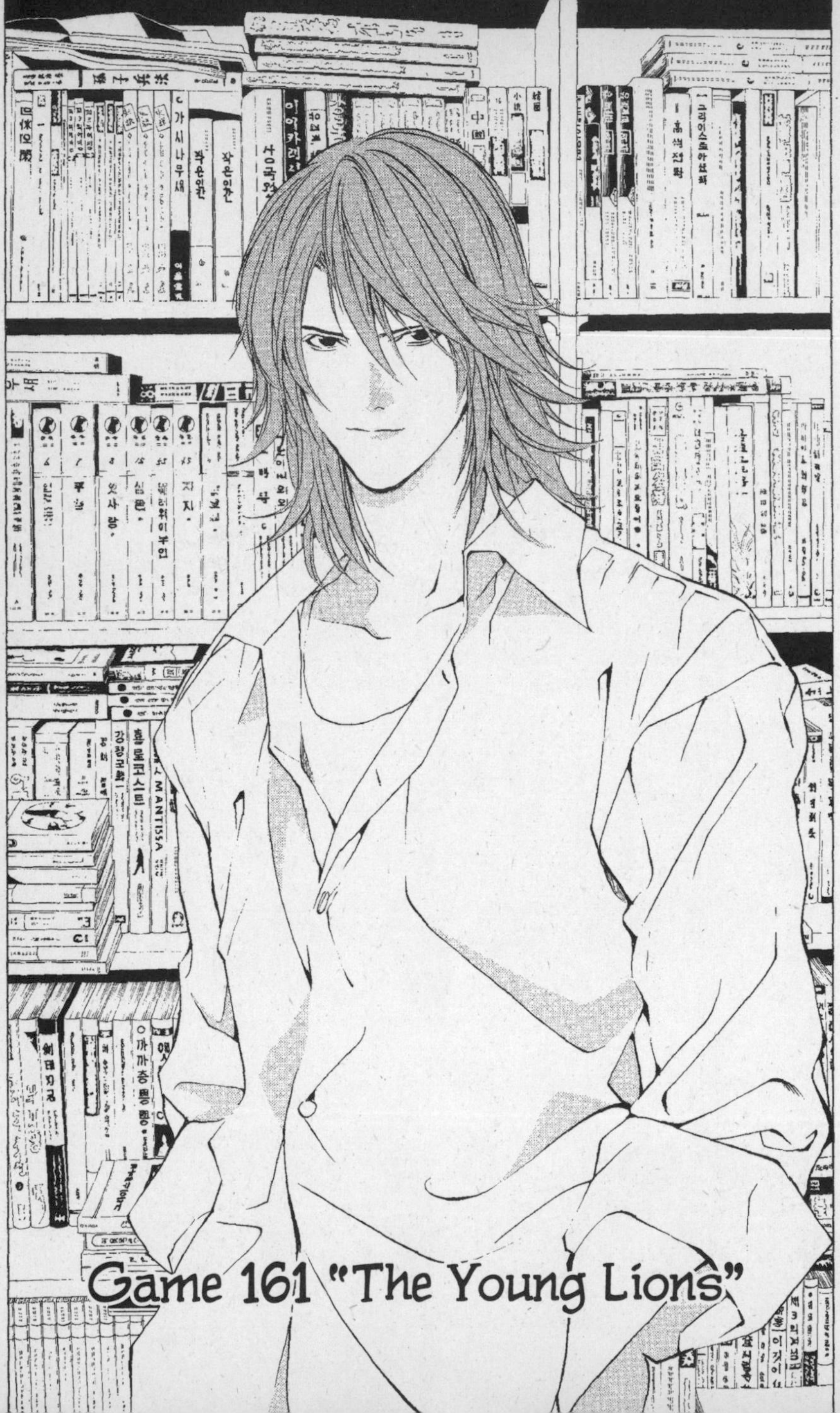

Game 161 "The Young Lions"

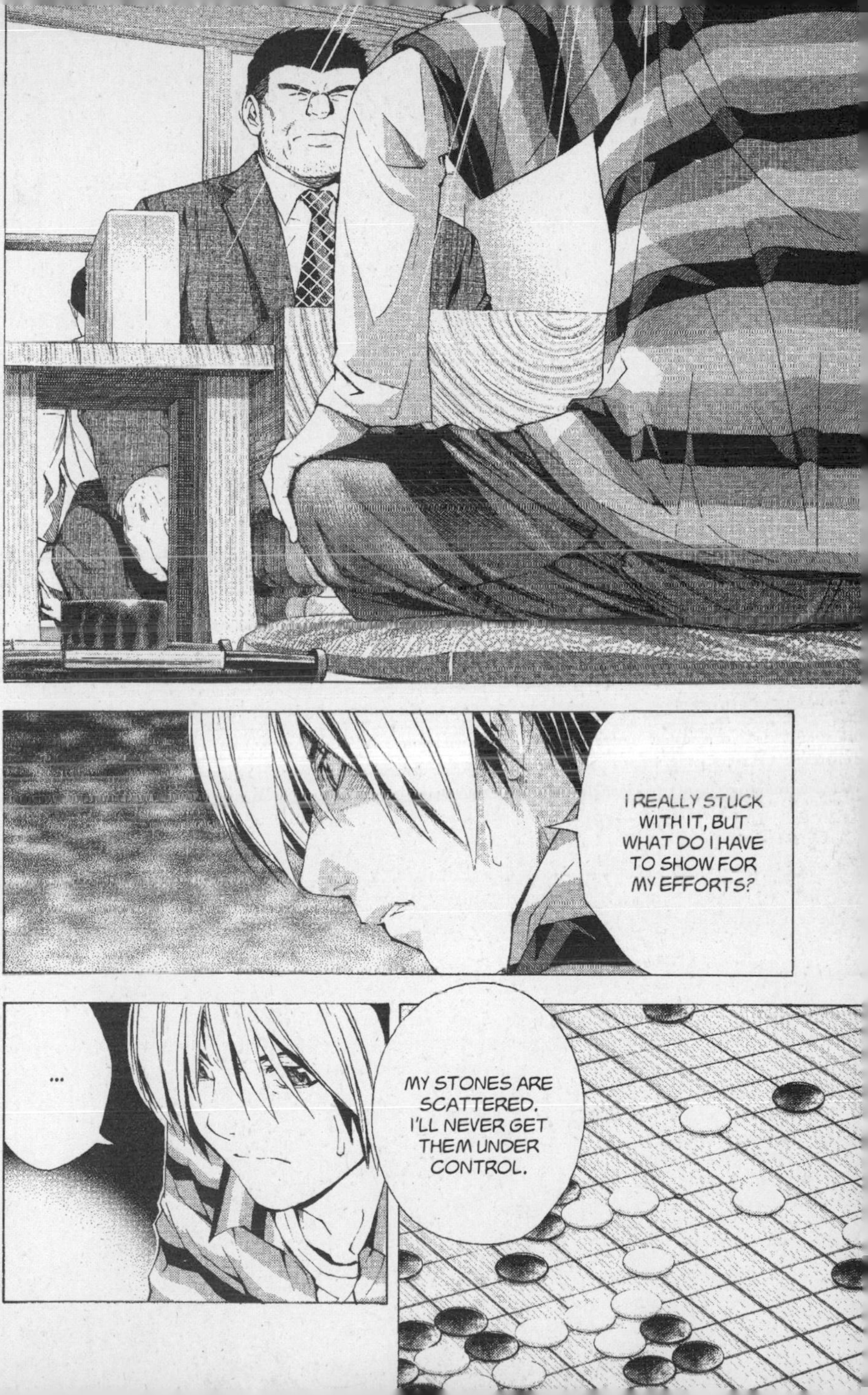
I REALLY STUCK WITH IT, BUT WHAT DO I HAVE TO SHOW FOR MY EFFORTS?
MY STONES ARE SCATTERED. I'LL NEVER GET THEM UNDER CONTROL.
...

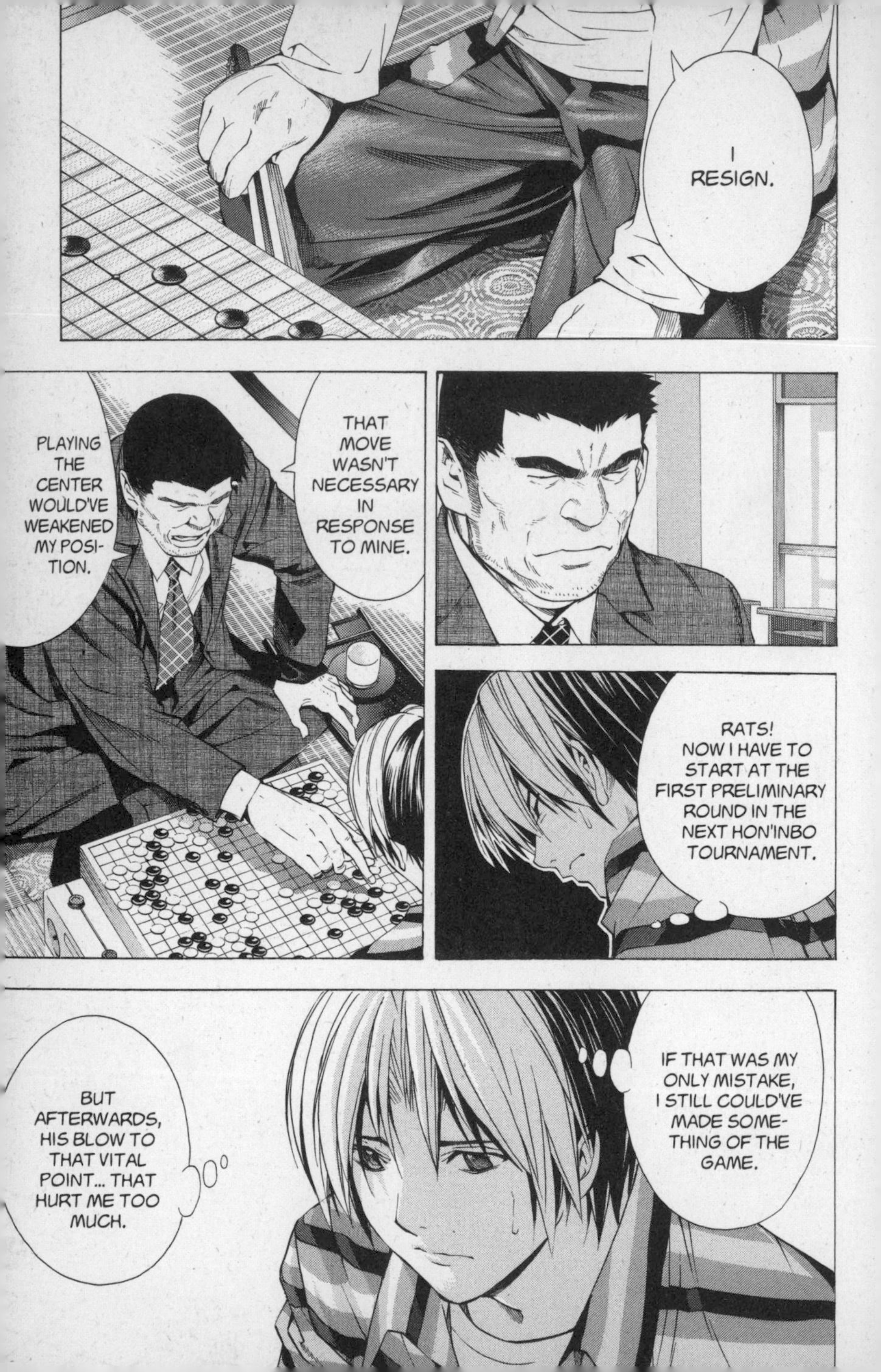
I RESIGN.
RATS! NOW I HAVE TO START AT THE FIRST PRELIMINARY ROUND IN THE NEXT HON'INBO TOURNAMENT.
THAT MOVE WASN'T NECESSARY IN RESPONSE TO MINE.
PLAYING THE CENTER WOULD'VE WEAKENED MY POSITION.
IF THAT WAS MY ONLY MISTAKE, I STILL COULD'VE MADE SOMETHING OF THE GAME.
BUT AFTERWARDS, HIS BLOW TO THAT VITAL POINT... THAT HURT ME TOO MUCH.

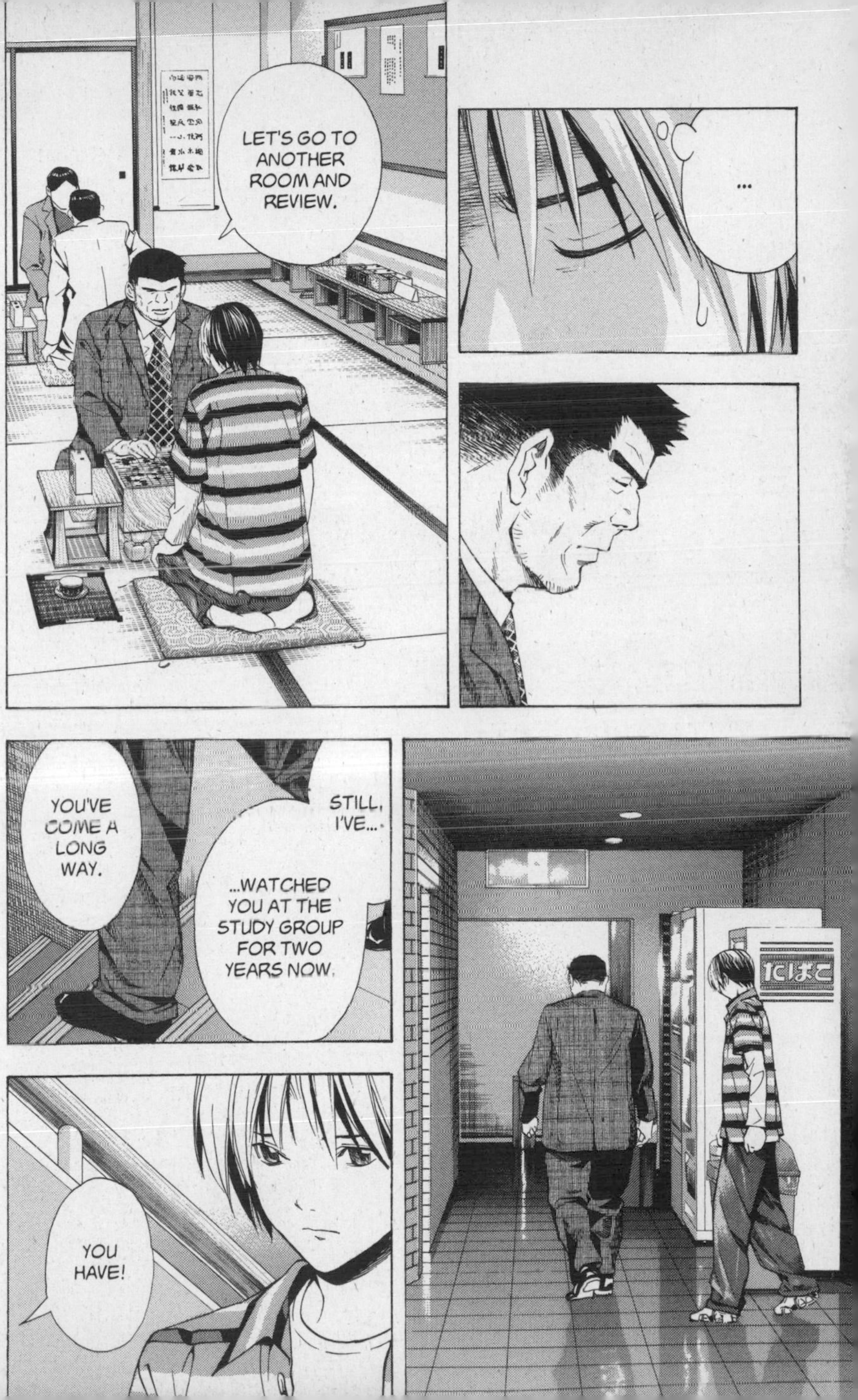
...
LET'S GO TO ANOTHER ROOM AND REVIEW.
STILL, I'VE...
...WATCHED YOU AT THE STUDY GROUP FOR TWO YEARS NOW.
YOU'VE COME A LONG WAY.
YOU HAVE!

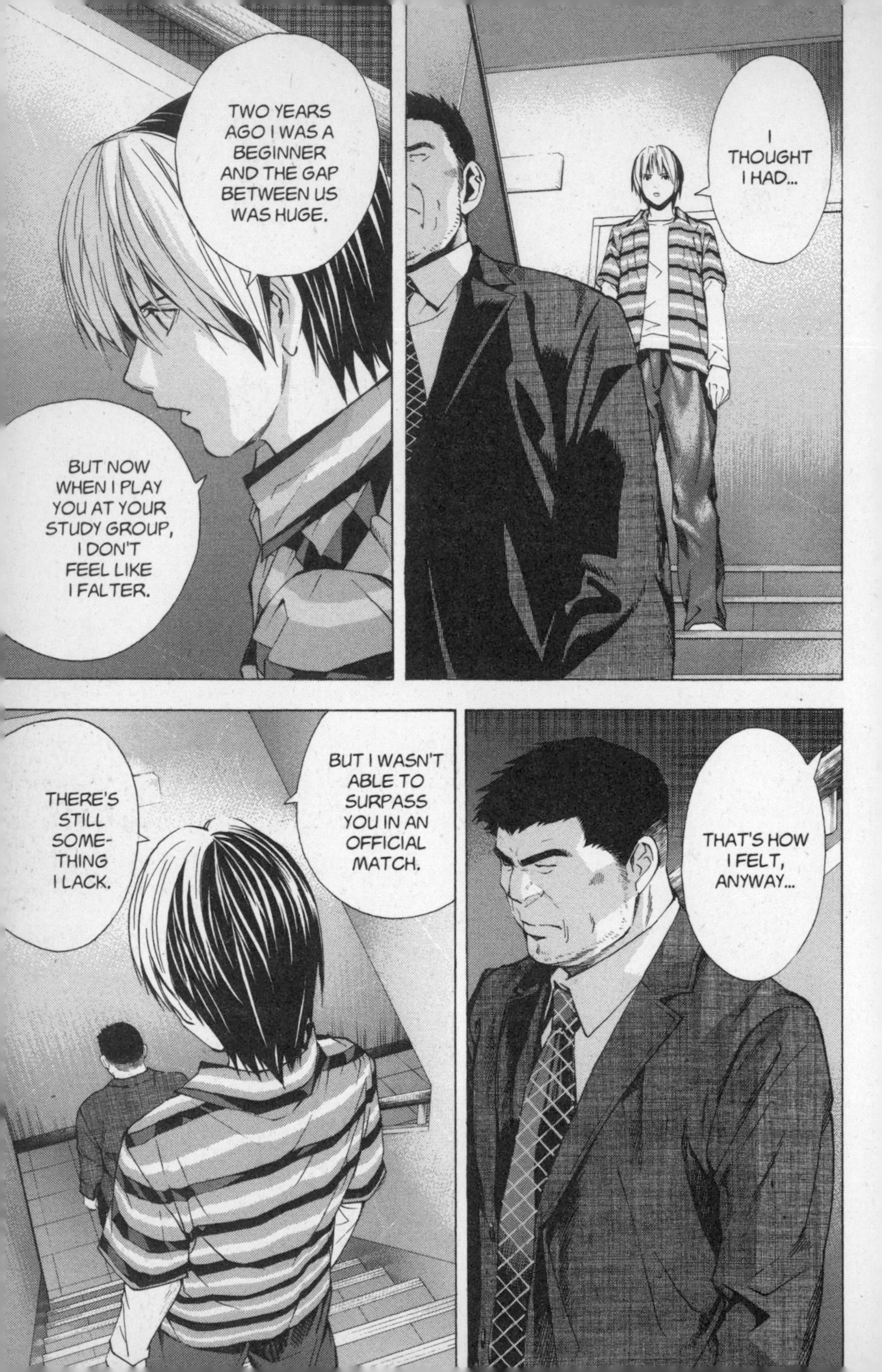
I THOUGHT I HAD...
TWO YEARS AGO I WAS A BEGINNER AND THE GAP BETWEEN US WAS HUGE.
BUT NOW WHEN I PLAY YOU AT YOUR STUDY GROUP, I DON'T FEEL LIKE I FALTER.
THAT'S HOW I FELT, ANYWAY...
BUT I WASN'T ABLE TO SURPASS YOU IN AN OFFICIAL MATCH.
THERE'S STILL SOME-THING I LACK.

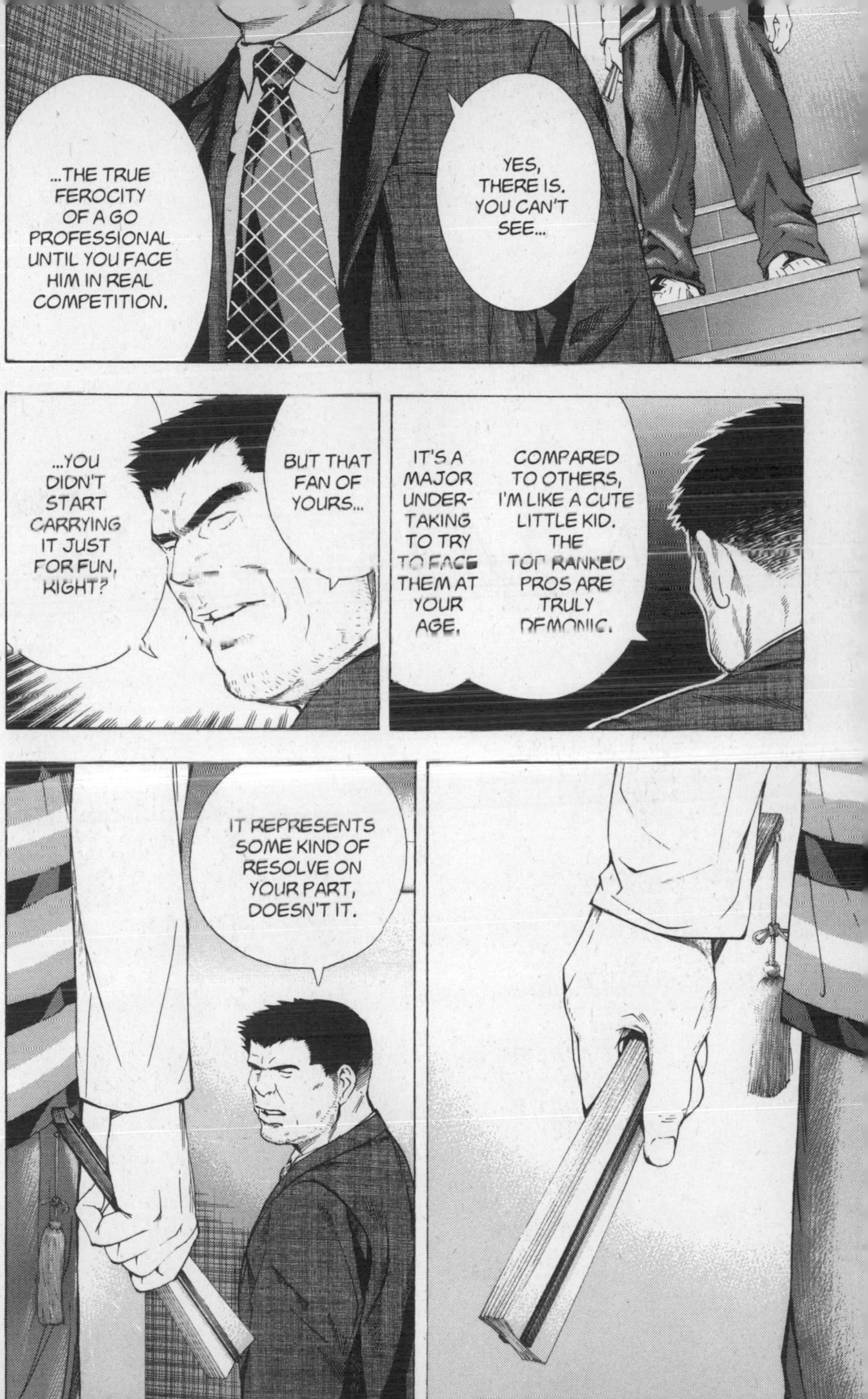
YES, THERE IS. YOU CAN'T SEE...
...THE TRUE FEROCITY OF A GO PROFESSIONAL UNTIL YOU FACE HIM IN REAL COMPETITION.
COMPARED TO OTHERS, I'M LIKE A CUTE LITTLE KID. THE TOP RANKED PROS ARE TRULY DEMONIC.
IT'S A MAJOR UNDER-TAKING TO TRY TO FACE THEM AT YOUR AGE.
BUT THAT FAN OF YOURS...
...YOU DIDN'T START CARRYING IT JUST FOR FUN, RIGHT?
IT REPRESENTS SOME KIND OF RESOLVE ON YOUR PART, DOESN'T IT.

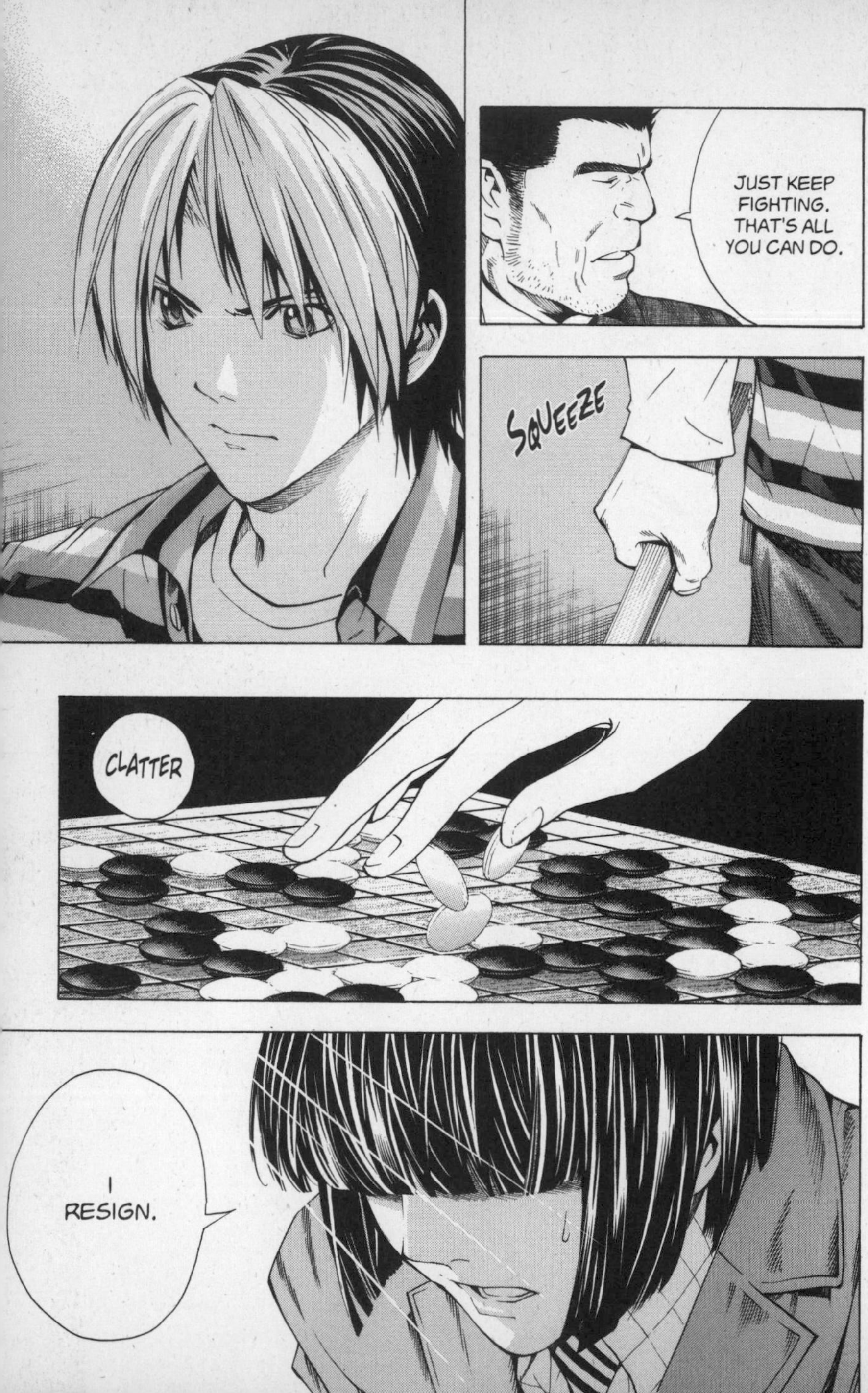
JUST KEEP FIGHTING. THAT'S ALL YOU CAN DO.
SQUEEZE
CLATTER
I RESIGN.

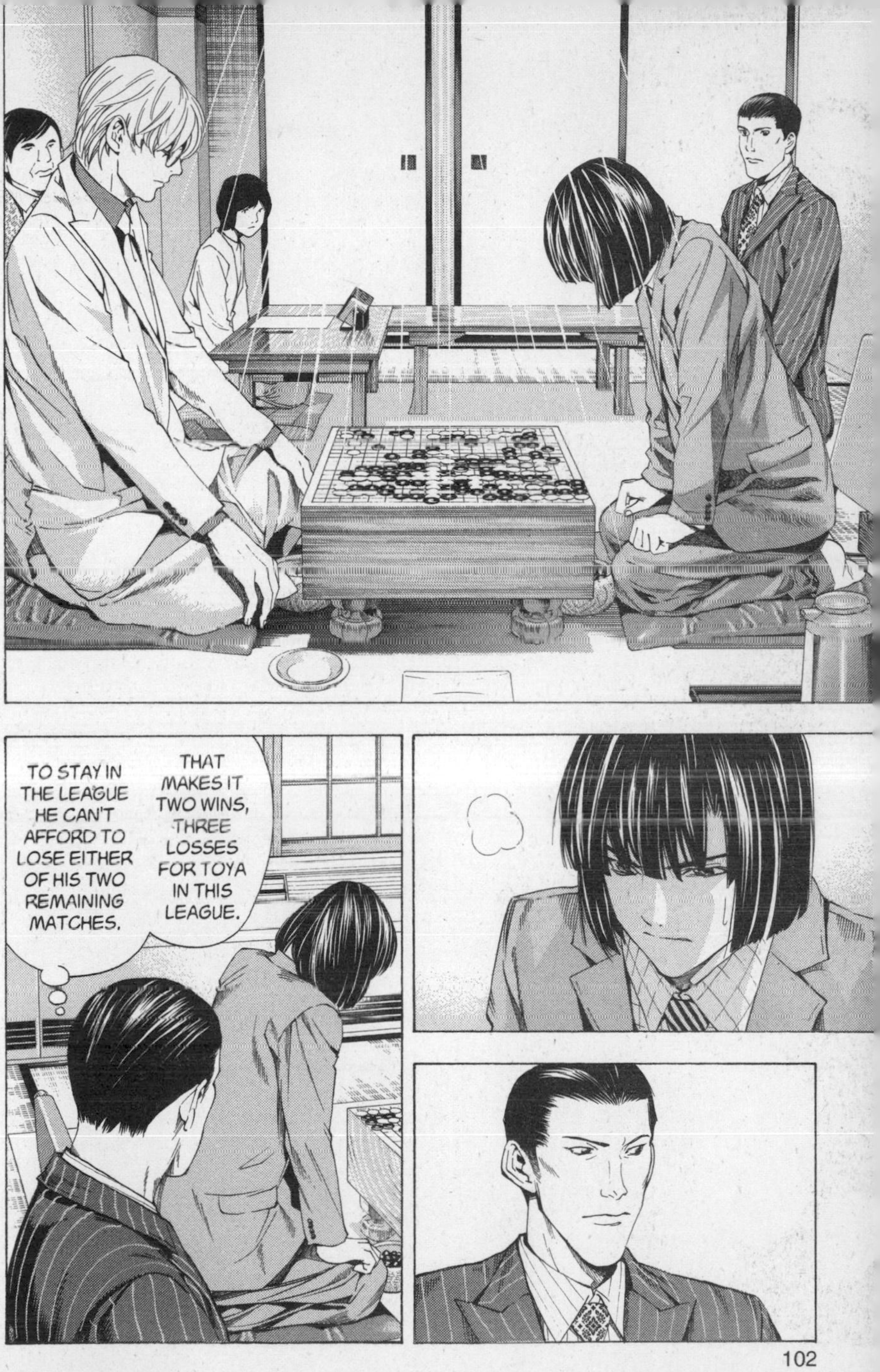
THAT MAKES IT TWO WINS, THREE LOSSES FOR TOYA IN THIS LEAGUE.
TO STAY IN THE LEAGUE HE CAN'T AFFORD TO LOSE EITHER OF HIS TWO REMAINING MATCHES.

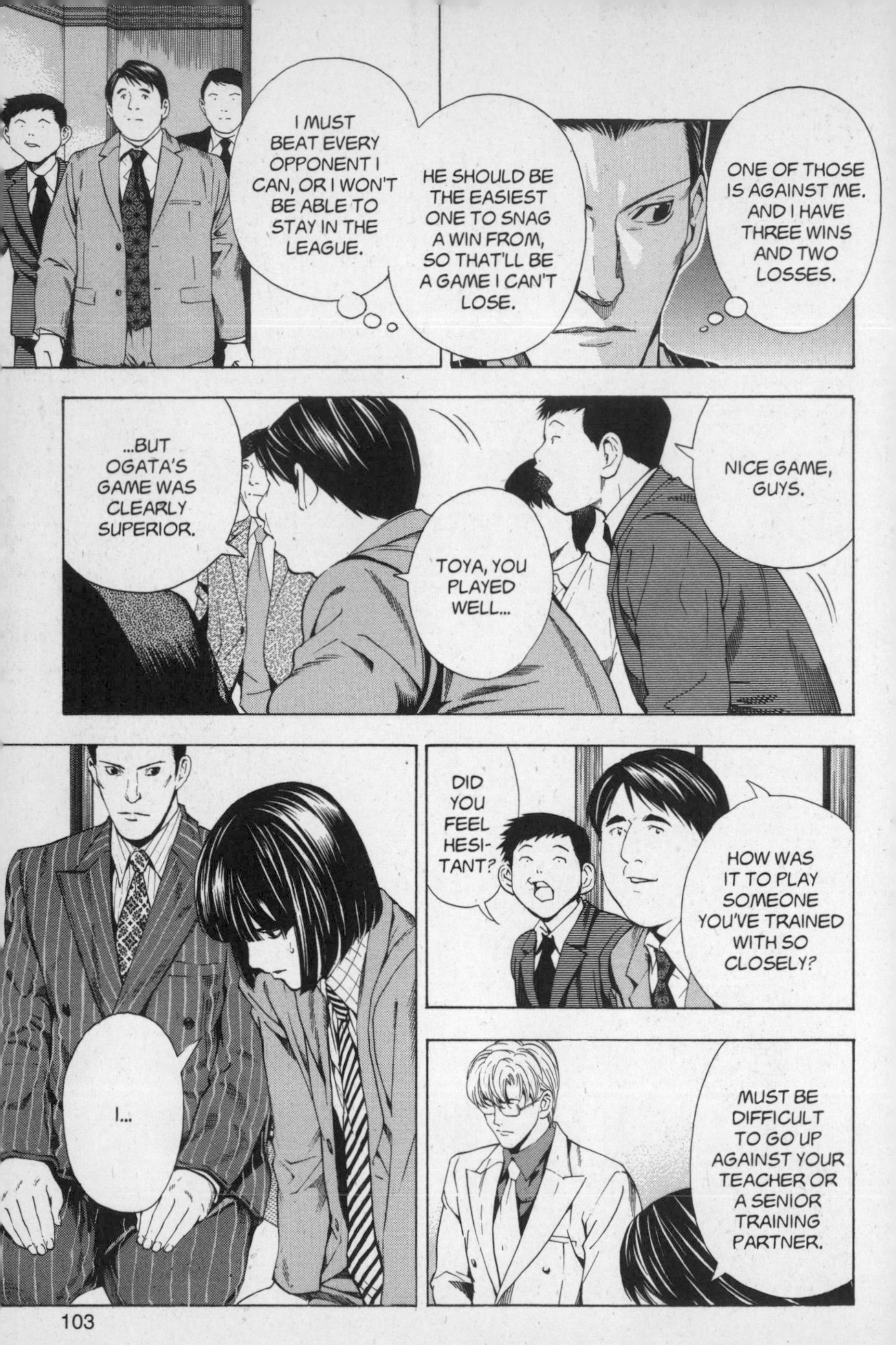
ONE OF THOSE IS AGAINST ME. AND I HAVE THREE WINS AND TWO LOSSES.
HE SHOULD BE THE EASIEST ONE TO SNAG A WIN FROM, SO THAT'LL BE A GAME I CAN'T LOSE.
I MUST BEAT EVERY OPPONENT I CAN, OR I WON'T BE ABLE TO STAY IN THE LEAGUE.
NICE GAME, GUYS.
TOYA, YOU PLAYED WELL...
...BUT OGATA'S GAME WAS CLEARLY SUPERIOR.
HOW WAS IT TO PLAY SOMEONE YOU'VE TRAINED WITH SO CLOSELY?
DID YOU FEEL HESI-TANT?
MUST BE DIFFICULT TO GO UP AGAINST YOUR TEACHER OR A SENIOR TRAINING PARTNER.
I...

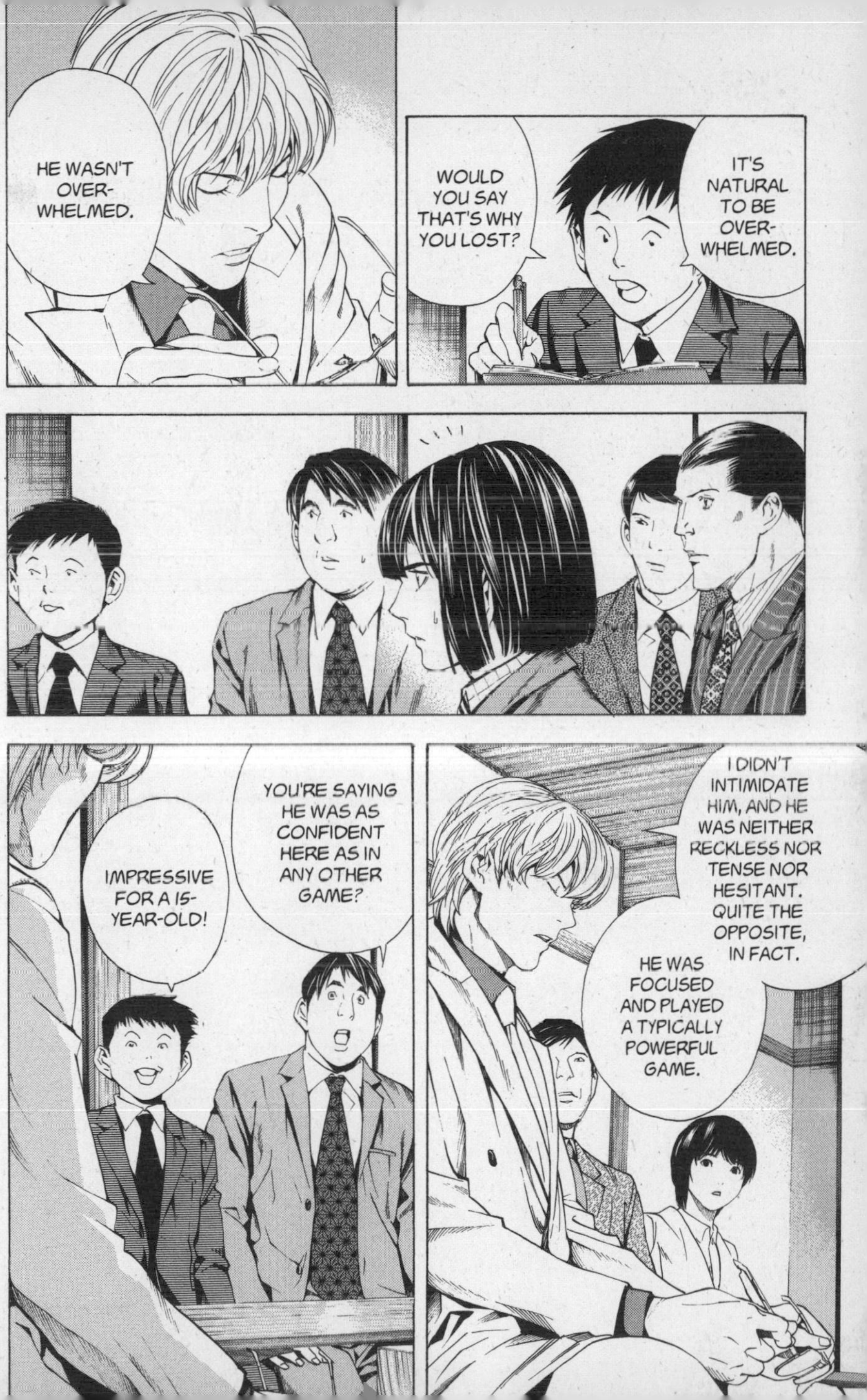
IT'S NATURAL TO BE OVER-WHELMED.
WOULD YOU SAY THAT'S WHY YOU LOST?
HE WASN'T OVER-WHELMED.
I DIDN'T INTIMIDATE HIM, AND HE WAS NEITHER RECKLESS NOR TENSE NOR HESITANT. QUITE THE OPPOSITE, IN FACT.
HE WAS FOCUSED AND PLAYED A TYPICALLY POWERFUL GAME.
YOU'RE SAYING HE WAS AS CONFIDENT HERE AS IN ANY OTHER GAME?
IMPRESSIVE FOR A 15-YEAR-OLD!

READ THIS WAY

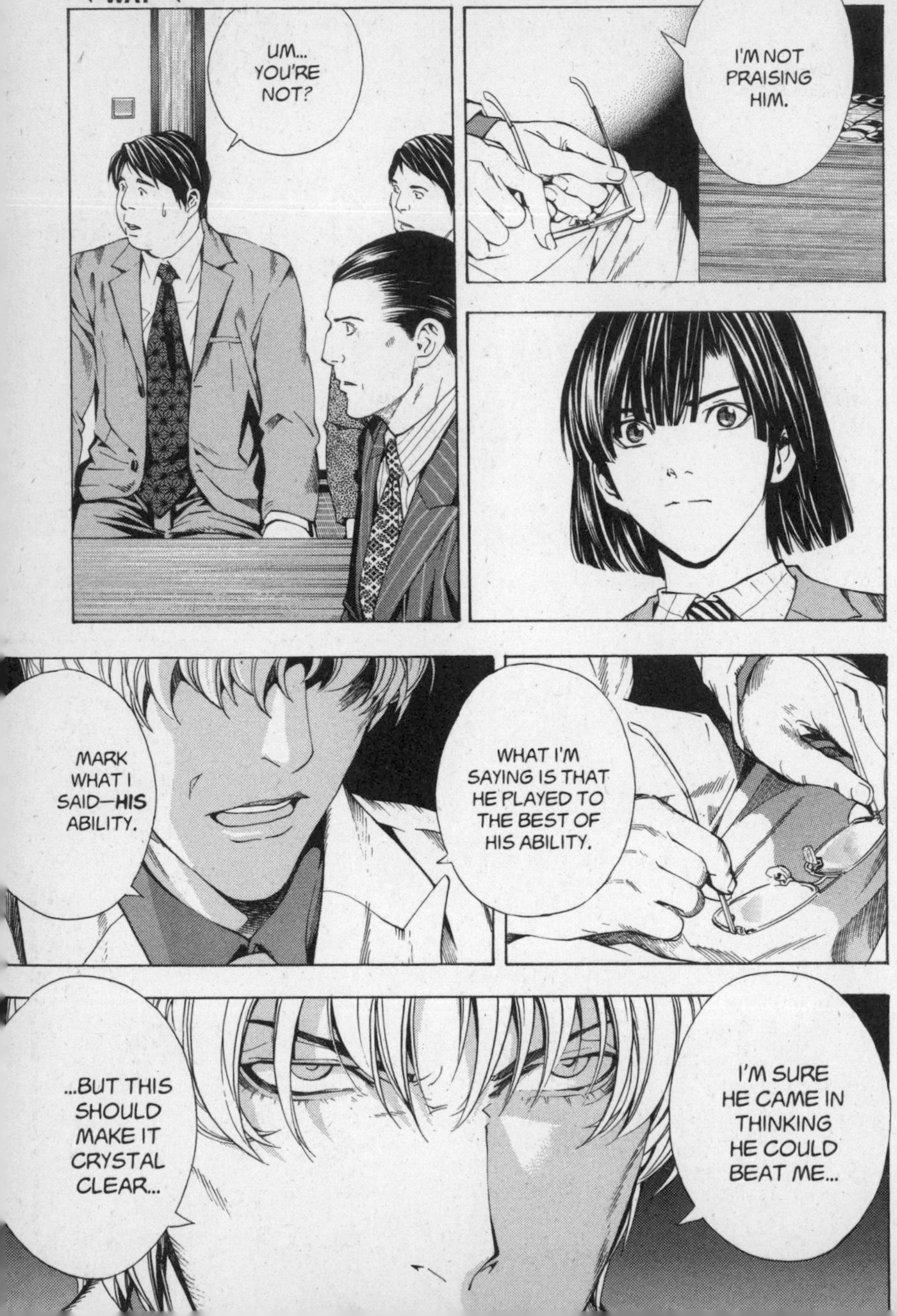
I'M NOT PRAISING HIM.
UM... YOU'RE NOT?
WHAT I'M SAYING IS THAT HE PLAYED TO THE BEST OF HIS ABILITY.
MARK WHAT I SAID—**HIS** ABILITY.
I'M SURE HE CAME IN THINKING HE COULD BEAT ME...
...BUT THIS SHOULD MAKE IT CRYSTAL CLEAR...

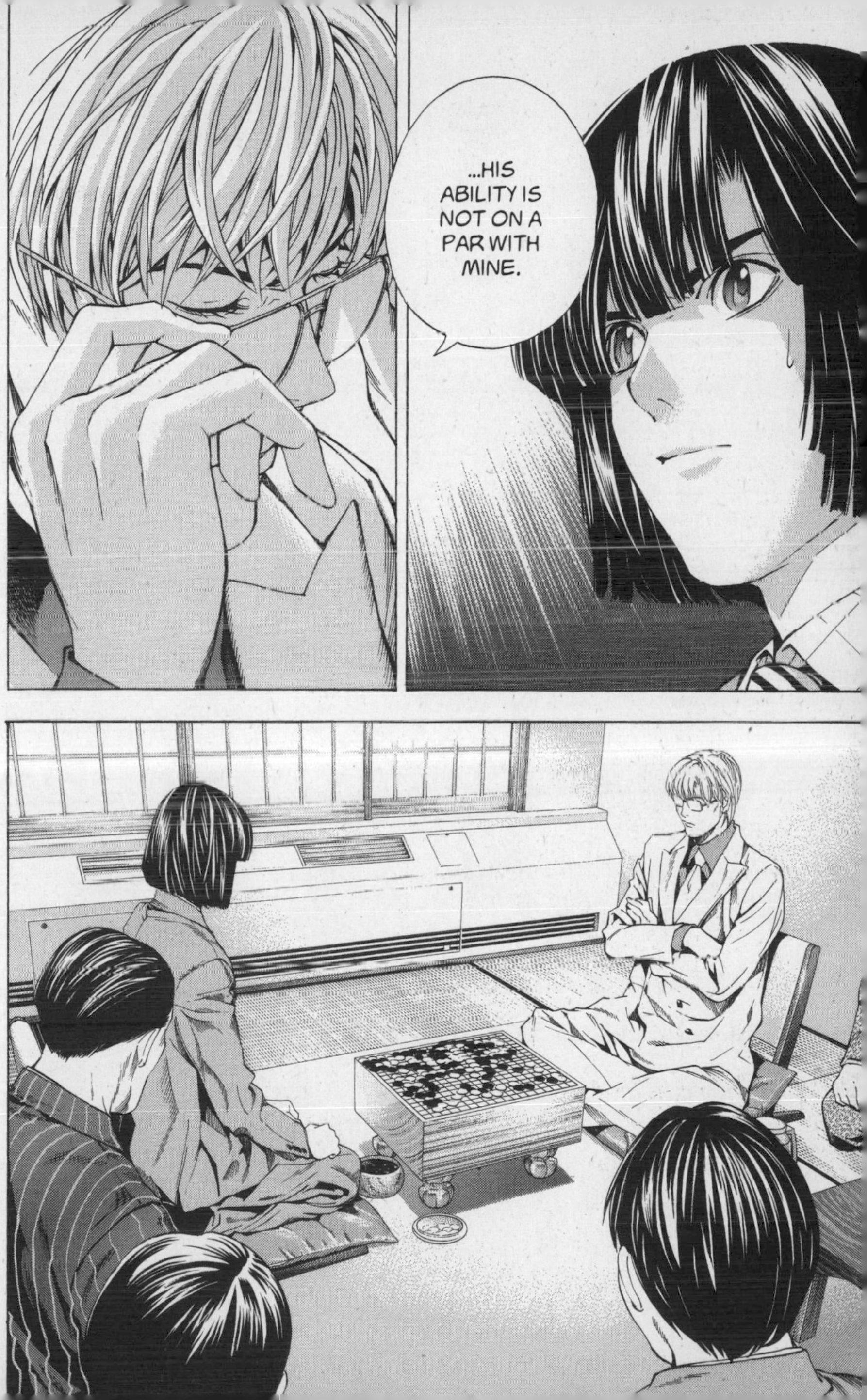
...HIS ABILITY IS NOT ON A PAR WITH MINE.

READ THIS WAY

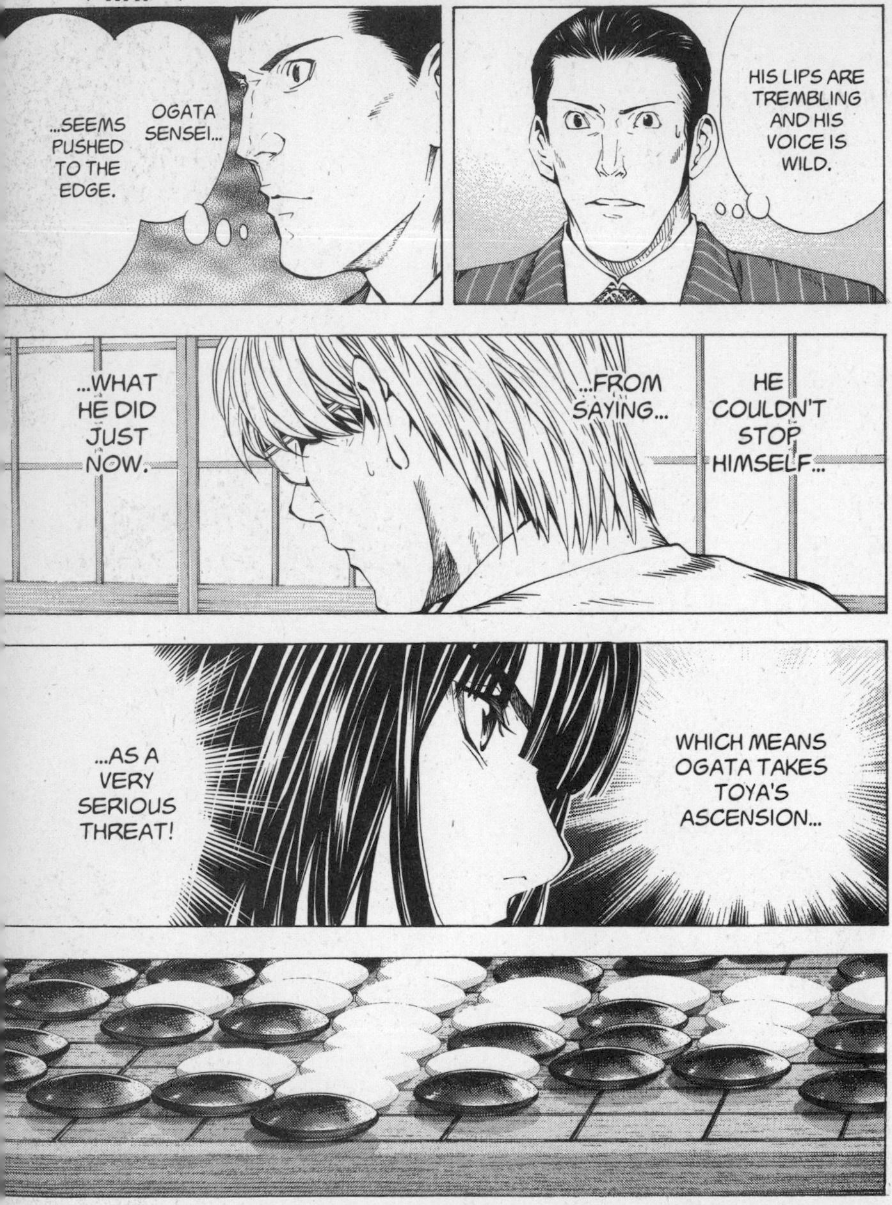
HIS LIPS ARE TREMBLING AND HIS VOICE IS WILD.
OGATA SENSEI...
...SEEMS PUSHED TO THE EDGE.
HE COULDN'T STOP HIMSELF...
...FROM SAYING...
...WHAT HE DID JUST NOW.
WHICH MEANS OGATA TAKES TOYA'S ASCENSION...
...AS A VERY SERIOUS THREAT!

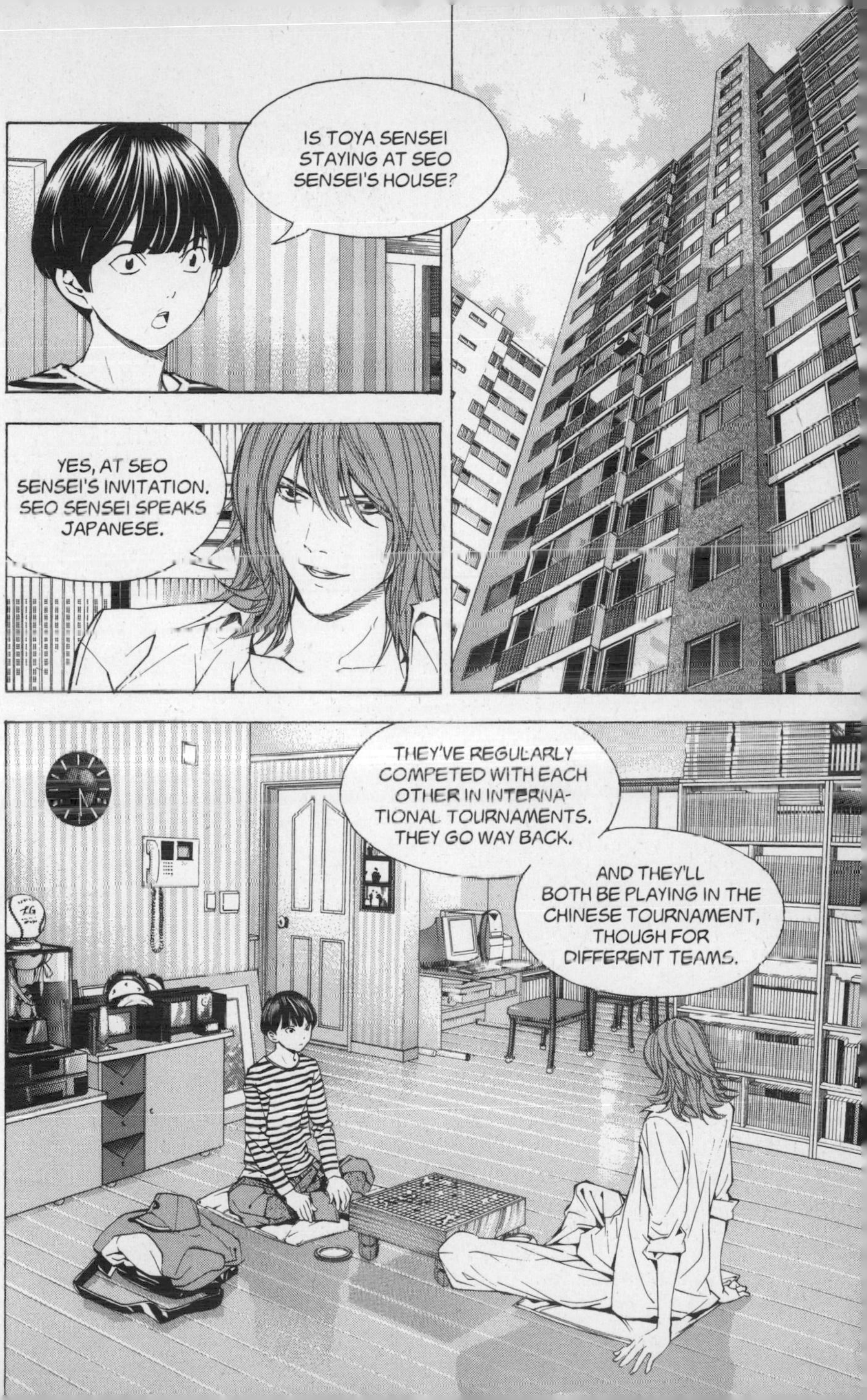
IS TOYA SENSEI STAYING AT SEO SENSEI'S HOUSE?
YES, AT SEO SENSEI'S INVITATION. SEO SENSEI SPEAKS JAPANESE.
THEY'VE REGULARLY COMPETED WITH EACH OTHER IN INTERNA-TIONAL TOURNAMENTS. THEY GO WAY BACK.
AND THEY'LL BOTH BE PLAYING IN THE CHINESE TOURNAMENT, THOUGH FOR DIFFERENT TEAMS.

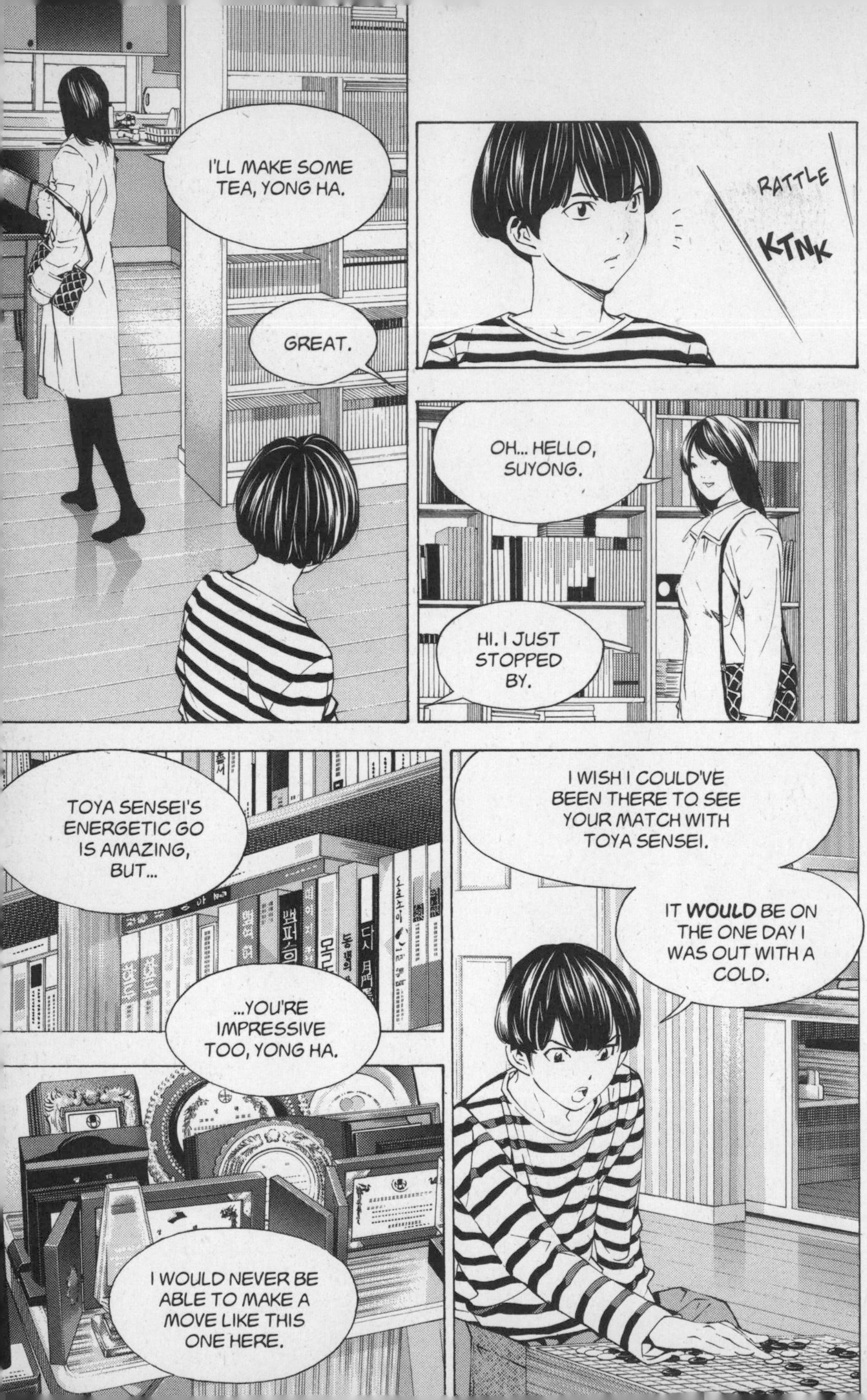
RATTLE
KTNK
OH... HELLO, SUYONG.
HI. I JUST STOPPED BY.
I'LL MAKE SOME TEA, YONG HA.
GREAT.
I WISH I COULD'VE BEEN THERE TO SEE YOUR MATCH WITH TOYA SENSEI.
IT **WOULD** BE ON THE ONE DAY I WAS OUT WITH A COLD.
TOYA SENSEI'S ENERGETIC GO IS AMAZING, BUT...
...YOU'RE IMPRESSIVE TOO, YONG HA.
I WOULD NEVER BE ABLE TO MAKE A MOVE LIKE THIS ONE HERE.

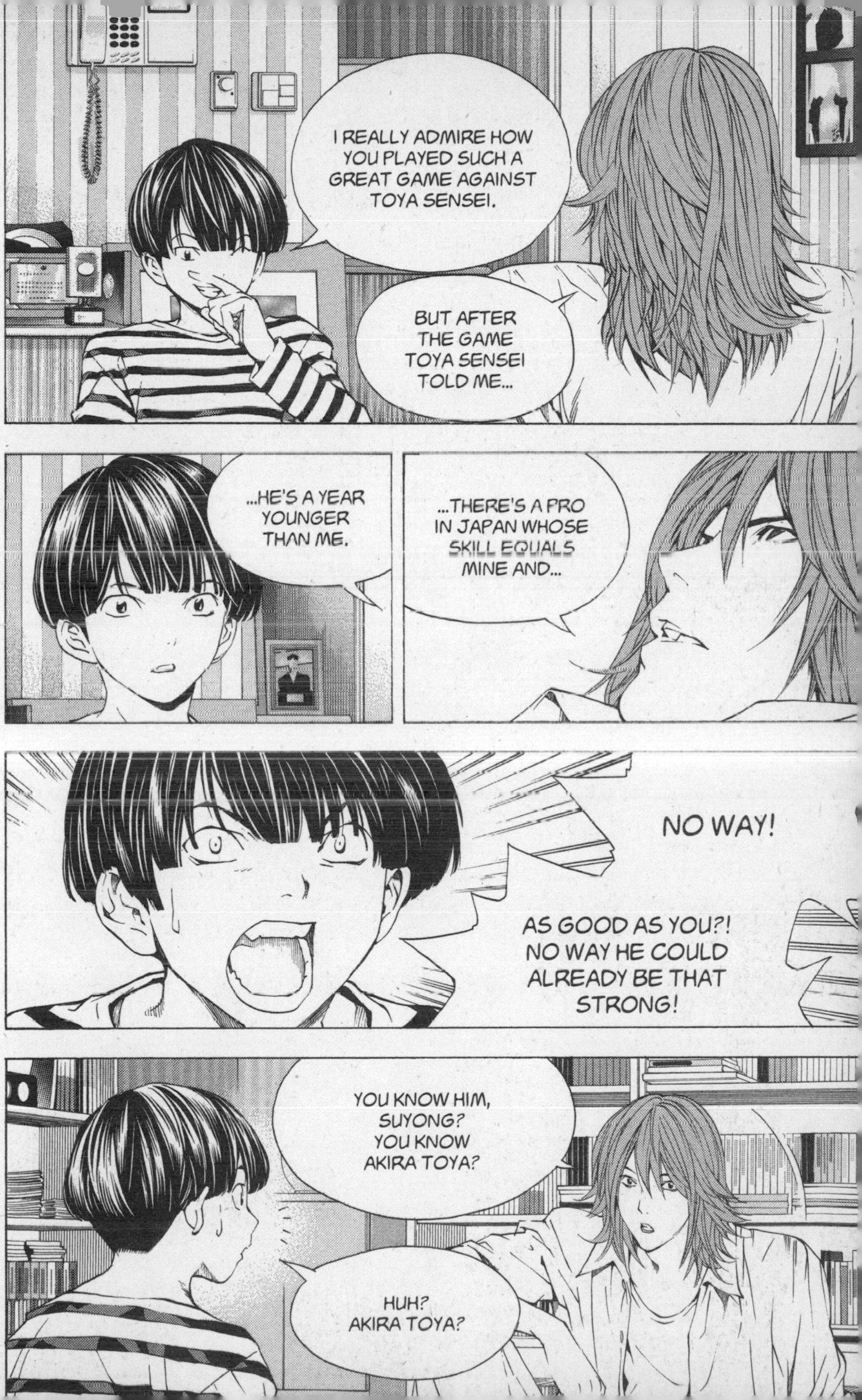
I REALLY ADMIRE HOW YOU PLAYED SUCH A GREAT GAME AGAINST TOYA SENSEI.
BUT AFTER THE GAME TOYA SENSEI TOLD ME...
...THERE'S A PRO IN JAPAN WHOSE SKILL EQUALS MINE AND...
...HE'S A YEAR YOUNGER THAN ME.
NO WAY!
AS GOOD AS YOU?! NO WAY HE COULD ALREADY BE THAT STRONG!
YOU KNOW HIM, SUYONG? YOU KNOW AKIRA TOYA?
HUH? AKIRA TOYA?

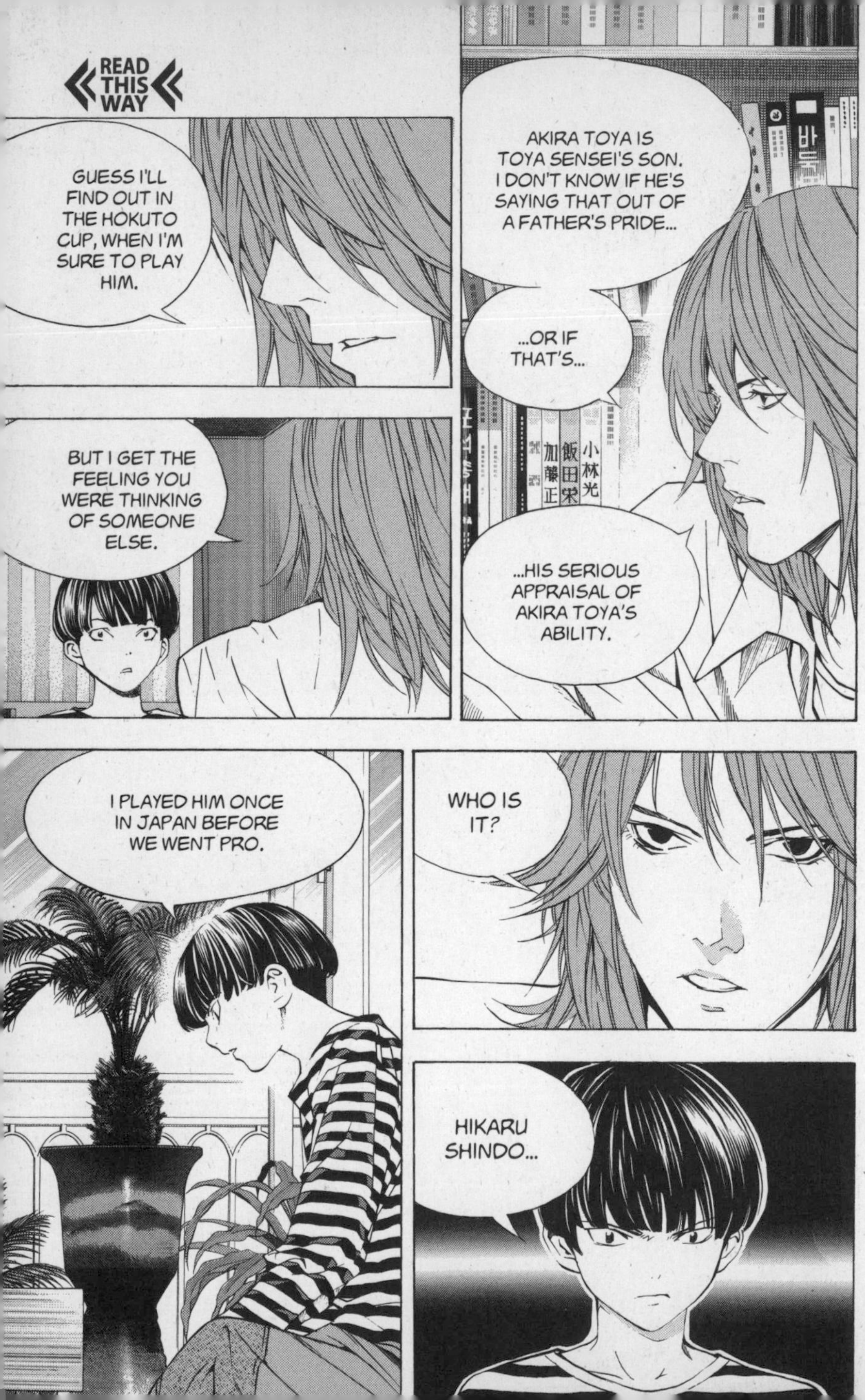
READ THIS WAY
AKIRA TOYA IS TOYA SENSEI'S SON. I DON'T KNOW IF HE'S SAYING THAT OUT OF A FATHER'S PRIDE...
...OR IF THAT'S...
...HIS SERIOUS APPRAISAL OF AKIRA TOYA'S ABILITY.
GUESS I'LL FIND OUT IN THE HOKUTO CUP, WHEN I'M SURE TO PLAY HIM.
BUT I GET THE FEELING YOU WERE THINKING OF SOMEONE ELSE.
WHO IS IT?
HIKARU SHINDO...
I PLAYED HIM ONCE IN JAPAN BEFORE WE WENT PRO.

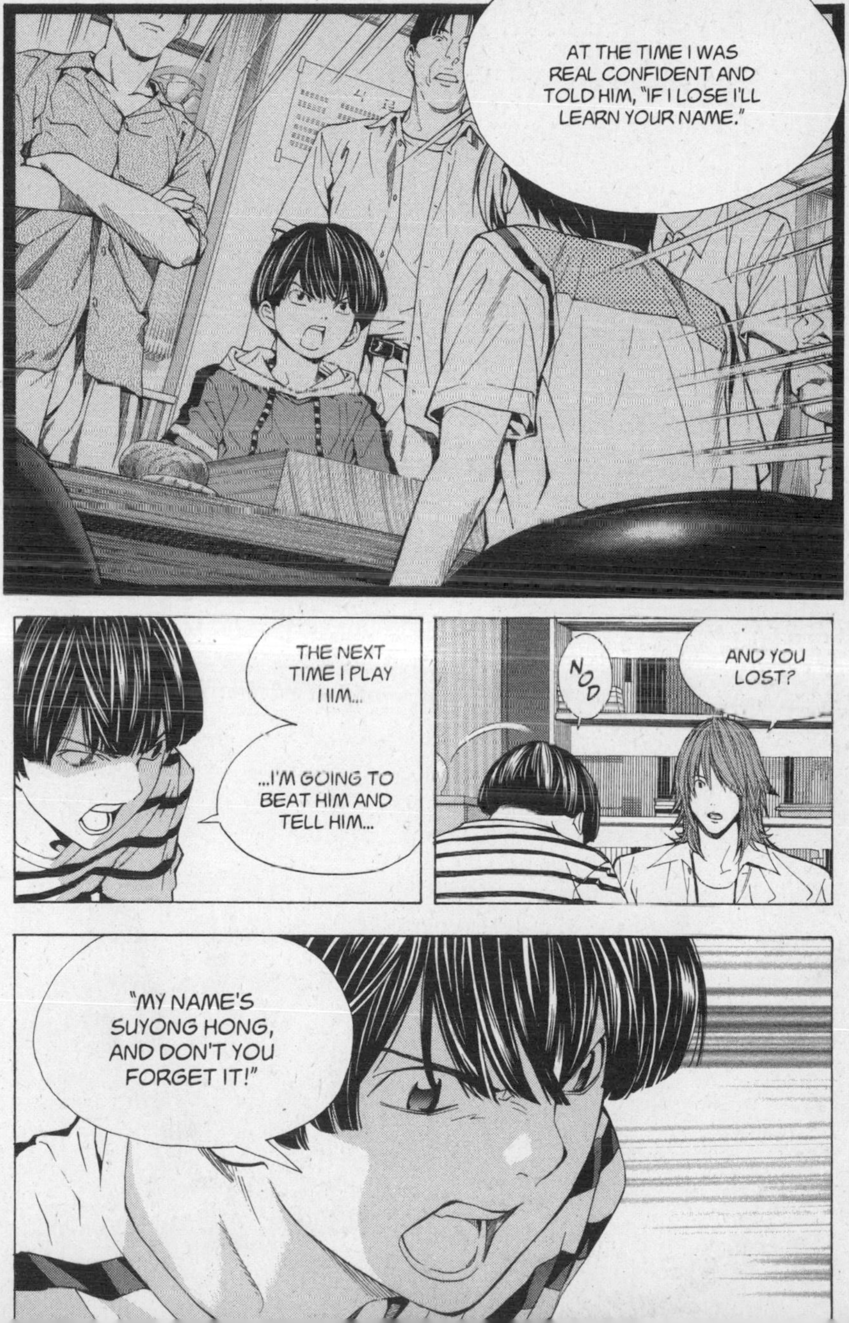
AT THE TIME I WAS REAL CONFIDENT AND TOLD HIM, "IF I LOSE I'LL LEARN YOUR NAME."
AND YOU LOST?
NOD
THE NEXT TIME I PLAY HIM...
...I'M GOING TO BEAT HIM AND TELL HIM...
"MY NAME'S SUYONG HONG, AND DON'T YOU FORGET IT!"

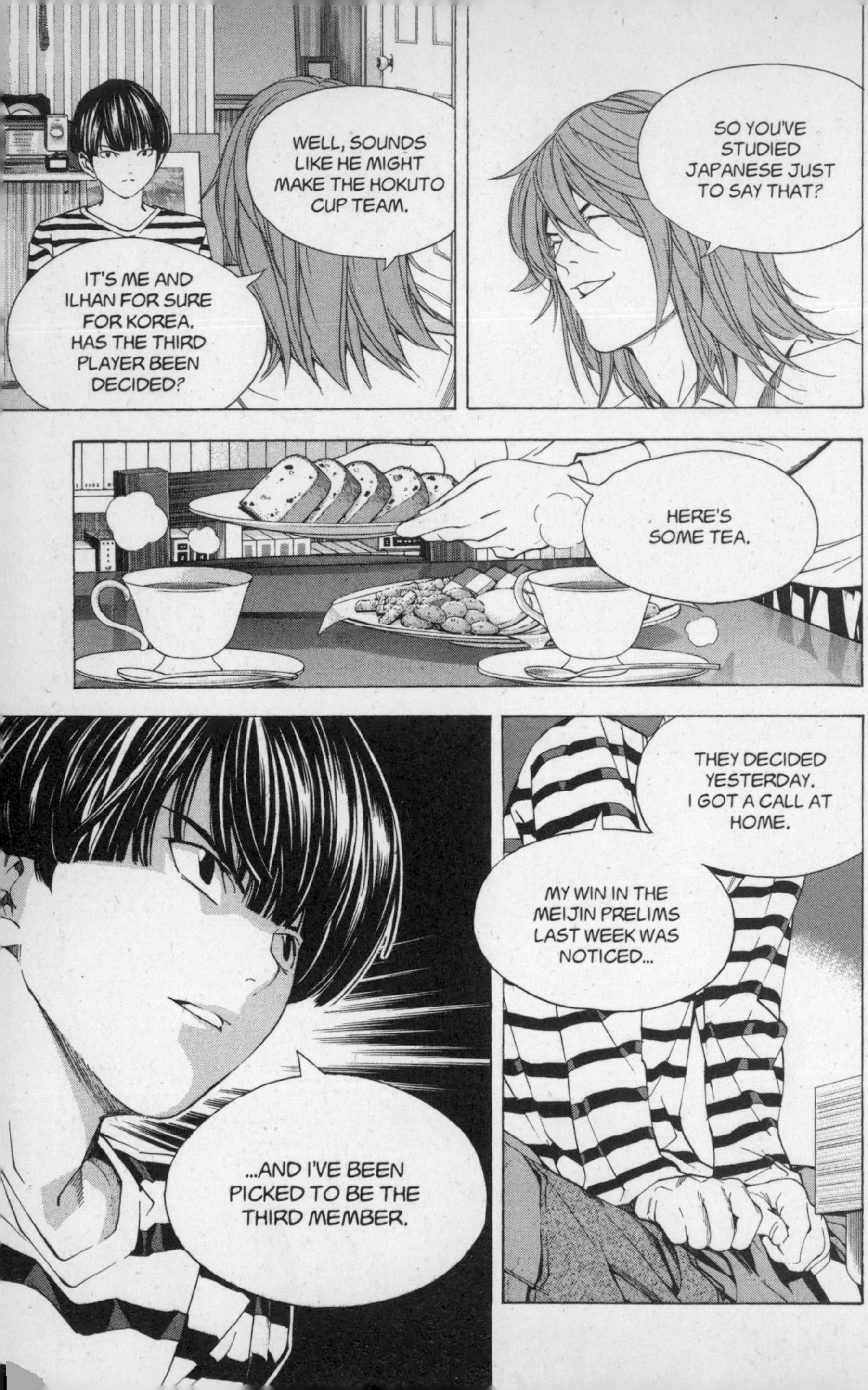
SO YOU'VE STUDIED JAPANESE JUST TO SAY THAT?
WELL, SOUNDS LIKE HE MIGHT MAKE THE HOKUTO CUP TEAM.
IT'S ME AND ILHAN FOR SURE FOR KOREA. HAS THE THIRD PLAYER BEEN DECIDED?
HERE'S SOME TEA.
THEY DECIDED YESTERDAY. I GOT A CALL AT HOME.
MY WIN IN THE MEIJIN PRELIMS LAST WEEK WAS NOTICED...
...AND I'VE BEEN PICKED TO BE THE THIRD MEMBER.

A WORD ABOUT HIKARU NO GO

THE KANSAI GO ASSOCIATION

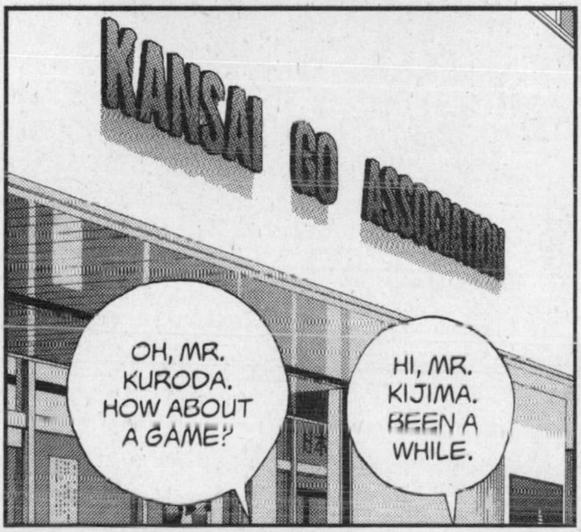
KANSAI GO ASSOCIATION
HI, MR. KIJIMA. BEEN A WHILE.
OH, MR. KURODA. HOW ABOUT A GAME?

IT'S A SEPARATE PROFESSIONAL ORGANIZATION FROM THE JAPAN GO ASSOCIATION.

IN KANSAI (WESTERN JAPAN), THERE'S ALSO THE "JAPAN GO ASSOCIATION KANSAI BRANCH." IT'S OFTEN CONFUSED WITH THE KANSAI GO ASSOCIATION. THE BUILDINGS ARE CLOSE TO EACH OTHER TOO. SINCE IT'S CONFUSING I DIDN'T EVEN MENTION THE KANSAI GO ASSOCIATION OR THE KANSAI BRANCH UNTIL VOLUME 17, THE ONE ABOUT SAI.

IF THE JAPAN GO ASSOCIATION AND THE KANSAI GO ASSOCIATION COULD MERGE, THEN TOKYO COULD HAVE THE "JAPAN GO ASSOCIATION," OSAKA COULD HAVE THE "KANSAI GO ASSOCIATION," AND NAGOYA COULD HAVE THE "CENTRAL GO ASSOCIATION," AND EVERYTHING WOULD BE EASIER TO UNDERSTAND.

RIGHT?

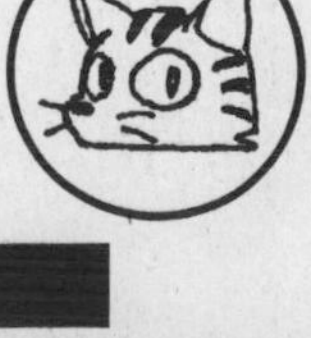

Game 162 "Graduation"

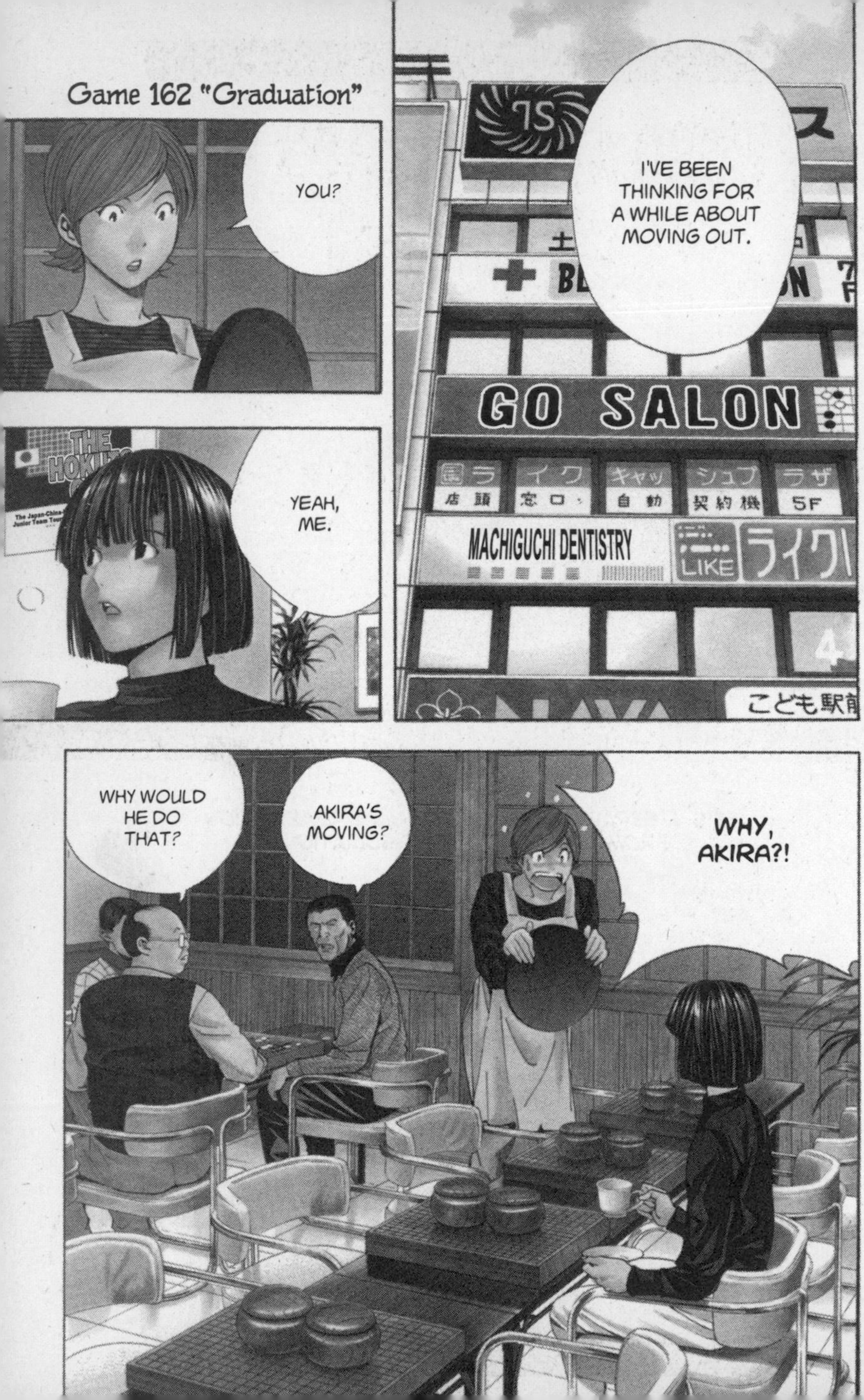
I'VE BEEN THINKING FOR A WHILE ABOUT MOVING OUT.
GO SALON
MACHIGUCHI DENTISTRY
YOU?
YEAH, ME.
WHY, AKIRA?!
AKIRA'S MOVING?
WHY WOULD HE DO THAT?

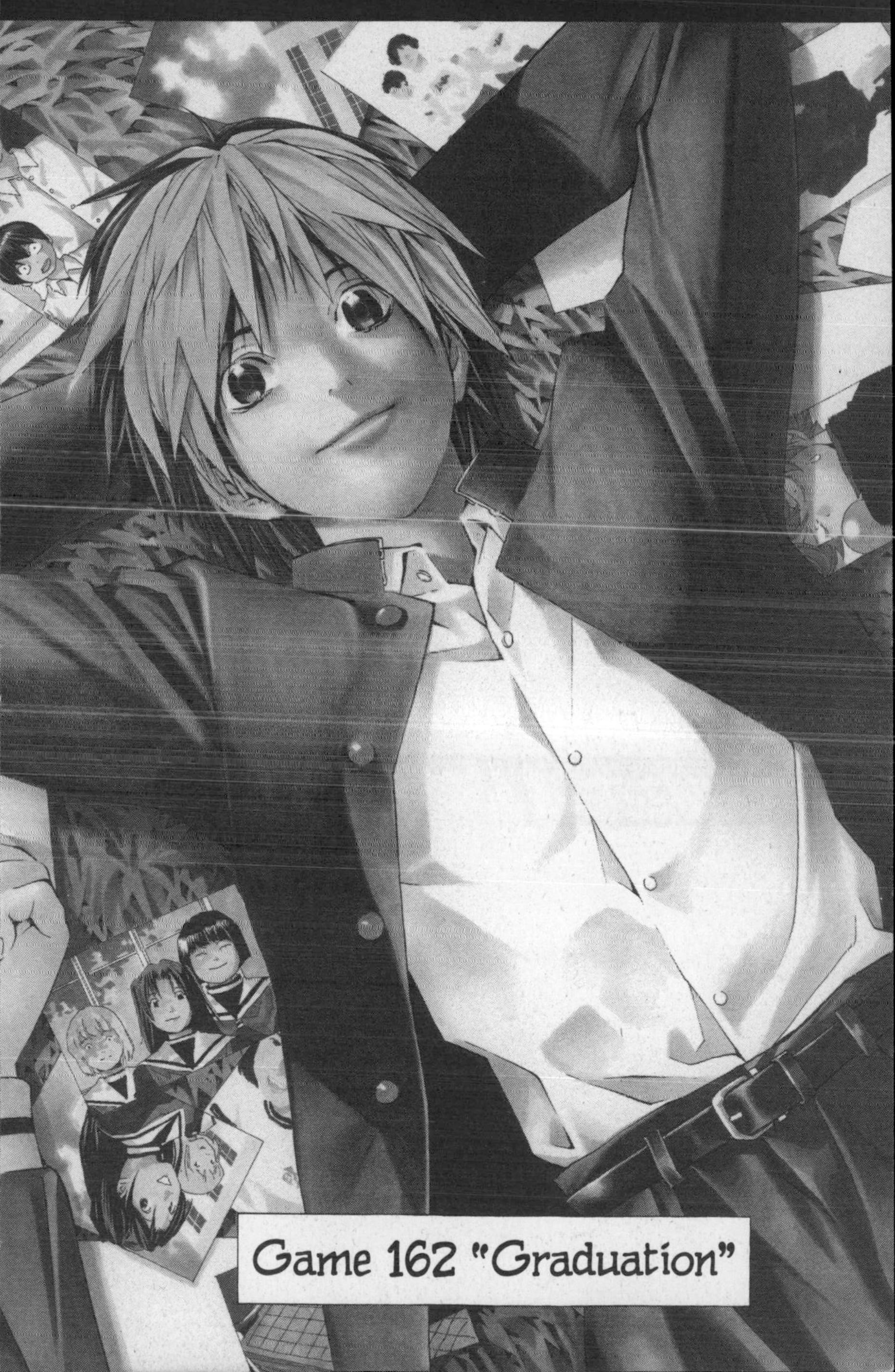
Game 162 "Graduation"

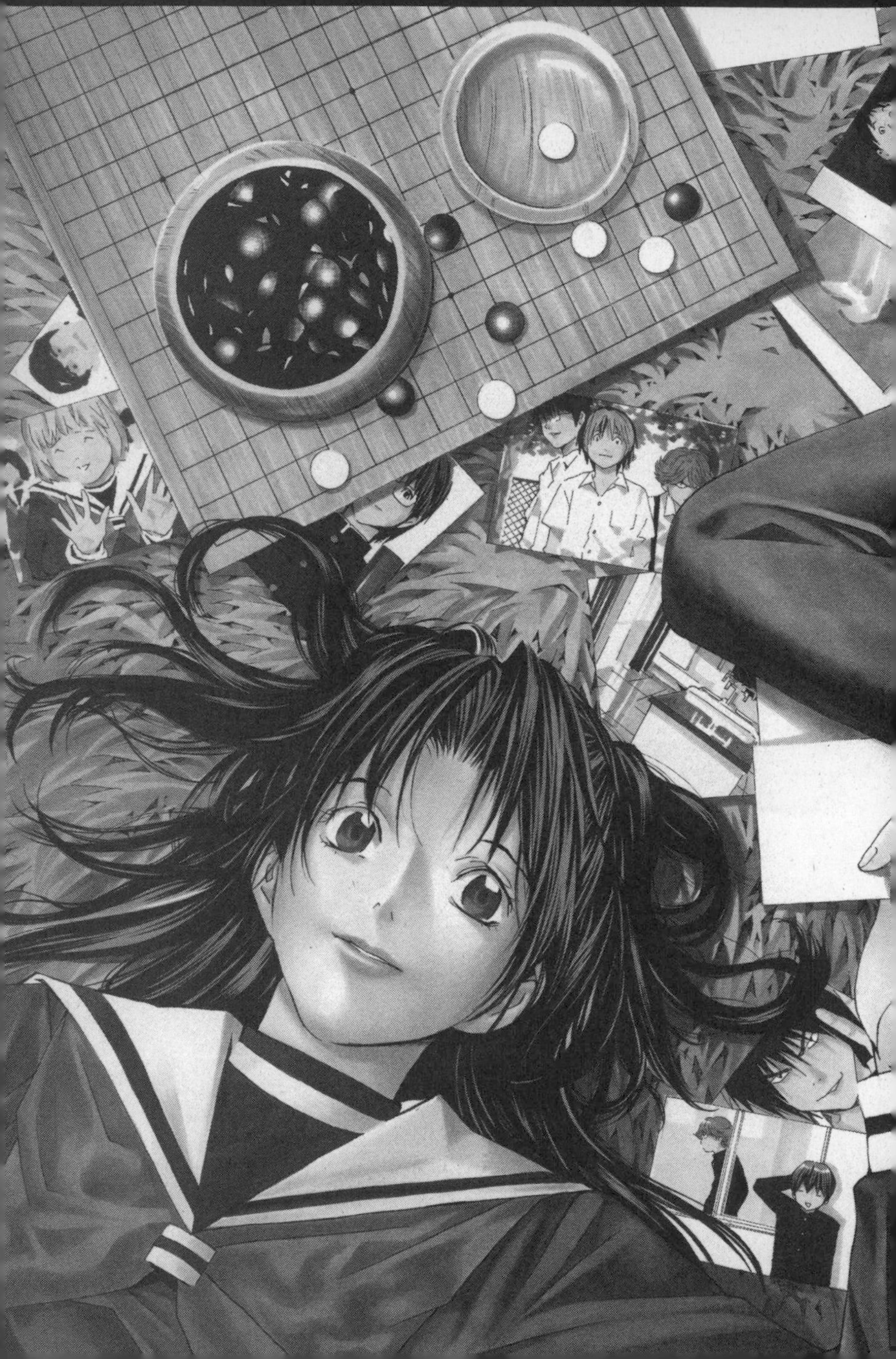

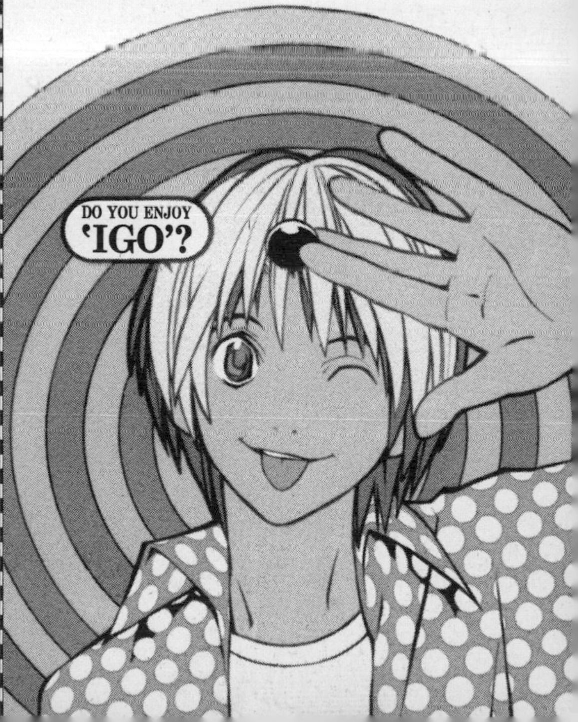
DO YOU ENJOY 'IGO'?

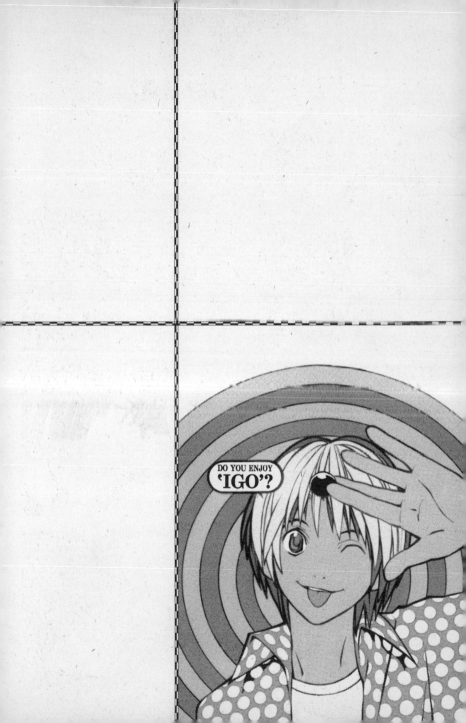

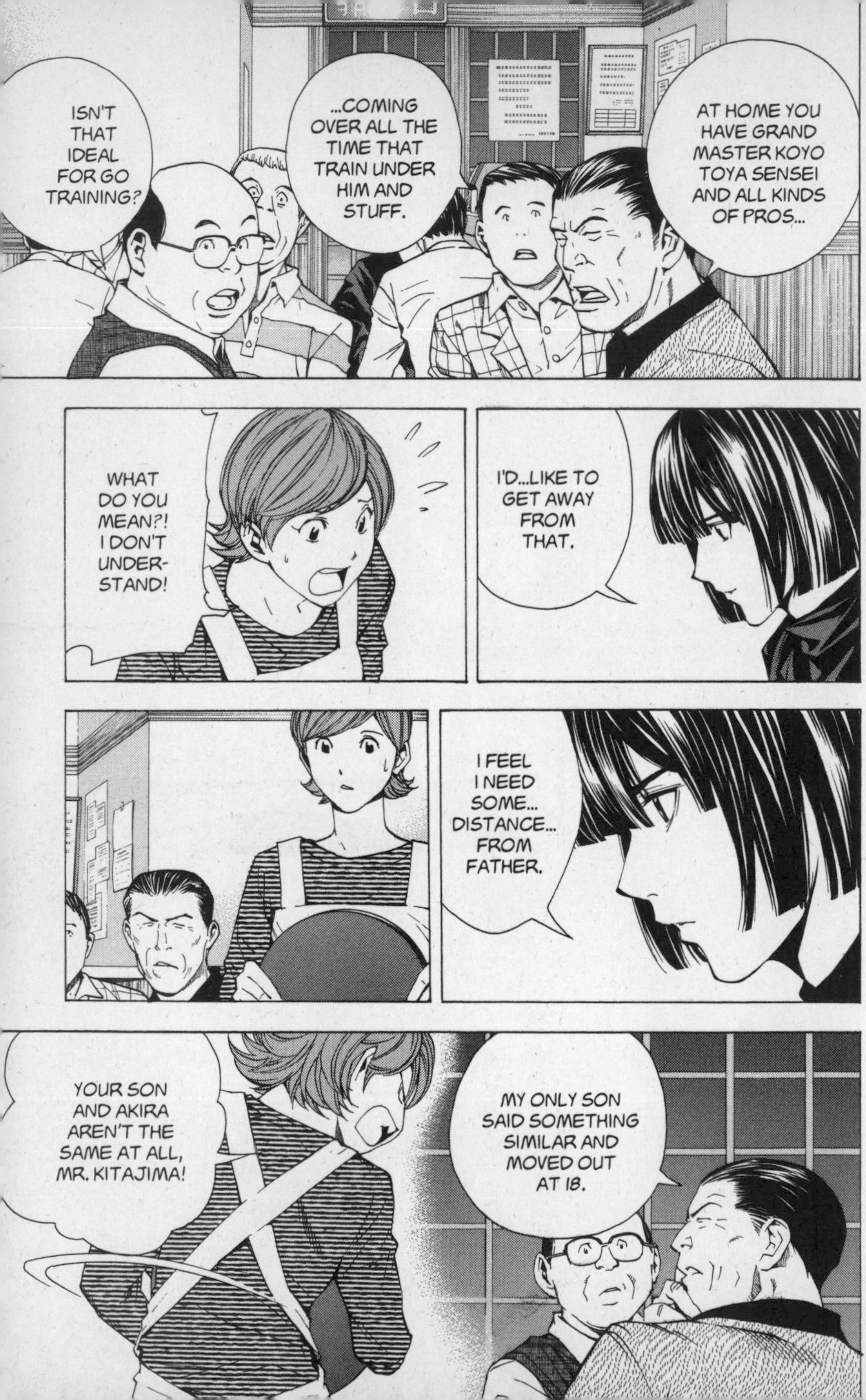
AT HOME YOU HAVE GRAND MASTER KOYO TOYA SENSEI AND ALL KINDS OF PROS...
...COMING OVER ALL THE TIME THAT TRAIN UNDER HIM AND STUFF.
ISN'T THAT IDEAL FOR GO TRAINING?
I'D...LIKE TO GET AWAY FROM THAT.
WHAT DO YOU MEAN?! I DON'T UNDER-STAND!
I FEEL I NEED SOME... DISTANCE... FROM FATHER.
MY ONLY SON SAID SOMETHING SIMILAR AND MOVED OUT AT 18.
YOUR SON AND AKIRA AREN'T THE SAME AT ALL, MR. KITAJIMA!

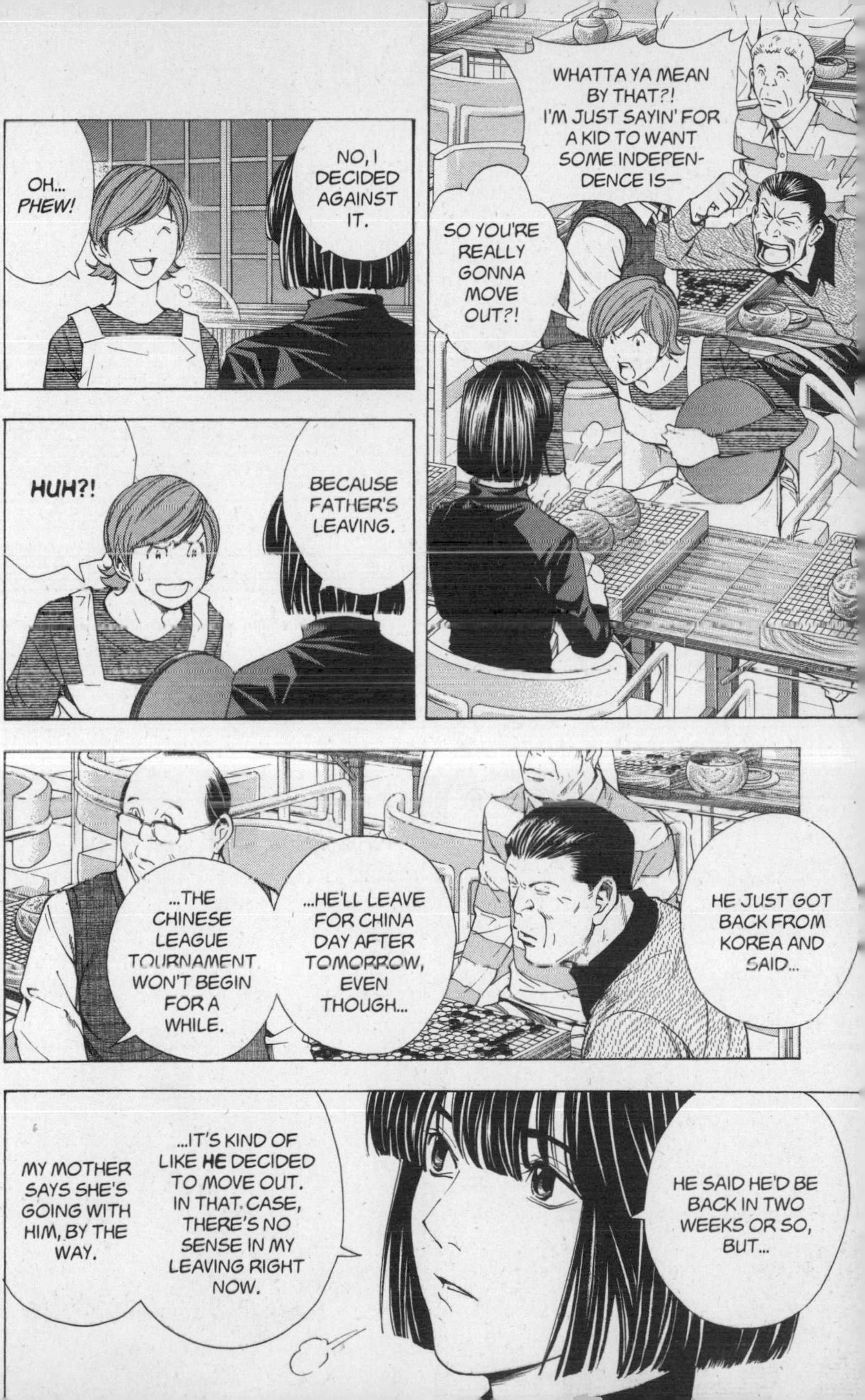
WHATTA YA MEAN BY THAT?! I'M JUST SAYIN' FOR A KID TO WANT SOME INDEPEN-DENCE IS—
SO YOU'RE REALLY GONNA MOVE OUT?!
NO, I DECIDED AGAINST IT.
OH... PHEW!
BECAUSE FATHER'S LEAVING.
HUH?!
HE JUST GOT BACK FROM KOREA AND SAID...
...HE'LL LEAVE FOR CHINA DAY AFTER TOMORROW, EVEN THOUGH...
...THE CHINESE LEAGUE TOURNAMENT WON'T BEGIN FOR A WHILE.
HE SAID HE'D BE BACK IN TWO WEEKS OR SO, BUT...
...IT'S KIND OF LIKE **HE** DECIDED TO MOVE OUT. IN THAT CASE, THERE'S NO SENSE IN MY LEAVING RIGHT NOW.
MY MOTHER SAYS SHE'S GOING WITH HIM, BY THE WAY.

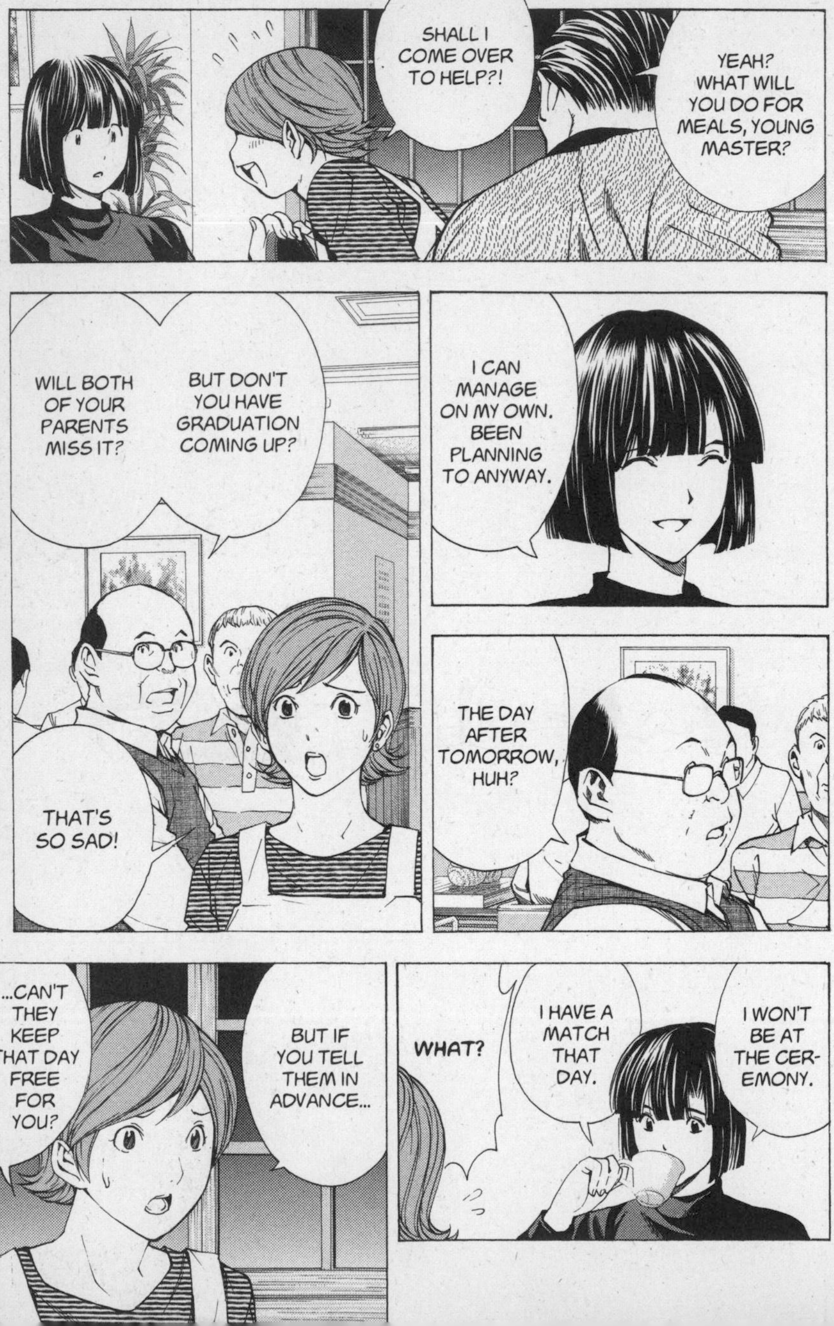
YEAH? WHAT WILL YOU DO FOR MEALS, YOUNG MASTER?
SHALL I COME OVER TO HELP?!
I CAN MANAGE ON MY OWN. BEEN PLANNING TO ANYWAY.
THE DAY AFTER TOMORROW, HUH?
BUT DON'T YOU HAVE GRADUATION COMING UP?
WILL BOTH OF YOUR PARENTS MISS IT?
THAT'S SO SAD!
I WON'T BE AT THE CER-EMONY.
I HAVE A MATCH THAT DAY.
WHAT?
BUT IF YOU TELL THEM IN ADVANCE...
...CAN'T THEY KEEP THAT DAY FREE FOR YOU?

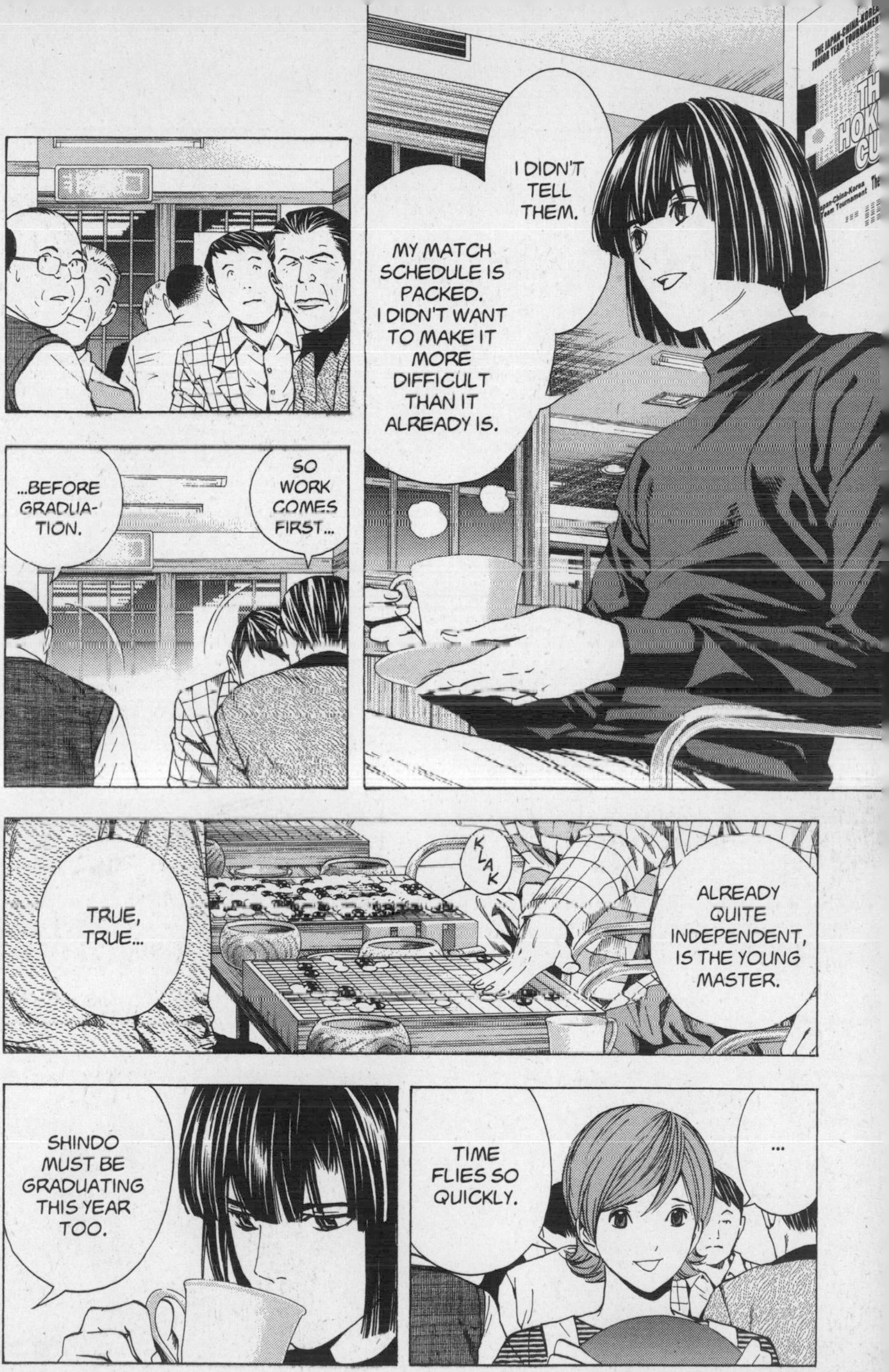
I DIDN'T TELL THEM.
MY MATCH SCHEDULE IS PACKED. I DIDN'T WANT TO MAKE IT MORE DIFFICULT THAN IT ALREADY IS.
SO WORK COMES FIRST...
...BEFORE GRADUATION.
ALREADY QUITE INDEPENDENT, IS THE YOUNG MASTER.
KLAK
TRUE, TRUE...
...
TIME FLIES SO QUICKLY.
SHINDO MUST BE GRADUATING THIS YEAR TOO.

READ THIS WAY

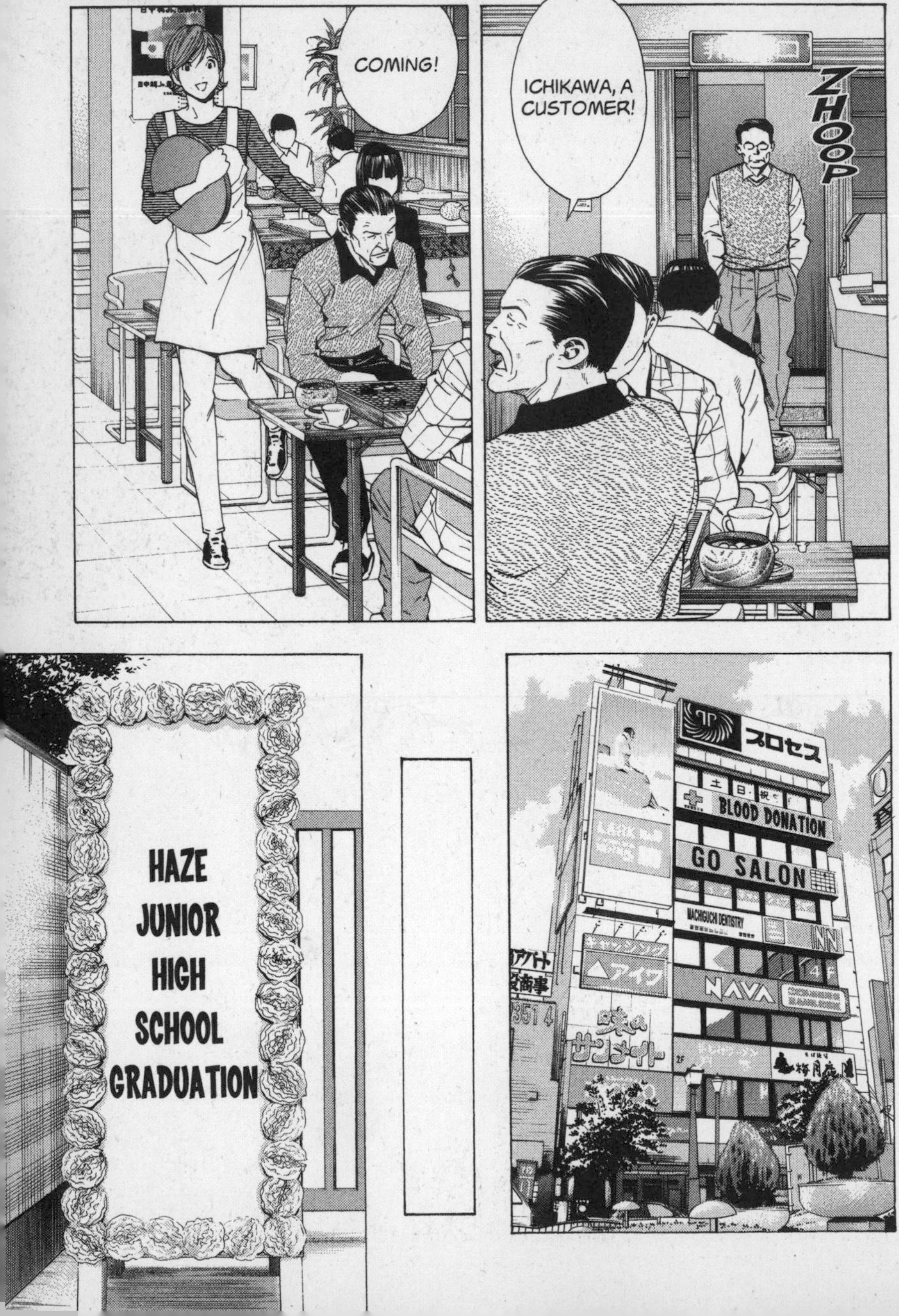
ICHIKAWA, A CUSTOMER!
ZHOOP
COMING!
プロセス
BLOOD DONATION
GO SALON
MACHIGUCHI DENTISTRY
アイワ
NAVA
HAZE JUNIOR HIGH SCHOOL GRADUATION

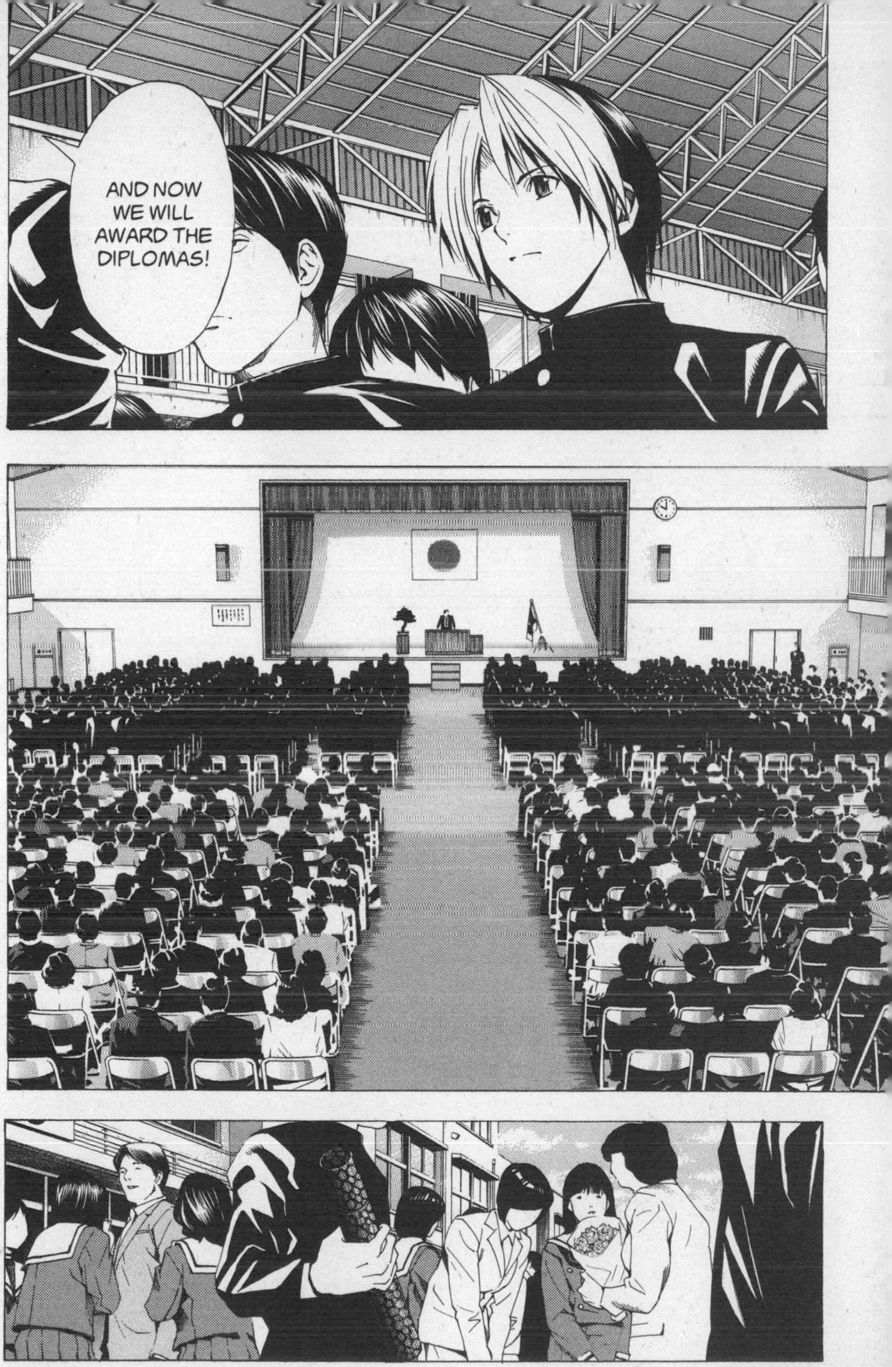
AND NOW WE WILL AWARD THE DIPLOMAS!

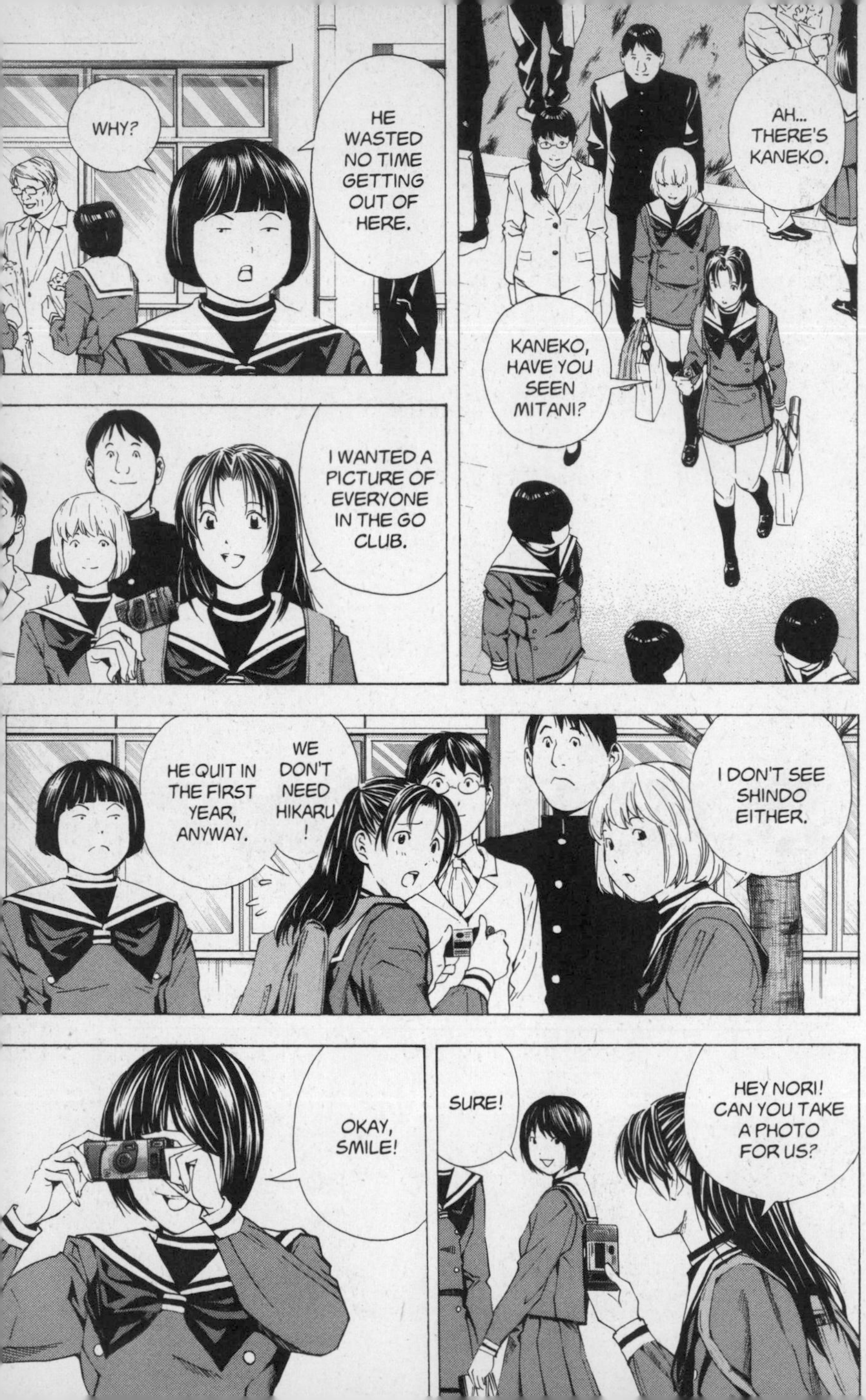
AH... THERE'S KANEKO.
KANEKO, HAVE YOU SEEN MITANI?
HE WASTED NO TIME GETTING OUT OF HERE.
WHY?
I WANTED A PICTURE OF EVERYONE IN THE GO CLUB.
I DON'T SEE SHINDO EITHER.
WE DON'T NEED HIKARU!
HE QUIT IN THE FIRST YEAR, ANYWAY.
HEY NORI! CAN YOU TAKE A PHOTO FOR US?
SURE!
OKAY, SMILE!

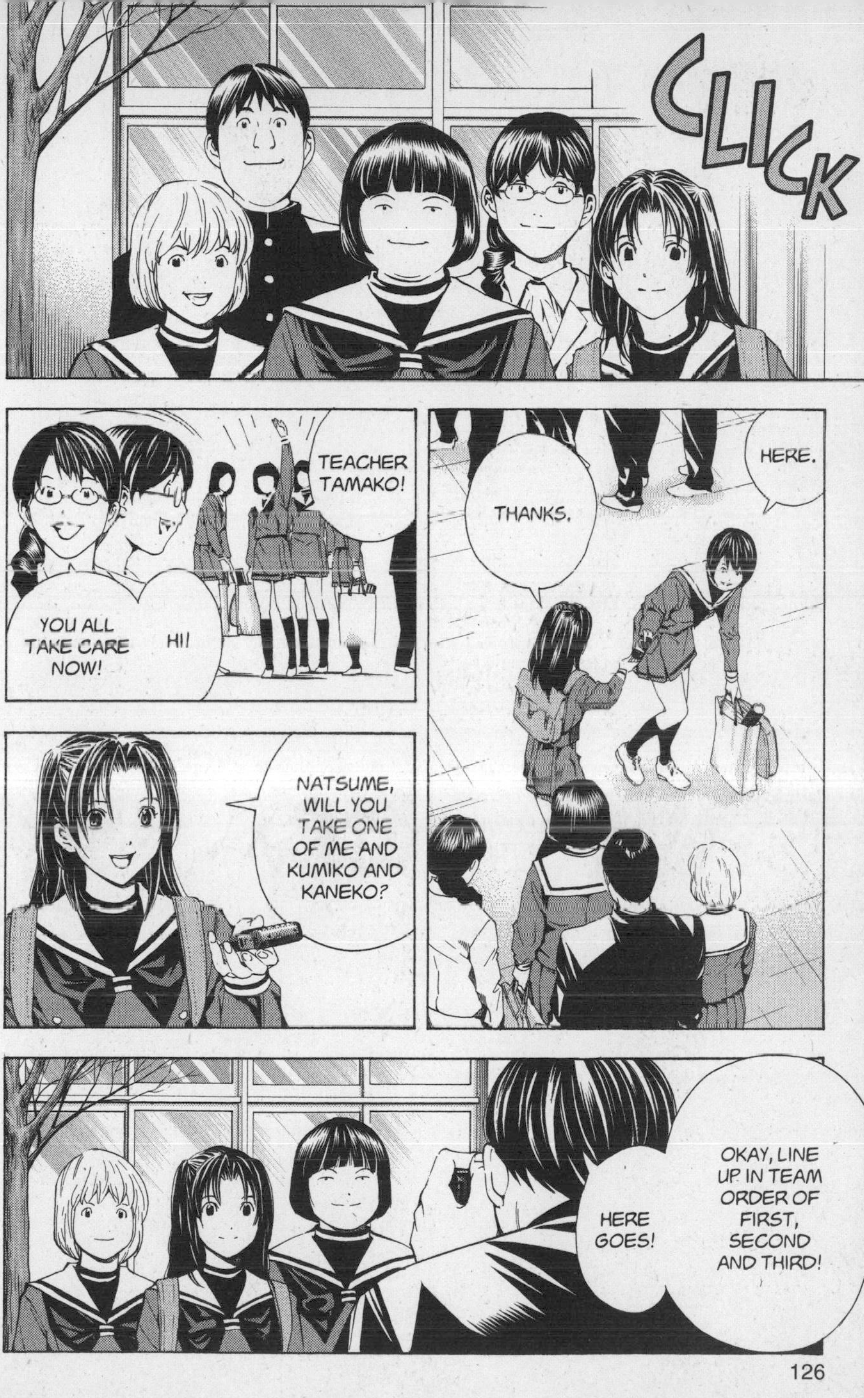
CLICK
HERE.
THANKS.
TEACHER TAMAKO!
HI!
YOU ALL TAKE CARE NOW!
NATSUME, WILL YOU TAKE ONE OF ME AND KUMIKO AND KANEKO?
OKAY, LINE UP IN TEAM ORDER OF FIRST, SECOND AND THIRD!
HERE GOES!

READ THIS WAY

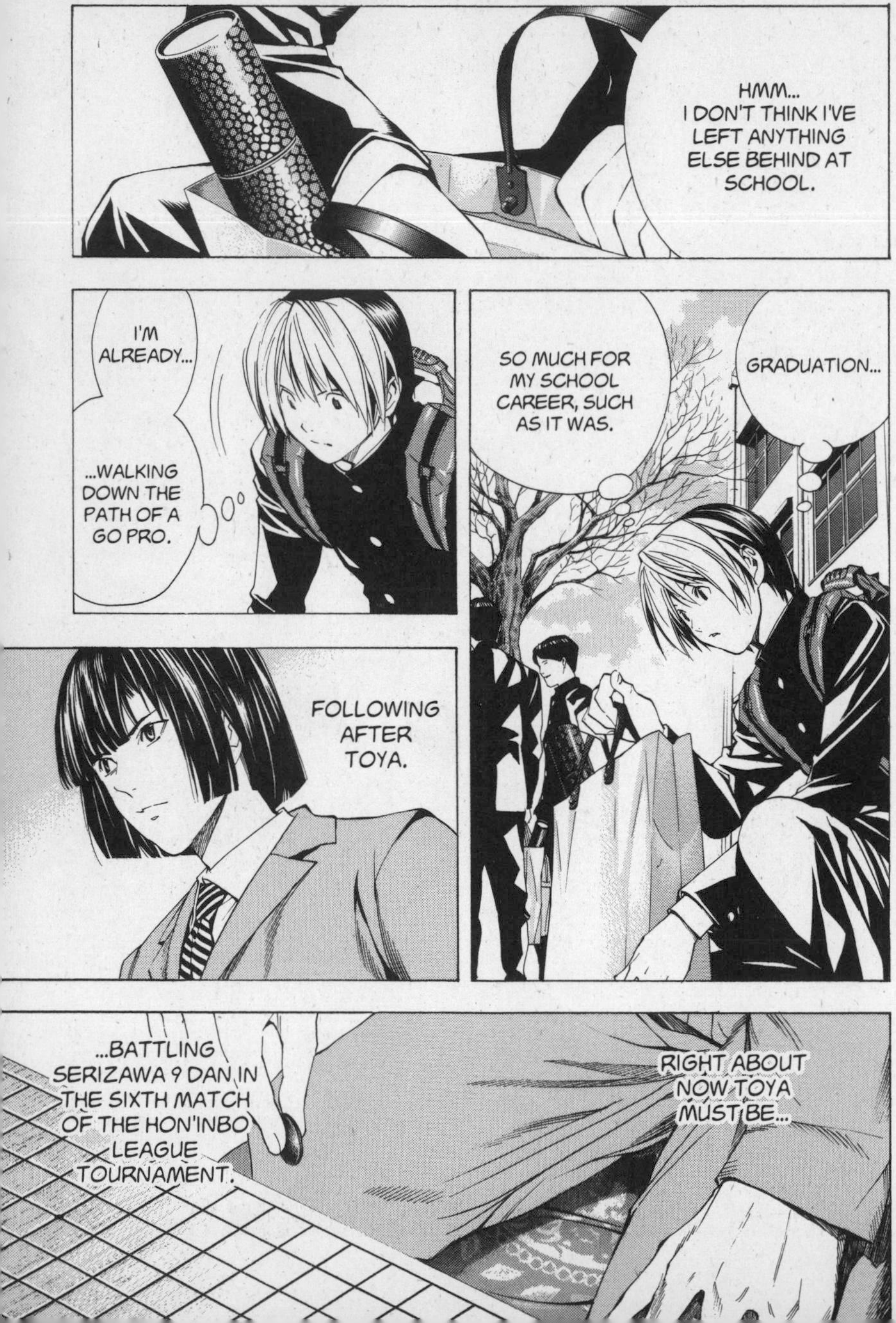
HMM... I DON'T THINK I'VE LEFT ANYTHING ELSE BEHIND AT SCHOOL.
GRADUATION...
SO MUCH FOR MY SCHOOL CAREER, SUCH AS IT WAS.
I'M ALREADY...
...WALKING DOWN THE PATH OF A GO PRO.
FOLLOWING AFTER TOYA.
RIGHT ABOUT NOW TOYA MUST BE...
...BATTLING SERIZAWA 9 DAN IN THE SIXTH MATCH OF THE HON'INBO LEAGUE TOURNAMENT.

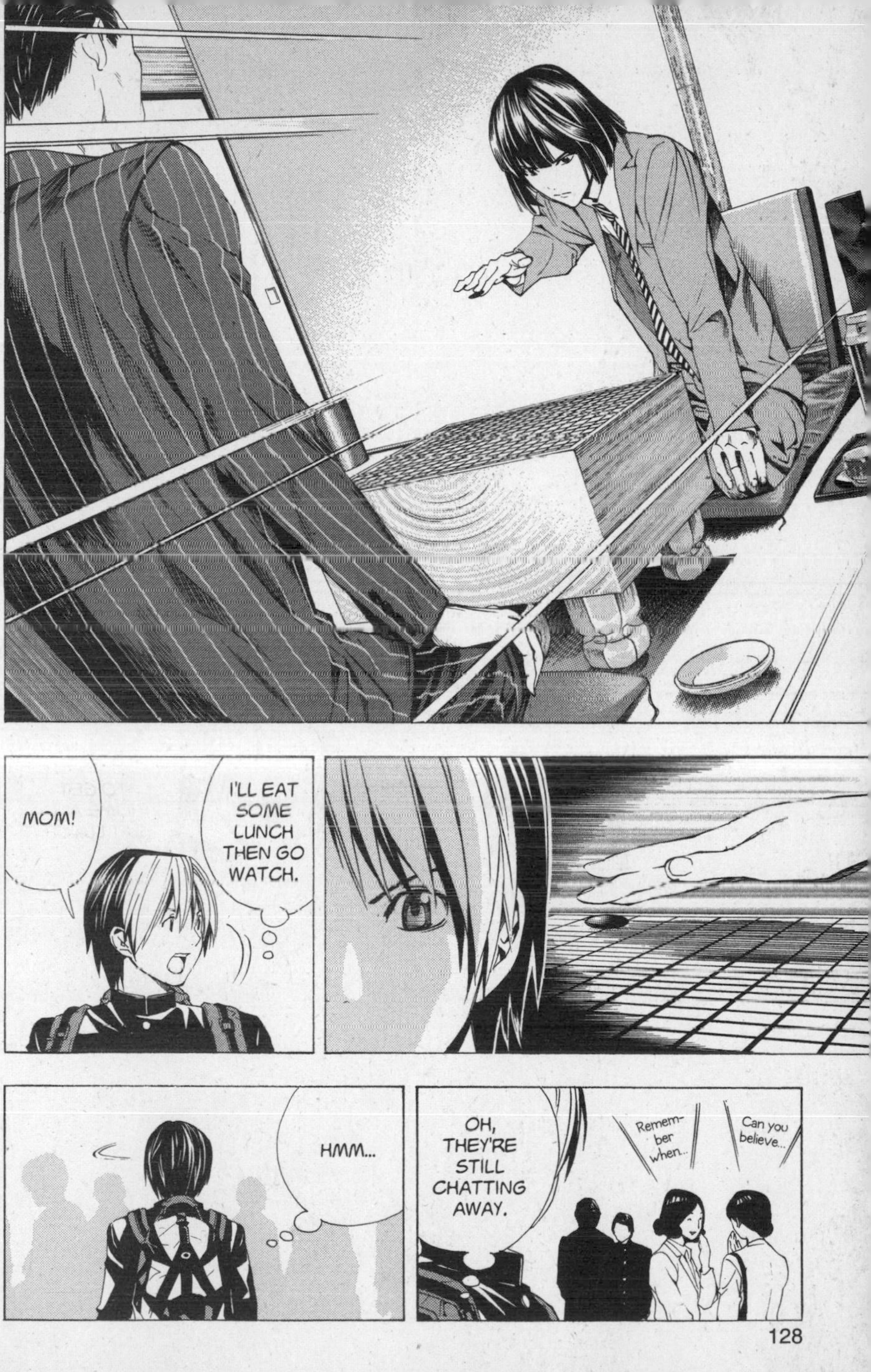

I'LL EAT SOME LUNCH THEN GO WATCH.
MOM!
Can you believe...
Remem-ber when...
OH, THEY'RE STILL CHATTING AWAY.
HMM...

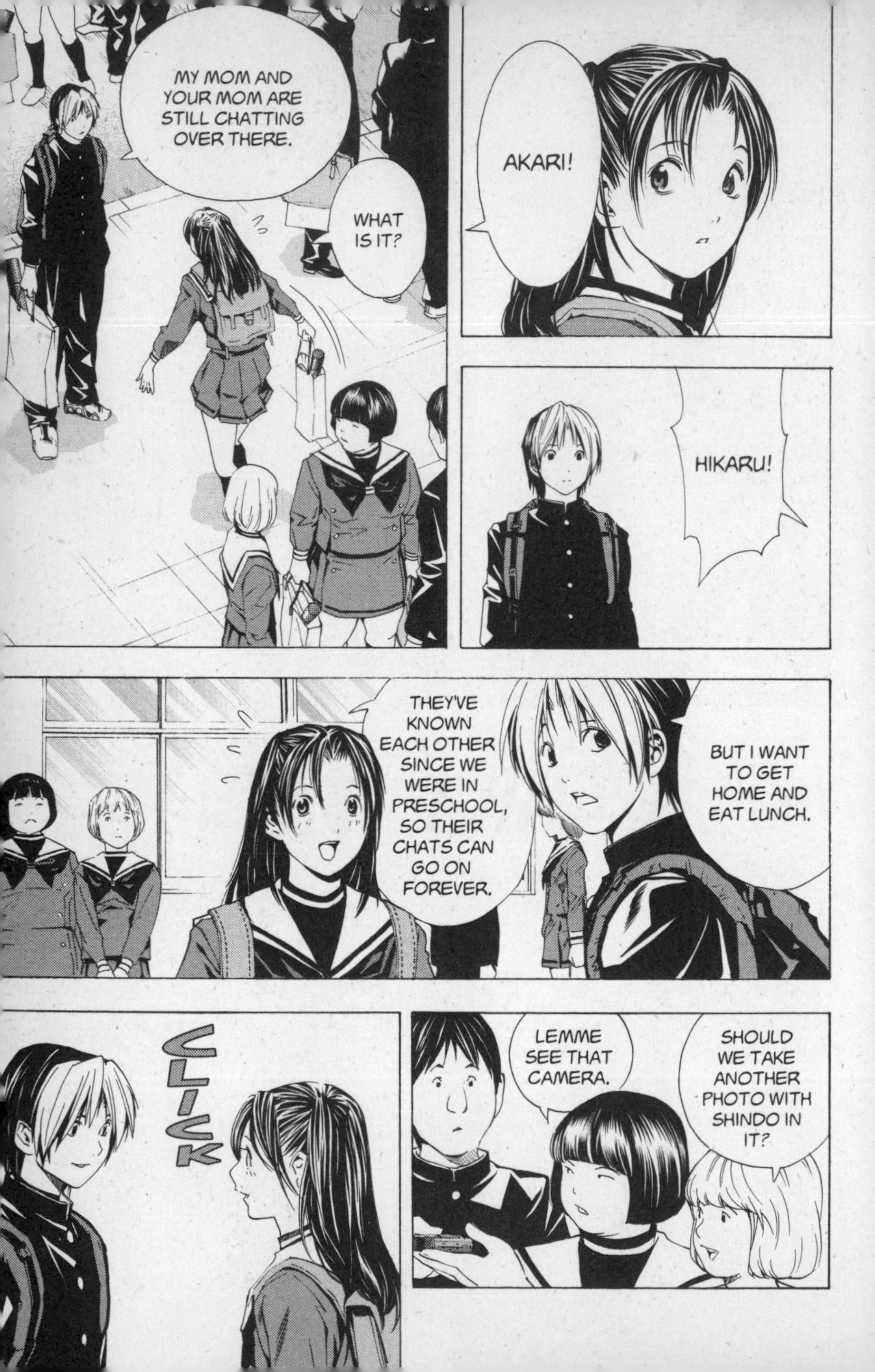
AKARI!
HIKARU!
WHAT IS IT?
MY MOM AND YOUR MOM ARE STILL CHATTING OVER THERE.
BUT I WANT TO GET HOME AND EAT LUNCH.
THEY'VE KNOWN EACH OTHER SINCE WE WERE IN PRESCHOOL, SO THEIR CHATS CAN GO ON FOREVER.
SHOULD WE TAKE ANOTHER PHOTO WITH SHINDO IN IT?
LEMME SEE THAT CAMERA.
CLICK

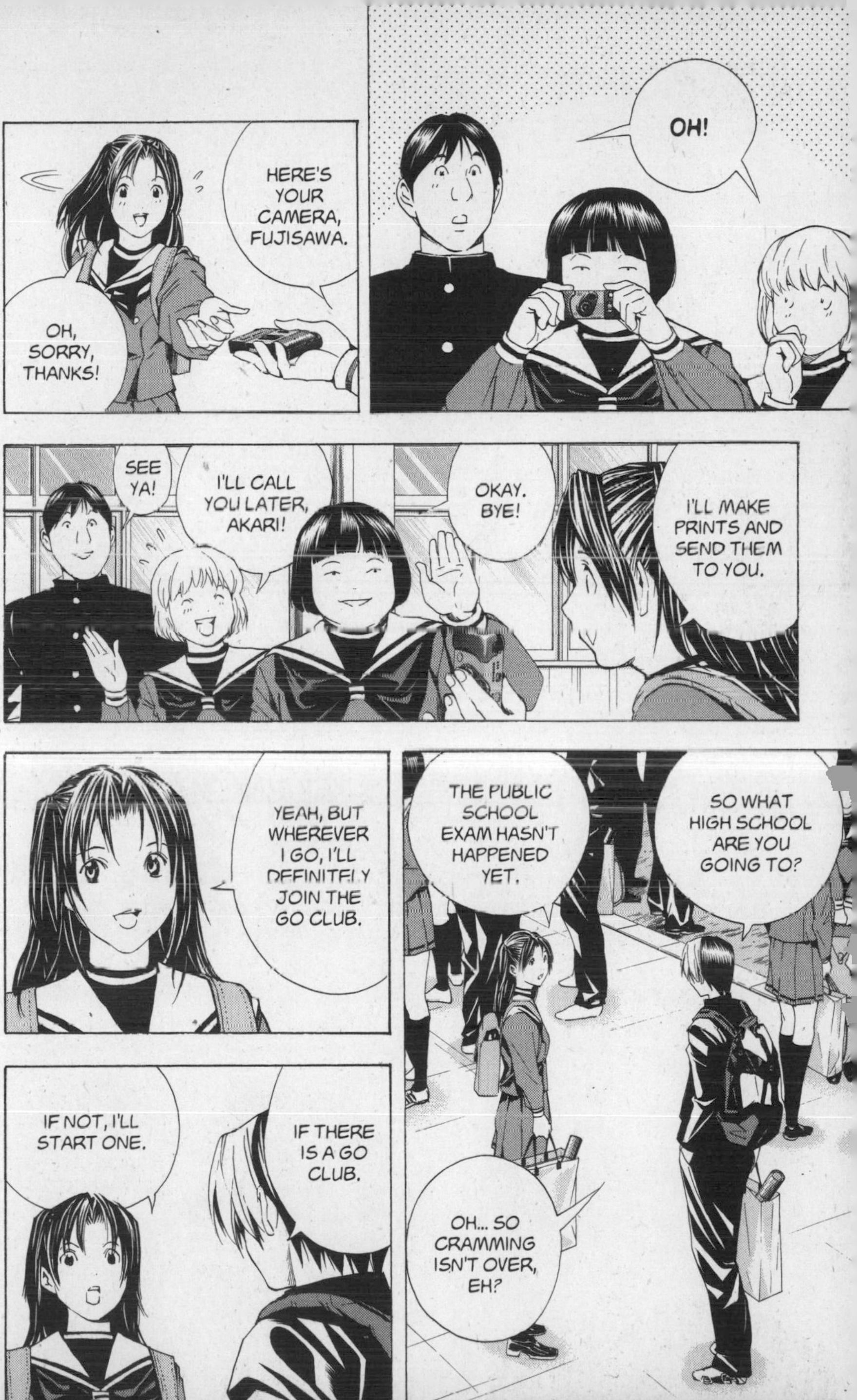
OH!
HERE'S YOUR CAMERA, FUJISAWA.
OH, SORRY, THANKS!
I'LL MAKE PRINTS AND SEND THEM TO YOU.
OKAY. BYE!
I'LL CALL YOU LATER, AKARI!
SEE YA!
SO WHAT HIGH SCHOOL ARE YOU GOING TO?
THE PUBLIC SCHOOL EXAM HASN'T HAPPENED YET.
OH... SO CRAMMING ISN'T OVER, EH?
YEAH, BUT WHEREVER I GO, I'LL DEFINITELY JOIN THE GO CLUB.
IF THERE IS A GO CLUB.
IF NOT, I'LL START ONE.

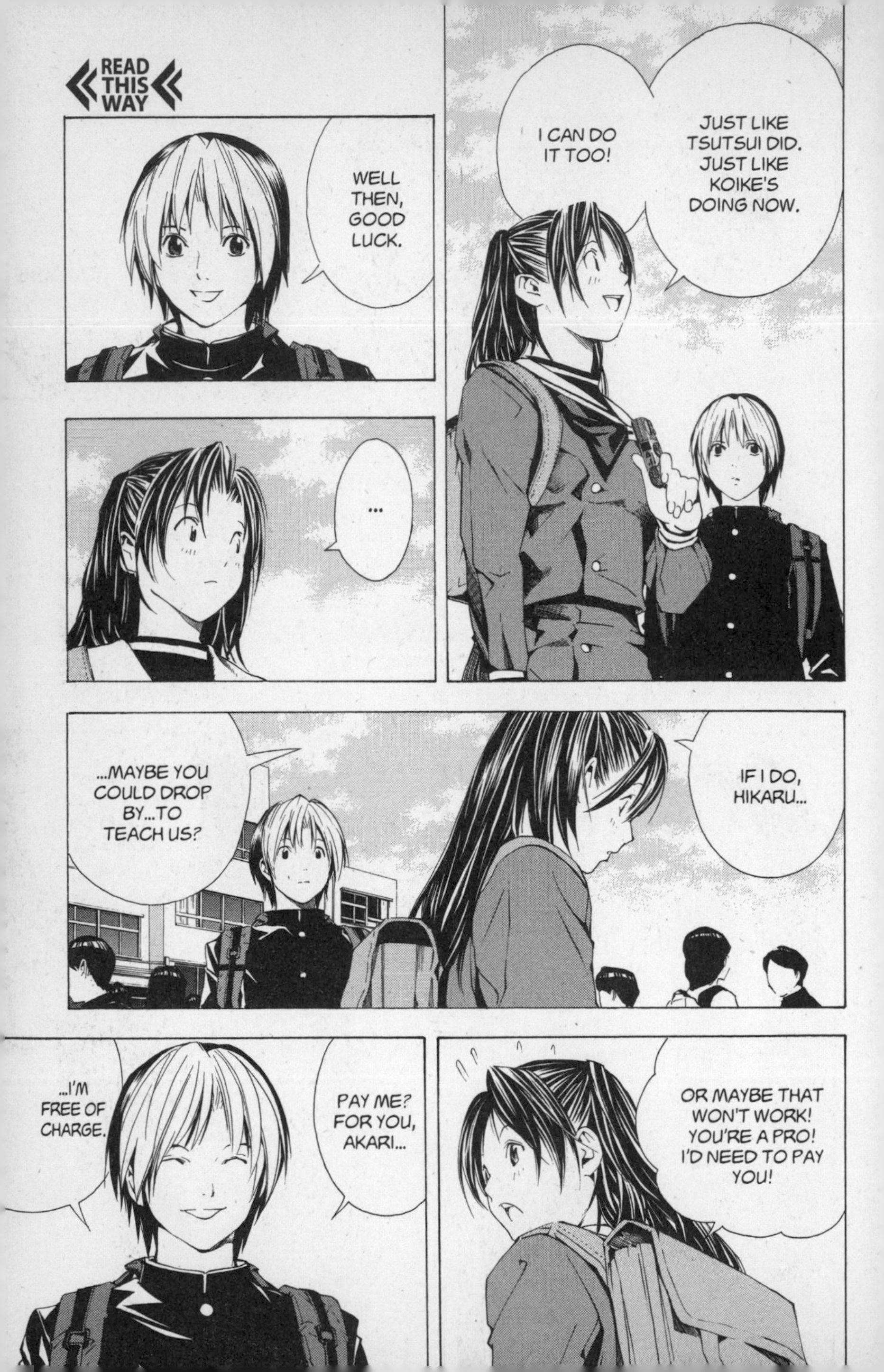
READ THIS WAY
JUST LIKE TSUTSUI DID. JUST LIKE KOIKE'S DOING NOW.
I CAN DO IT TOO!
WELL THEN, GOOD LUCK.
...
IF I DO, HIKARU...
...MAYBE YOU COULD DROP BY...TO TEACH US?
OR MAYBE THAT WON'T WORK! YOU'RE A PRO! I'D NEED TO PAY YOU!
PAY ME? FOR YOU, AKARI...
...I'M FREE OF CHARGE.

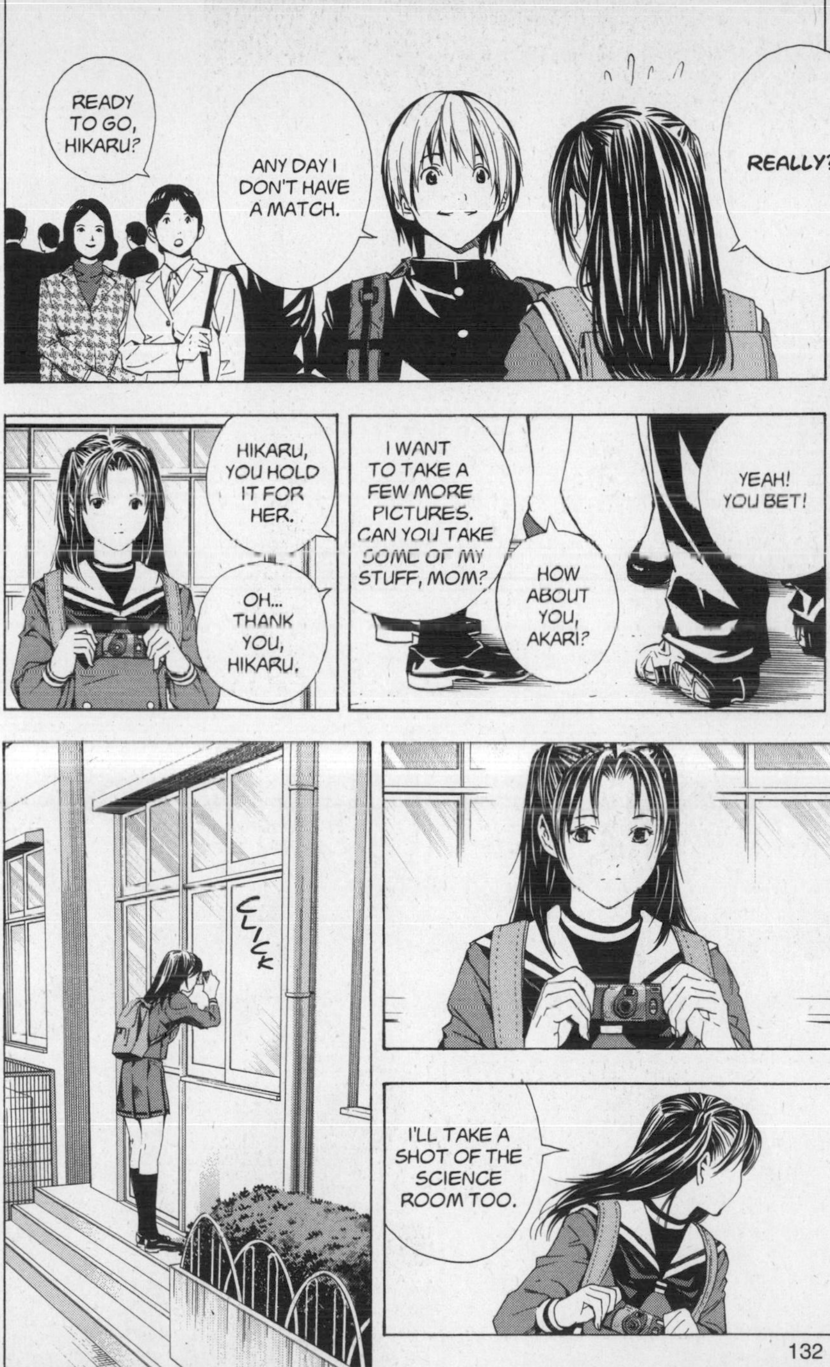
REALLY?!
ANY DAY I DON'T HAVE A MATCH.
READY TO GO, HIKARU?
YEAH! YOU BET!
I WANT TO TAKE A FEW MORE PICTURES. CAN YOU TAKE SOME OF MY STUFF, MOM?
HOW ABOUT YOU, AKARI?
HIKARU, YOU HOLD IT FOR HER.
OH... THANK YOU, HIKARU.
I'LL TAKE A SHOT OF THE SCIENCE ROOM TOO.
CLICK

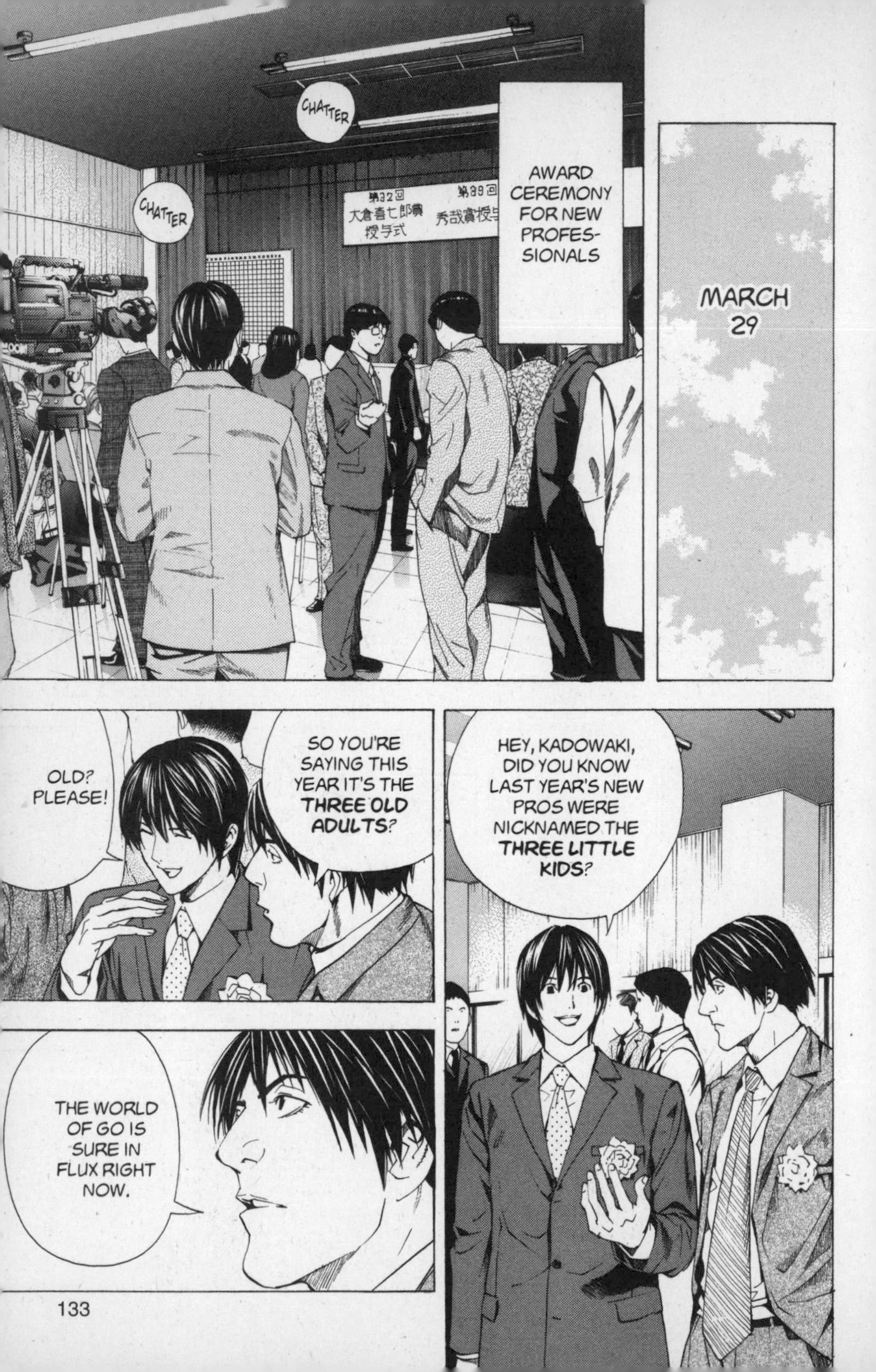
MARCH 29
AWARD CEREMONY FOR NEW PROFES-SIONALS
CHATTER
第32回 大倉喜七郎賞 授与式
第39回 秀哉賞授与
CHATTER
HEY, KADOWAKI, DID YOU KNOW LAST YEAR'S NEW PROS WERE NICKNAMED THE **THREE LITTLE KIDS**?
SO YOU'RE SAYING THIS YEAR IT'S THE **THREE OLD ADULTS**?
OLD? PLEASE!
THE WORLD OF GO IS SURE IN FLUX RIGHT NOW.

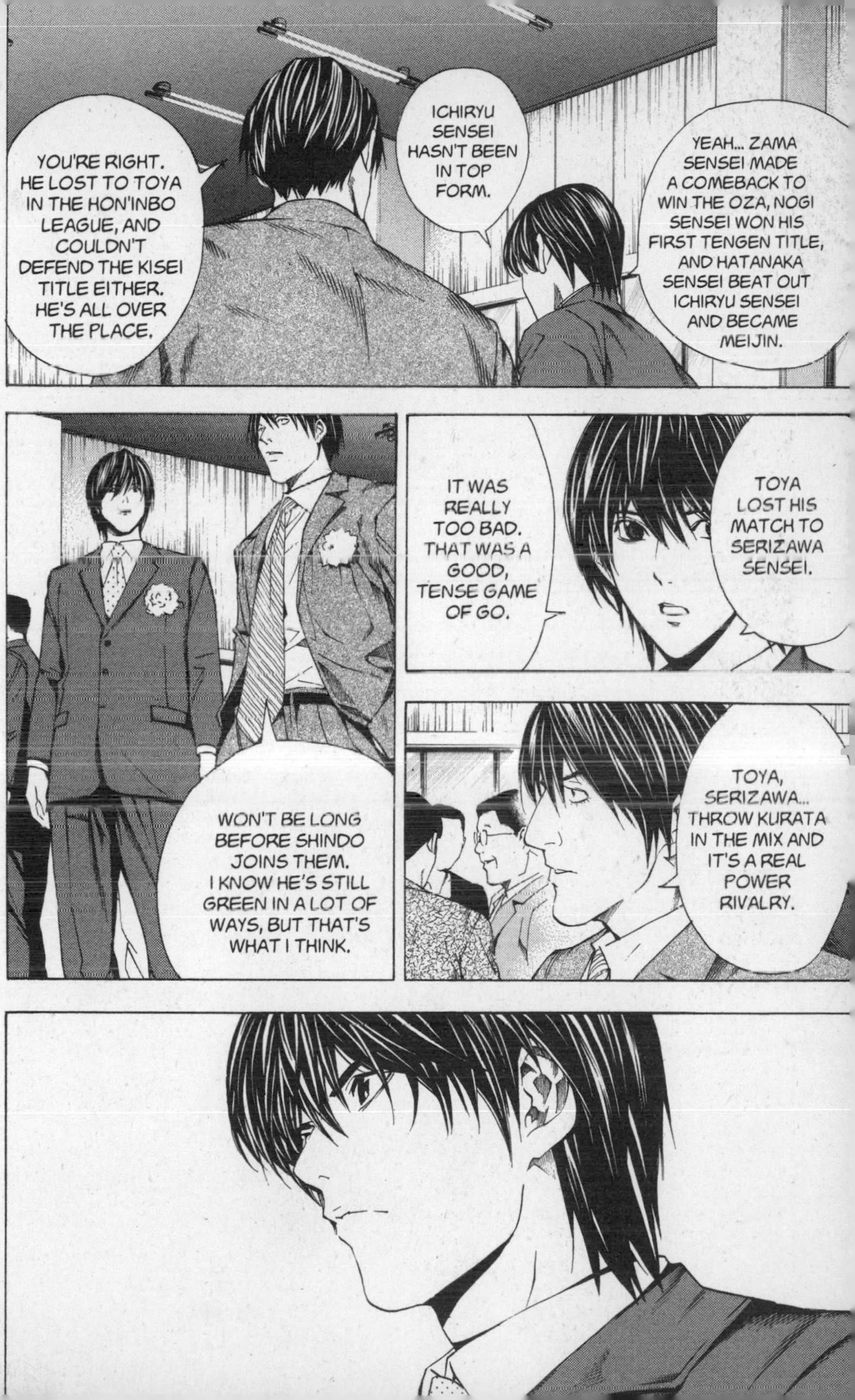
YEAH... ZAMA SENSEI MADE A COMEBACK TO WIN THE OZA, NOGI SENSEI WON HIS FIRST TENGEN TITLE, AND HATANAKA SENSEI BEAT OUT ICHIRYU SENSEI AND BECAME MEIJIN.
ICHIRYU SENSEI HASN'T BEEN IN TOP FORM.
YOU'RE RIGHT. HE LOST TO TOYA IN THE HON'INBO LEAGUE, AND COULDN'T DEFEND THE KISEI TITLE EITHER. HE'S ALL OVER THE PLACE.
TOYA LOST HIS MATCH TO SERIZAWA SENSEI.
IT WAS REALLY TOO BAD. THAT WAS A GOOD, TENSE GAME OF GO.
TOYA, SERIZAWA... THROW KURATA IN THE MIX AND IT'S A REAL POWER RIVALRY.
WON'T BE LONG BEFORE SHINDO JOINS THEM. I KNOW HE'S STILL GREEN IN A LOT OF WAYS, BUT THAT'S WHAT I THINK.

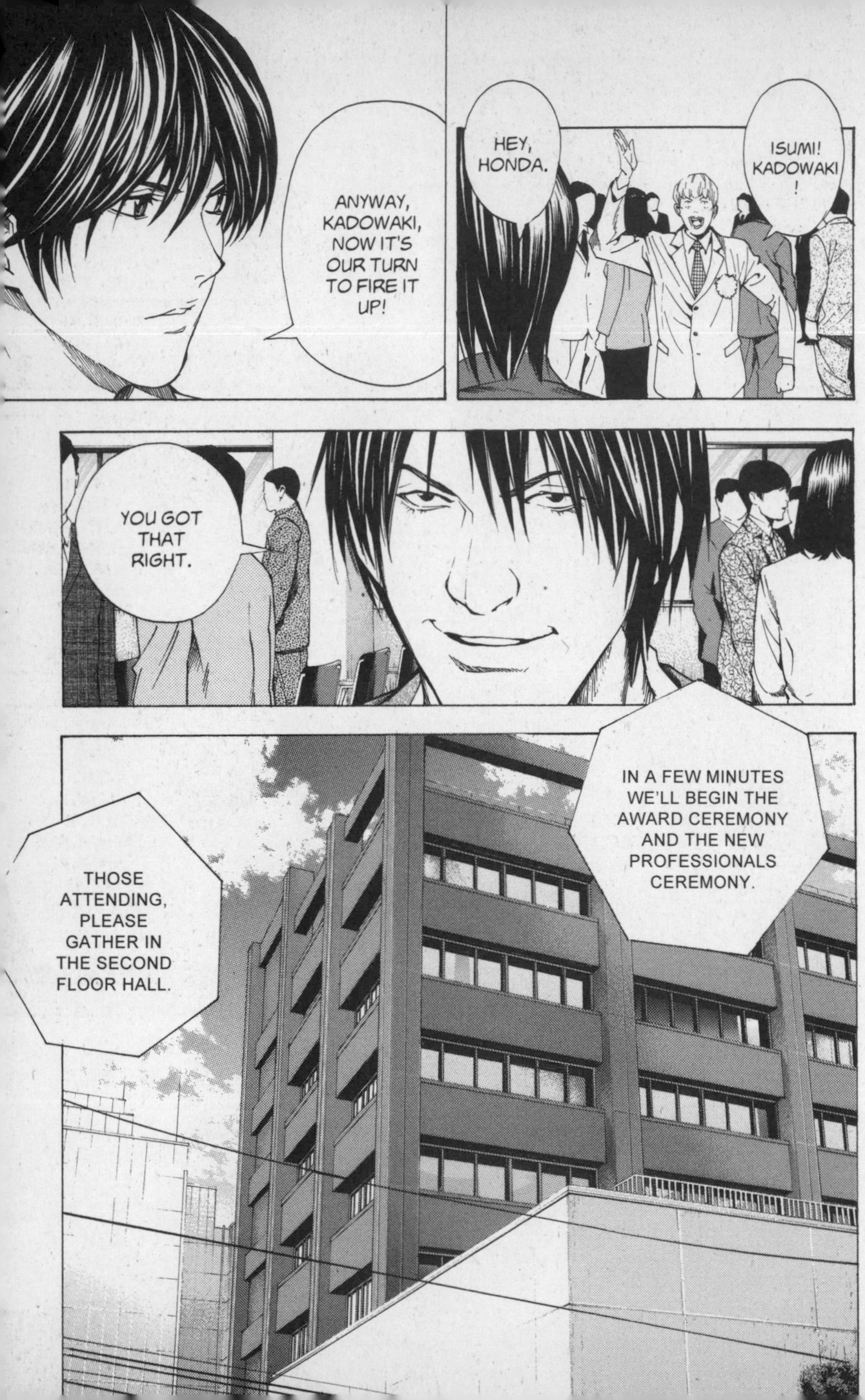
ISUMI! KADOWAKI !
HEY, HONDA.
ANYWAY, KADOWAKI, NOW IT'S OUR TURN TO FIRE IT UP!
YOU GOT THAT RIGHT.
IN A FEW MINUTES WE'LL BEGIN THE AWARD CEREMONY AND THE NEW PROFESSIONALS CEREMONY.
THOSE ATTENDING, PLEASE GATHER IN THE SECOND FLOOR HALL.

A WORD ABOUT HIKARU NO GO

THE SYSTEM OF TOURNAMENT MATCHES 1

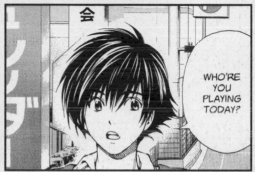

WHO'RE YOU PLAYING TODAY?
KAWASAKI 3 DAN.
IT'S THE THIRD ROUND OF THE FIRST PRELIMS FOR THE HON'INBO TOURNAMENT.
OH. I'M PLAYING TOYAMA 2 DAN IN THE SECOND ROUND OF THE FIRST PRELIMS FOR THE MEIJIN TOURNAMENT.

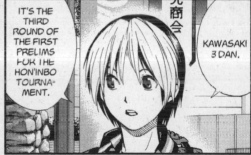

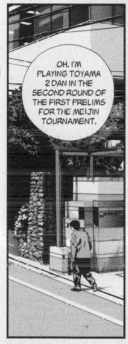

IT IS VERY COMPLICATED.

PROFESSIONAL GO PLAYERS COMPETE IN CLOSE TO 30 TOURNAMENTS, INCLUDING INTERNATIONAL ONES. AND THEY ALL PROCEED SLOWLY AND SIMULTANEOUSLY.

SO IT IS DIFFICULT TO GRASP THE OVERALL PICTURE. AND THE COMPLICATED MATCH LINEUPS ARE NO HELP!

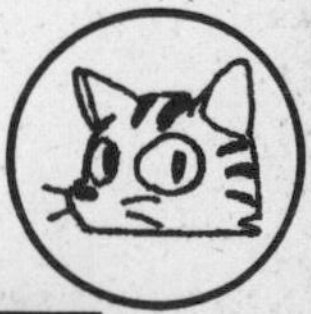

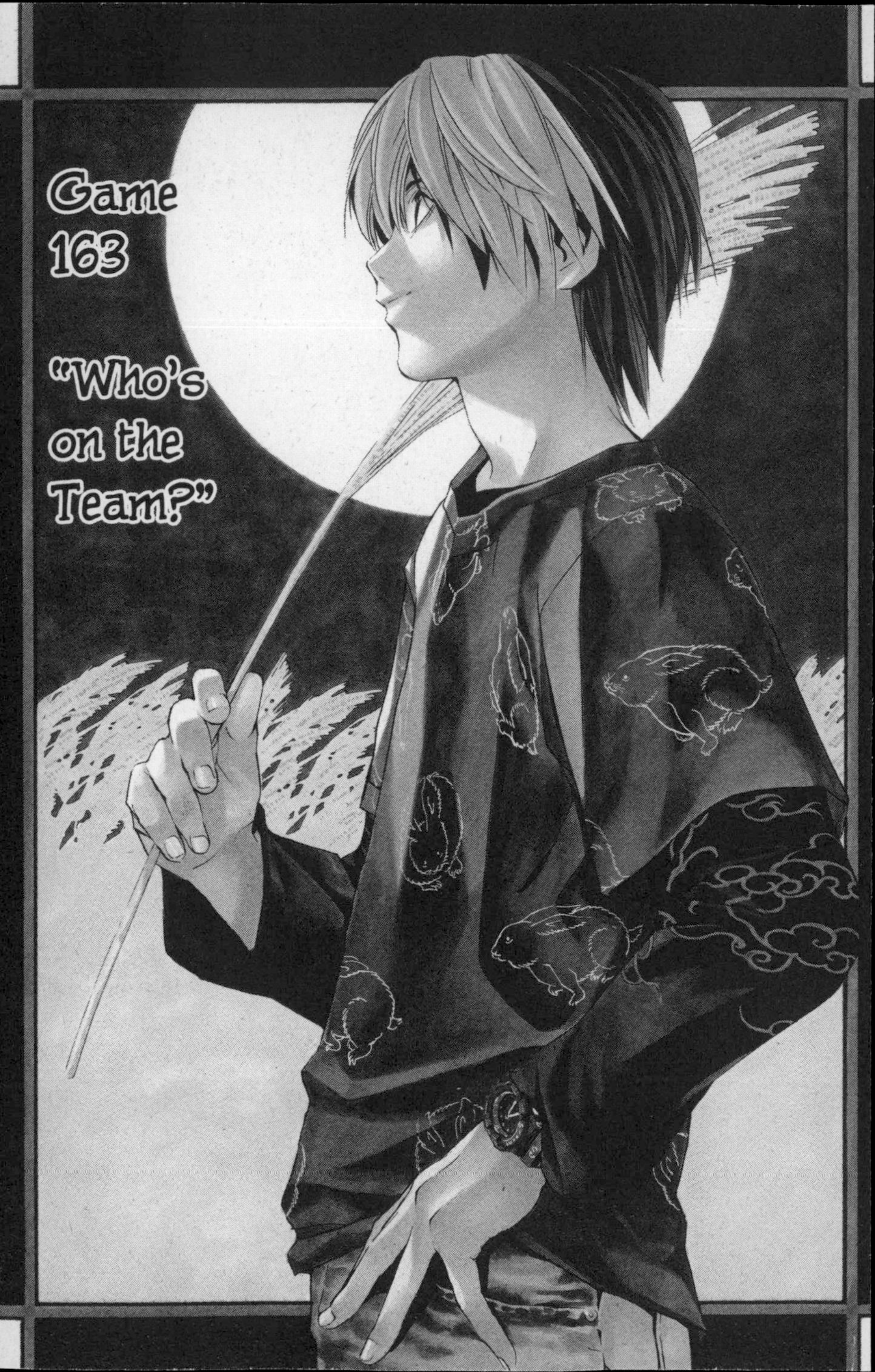
Game 163
"Who's on the Team?"

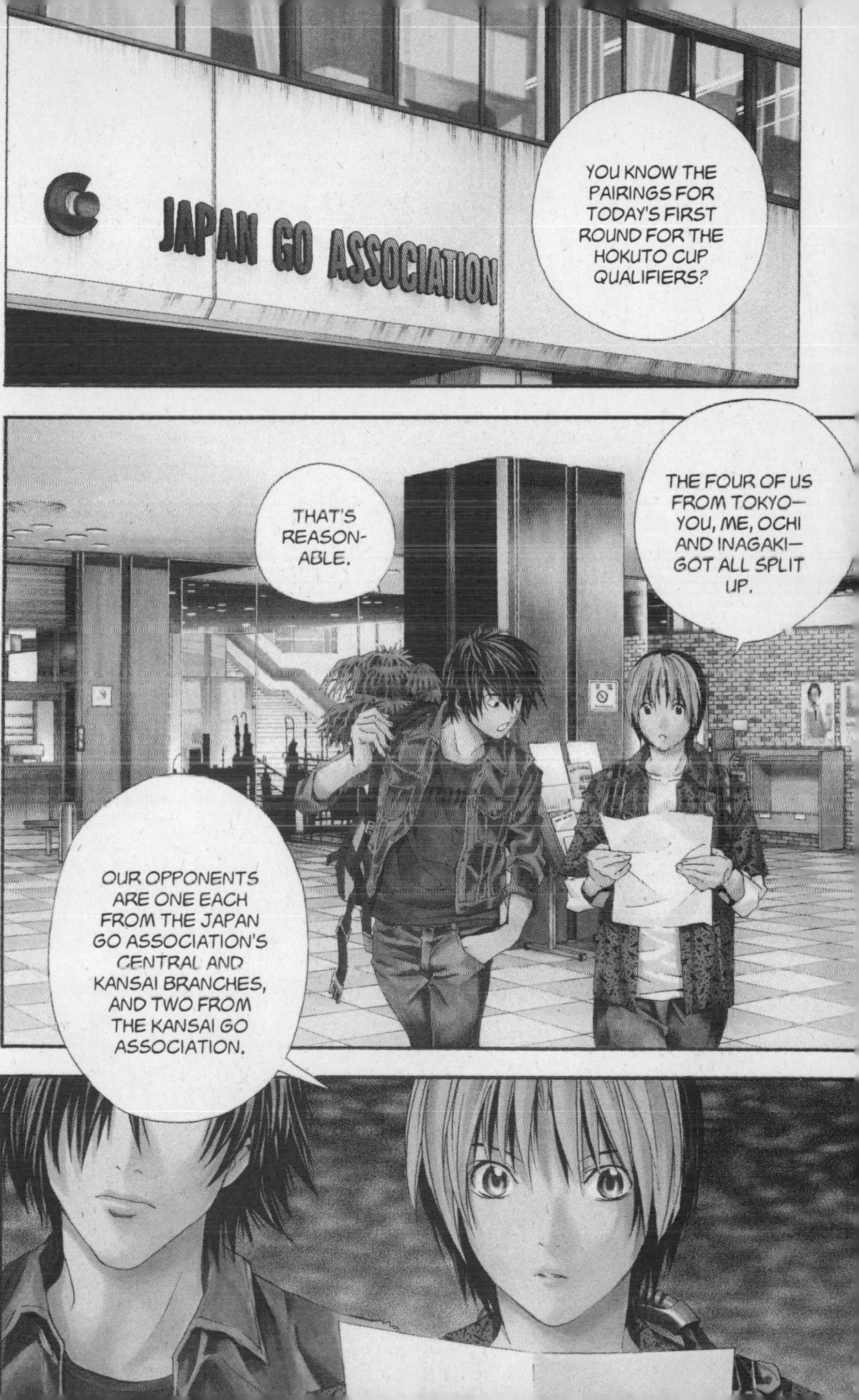
JAPAN GO ASSOCIATION
YOU KNOW THE PAIRINGS FOR TODAY'S FIRST ROUND FOR THE HOKUTO CUP QUALIFIERS?
THE FOUR OF US FROM TOKYO—YOU, ME, OCHI AND INAGAKI—GOT ALL SPLIT UP.
THAT'S REASON-ABLE.
OUR OPPONENTS ARE ONE EACH FROM THE JAPAN GO ASSOCIATION'S CENTRAL AND KANSAI BRANCHES, AND TWO FROM THE KANSAI GO ASSOCIATION.

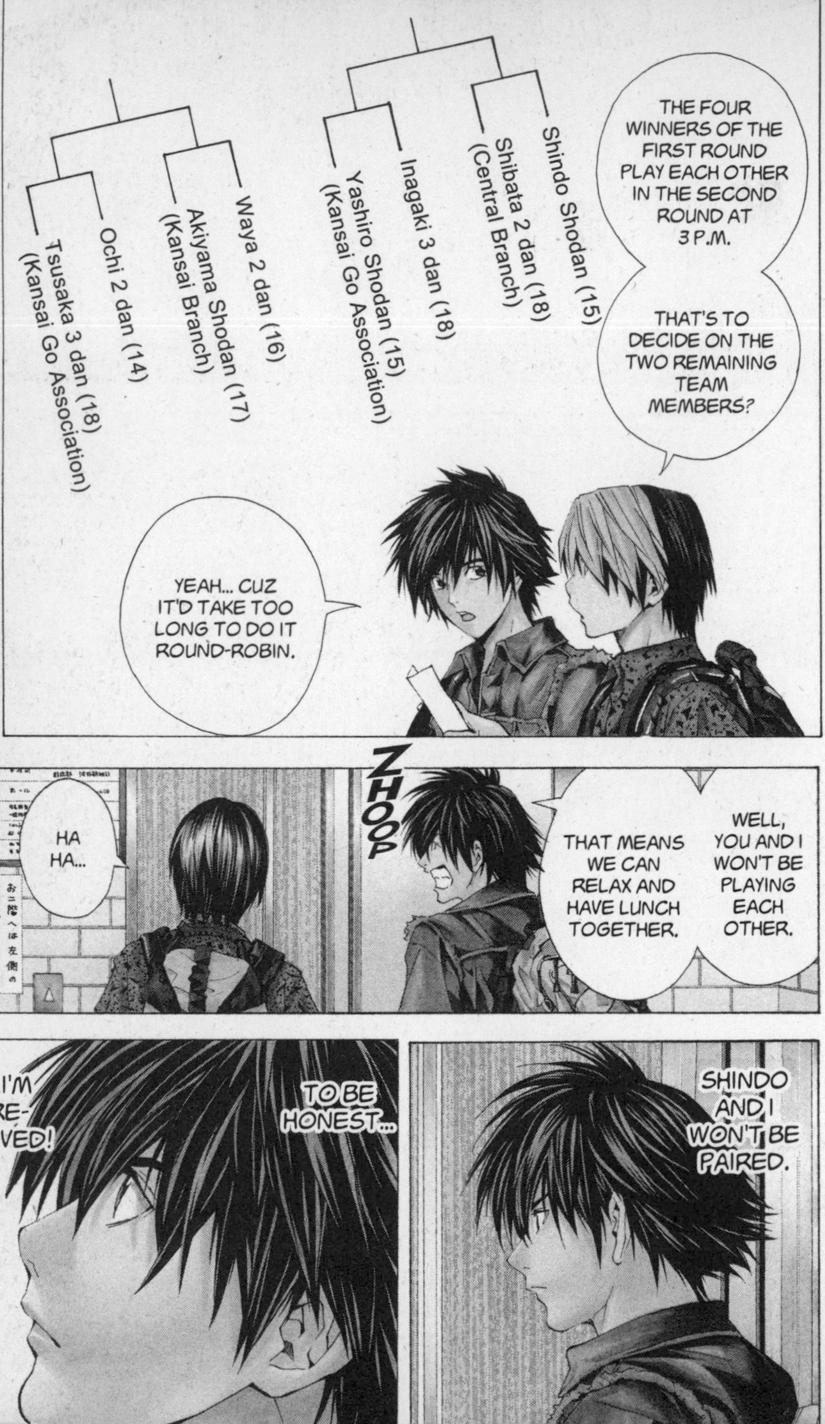
Shindo Shodan (15)
Shibata 2 dan (18) (Central Branch)
Inagaki 3 dan (18)
Yashiro Shodan (15) (Kansai Go Association)
Waya 2 dan (16)
Akiyama Shodan (17) (Kansai Branch)
Ochi 2 dan (14)
Tsusaka 3 dan (18) (Kansai Go Association)
THE FOUR WINNERS OF THE FIRST ROUND PLAY EACH OTHER IN THE SECOND ROUND AT 3 P.M.
THAT'S TO DECIDE ON THE TWO REMAINING TEAM MEMBERS?
YEAH... CUZ IT'D TAKE TOO LONG TO DO IT ROUND-ROBIN.
WELL, YOU AND I WON'T BE PLAYING EACH OTHER.
THAT MEANS WE CAN RELAX AND HAVE LUNCH TOGETHER.
ZHOOP
HA HA...
お二階へは左側の階段がご便利です
SHINDO AND I WON'T BE PAIRED.
TO BE HONEST...
...I'M RE- LIEVED!

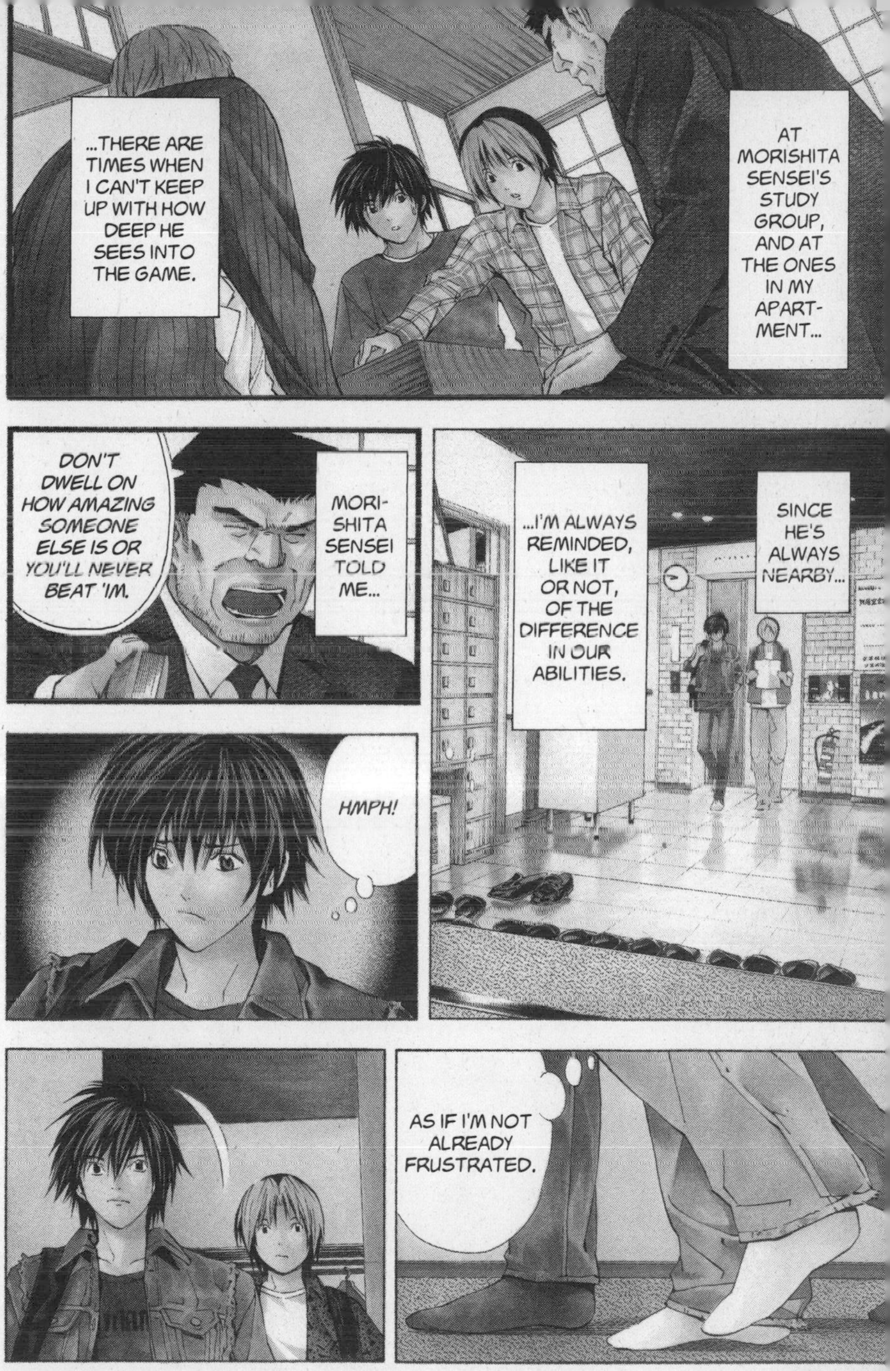
AT MORISHITA SENSEI'S STUDY GROUP, AND AT THE ONES IN MY APARTMENT...
...THERE ARE TIMES WHEN I CAN'T KEEP UP WITH HOW DEEP HE SEES INTO THE GAME.
SINCE HE'S ALWAYS NEARBY...
...I'M ALWAYS REMINDED, LIKE IT OR NOT, OF THE DIFFERENCE IN OUR ABILITIES.
MORISHITA SENSEI TOLD ME...
DON'T DWELL ON HOW AMAZING SOMEONE ELSE IS OR YOU'LL NEVER BEAT 'IM.
HMPH!
AS IF I'M NOT ALREADY FRUSTRATED.

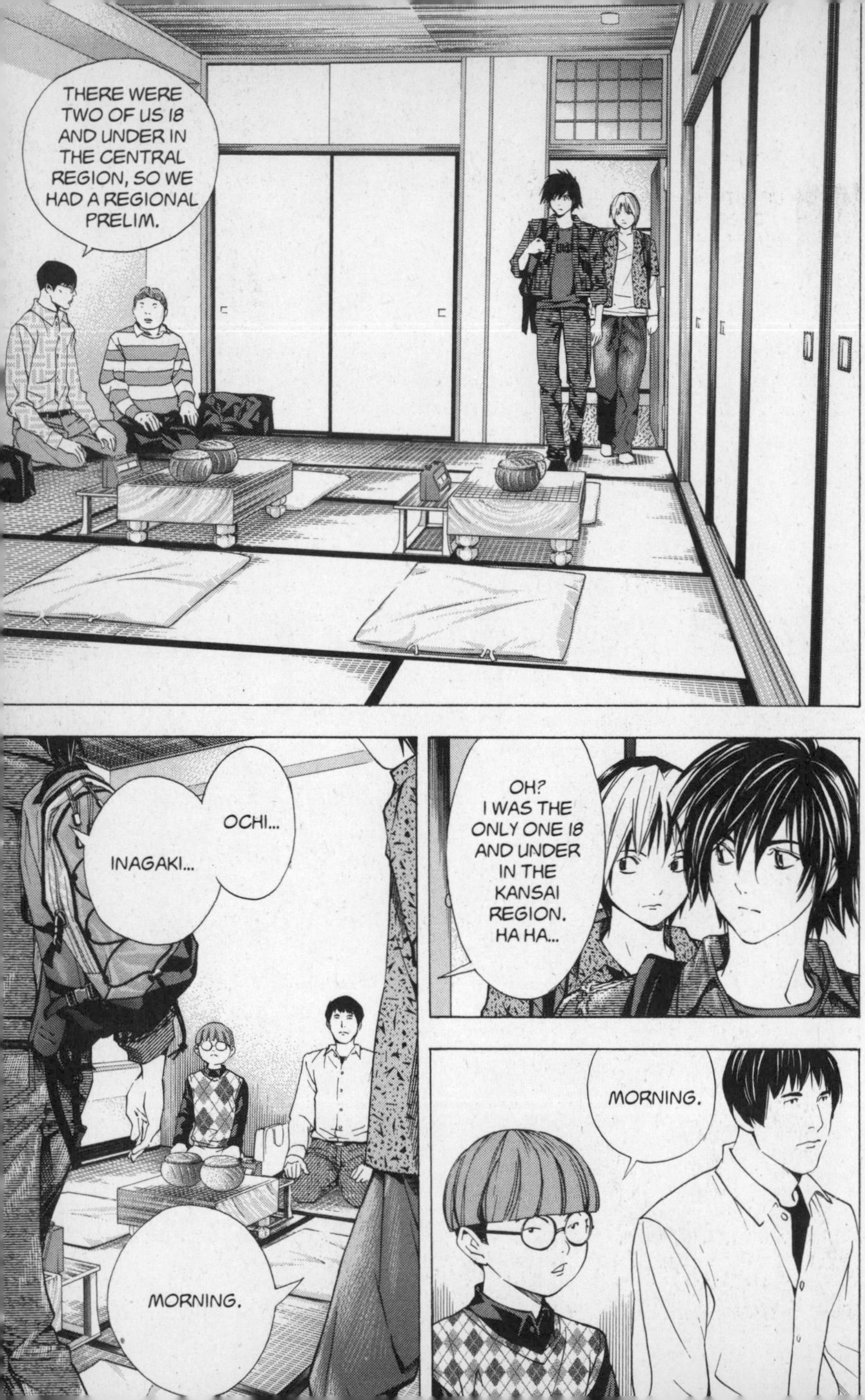
THERE WERE TWO OF US 18 AND UNDER IN THE CENTRAL REGION, SO WE HAD A REGIONAL PRELIM.
OH? I WAS THE ONLY ONE 18 AND UNDER IN THE KANSAI REGION. HA HA...
MORNING.
OCHI...
INAGAKI...
MORNING.

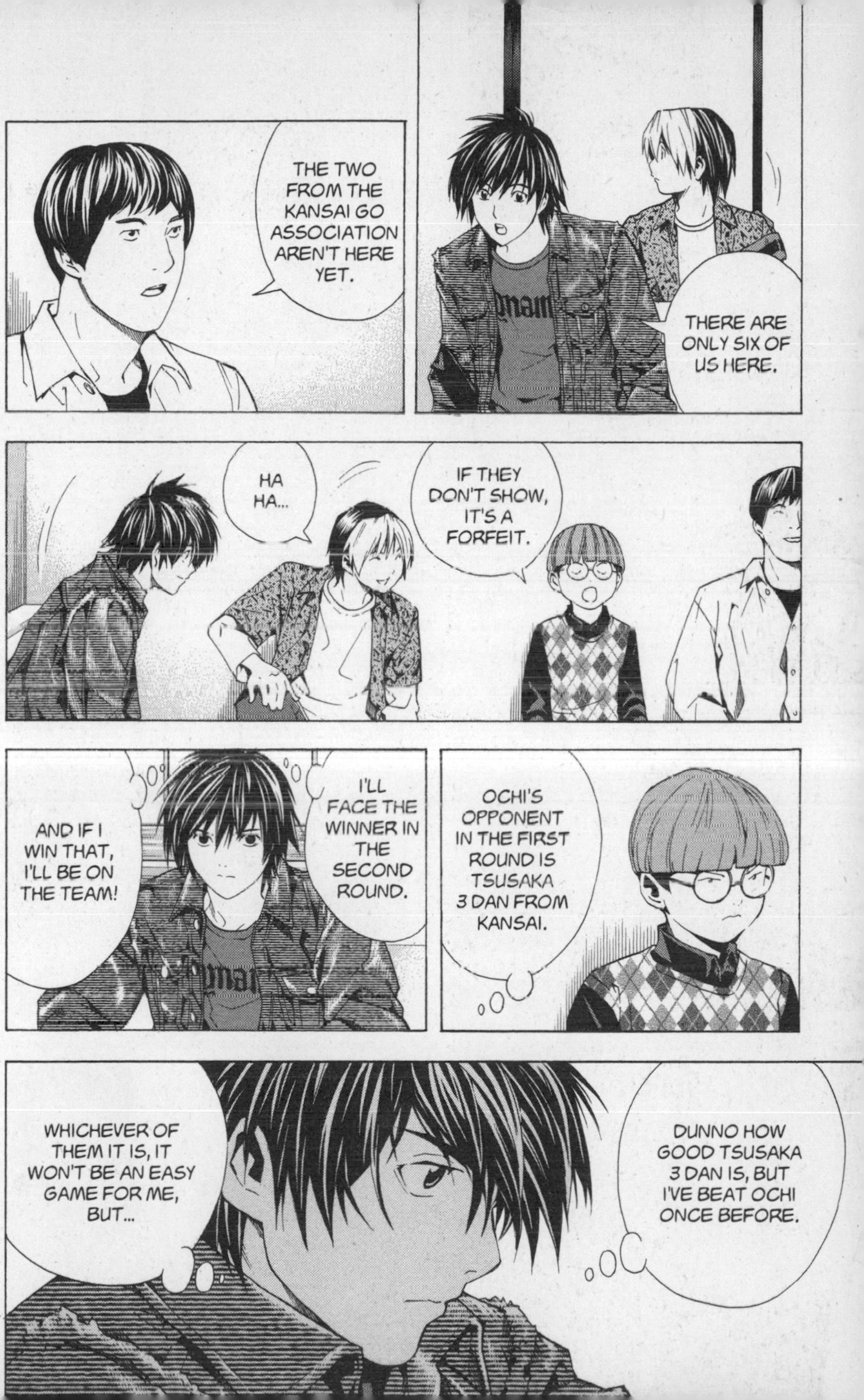
THERE ARE ONLY SIX OF US HERE.
THE TWO FROM THE KANSAI GO ASSOCIATION AREN'T HERE YET.
IF THEY DON'T SHOW, IT'S A FORFEIT.
HA HA...
OCHI'S OPPONENT IN THE FIRST ROUND IS TSUSAKA 3 DAN FROM KANSAI.
I'LL FACE THE WINNER IN THE SECOND ROUND.
AND IF I WIN THAT, I'LL BE ON THE TEAM!
DUNNO HOW GOOD TSUSAKA 3 DAN IS, BUT I'VE BEAT OCHI ONCE BEFORE.
WHICHEVER OF THEM IT IS, IT WON'T BE AN EASY GAME FOR ME, BUT...

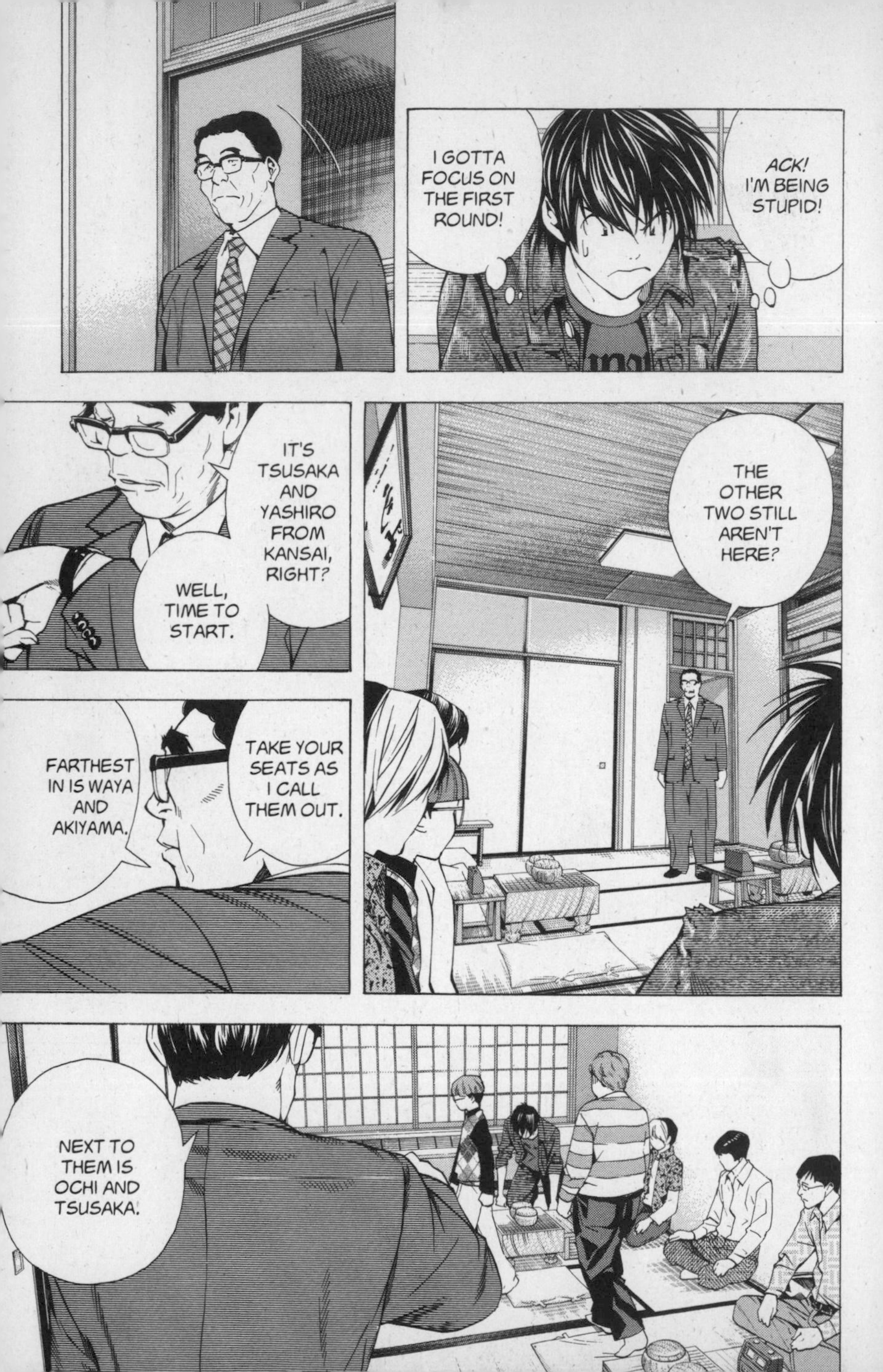
ACK! I'M BEING STUPID!
I GOTTA FOCUS ON THE FIRST ROUND!
THE OTHER TWO STILL AREN'T HERE?
IT'S TSUSAKA AND YASHIRO FROM KANSAI, RIGHT?
WELL, TIME TO START.
TAKE YOUR SEATS AS I CALL THEM OUT.
FARTHEST IN IS WAYA AND AKIYAMA.
NEXT TO THEM IS OCHI AND TSUSAKA.

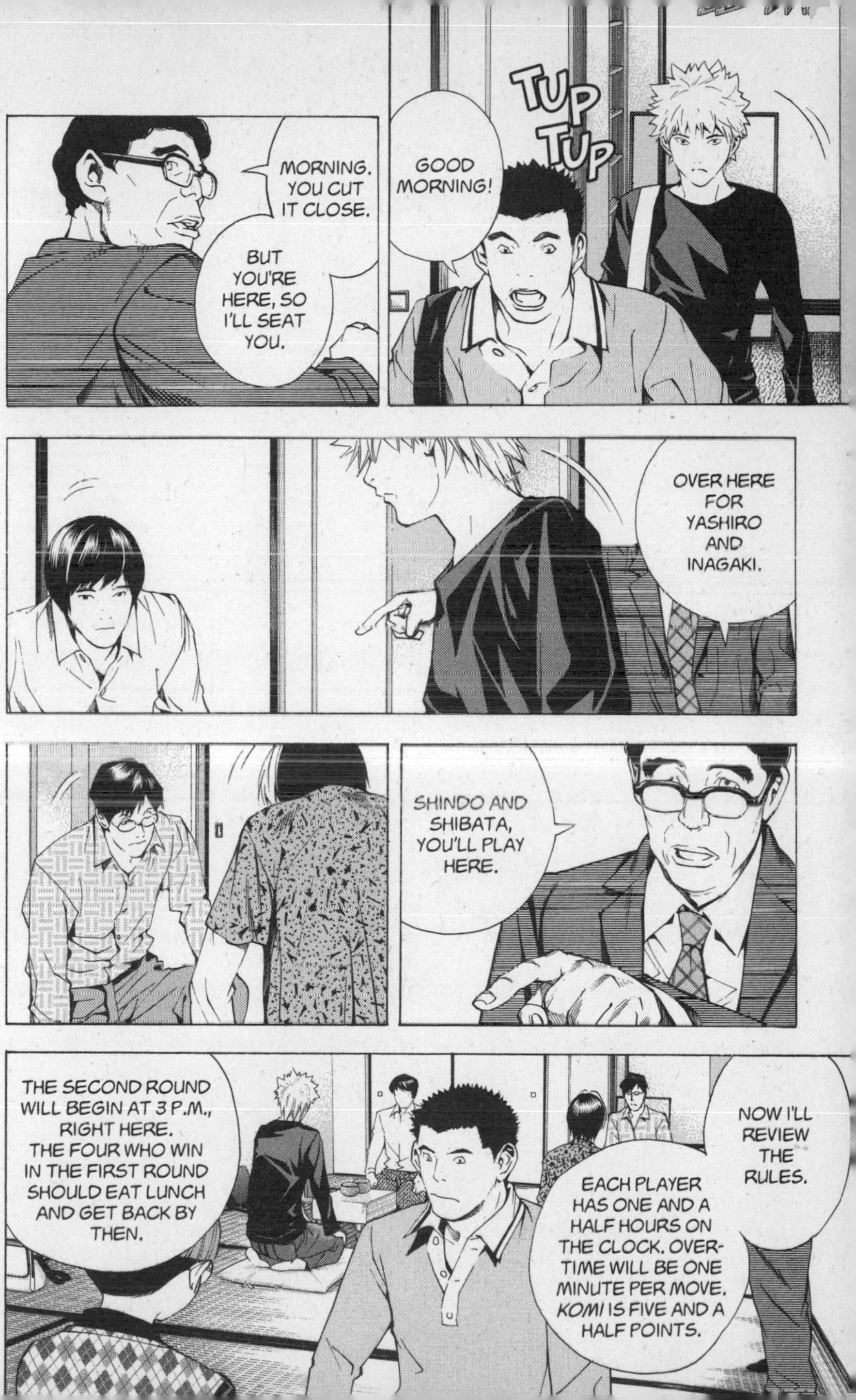
TUP TUP
GOOD MORNING!
MORNING. YOU CUT IT CLOSE.
BUT YOU'RE HERE, SO I'LL SEAT YOU.
OVER HERE FOR YASHIRO AND INAGAKI.
SHINDO AND SHIBATA, YOU'LL PLAY HERE.
NOW I'LL REVIEW THE RULES.
EACH PLAYER HAS ONE AND A HALF HOURS ON THE CLOCK. OVERTIME WILL BE ONE MINUTE PER MOVE. *KOMI* IS FIVE AND A HALF POINTS.
THE SECOND ROUND WILL BEGIN AT 3 P.M., RIGHT HERE. THE FOUR WHO WIN IN THE FIRST ROUND SHOULD EAT LUNCH AND GET BACK BY THEN.

SO NOW, PLEASE BEGIN.
CLATTER
CLATTER
CLATTER
CLUNK
ONEGAI-SHIMASU.
ONEGAI-SHIMASU.
ONEGAI-SHIMASU.
KCHK
1:30
KLAK

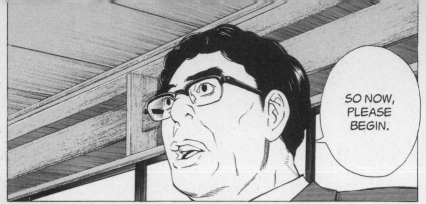

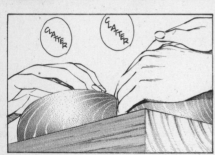

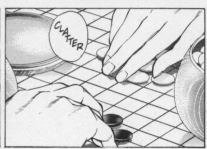

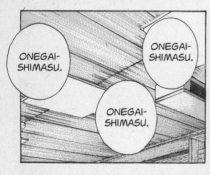

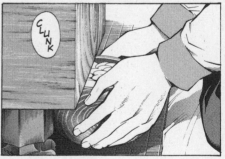

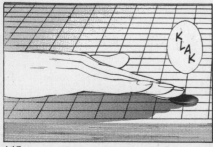

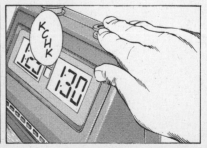

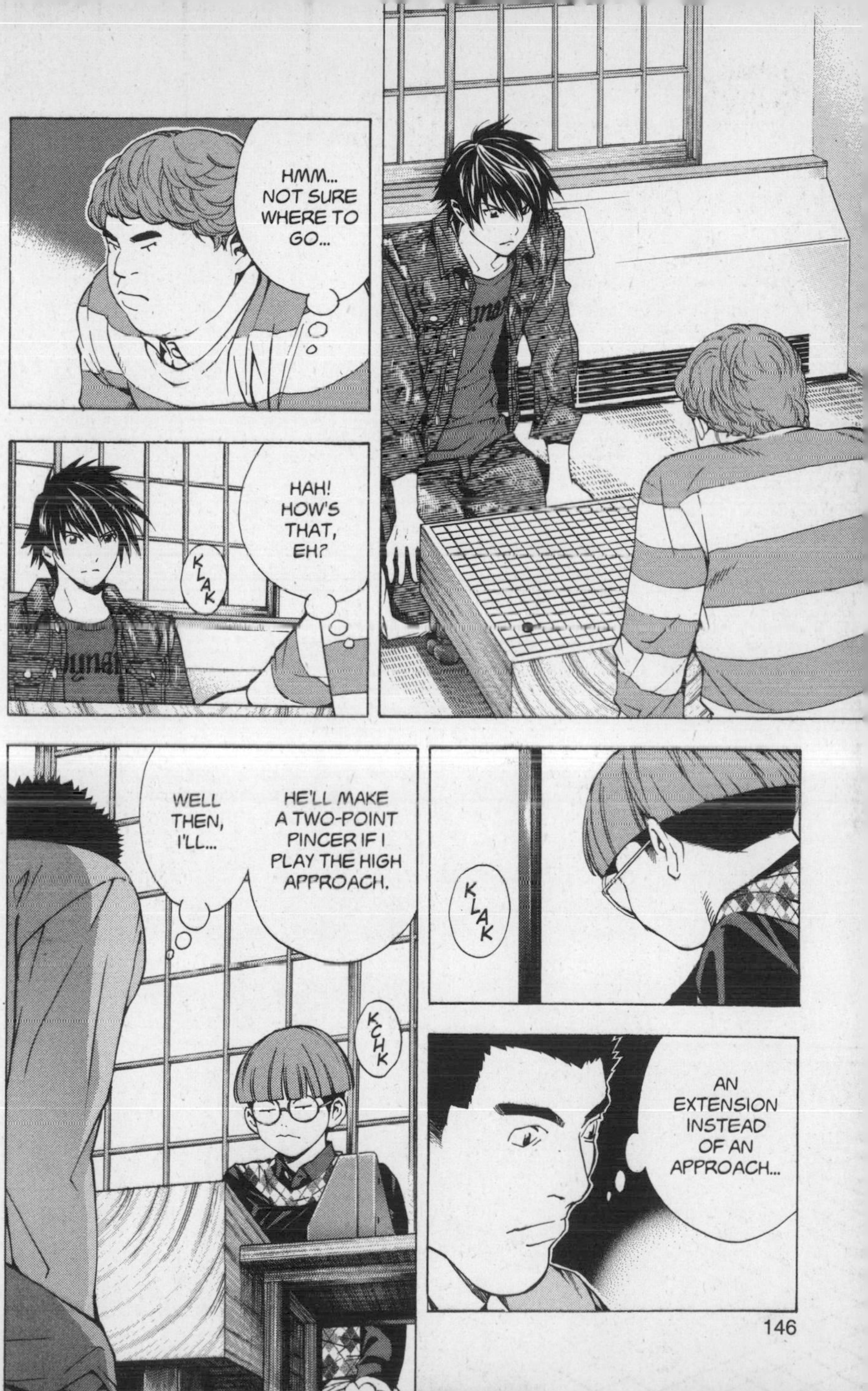
HMM... NOT SURE WHERE TO GO...
KLAK
HAH! HOW'S THAT, EH?
KLAK
AN EXTENSION INSTEAD OF AN APPROACH...
HE'LL MAKE A TWO-POINT PINCER IF I PLAY THE HIGH APPROACH.
WELL THEN, I'LL...
KCHK

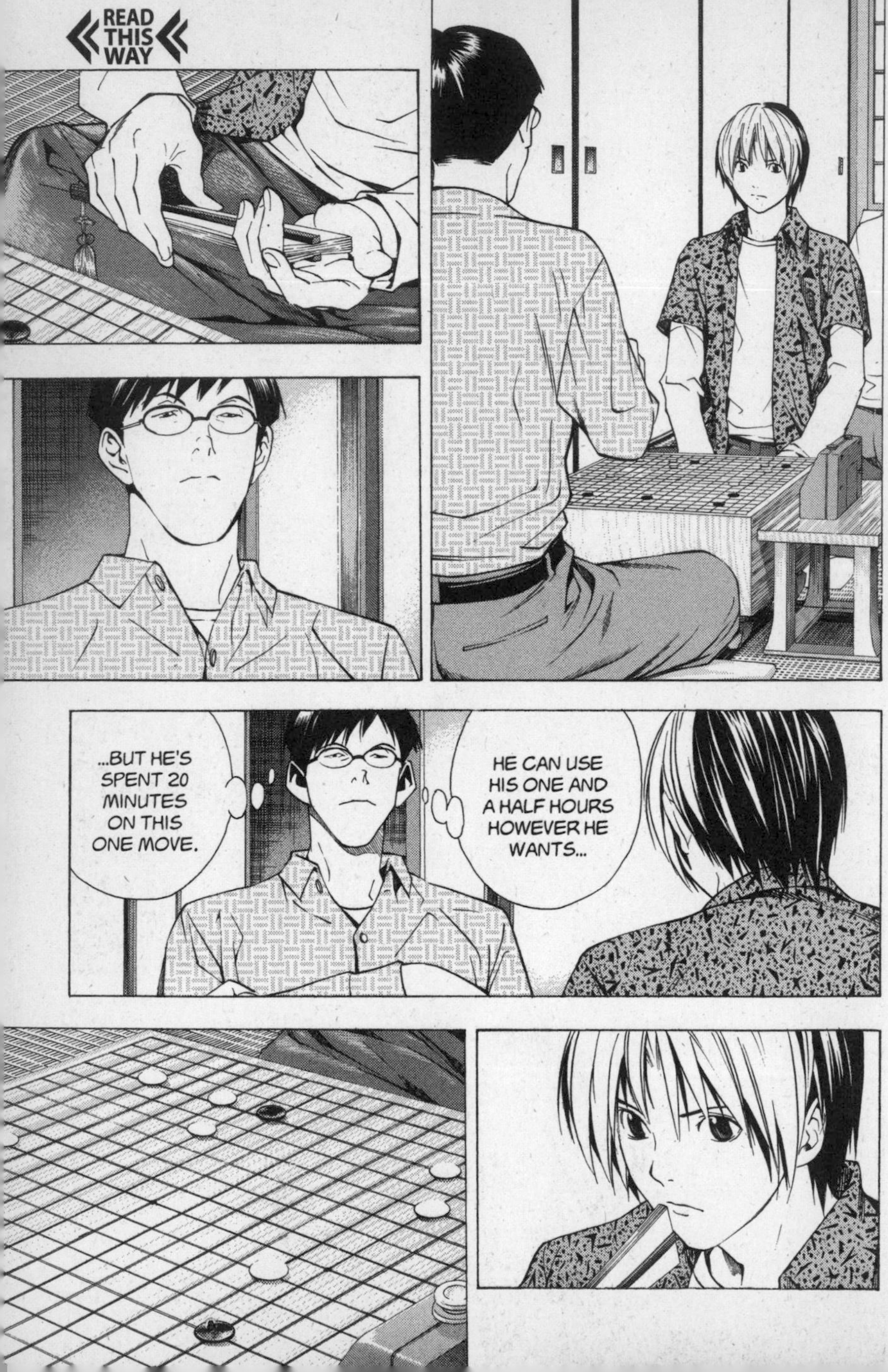
READ THIS WAY
HE CAN USE HIS ONE AND A HALF HOURS HOWEVER HE WANTS...
...BUT HE'S SPENT 20 MINUTES ON THIS ONE MOVE.

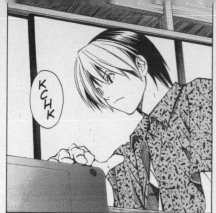
KCHK

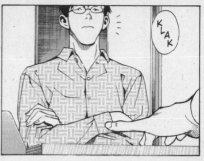
KLAK

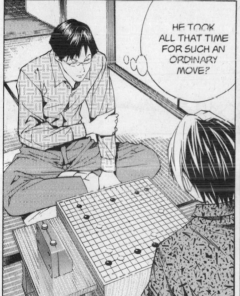
HE TOOK ALL THAT TIME FOR SUCH AN ORDINARY MOVE?

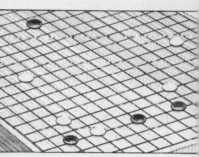

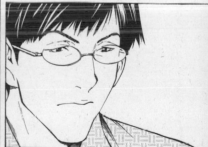

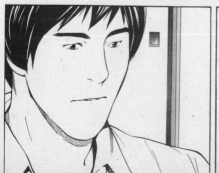

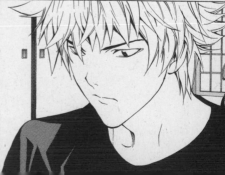

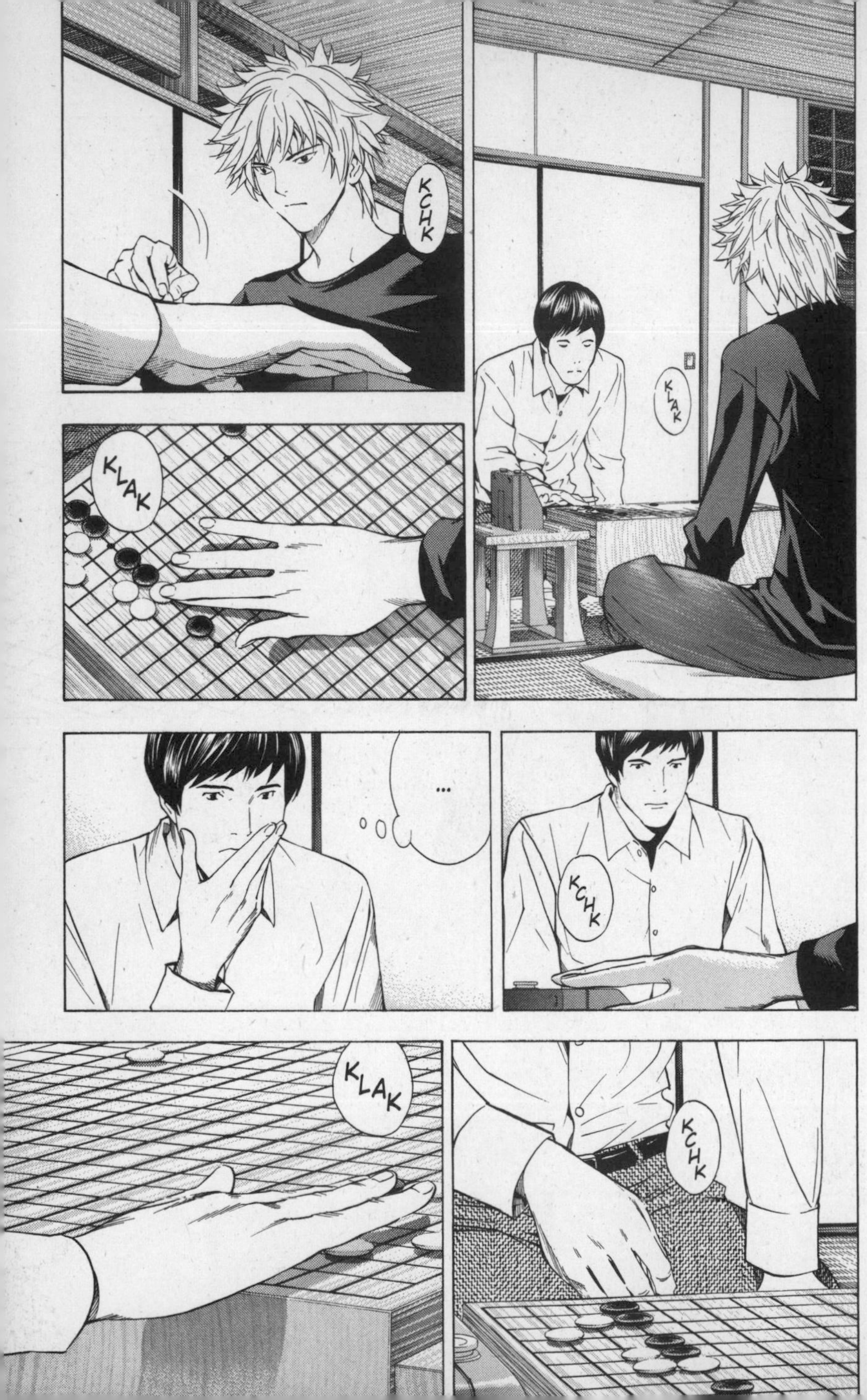
KLAK
KCHK
KLAK
KCHK
...
KCHK
KLAK

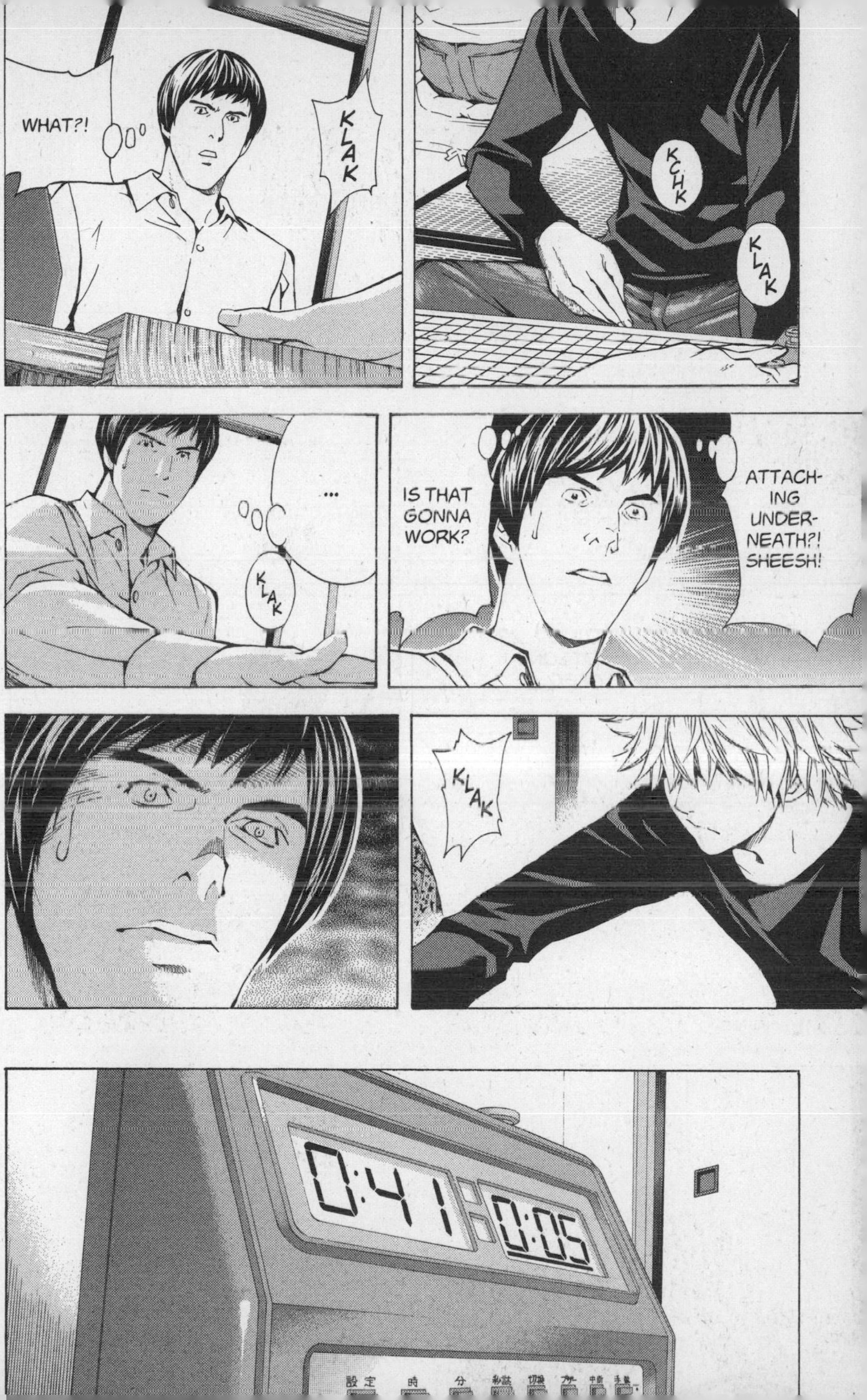
KCHK
KLAK
KLAK
WHAT?!
ATTACH-ING UNDER-NEATH?! SHEESH!
IS THAT GONNA WORK?
...
KLAK
KLAK
0:41
0:05

READ THIS WAY

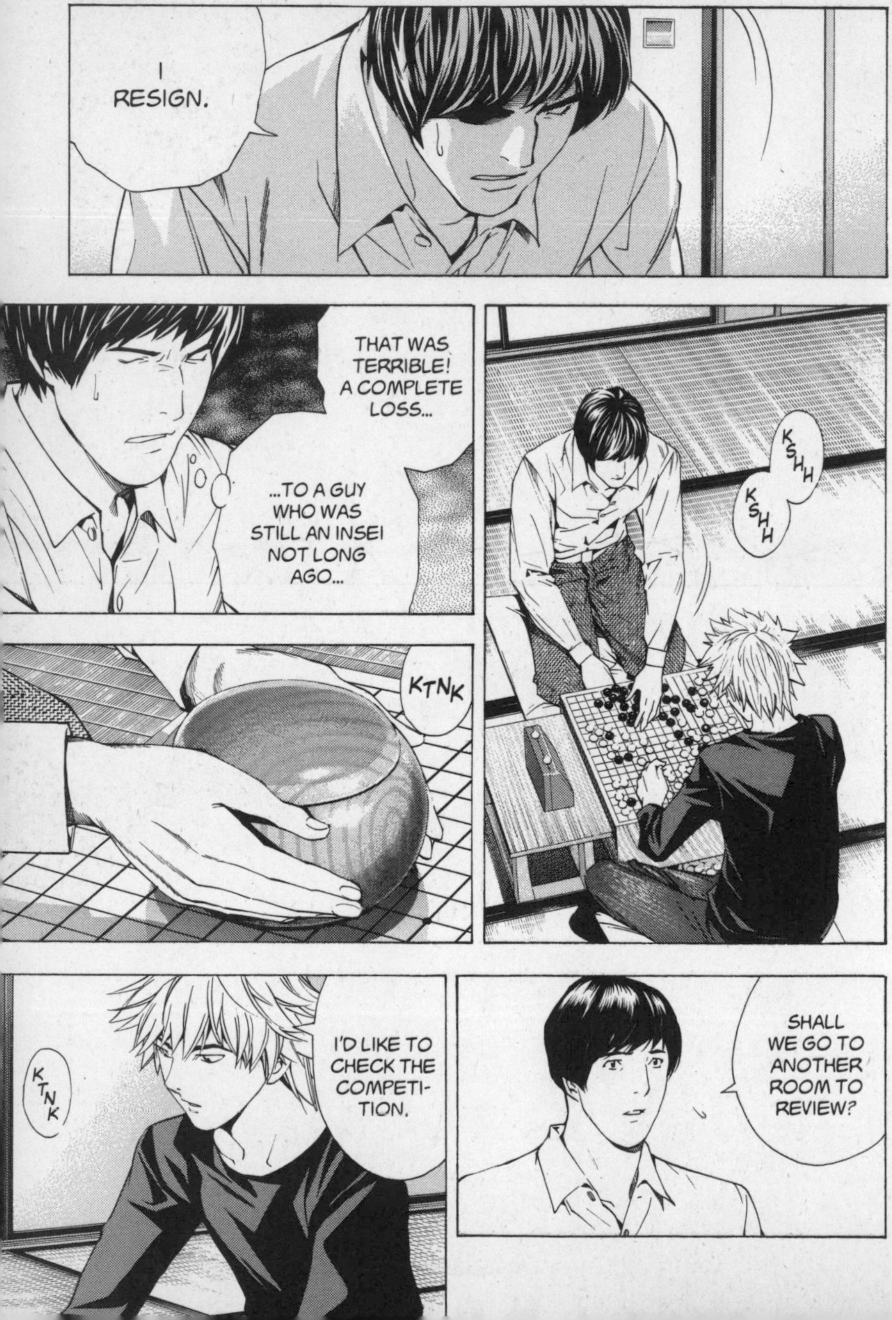

I RESIGN.
KSHH
KSHH
THAT WAS TERRIBLE! A COMPLETE LOSS...
...TO A GUY WHO WAS STILL AN INSEI NOT LONG AGO...
KTNK
SHALL WE GO TO ANOTHER ROOM TO REVIEW?
I'D LIKE TO CHECK THE COMPETI-TION.
KTNK

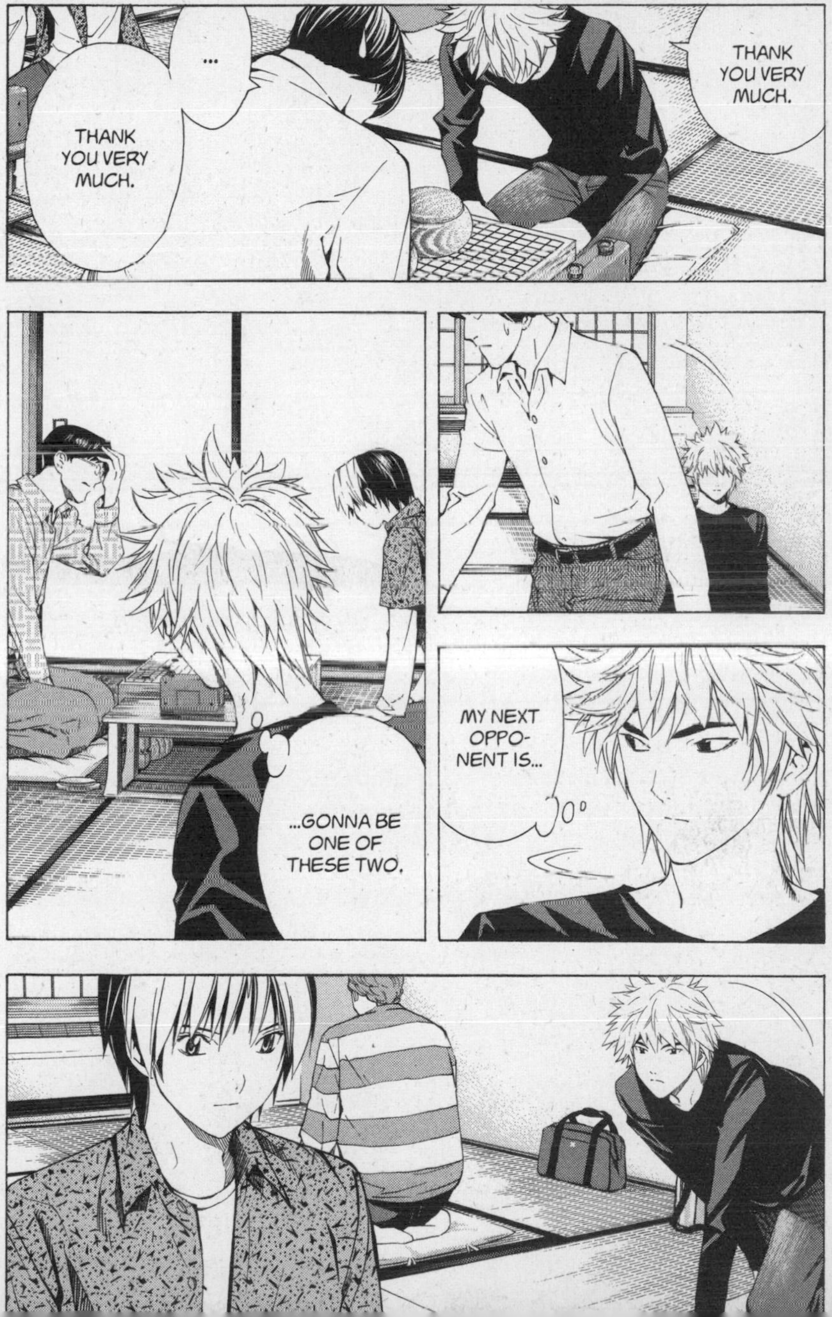
THANK YOU VERY MUCH.
...
THANK YOU VERY MUCH.
MY NEXT OPPO-NENT IS...
...GONNA BE ONE OF THESE TWO.

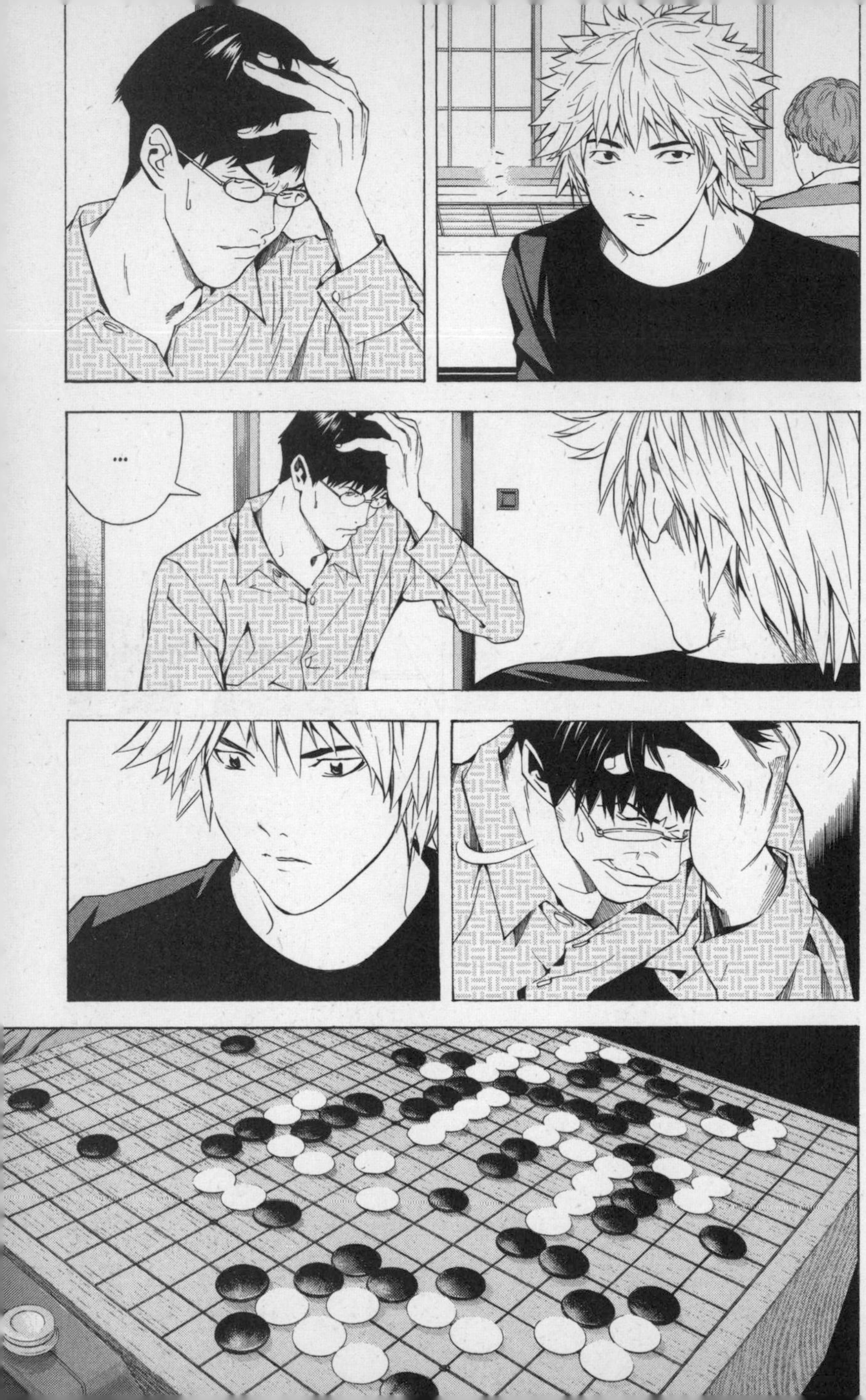
...

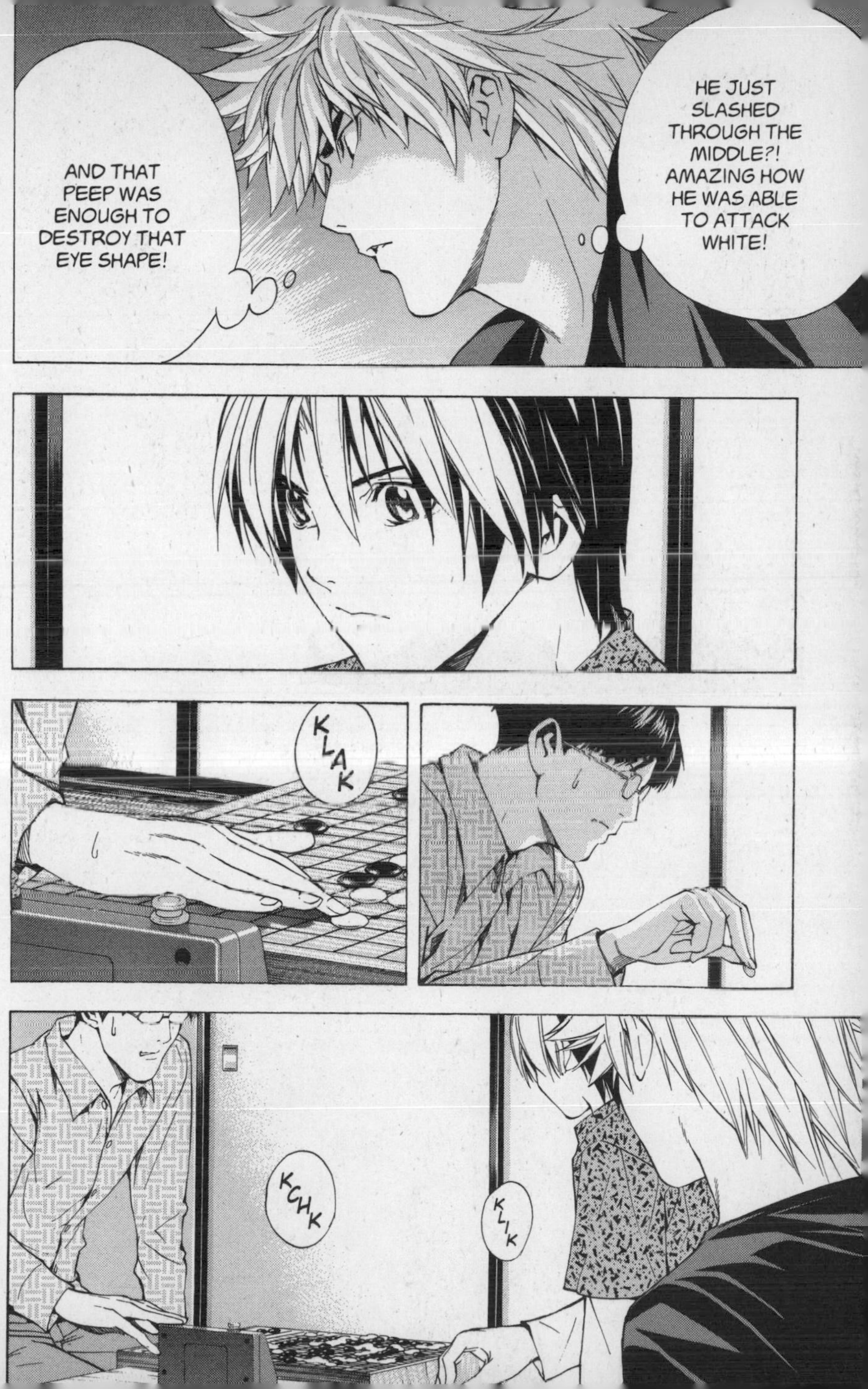
HE JUST SLASHED THROUGH THE MIDDLE?! AMAZING HOW HE WAS ABLE TO ATTACK WHITE!
AND THAT PEEP WAS ENOUGH TO DESTROY THAT EYE SHAPE!
KLAK
KLIK
KCHK

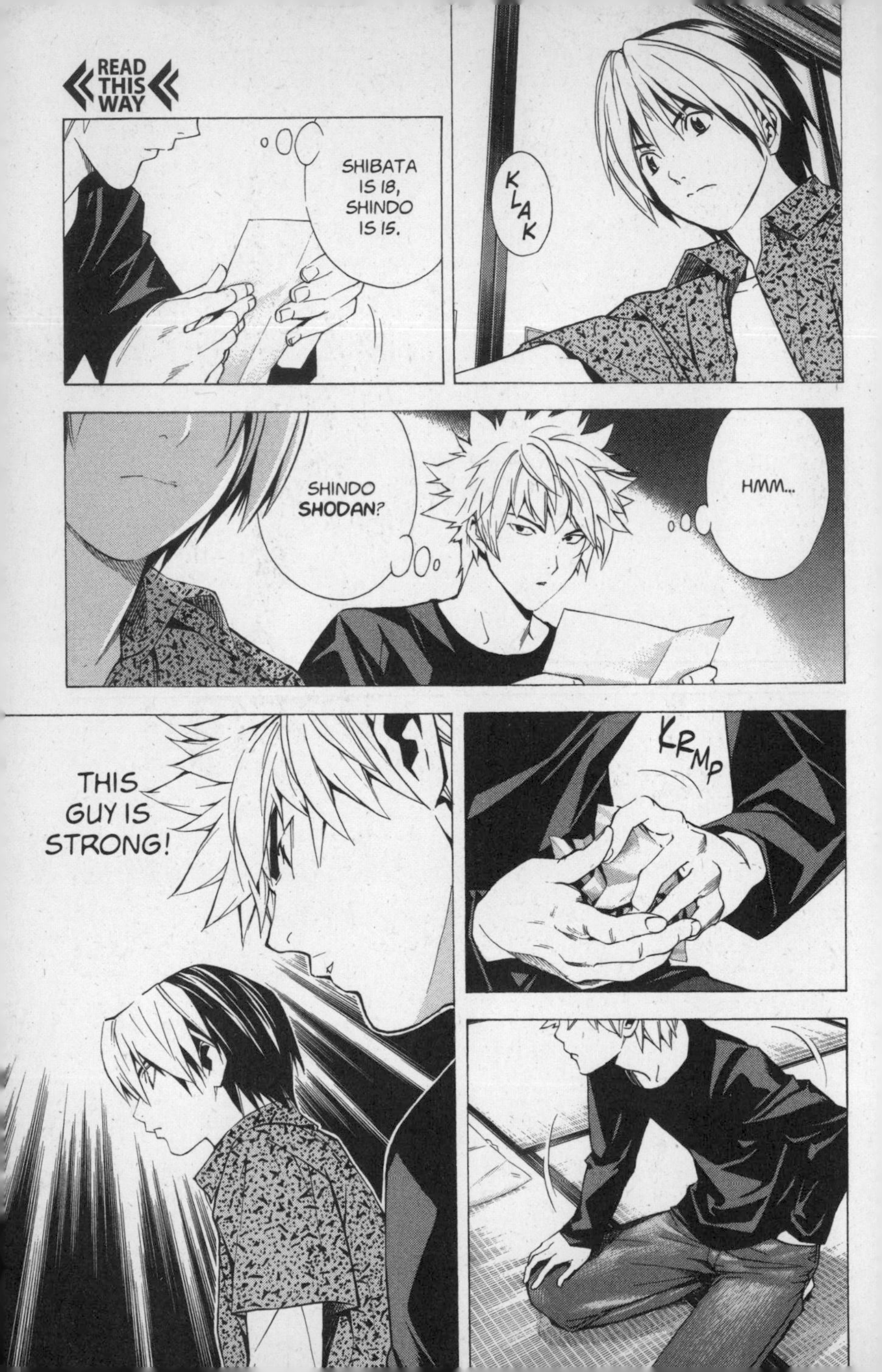
READ THIS WAY
KLAK
SHIBATA IS 18, SHINDO IS 15.
HMM...
SHINDO SHODAN?
KRMP
THIS GUY IS STRONG!

A WORD ABOUT HIKARU NO GO

THE SYSTEM OF TOURNAMENT MATCHES ❷

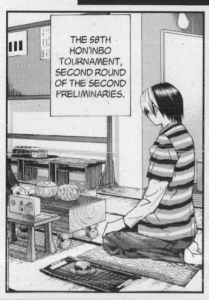

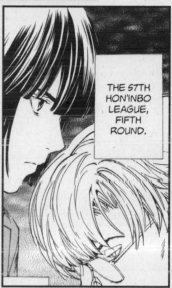

THE 57TH HON'INBO LEAGUE, FIFTH ROUND.
THE 58TH HON'INBO TOURNAMENT, SECOND ROUND OF THE SECOND PRELIMINARIES.

THE SEVEN MAJOR TITLES ARE EVEN MORE COMPLEX THAN OTHER TOURNAMENTS.

TAKE THE HON'INBO TOURNAMENT, FOR EXAMPLE. IT ACTUALLY TAKES TWO YEARS AND TWO MONTHS TO GET FROM THE FIRST GAME IN THE FIRST PRELIMINARY TO THE FINAL DECIDING MATCH, BUT A NEW FIRST PRELIMINARY BEGINS EVERY YEAR. IN OTHER WORDS, THE SEVENTH MATCH OF THE FINALS OF THE 56TH EDITION, THE THIRD PRELIMINARIES OF THE 57TH EDITION AND THE FIRST PRELIMINARIES OF THE 58TH EDITION ARE ALL TAKING PLACE AT THE SAME TIME.

THAT'S WHY IN "GAME 159" AKIRA'S HON'INBO LEAGUE MATCH IN THE 57TH EDITION AND HIKARU'S MATCH IN THE SECOND PRELIMINARIES OF THE 58TH HAPPENED ON THE SAME DAY.

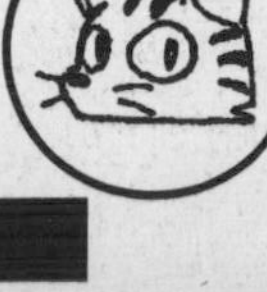

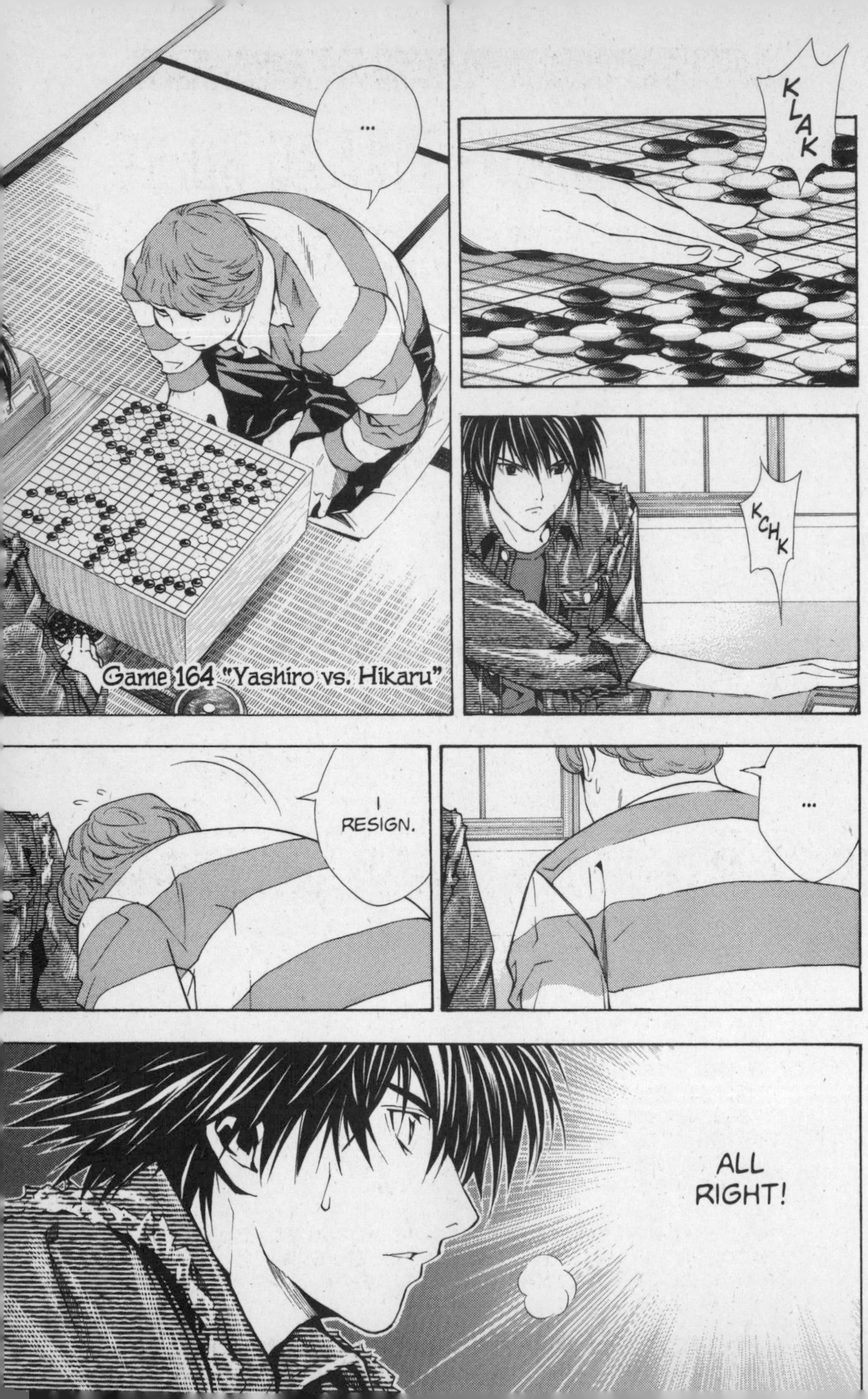
KLAK
KCHK
...
Game 164 "Yashiro vs. Hikaru"
...
I RESIGN.
ALL RIGHT!

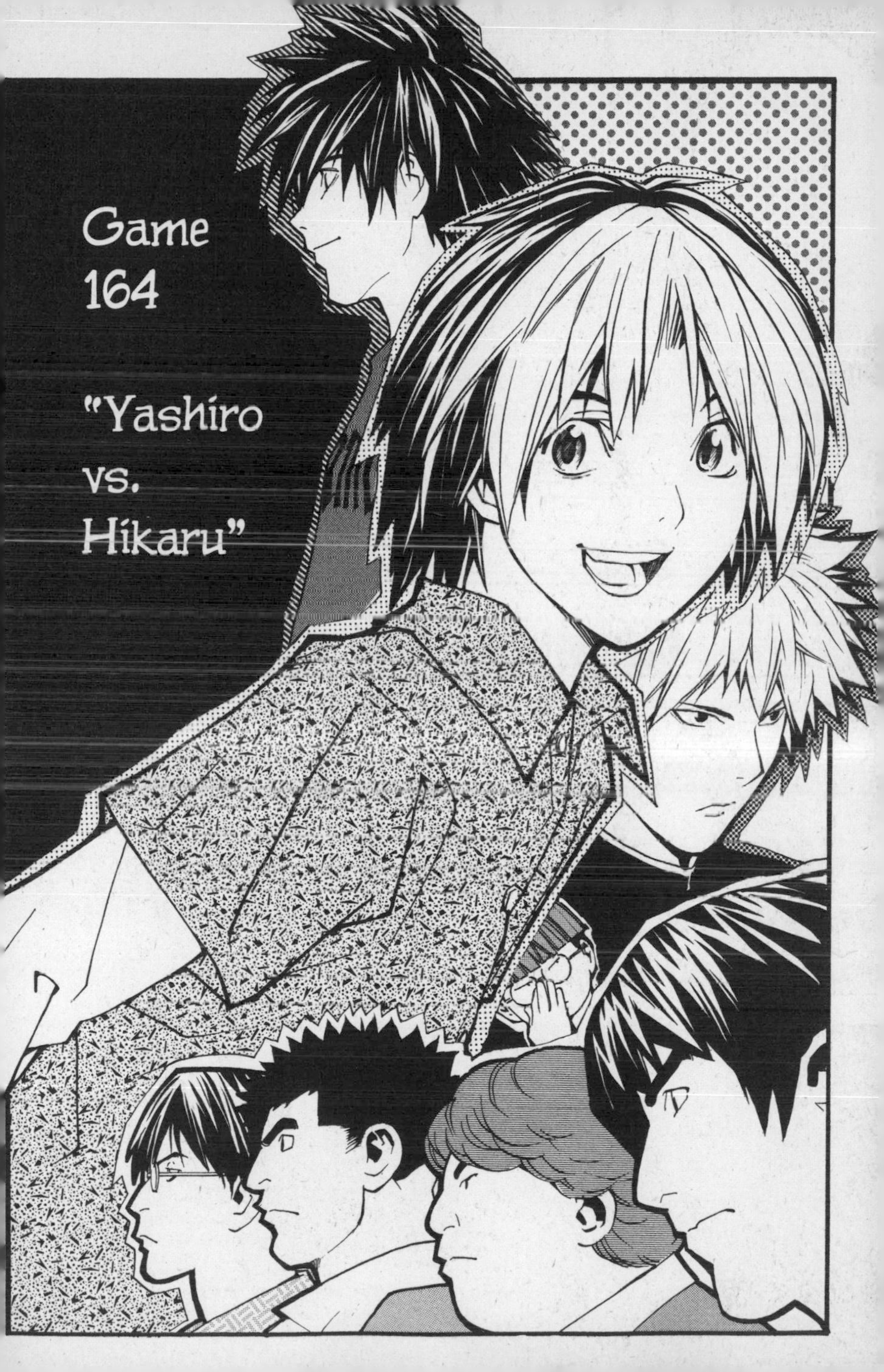
Game 164
"Yashiro vs. Hikaru"

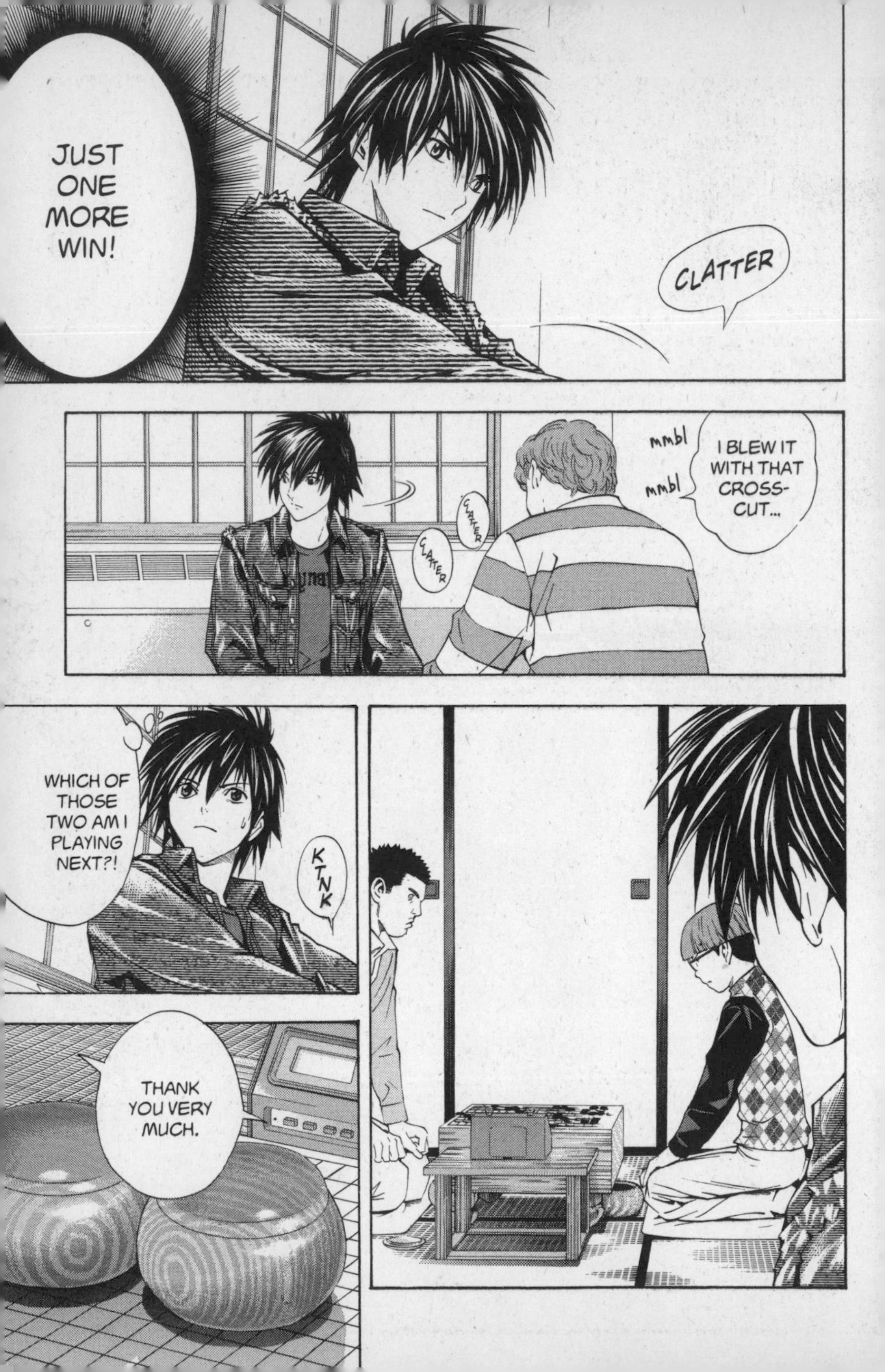
CLATTER
JUST ONE MORE WIN!
I BLEW IT WITH THAT CROSS-CUT...
mmbl
mmbl
CLATTER
CLATTER
KTNK
WHICH OF THOSE TWO AM I PLAYING NEXT?!
THANK YOU VERY MUCH.

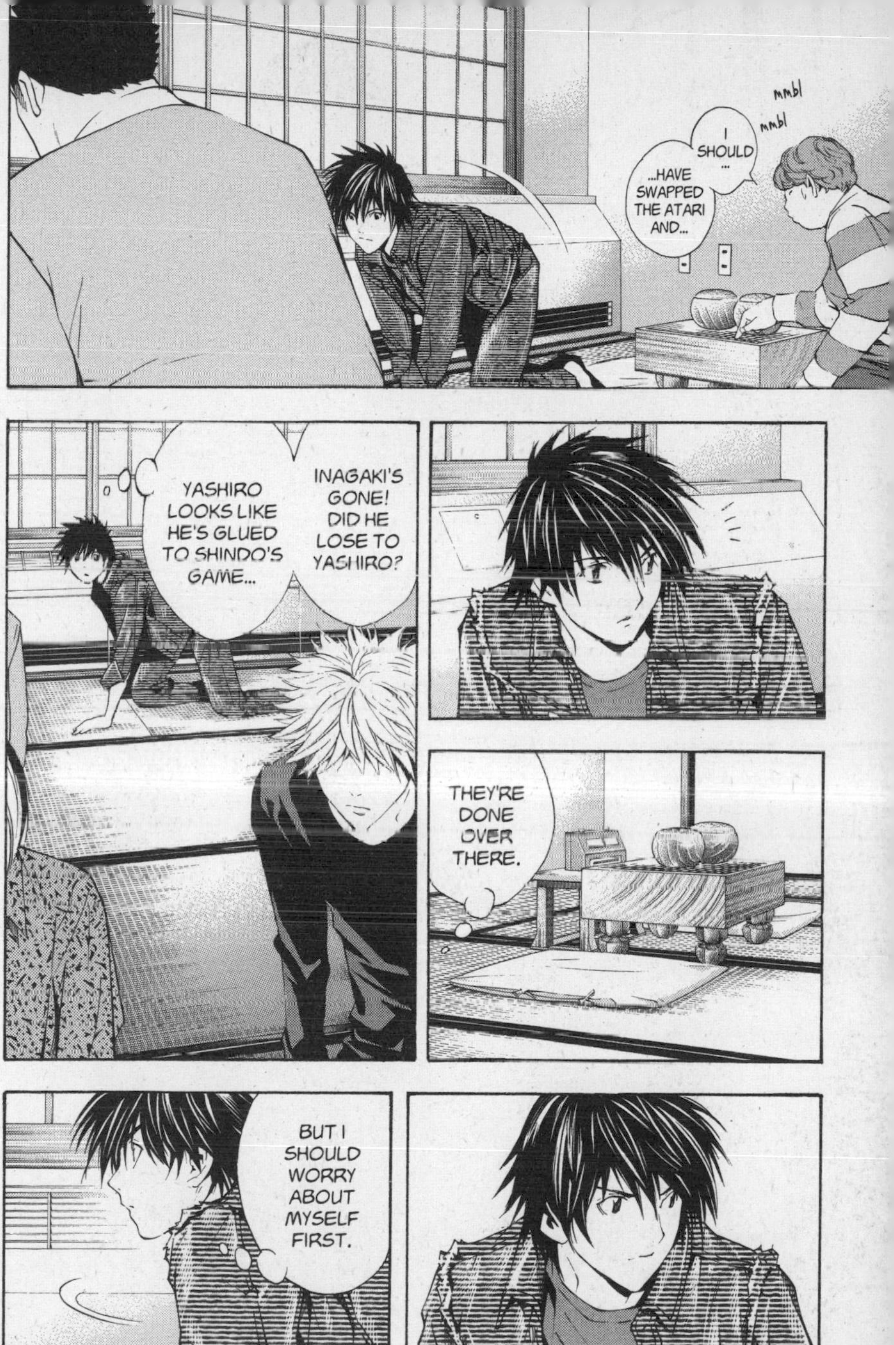
mmbl
mmbl
I SHOULD ...
...HAVE SWAPPED THE ATARI AND...
THEY'RE DONE OVER THERE.
INAGAKI'S GONE! DID HE LOSE TO YASHIRO?
YASHIRO LOOKS LIKE HE'S GLUED TO SHINDO'S GAME...
BUT I SHOULD WORRY ABOUT MYSELF FIRST.

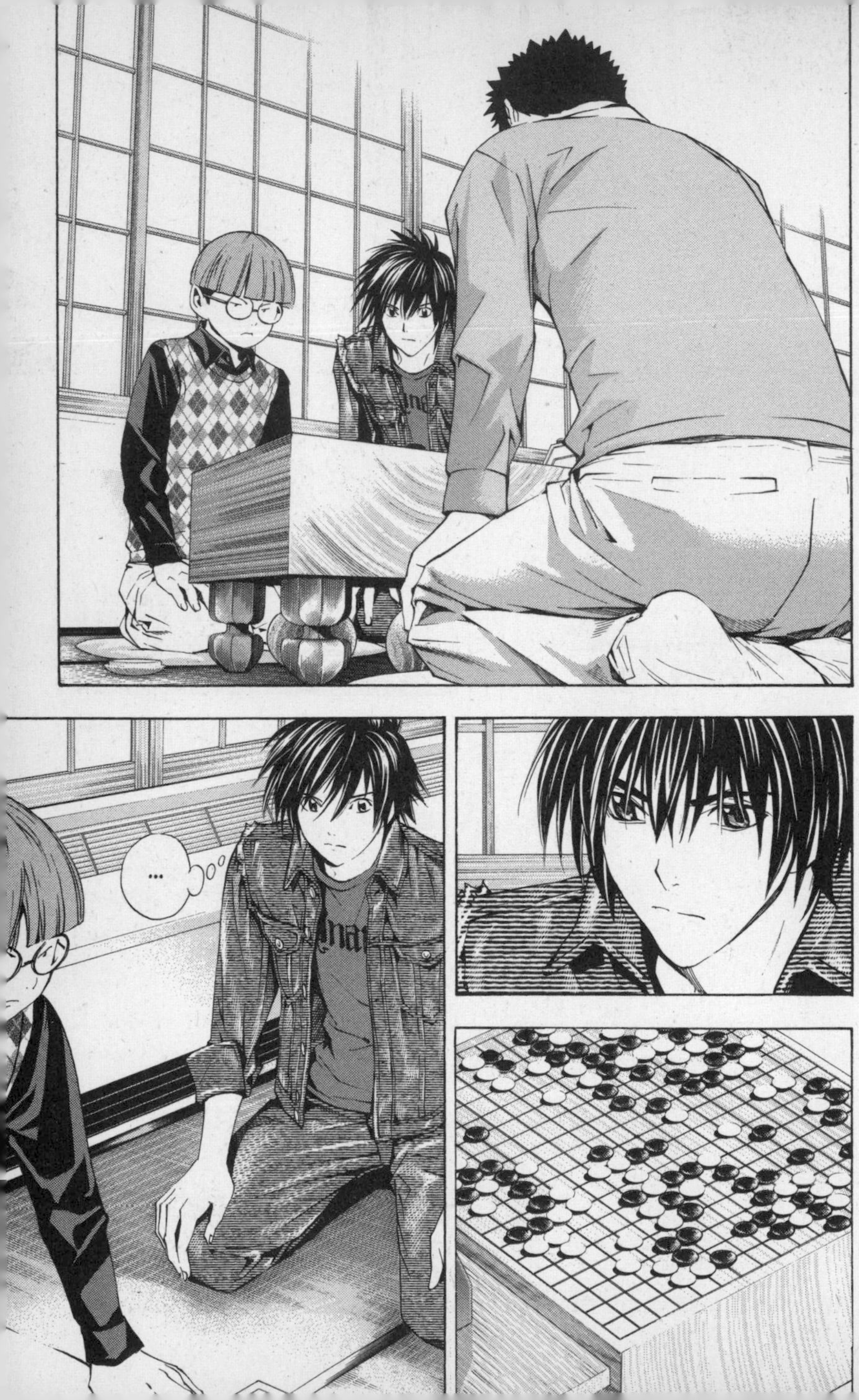
...

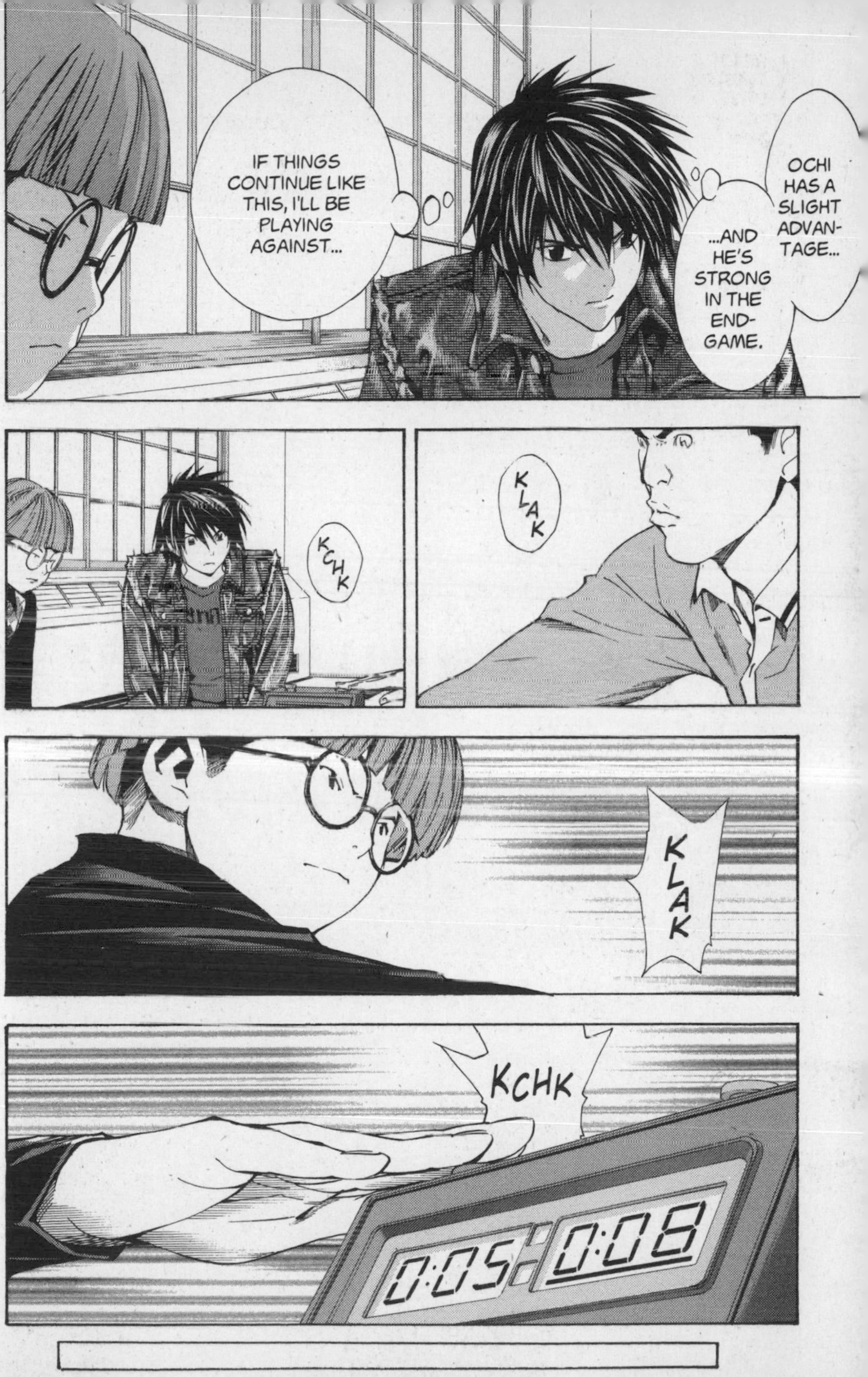
OCHI HAS A SLIGHT ADVANTAGE...
...AND HE'S STRONG IN THE END-GAME.
IF THINGS CONTINUE LIKE THIS, I'LL BE PLAYING AGAINST...
KLAK
KCHK
KLAK
KCHK
0:05 0:08

READ THIS WAY

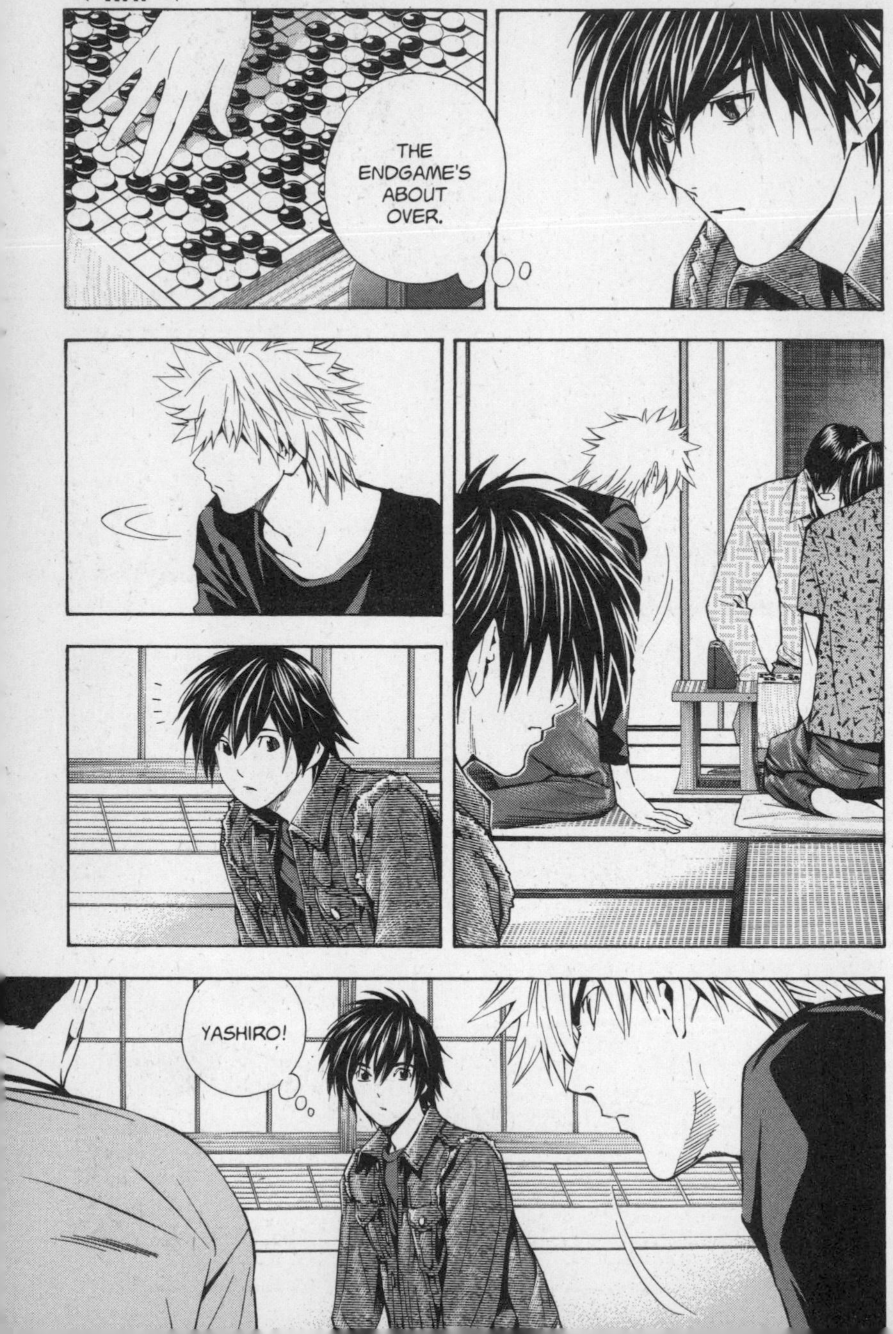
THE ENDGAME'S ABOUT OVER.
YASHIRO!

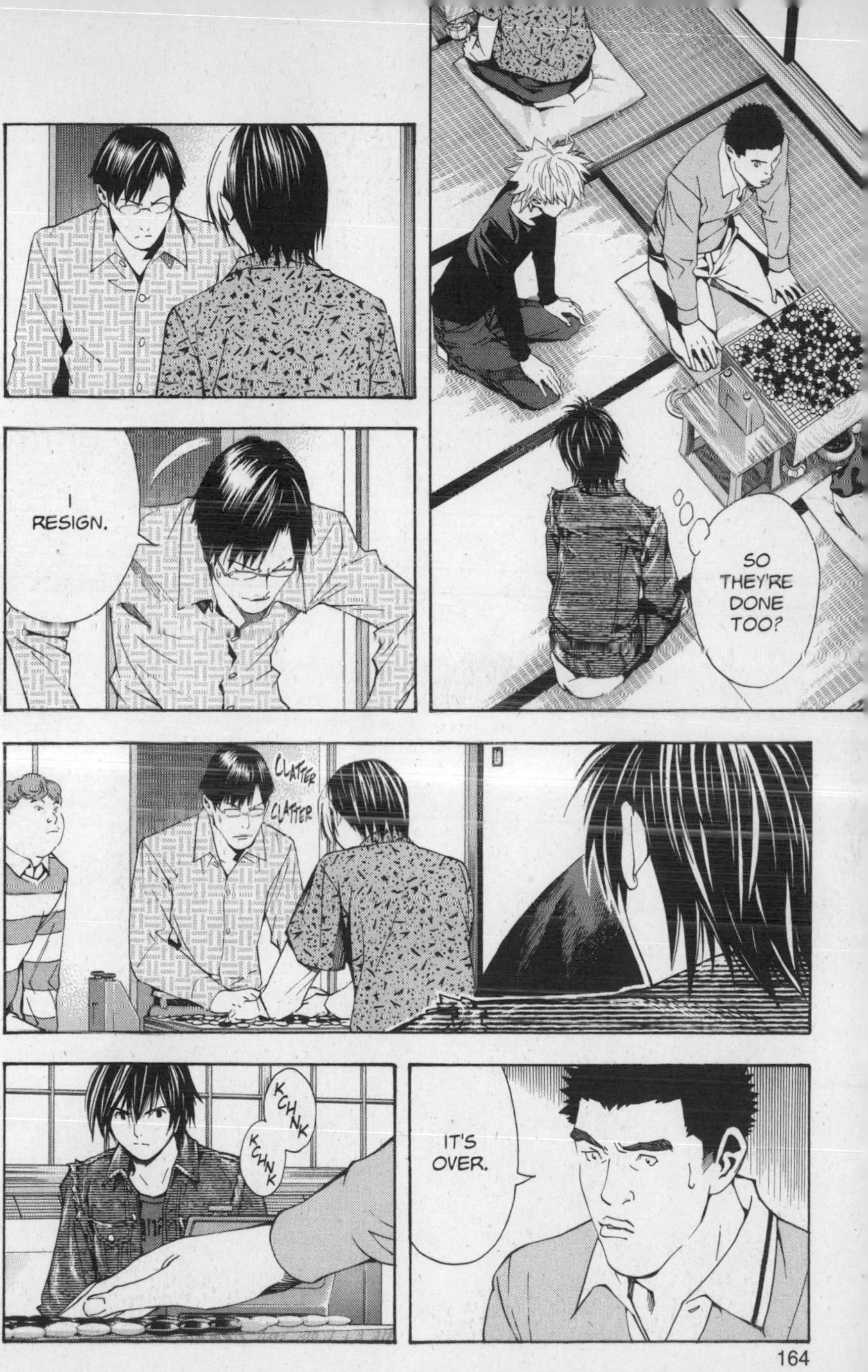
SO THEY'RE DONE TOO?
I RESIGN.
CLATTER
CLATTER
IT'S OVER.
KCHNK
KCHNK

READ THIS WAY

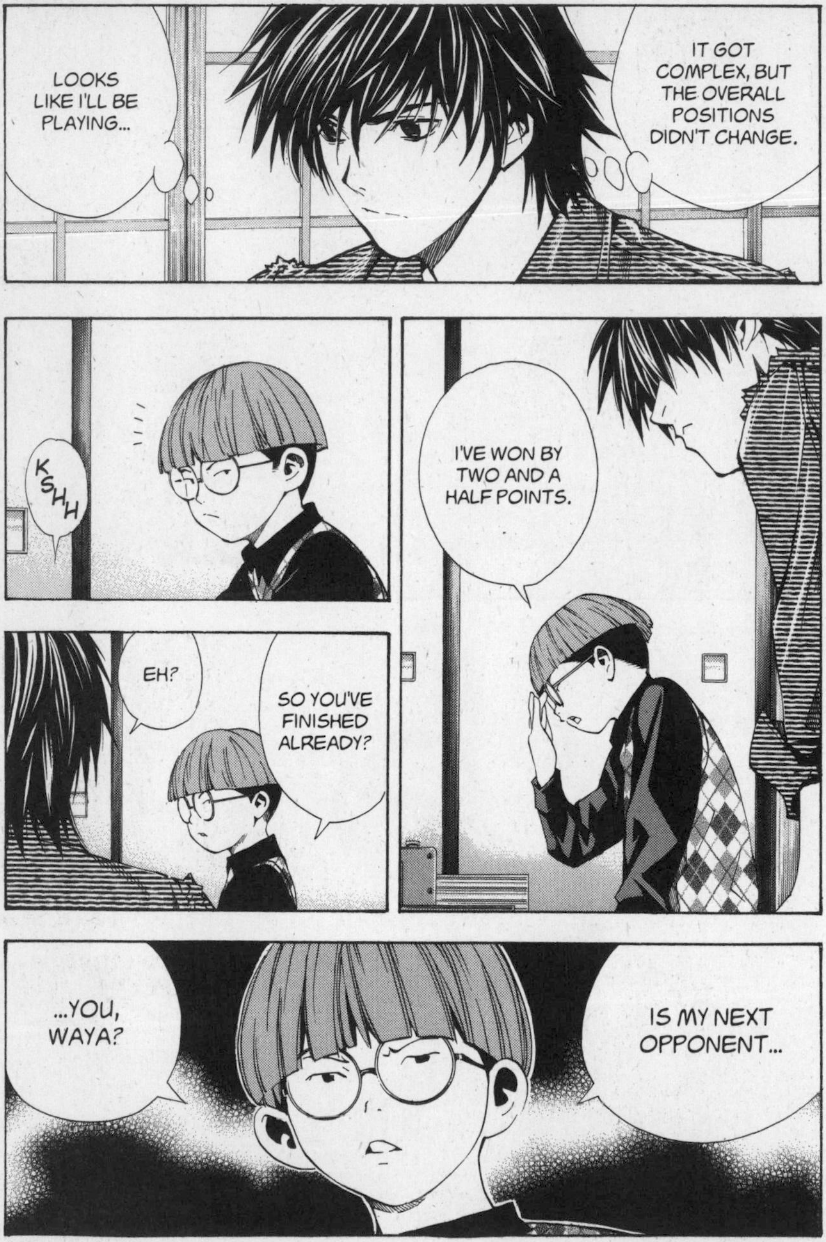
IT GOT COMPLEX, BUT THE OVERALL POSITIONS DIDN'T CHANGE.
LOOKS LIKE I'LL BE PLAYING...
I'VE WON BY TWO AND A HALF POINTS.
KSHH
SO YOU'VE FINISHED ALREADY?
EH?
IS MY NEXT OPPONENT...
...YOU, WAYA?

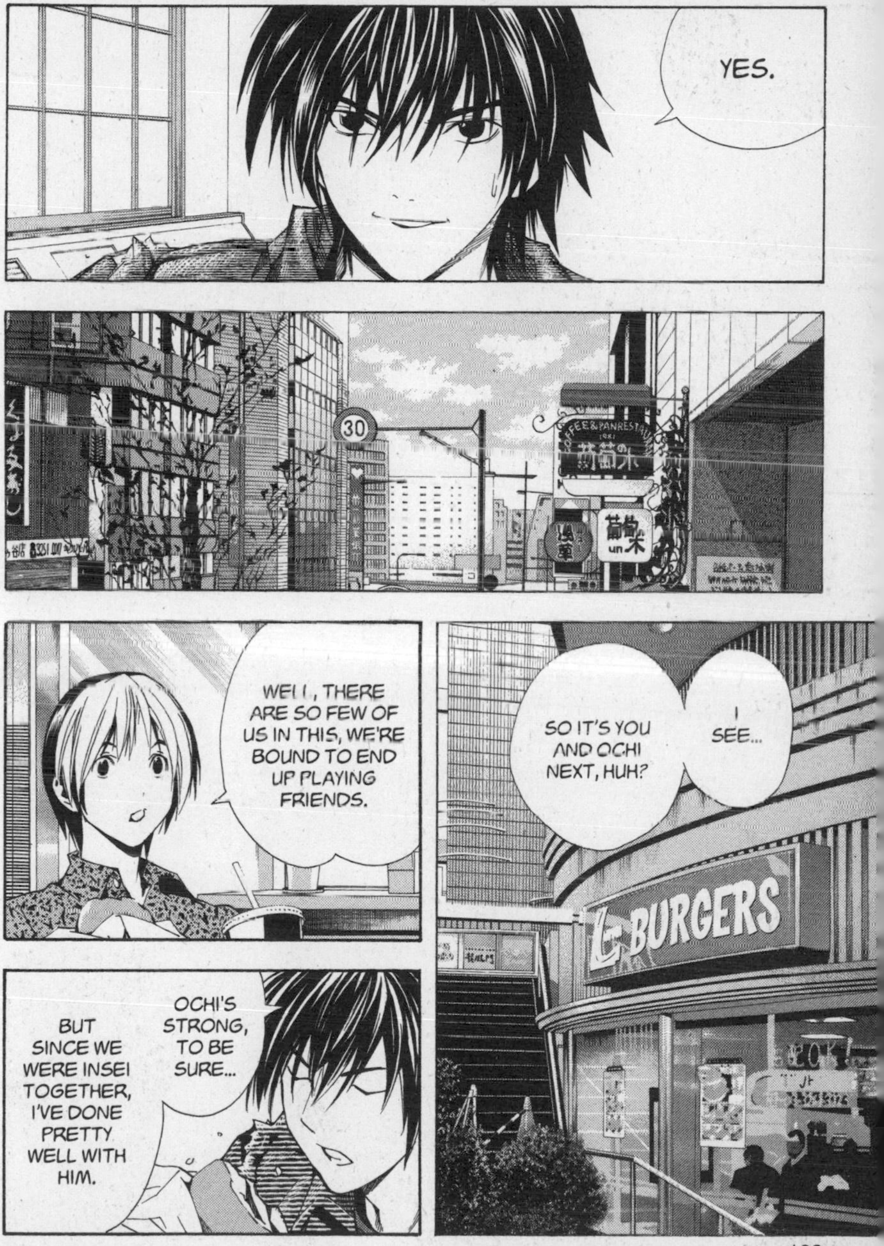
YES.
30
I SEE...
SO IT'S YOU AND OCHI NEXT, HUH?
BURGERS
WELL, THERE ARE SO FEW OF US IN THIS, WE'RE BOUND TO END UP PLAYING FRIENDS.
OCHI'S STRONG, TO BE SURE...
BUT SINCE WE WERE INSEI TOGETHER, I'VE DONE PRETTY WELL WITH HIM.

READ THIS WAY

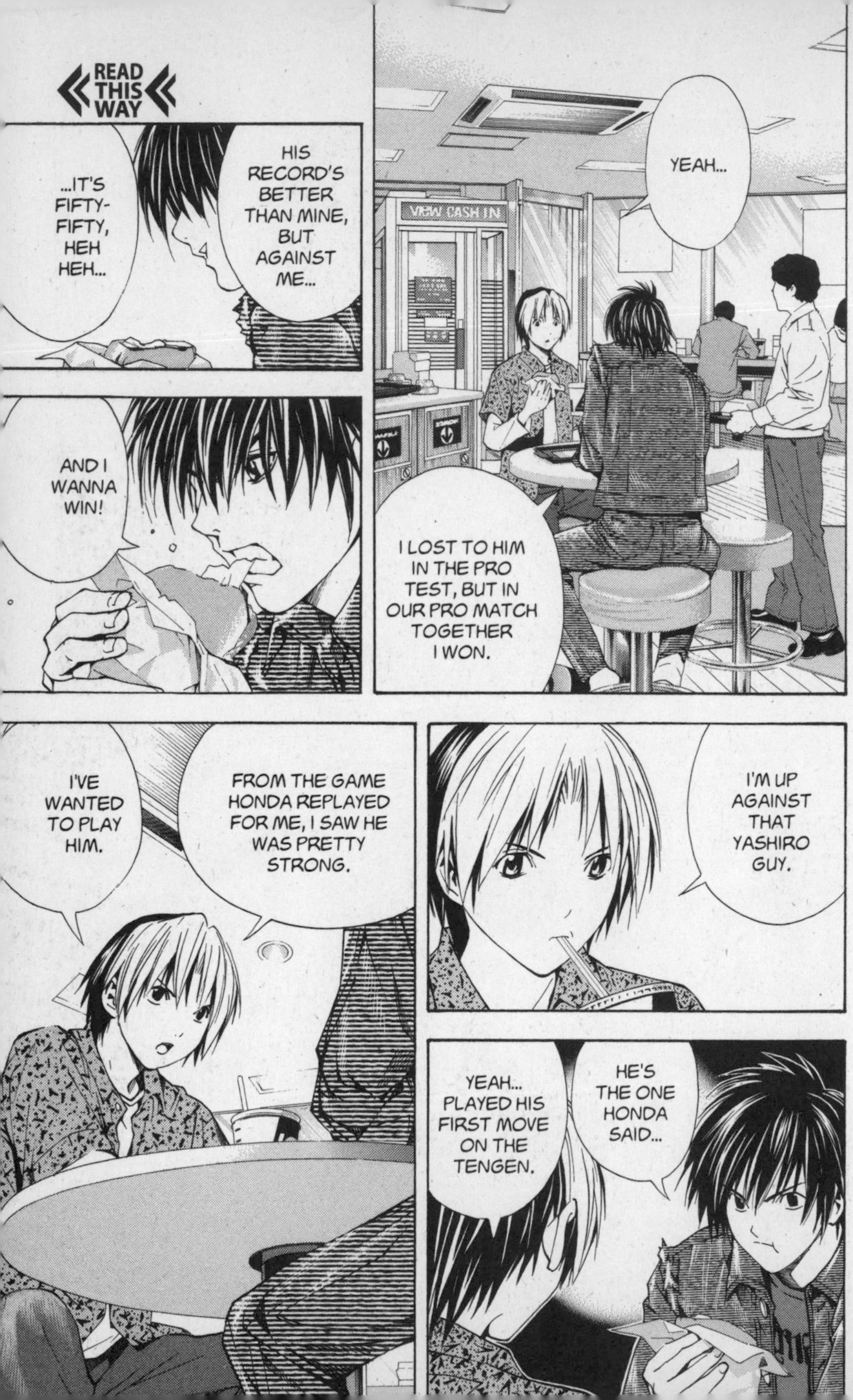
YEAH...
VIEW CASH IN
I LOST TO HIM IN THE PRO TEST, BUT IN OUR PRO MATCH TOGETHER I WON.
HIS RECORD'S BETTER THAN MINE, BUT AGAINST ME...
...IT'S FIFTY-FIFTY, HEH HEH...
AND I WANNA WIN!
I'M UP AGAINST THAT YASHIRO GUY.
HE'S THE ONE HONDA SAID...
YEAH... PLAYED HIS FIRST MOVE ON THE TENGEN.
FROM THE GAME HONDA REPLAYED FOR ME, I SAW HE WAS PRETTY STRONG.
I'VE WANTED TO PLAY HIM.

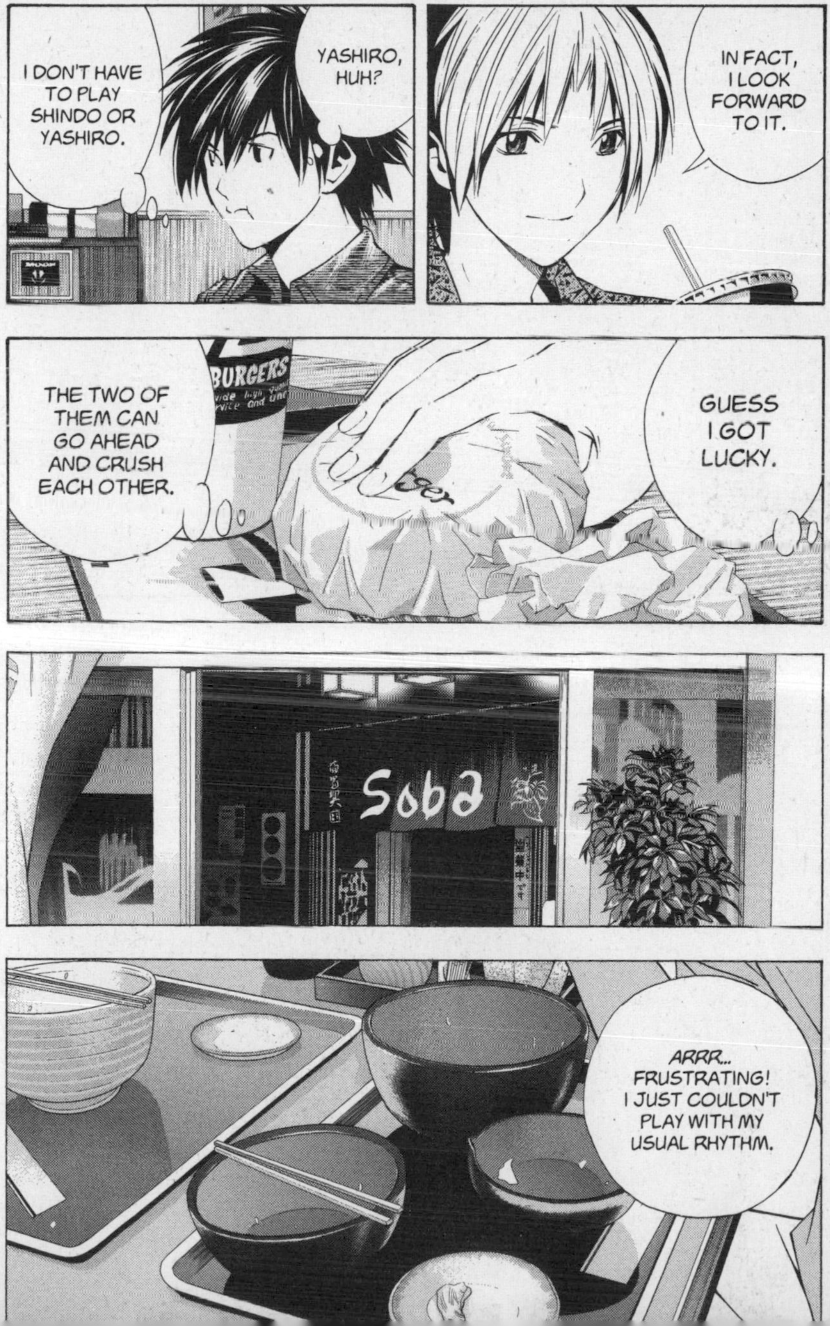
IN FACT, I LOOK FORWARD TO IT.
YASHIRO, HUH?
I DON'T HAVE TO PLAY SHINDO OR YASHIRO.
GUESS I GOT LUCKY.
BURGERS
THE TWO OF THEM CAN GO AHEAD AND CRUSH EACH OTHER.
Soba
ARRR... FRUSTRATING! I JUST COULDN'T PLAY WITH MY USUAL RHYTHM.

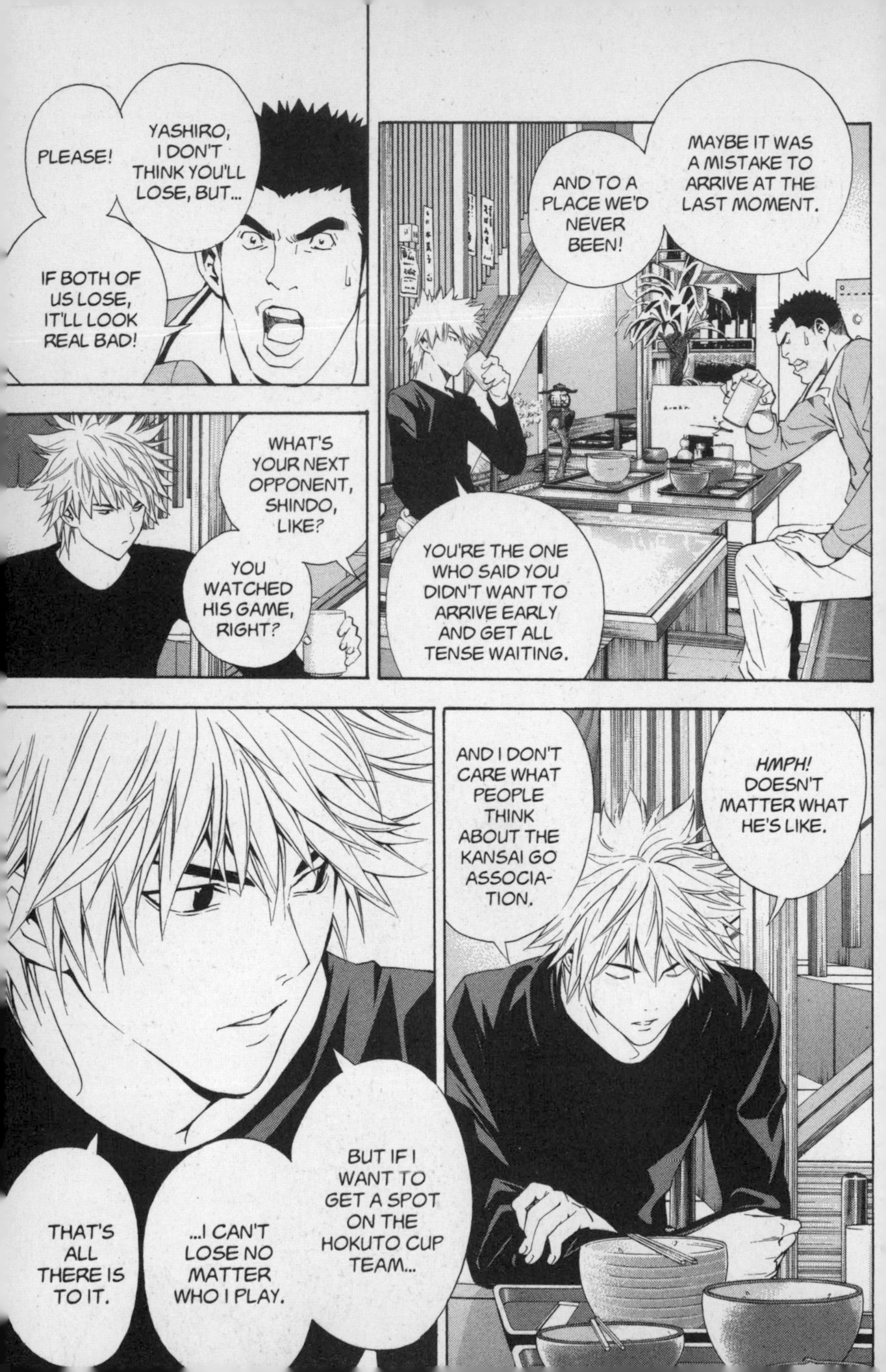
MAYBE IT WAS A MISTAKE TO ARRIVE AT THE LAST MOMENT.
AND TO A PLACE WE'D NEVER BEEN!
YOU'RE THE ONE WHO SAID YOU DIDN'T WANT TO ARRIVE EARLY AND GET ALL TENSE WAITING.
YASHIRO, I DON'T THINK YOU'LL LOSE, BUT...
PLEASE!
IF BOTH OF US LOSE, IT'LL LOOK REAL BAD!
WHAT'S YOUR NEXT OPPONENT, SHINDO, LIKE?
YOU WATCHED HIS GAME, RIGHT?
HMPH! DOESN'T MATTER WHAT HE'S LIKE.
AND I DON'T CARE WHAT PEOPLE THINK ABOUT THE KANSAI GO ASSOCIA-TION.
BUT IF I WANT TO GET A SPOT ON THE HOKUTO CUP TEAM...
...I CAN'T LOSE NO MATTER WHO I PLAY.
THAT'S ALL THERE IS TO IT.

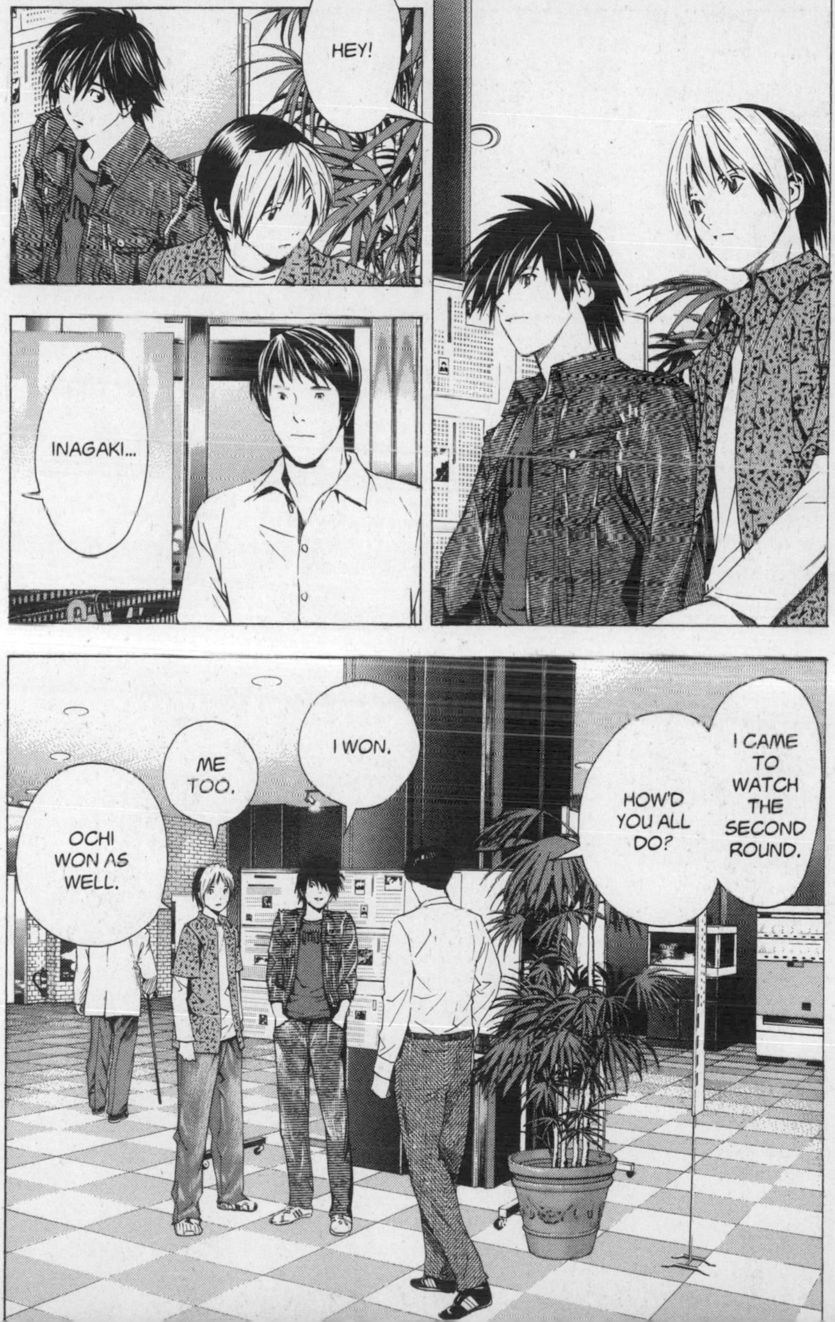
HEY!
INAGAKI...
I CAME TO WATCH THE SECOND ROUND.
HOW'D YOU ALL DO?
I WON.
ME TOO.
OCHI WON AS WELL.

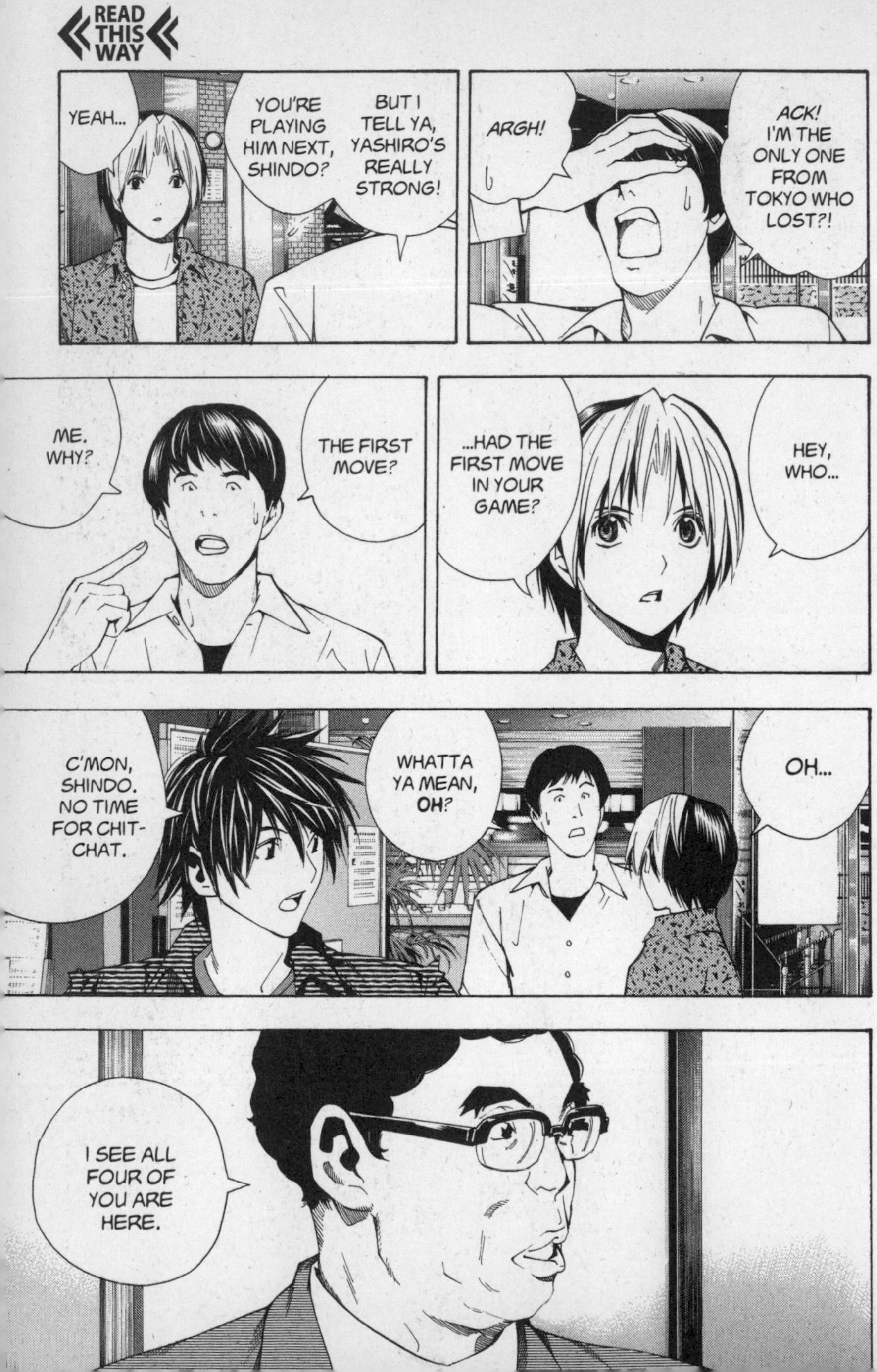
READ THIS WAY
ACK! I'M THE ONLY ONE FROM TOKYO WHO LOST?!
ARGH!
BUT I TELL YA, YASHIRO'S REALLY STRONG!
YOU'RE PLAYING HIM NEXT, SHINDO?
YEAH...
HEY, WHO...
...HAD THE FIRST MOVE IN YOUR GAME?
THE FIRST MOVE?
ME. WHY?
OH...
WHATTA YA MEAN, **OH**?
C'MON, SHINDO. NO TIME FOR CHIT-CHAT.
I SEE ALL FOUR OF YOU ARE HERE.

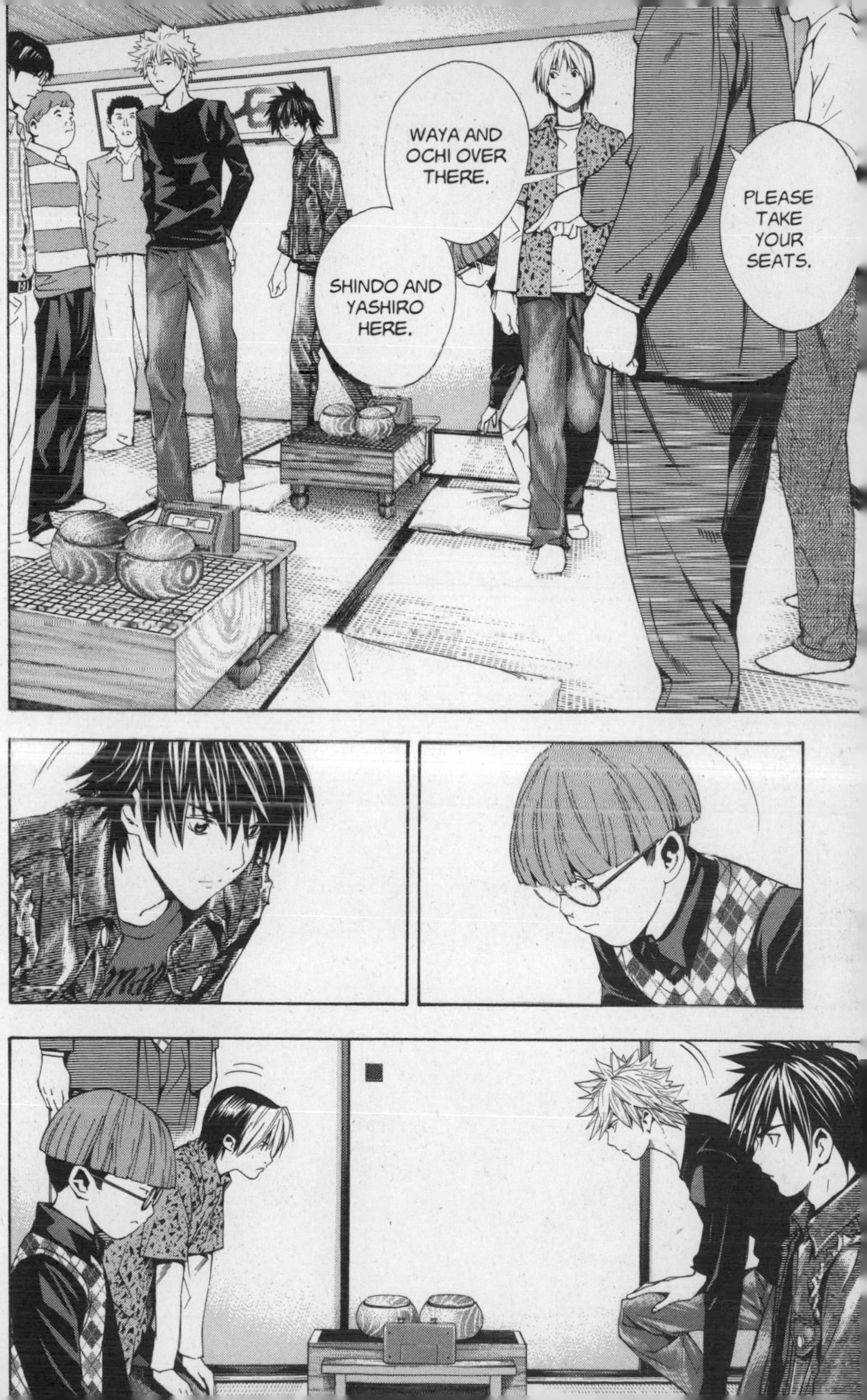
PLEASE TAKE YOUR SEATS.
WAYA AND OCHI OVER THERE.
SHINDO AND YASHIRO HERE.

READ THIS WAY

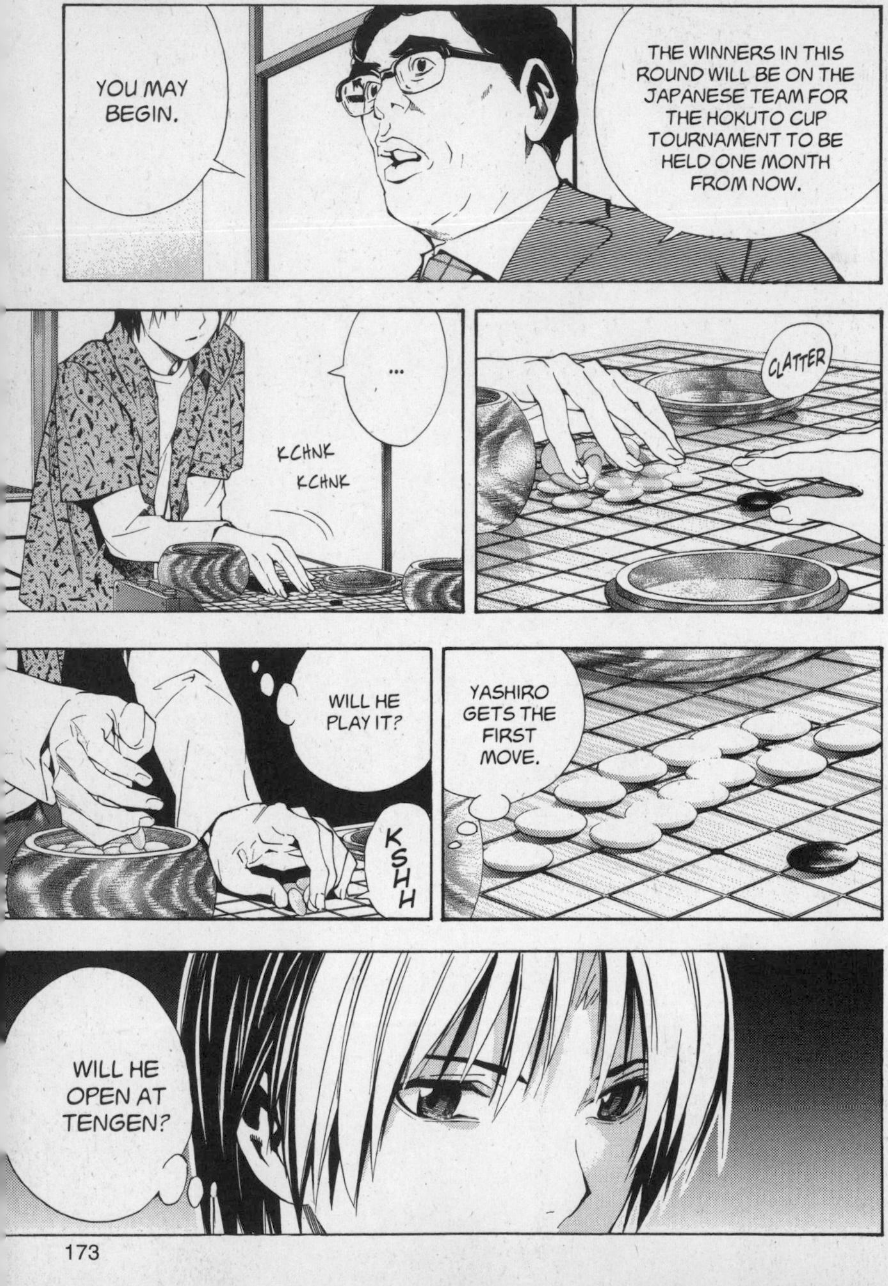
THE WINNERS IN THIS ROUND WILL BE ON THE JAPANESE TEAM FOR THE HOKUTO CUP TOURNAMENT TO BE HELD ONE MONTH FROM NOW.
YOU MAY BEGIN.
CLATTER
...
KCHNK
KCHNK
YASHIRO GETS THE FIRST MOVE.
WILL HE PLAY IT?
KSHH
WILL HE OPEN AT TENGEN?

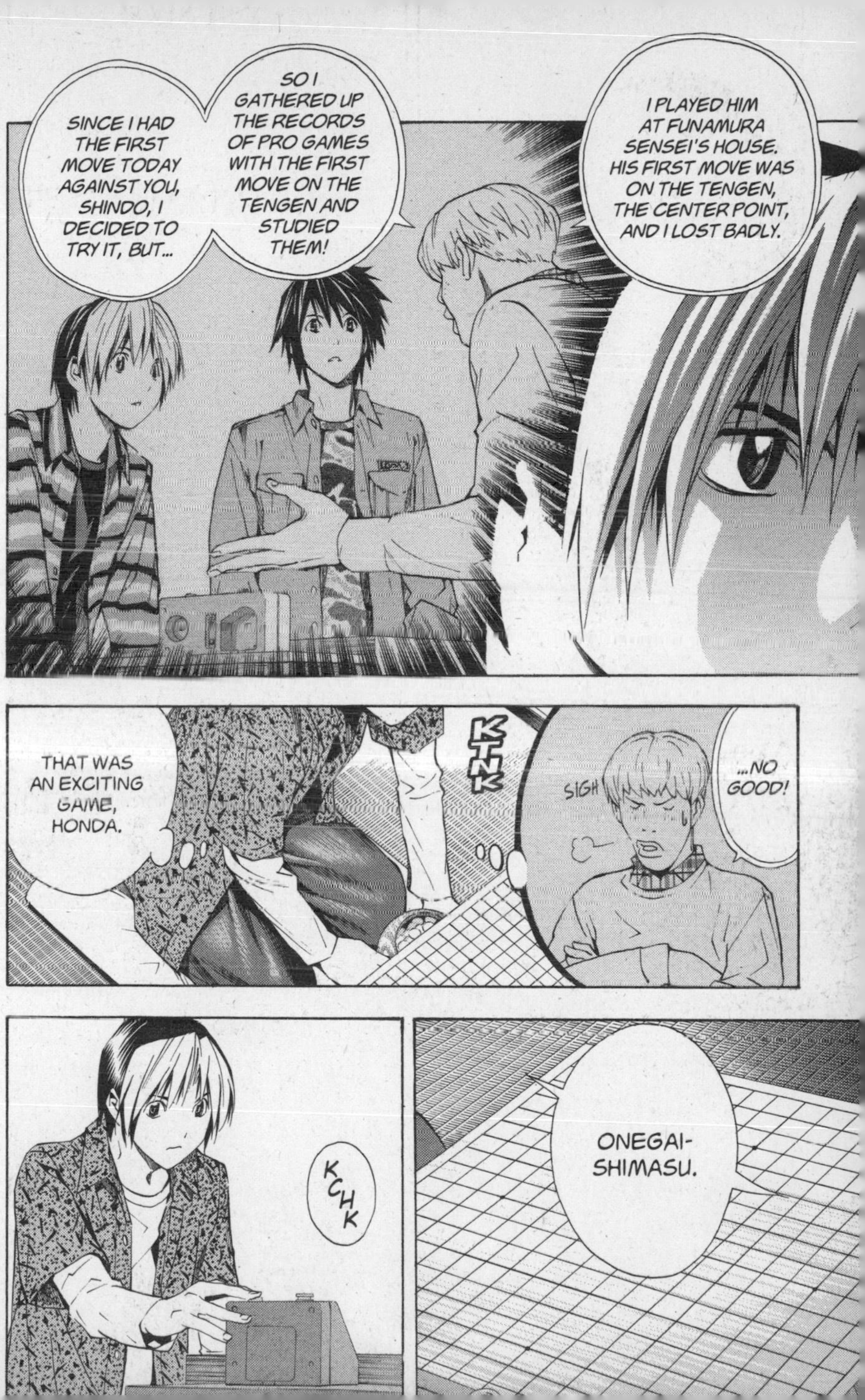
I PLAYED HIM AT FUNAMURA SENSEI'S HOUSE. HIS FIRST MOVE WAS ON THE TENGEN, THE CENTER POINT, AND I LOST BADLY.
SO I GATHERED UP THE RECORDS OF PRO GAMES WITH THE FIRST MOVE ON THE TENGEN AND STUDIED THEM!
SINCE I HAD THE FIRST MOVE TODAY AGAINST YOU, SHINDO, I DECIDED TO TRY IT, BUT...
...NO GOOD!
SIGH
KTNK
THAT WAS AN EXCITING GAME, HONDA.
ONEGAI-SHIMASU.
KCHK

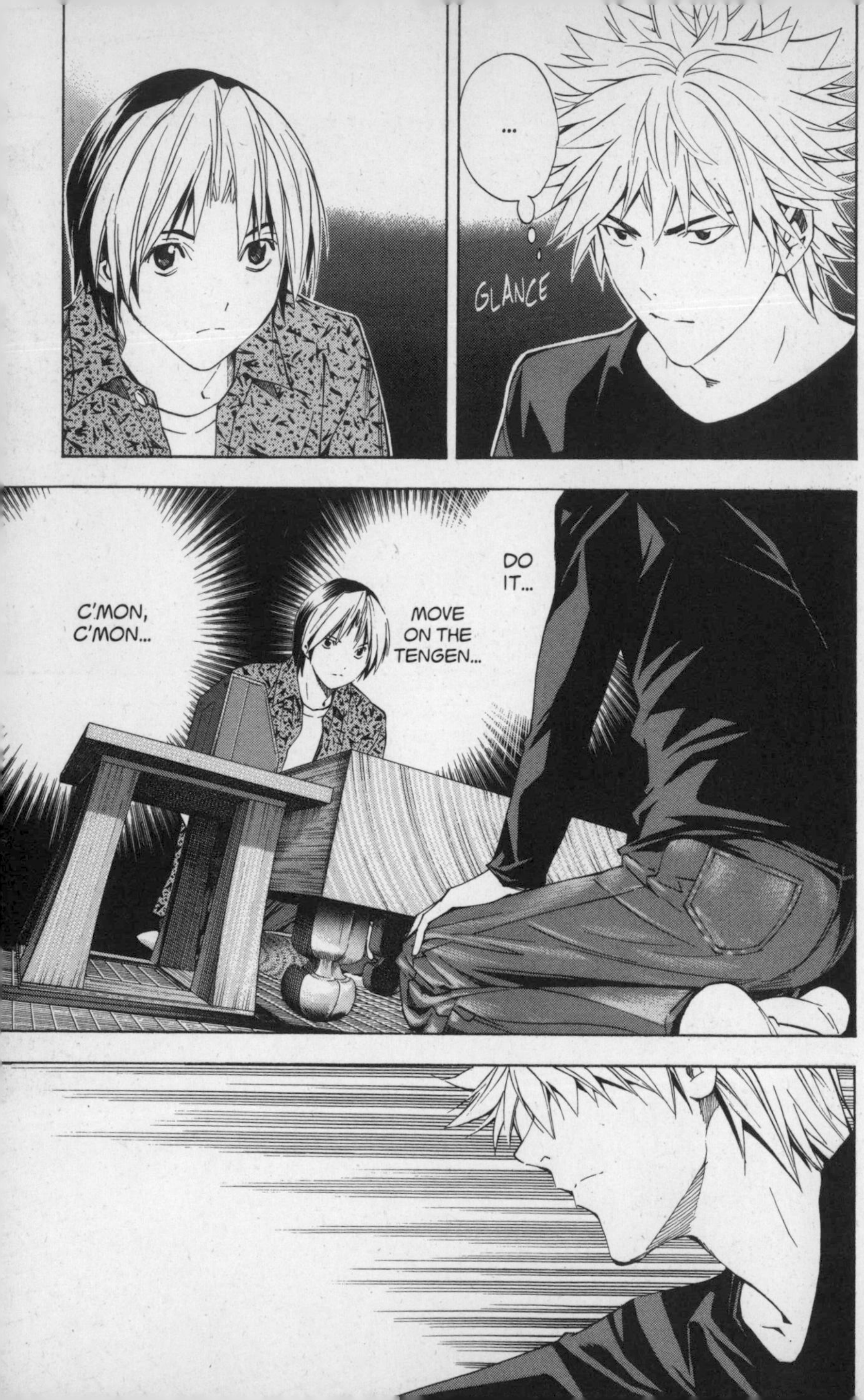
...
GLANCE
DO IT...
MOVE ON THE TENGEN...
C'MON, C'MON...

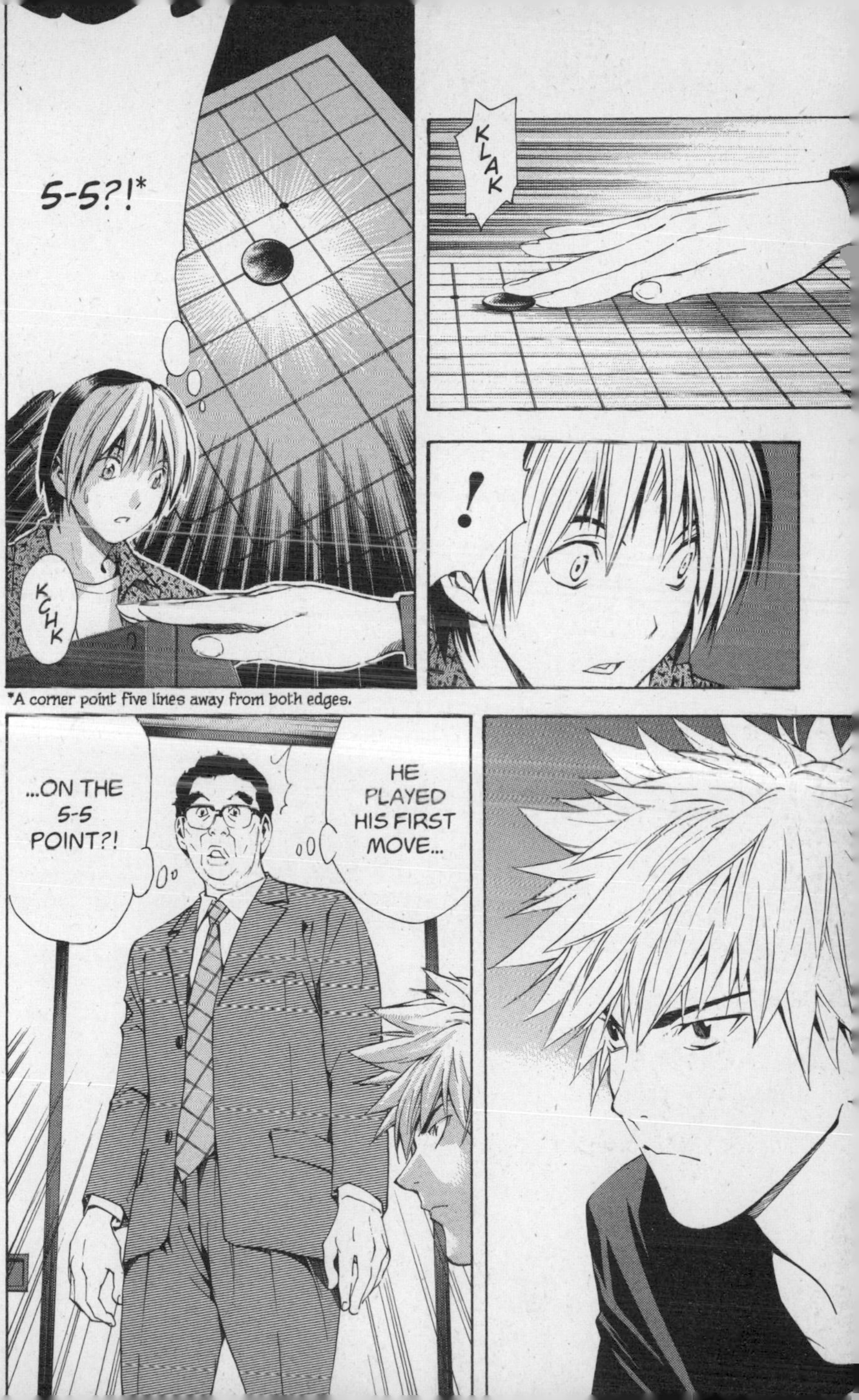
KLAK
!
5-5?!*
KCHK
HE PLAYED HIS FIRST MOVE...
...ON THE 5-5 POINT?!
*A corner point five lines away from both edges.

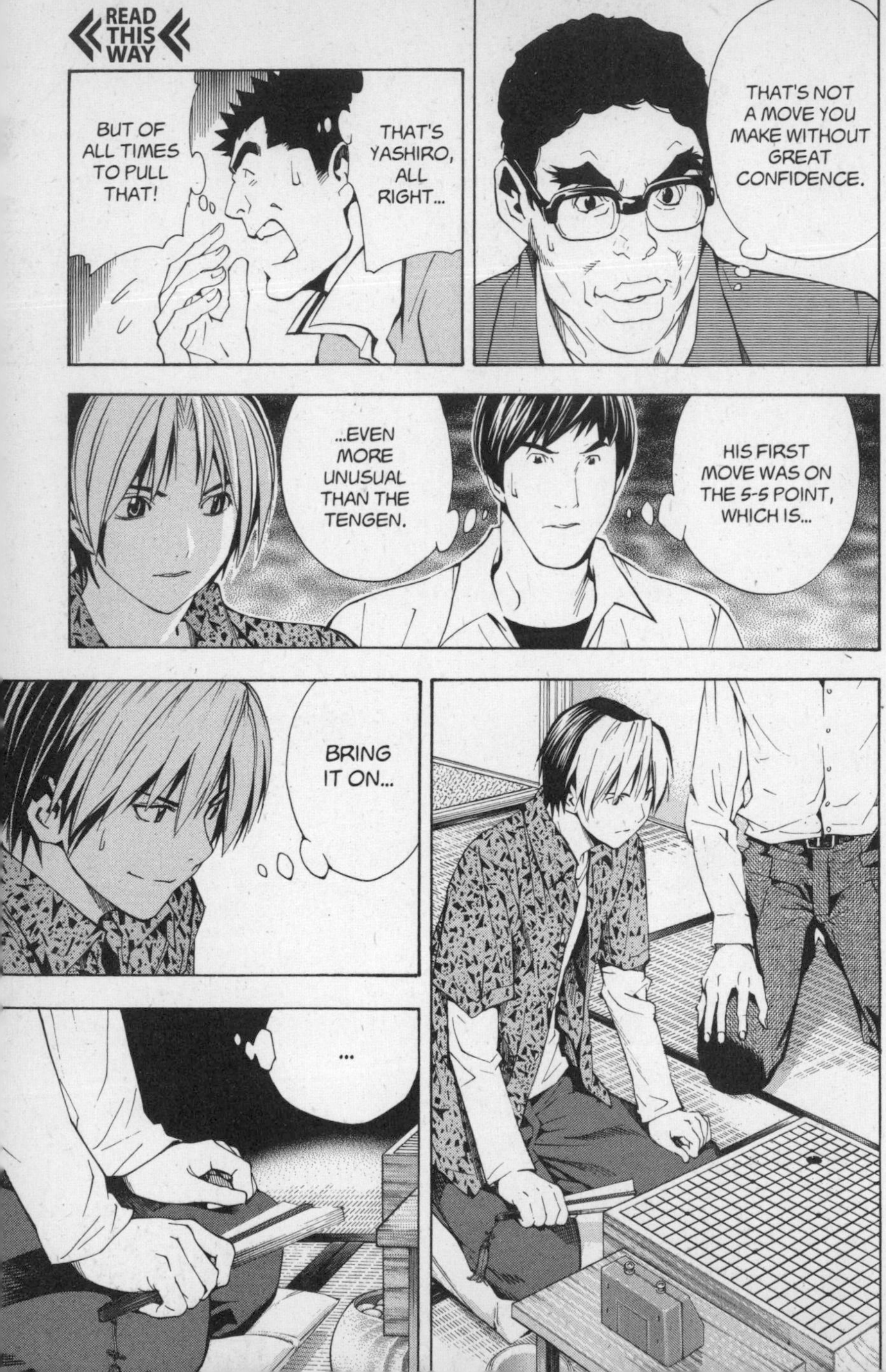
READ THIS WAY
THAT'S NOT A MOVE YOU MAKE WITHOUT GREAT CONFIDENCE.
THAT'S YASHIRO, ALL RIGHT...
BUT OF ALL TIMES TO PULL THAT!
HIS FIRST MOVE WAS ON THE 5-5 POINT, WHICH IS...
...EVEN MORE UNUSUAL THAN THE TENGEN.
BRING IT ON...
...

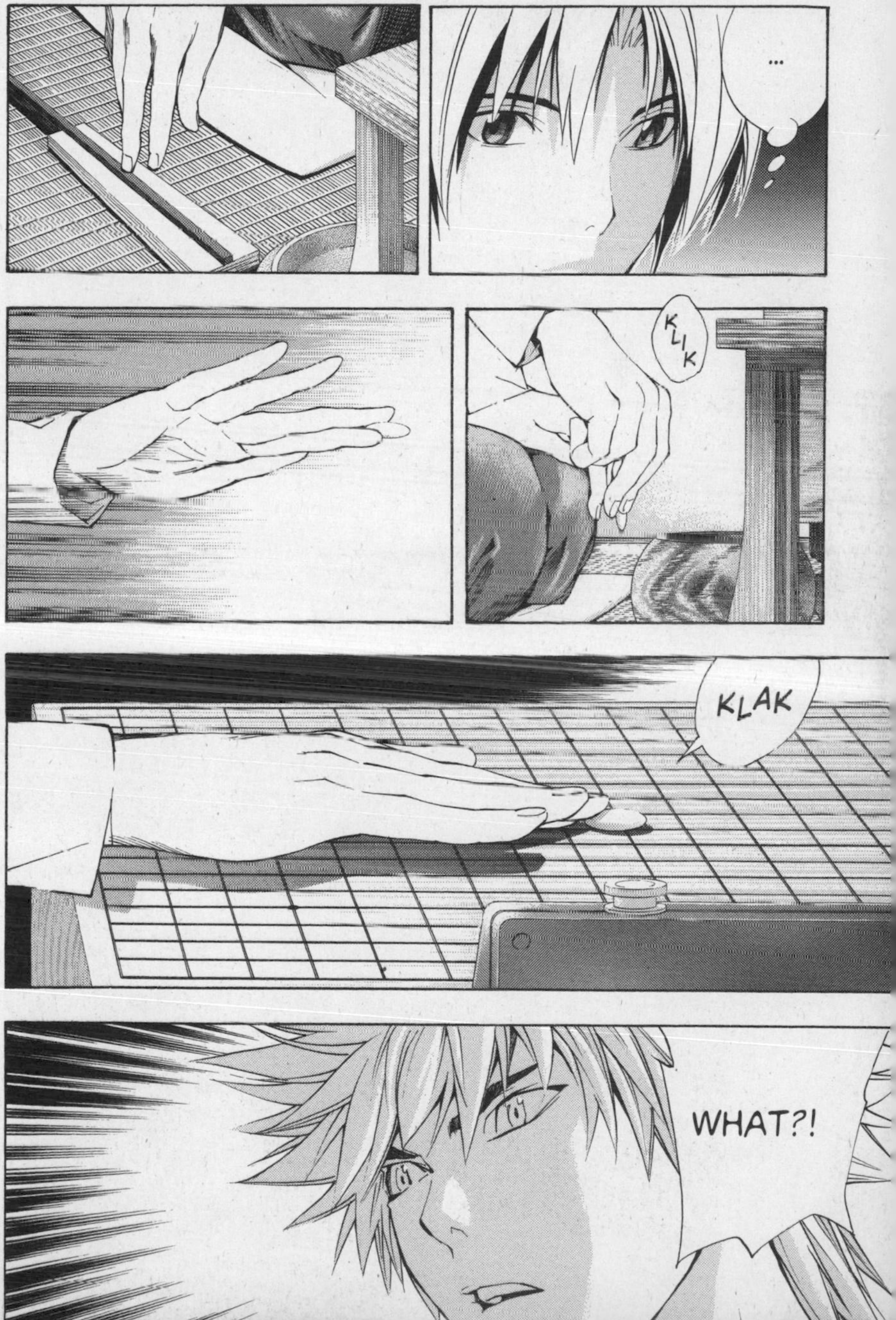
...
KLIK
KLAK
WHAT?!

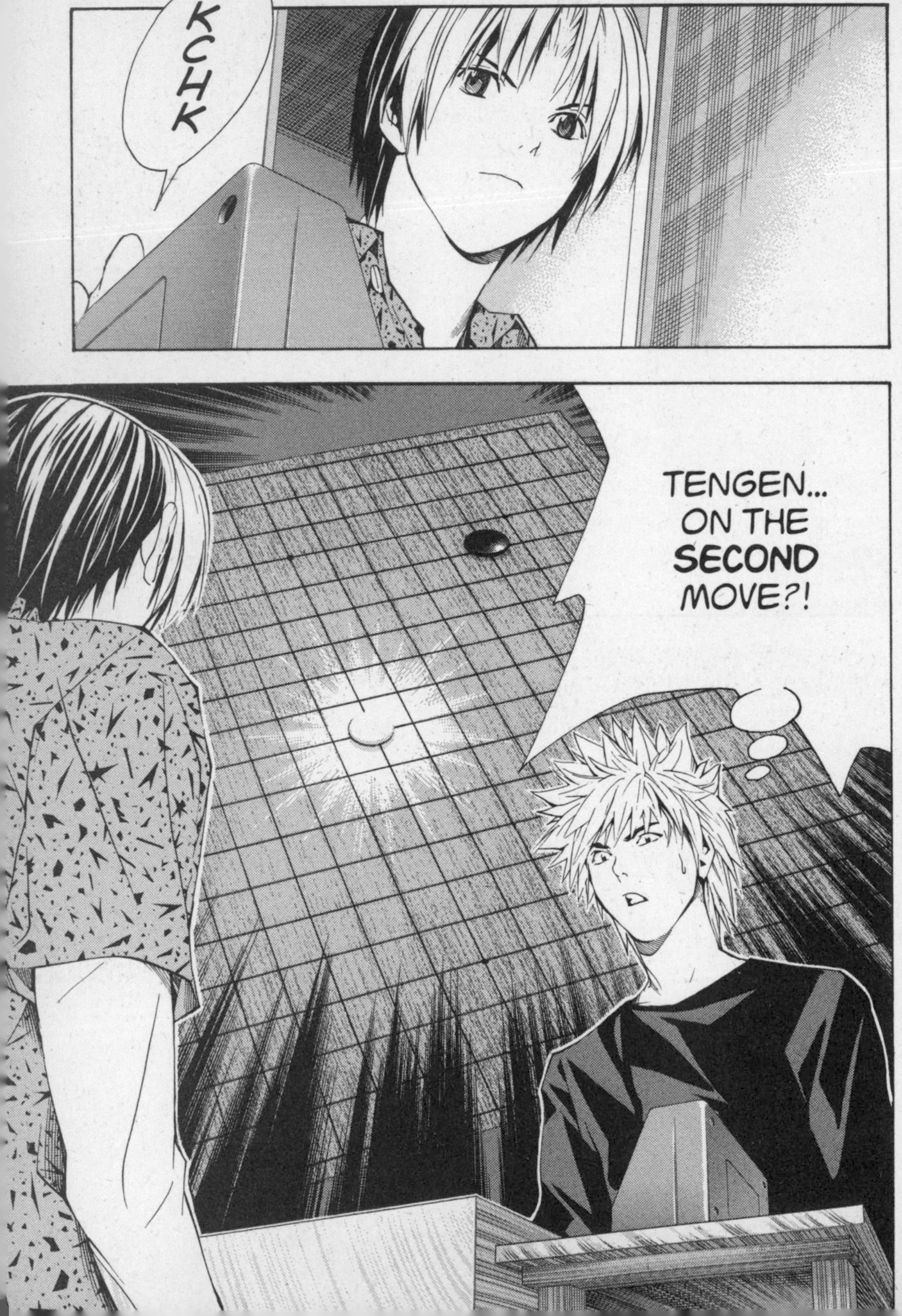
KCHK
TENGEN... ON THE SECOND MOVE?!

A WORD ABOUT HIKARU NO GO

THE SYSTEM OF TOURNAMENT MATCHES ③

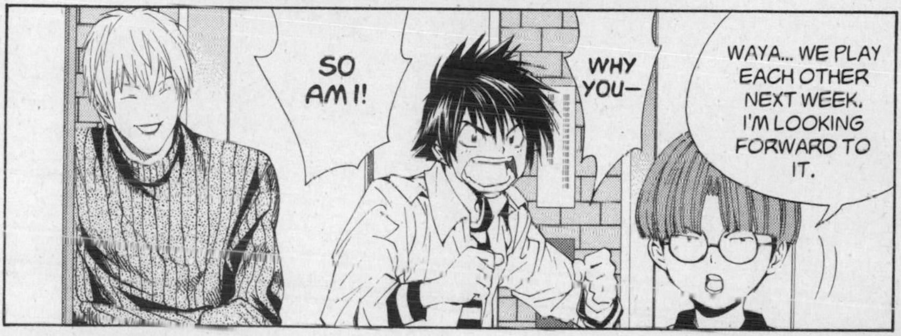
WAYA... WE PLAY EACH OTHER NEXT WEEK. I'M LOOKING FORWARD TO IT.
WHY YOU—
SO AM I!

IN MANY TOURNAMENTS IT TAKES ABOUT A YEAR TO GO FROM THE FIRST ROUND TO THE FINALS. BUT WITH THE SEVEN MAJOR TITLES IT TAKES ABOUT A YEAR AND A HALF TO TWO YEARS. THAT'S WHY THE PRELIMINARIES FOR THE FOLLOWING YEAR'S TOURNAMENT (AS WELL AS THE ONE AFTER THAT) END UP HAPPENING AT THE SAME TIME AS THE CURRENT TOURNAMENT.

AND ALL THESE TOURNAMENTS HAPPEN CONCURRENTLY, WITH DIFFERENT SYSTEMS FOR THE PRELIMINARIES IN EACH ONE.

SO WHEN READERS ASK QUESTIONS LIKE:
"HOW DO THE TOURNAMENT PRELIMINARIES HAPPEN?"
OR
"WHAT ARE THE PLAYERS' MATCH SCHEDULES LIKE?"
I REPLY...

"SORRY. IT'S BEYOND ME TO EXPLAIN IT." (HOTTA)

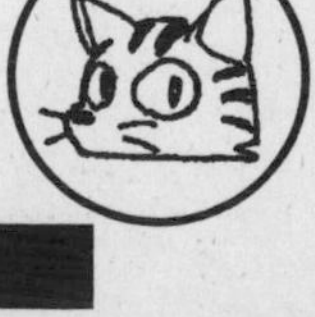

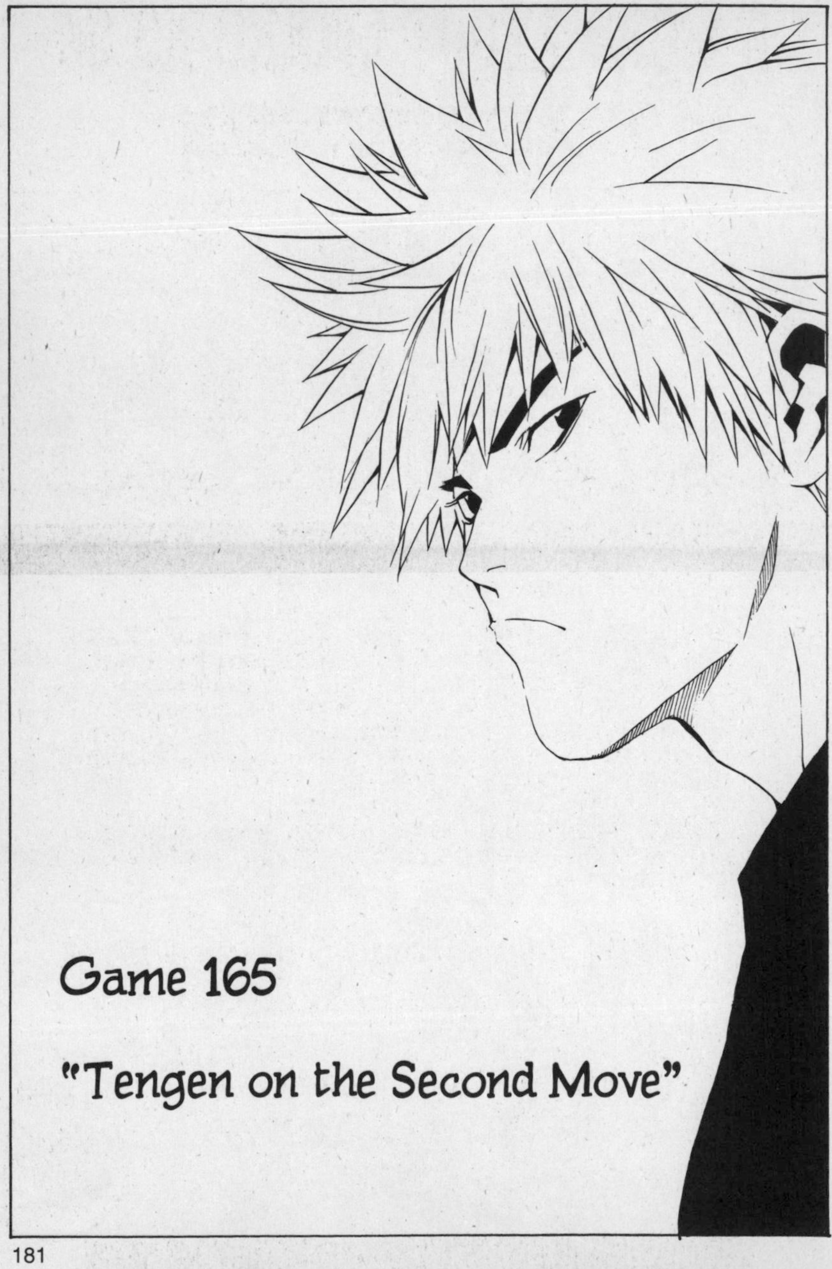

Game 165

"Tengen on the Second Move"

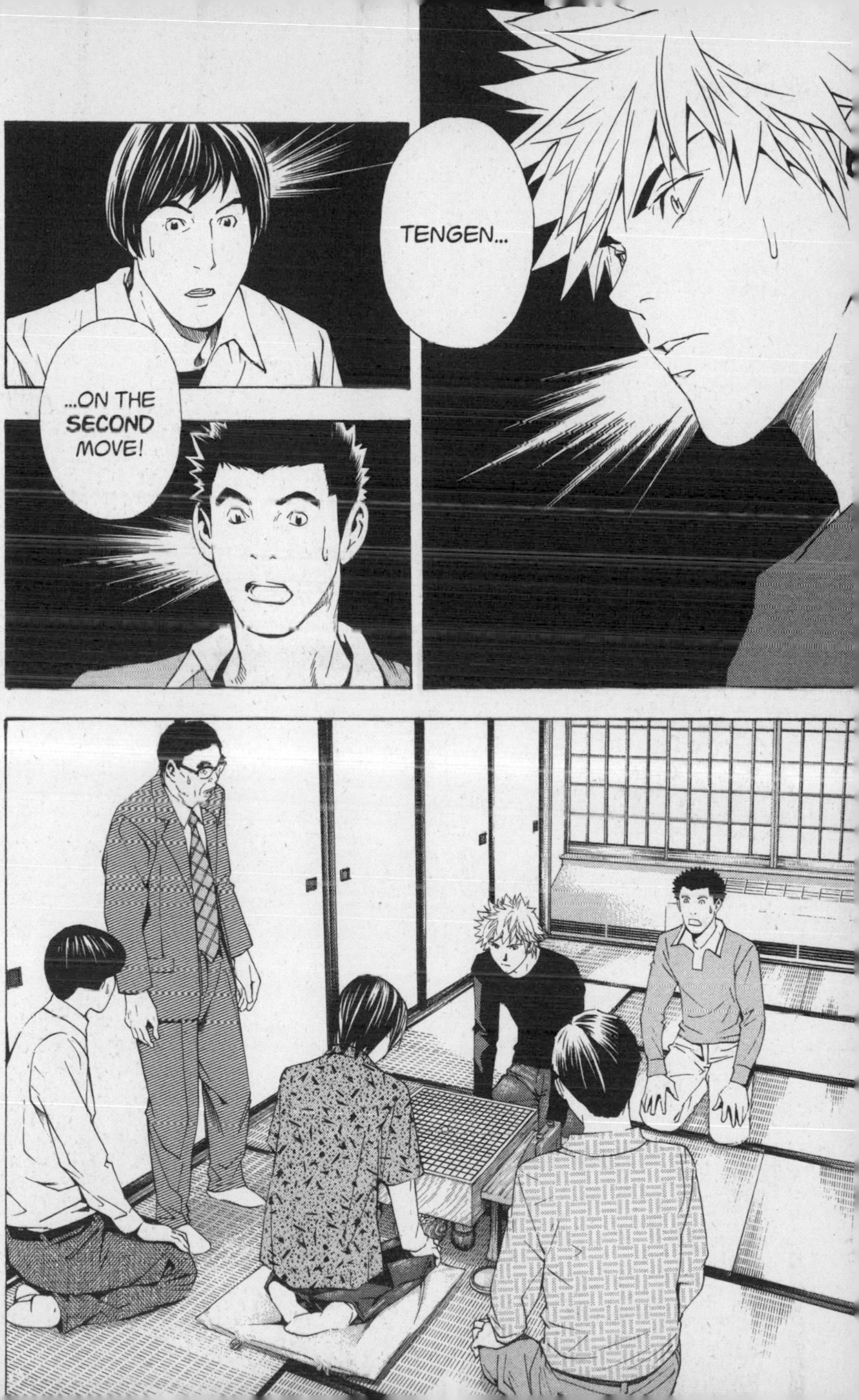
TENGEN...
...ON THE SECOND MOVE!

READ THIS WAY

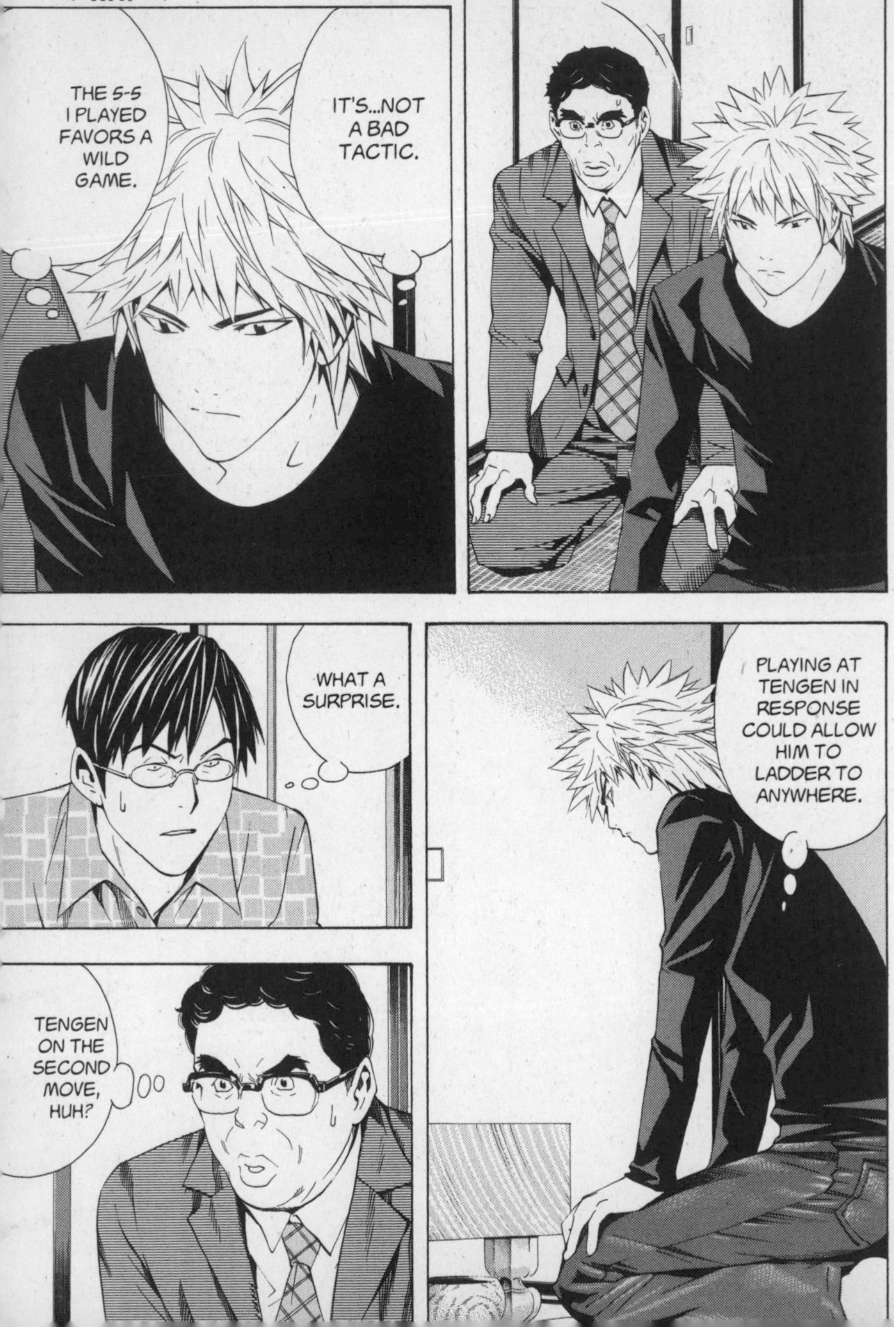
IT'S...NOT A BAD TACTIC.
THE 5-5 I PLAYED FAVORS A WILD GAME.
PLAYING AT TENGEN IN RESPONSE COULD ALLOW HIM TO LADDER TO ANYWHERE.
WHAT A SURPRISE.
TENGEN ON THE SECOND MOVE, HUH?

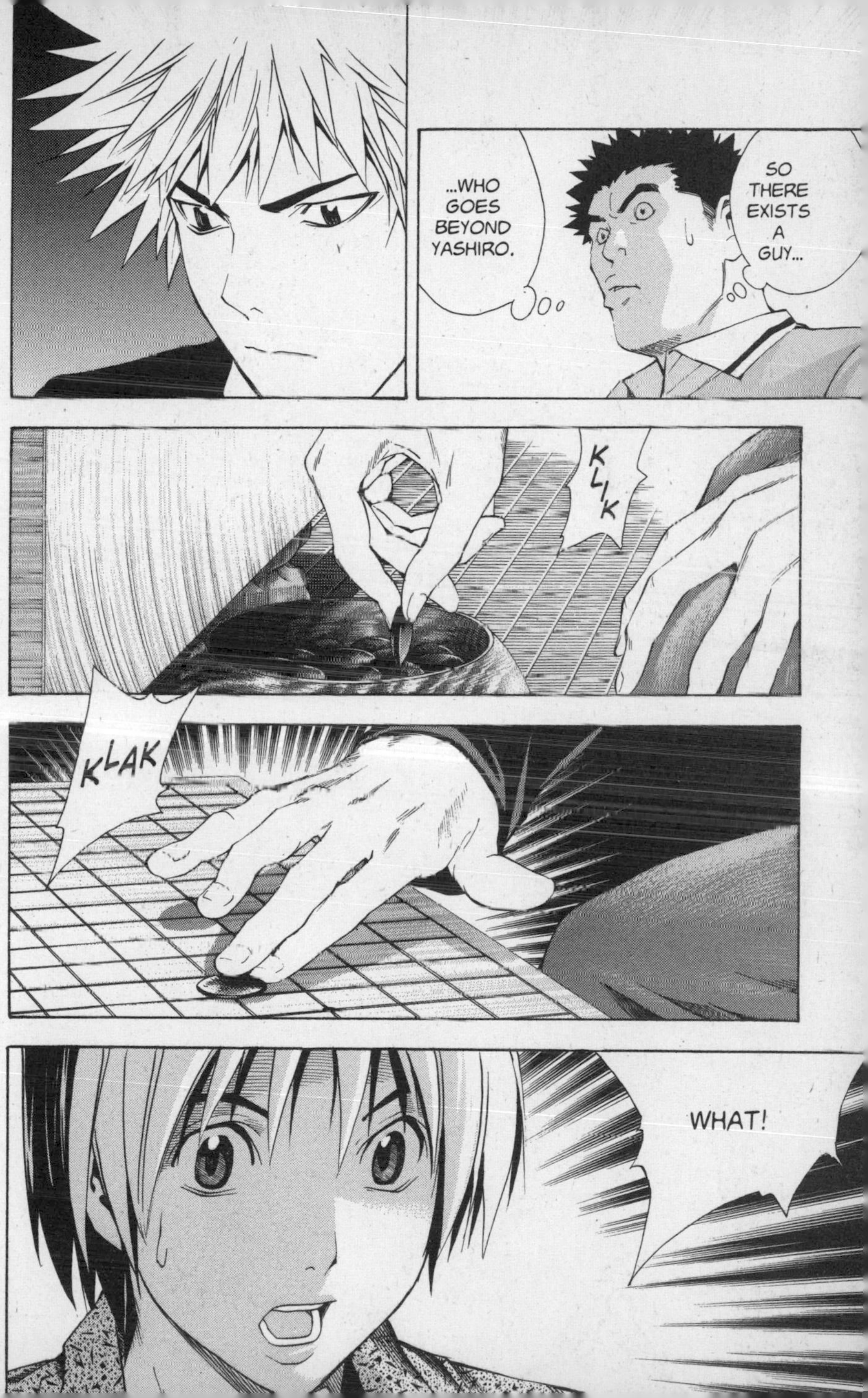
SO THERE EXISTS A GUY...
...WHO GOES BEYOND YASHIRO.
KLIK
KLAK
WHAT!

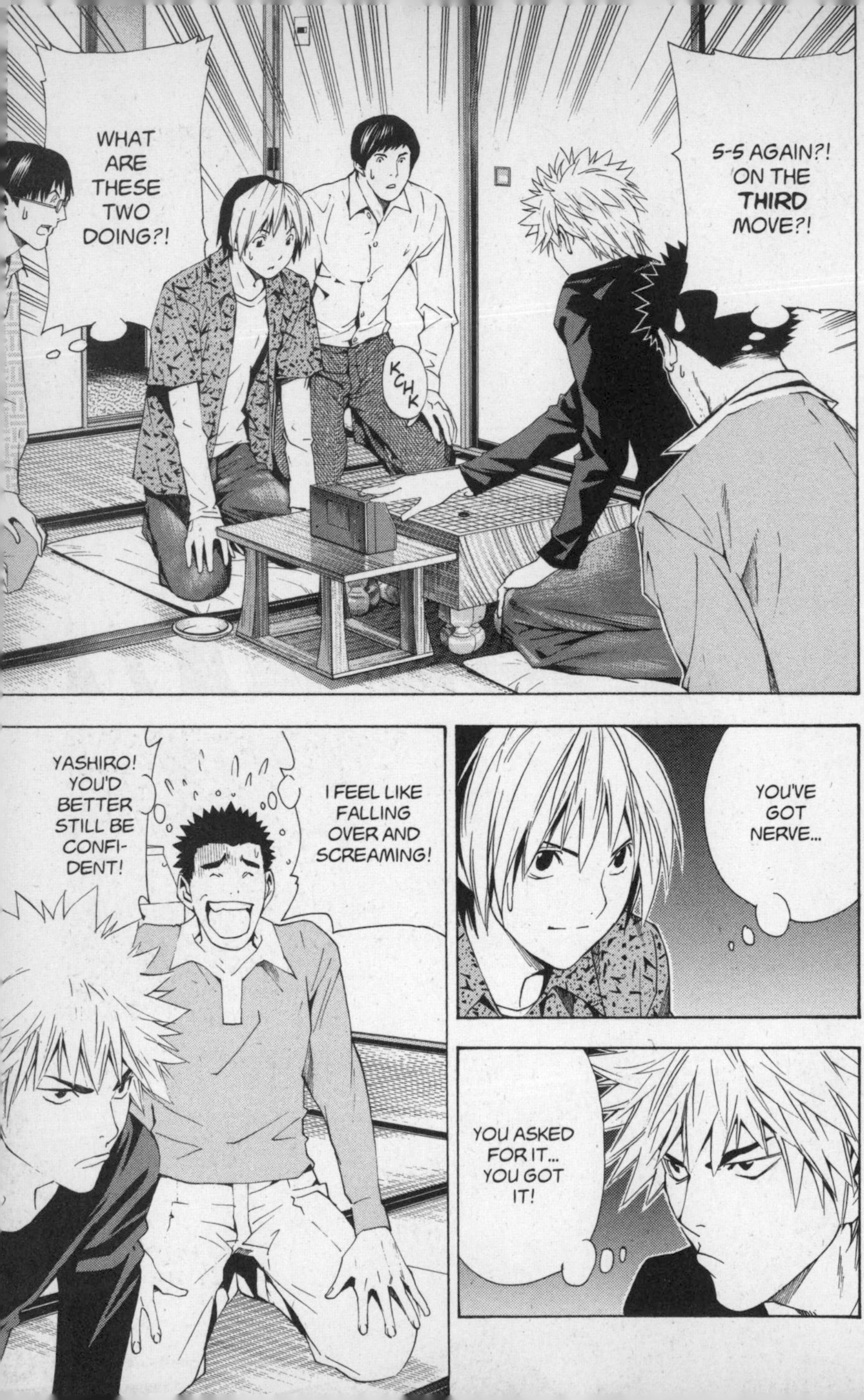
5-5 AGAIN?! ON THE **THIRD** MOVE?!
KCHK
WHAT ARE THESE TWO DOING?!
YOU'VE GOT NERVE...
YOU ASKED FOR IT... YOU GOT IT!
I FEEL LIKE FALLING OVER AND SCREAMING!
YASHIRO! YOU'D BETTER STILL BE CONFI-DENT!

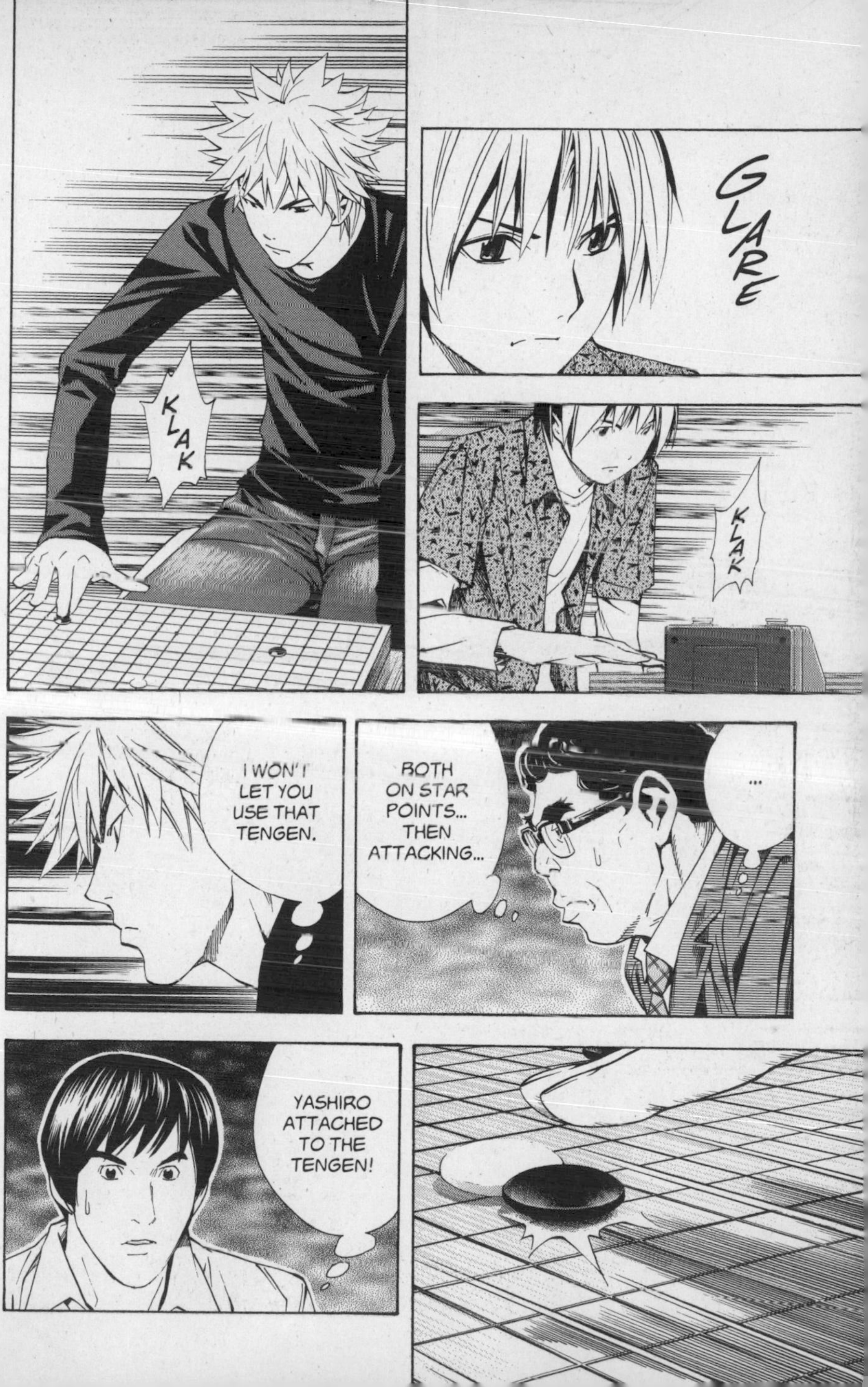
GLARE
KLAK
KLAK
...
BOTH ON STAR POINTS... THEN ATTACKING...
I WON'T LET YOU USE THAT TENGEN.
YASHIRO ATTACHED TO THE TENGEN!

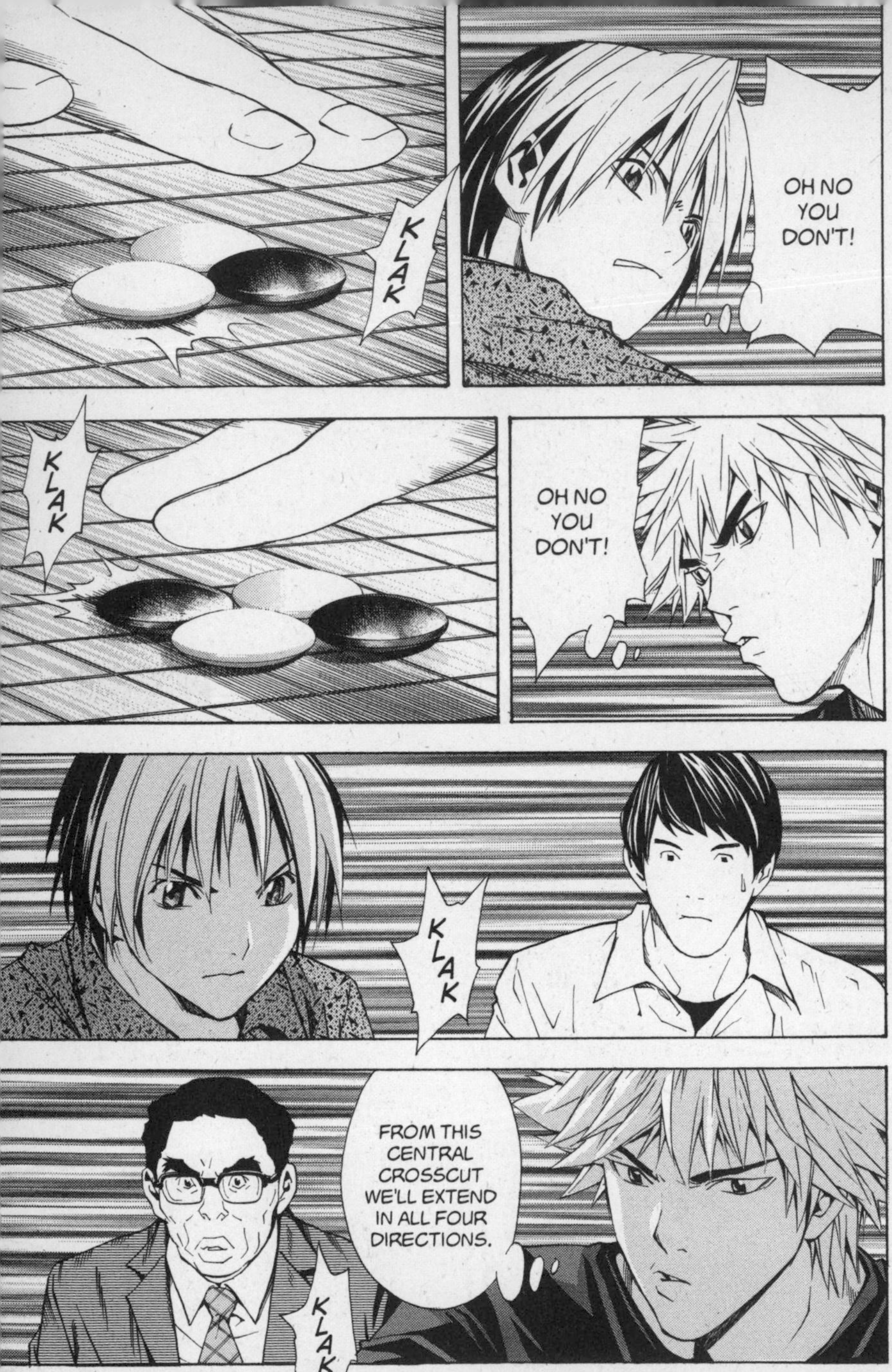
OH NO YOU DON'T!
KLAK
OH NO YOU DON'T!
KLAK
KLAK
FROM THIS CENTRAL CROSSCUT WE'LL EXTEND IN ALL FOUR DIRECTIONS.
KLAK

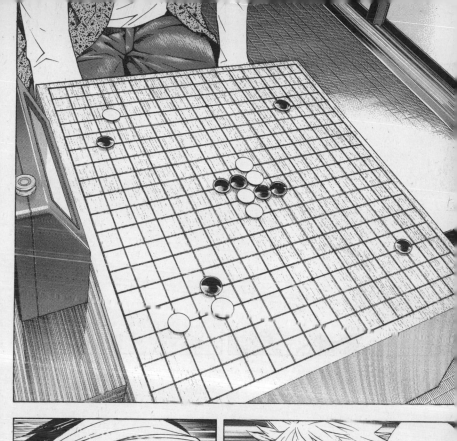

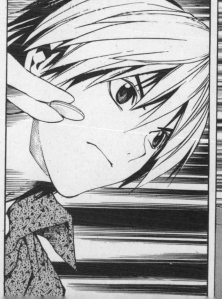

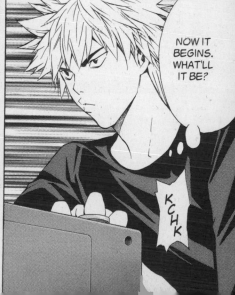

NOW IT BEGINS. WHAT'LL IT BE?

KCHK

READ THIS WAY

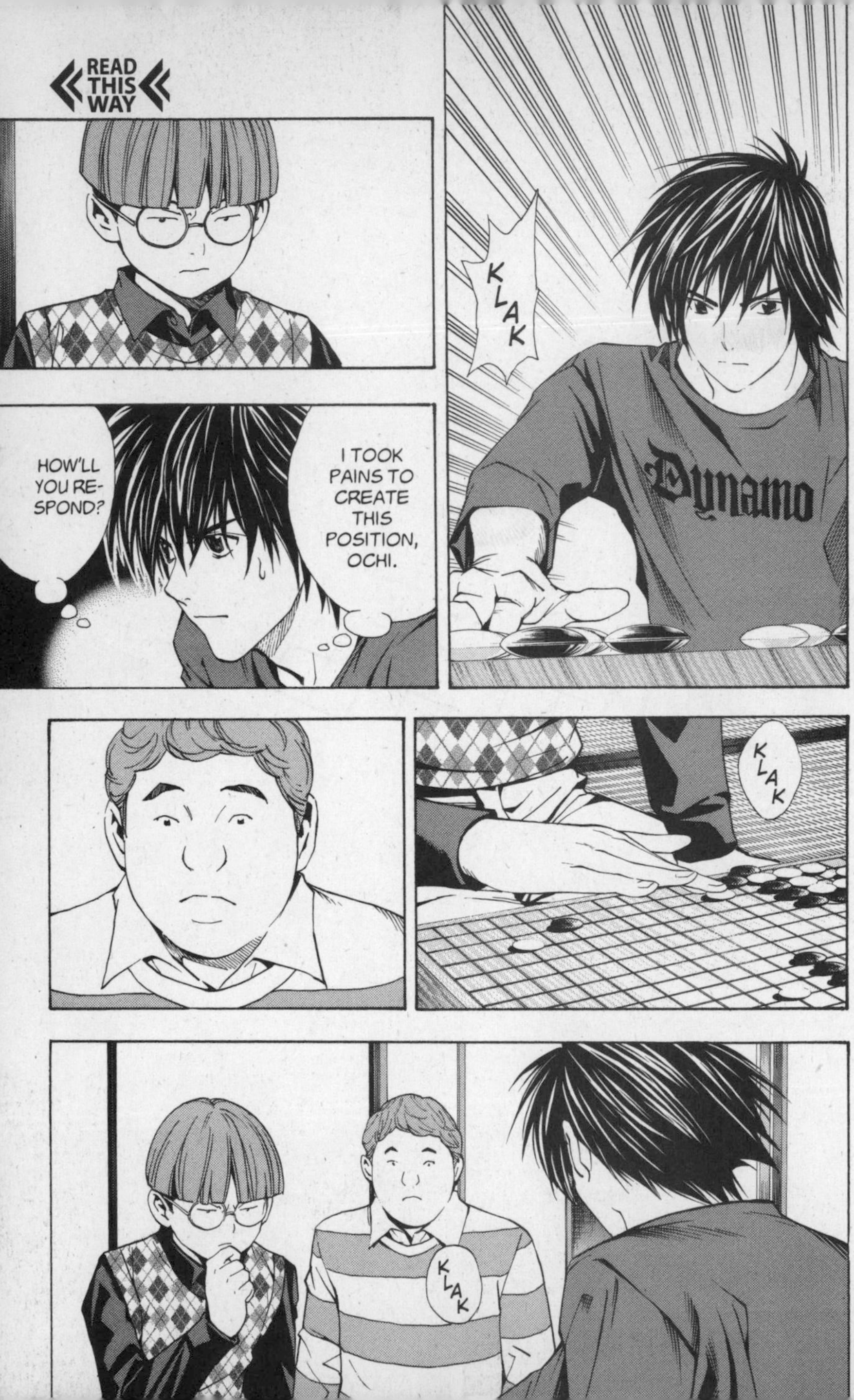
KLAK
I TOOK PAINS TO CREATE THIS POSITION, OCHI.
HOW'LL YOU RE-SPOND?
KLAK
KLAK

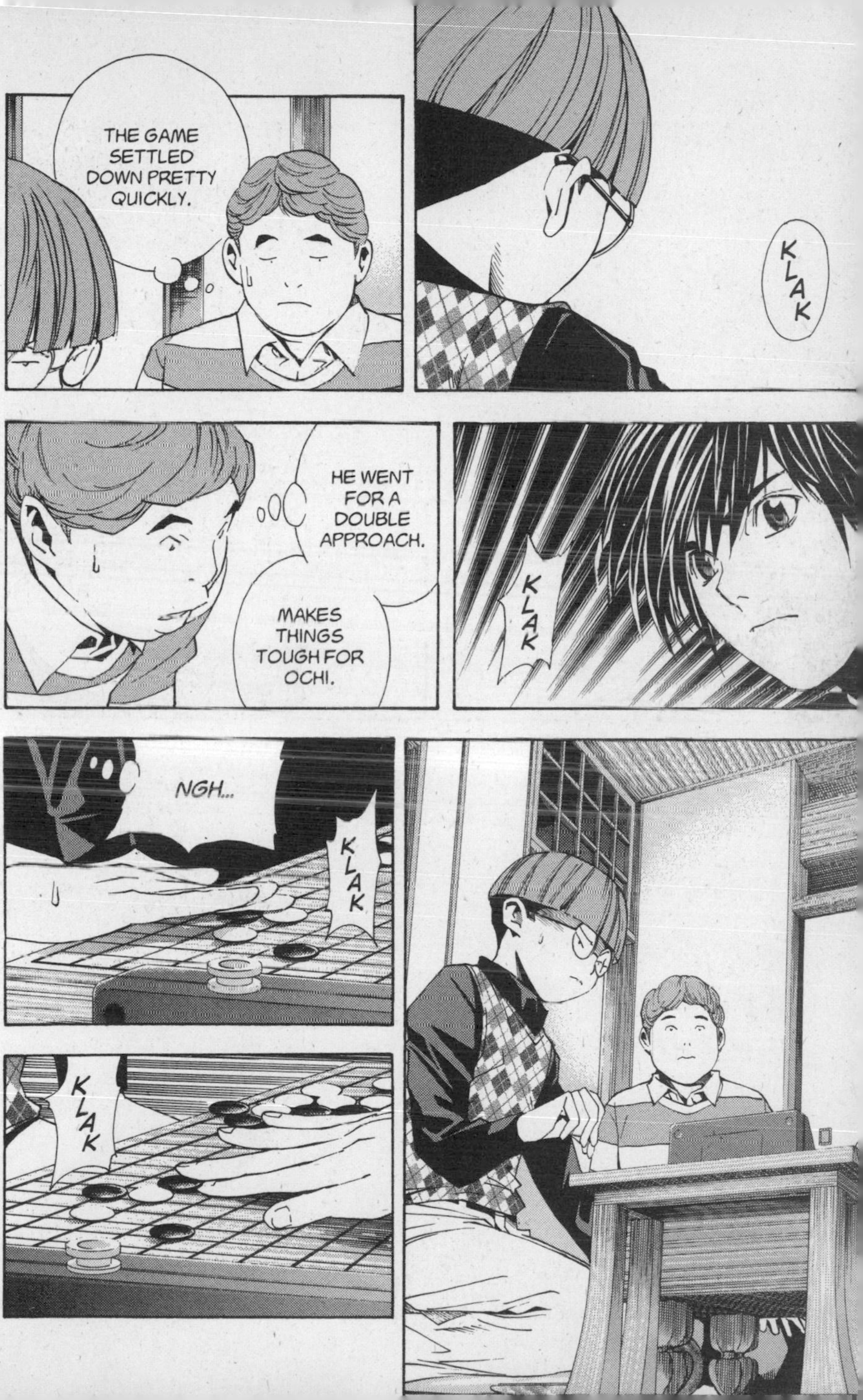
KLAK
THE GAME SETTLED DOWN PRETTY QUICKLY.
KLAK
HE WENT FOR A DOUBLE APPROACH.
MAKES THINGS TOUGH FOR OCHI.
NGH...
KLAK
KLAK

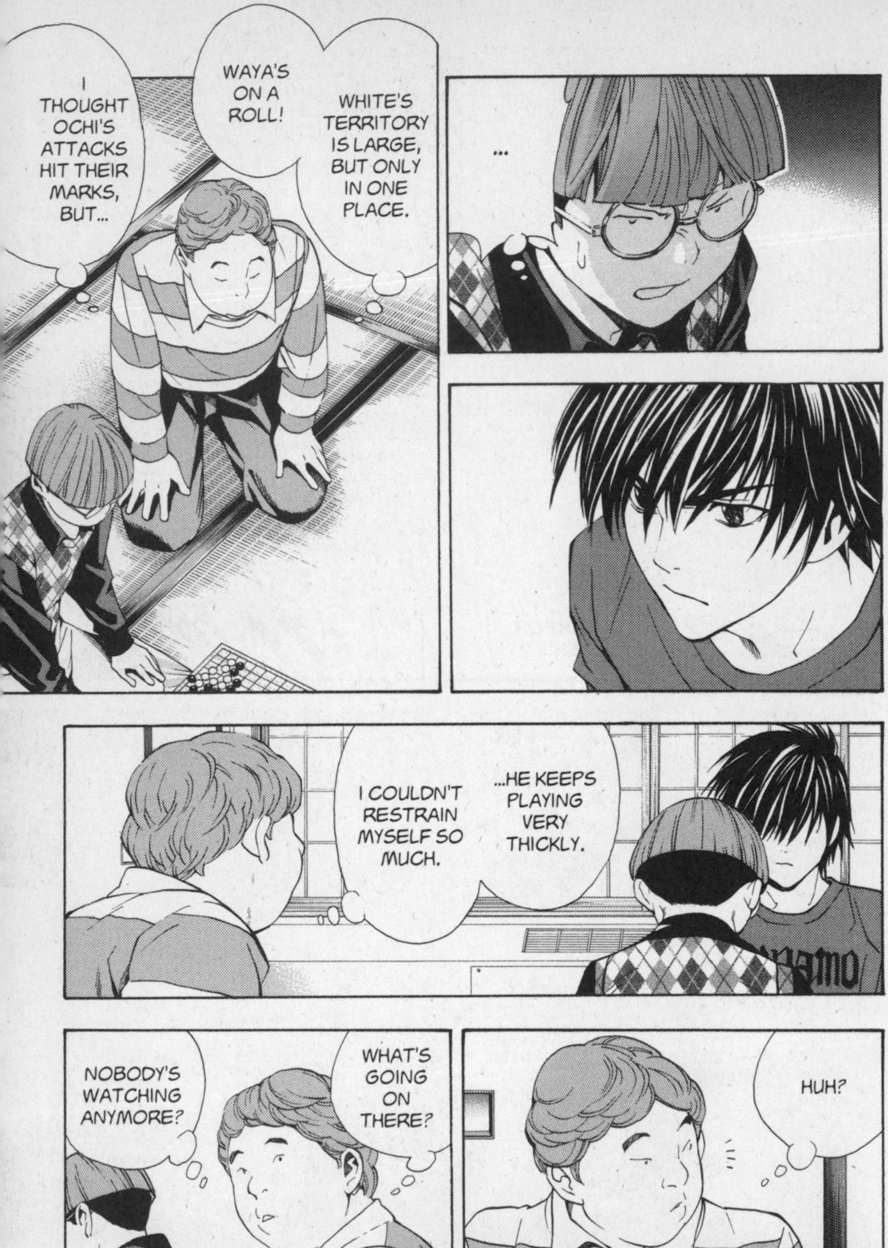
...
WHITE'S TERRITORY IS LARGE, BUT ONLY IN ONE PLACE.
WAYA'S ON A ROLL!
I THOUGHT OCHI'S ATTACKS HIT THEIR MARKS, BUT...
...HE KEEPS PLAYING VERY THICKLY.
I COULDN'T RESTRAIN MYSELF SO MUCH.
HUH?
WHAT'S GOING ON THERE?
NOBODY'S WATCHING ANYMORE?

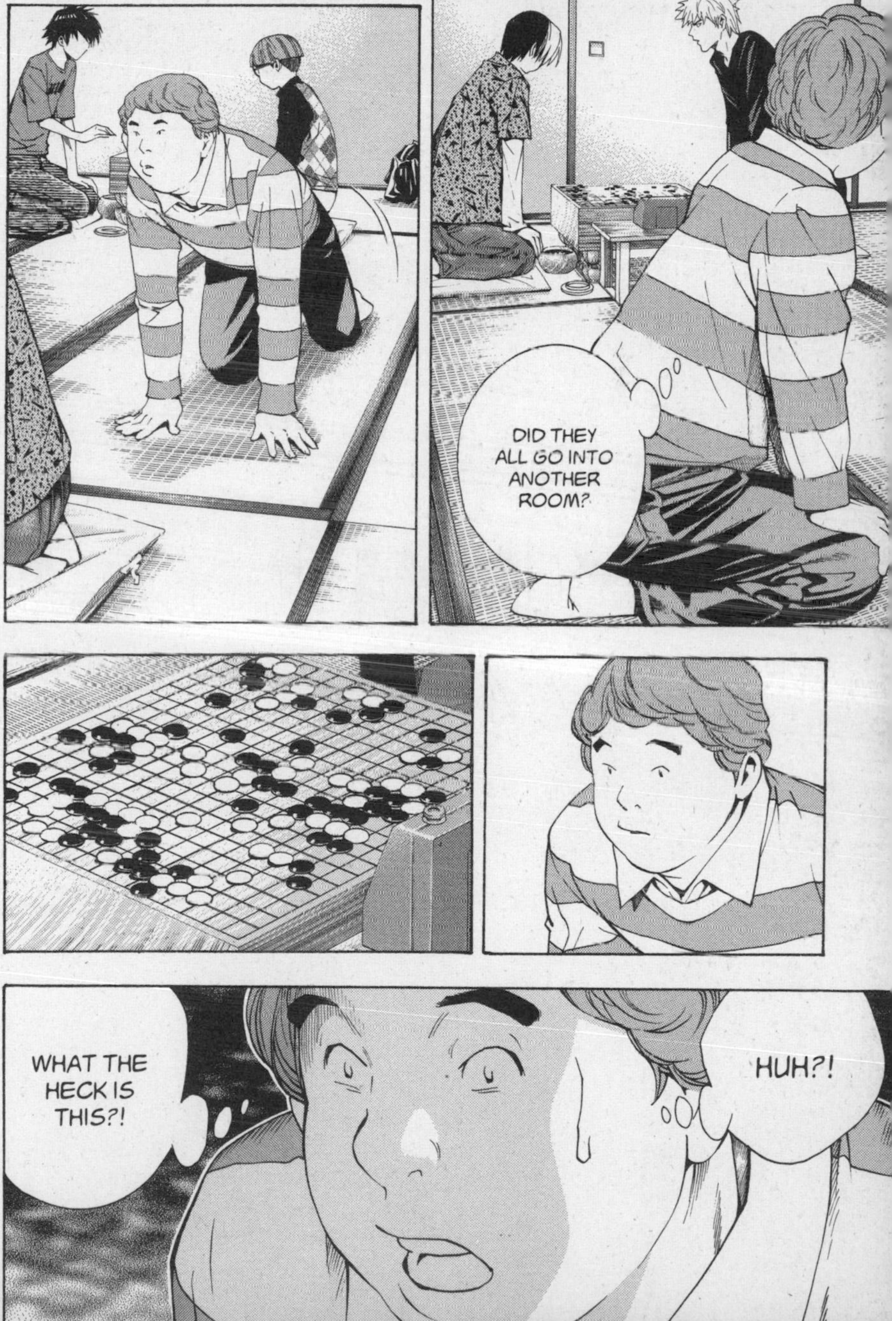
DID THEY ALL GO INTO ANOTHER ROOM?
HUH?!
WHAT THE HECK IS THIS?!

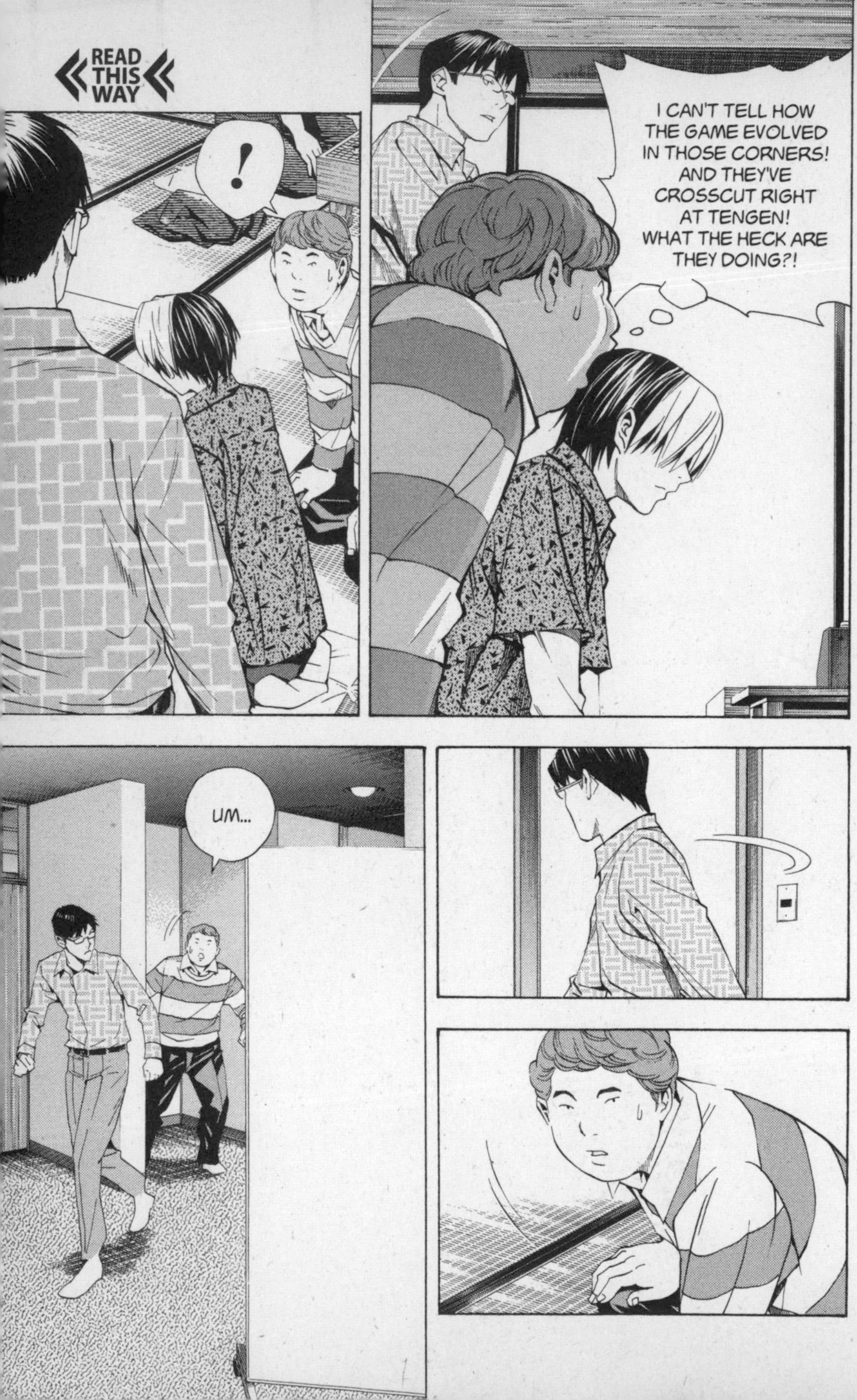
READ THIS WAY
I CAN'T TELL HOW THE GAME EVOLVED IN THOSE CORNERS! AND THEY'VE CROSSCUT RIGHT AT TENGEN! WHAT THE HECK ARE THEY DOING?!
!
UM...

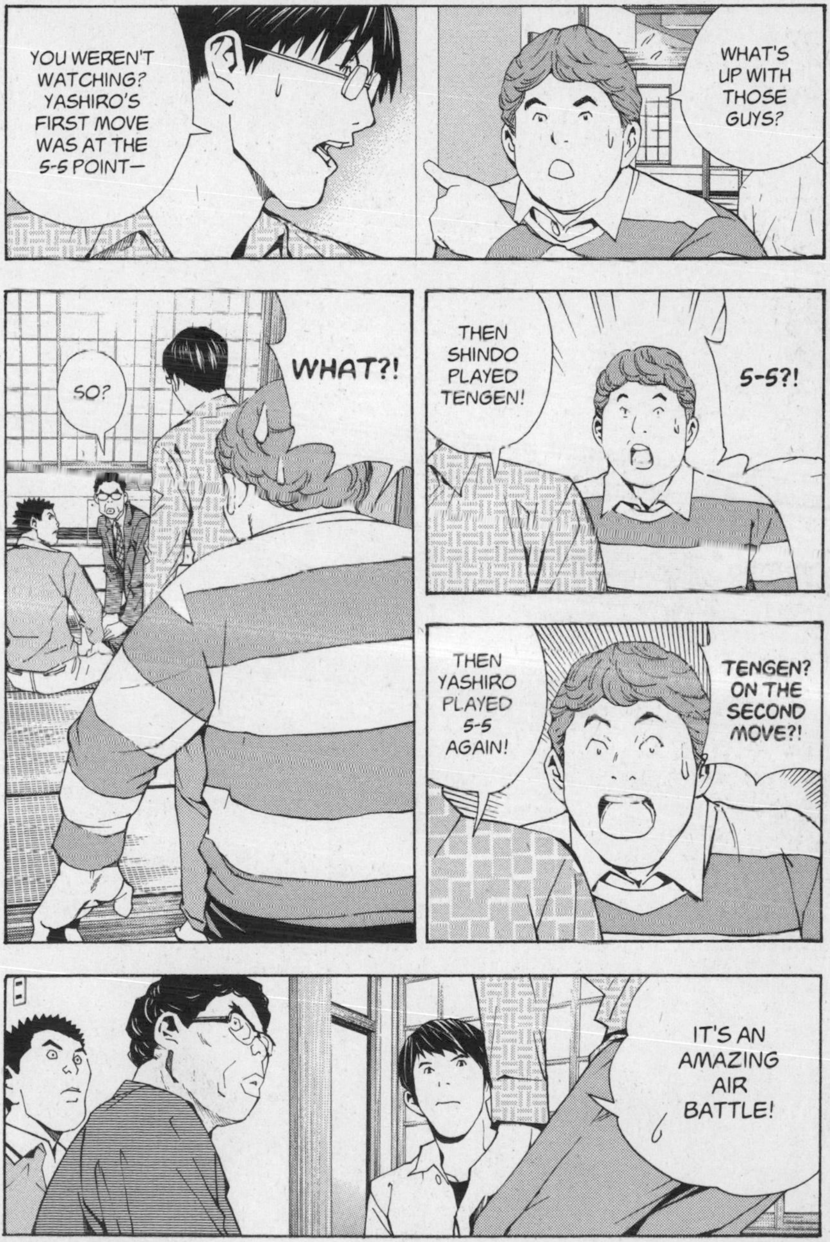
WHAT'S UP WITH THOSE GUYS?
YOU WEREN'T WATCHING? YASHIRO'S FIRST MOVE WAS AT THE 5-5 POINT—
5-5?!
THEN SHINDO PLAYED TENGEN!
TENGEN? ON THE SECOND MOVE?!
THEN YASHIRO PLAYED 5-5 AGAIN!
WHAT?!
SO?
IT'S AN AMAZING AIR BATTLE!

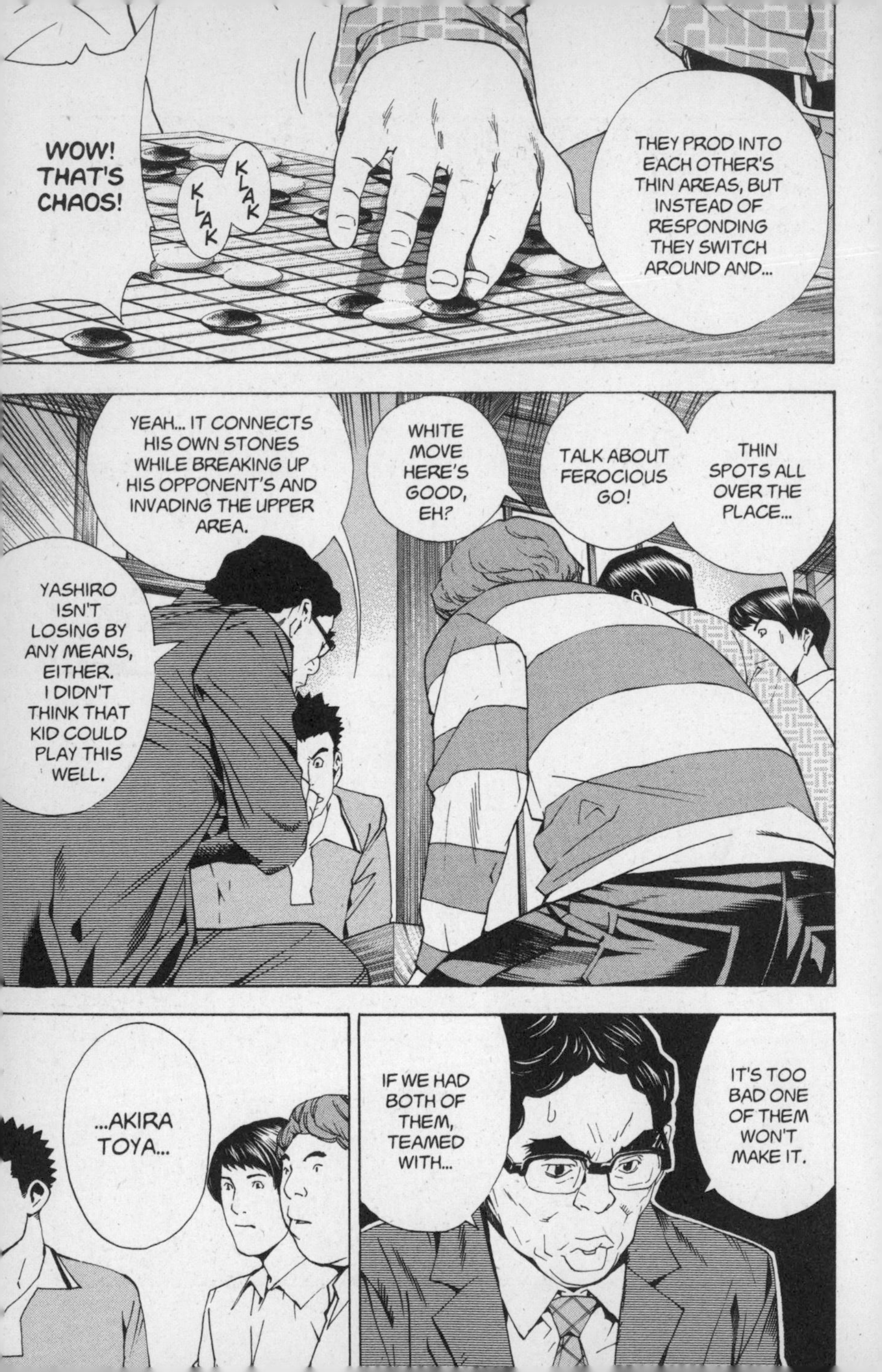
THEY PROD INTO EACH OTHER'S THIN AREAS, BUT INSTEAD OF RESPONDING THEY SWITCH AROUND AND...
KLAK KLAK
WOW! THAT'S CHAOS!
THIN SPOTS ALL OVER THE PLACE...
TALK ABOUT FEROCIOUS GO!
WHITE MOVE HERE'S GOOD, EH?
YEAH... IT CONNECTS HIS OWN STONES WHILE BREAKING UP HIS OPPONENT'S AND INVADING THE UPPER AREA.
YASHIRO ISN'T LOSING BY ANY MEANS, EITHER. I DIDN'T THINK THAT KID COULD PLAY THIS WELL.
IT'S TOO BAD ONE OF THEM WON'T MAKE IT.
IF WE HAD BOTH OF THEM, TEAMED WITH...
...AKIRA TOYA...

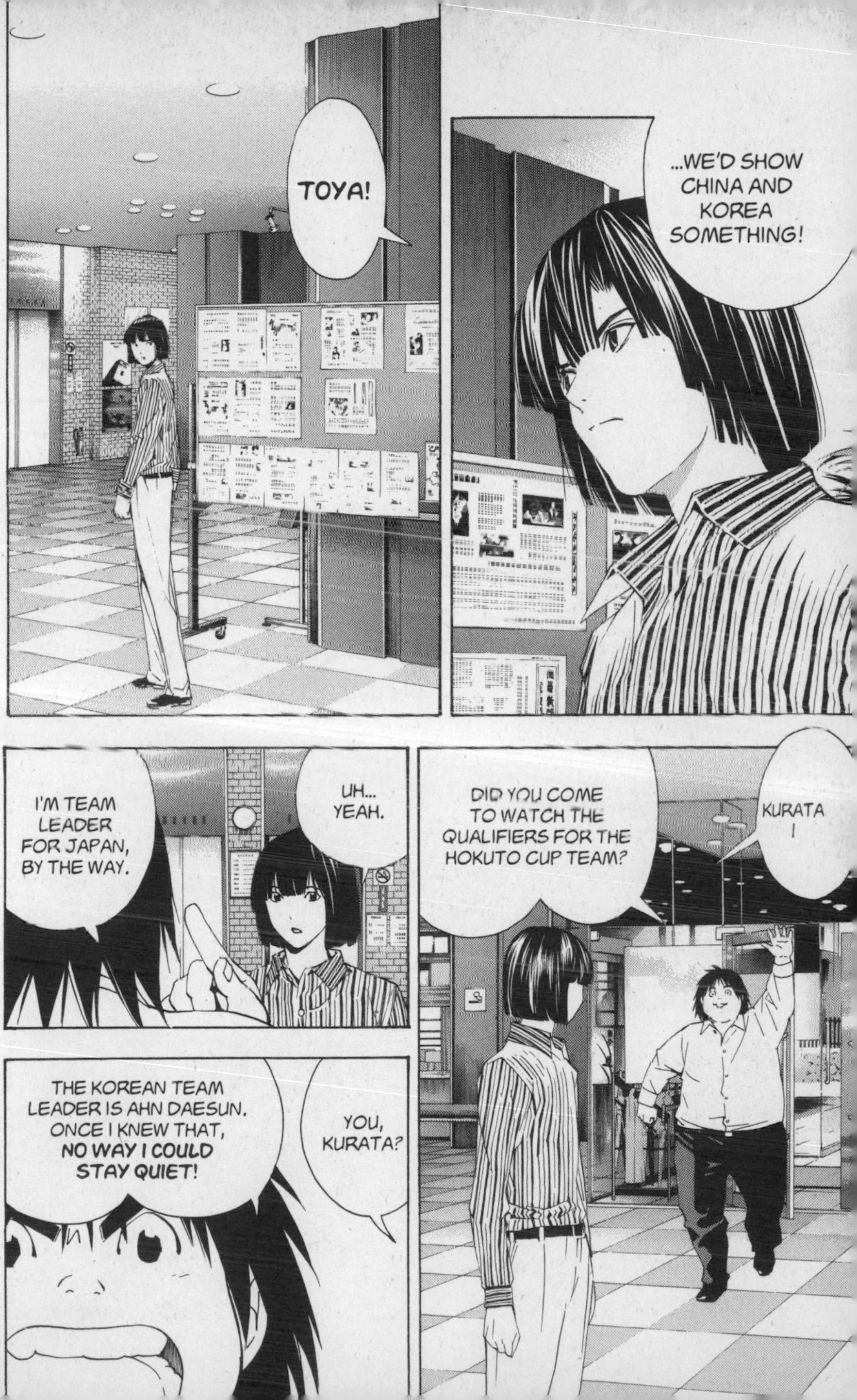
...WE'D SHOW CHINA AND KOREA SOMETHING!
TOYA!
KURATA!
DID YOU COME TO WATCH THE QUALIFIERS FOR THE HOKUTO CUP TEAM?
UH... YEAH.
I'M TEAM LEADER FOR JAPAN, BY THE WAY.
YOU, KURATA?
THE KOREAN TEAM LEADER IS AHN DAESUN. ONCE I KNEW THAT, **NO WAY I COULD STAY QUIET!**

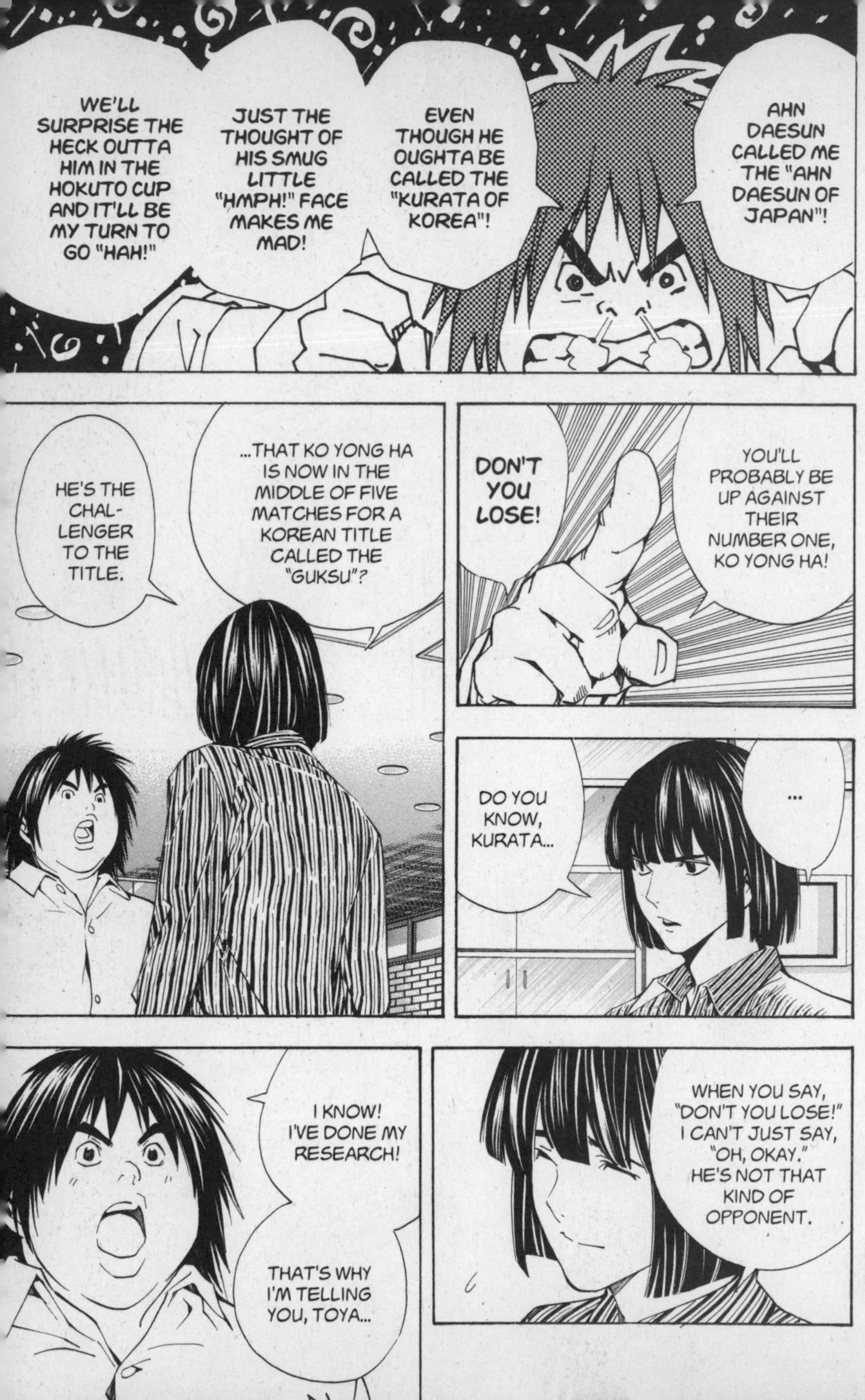
AHN DAESUN CALLED ME THE "AHN DAESUN OF JAPAN"!
EVEN THOUGH HE OUGHTA BE CALLED THE "KURATA OF KOREA"!
JUST THE THOUGHT OF HIS SMUG LITTLE "HMPH!" FACE MAKES ME MAD!
WE'LL SURPRISE THE HECK OUTTA HIM IN THE HOKUTO CUP AND IT'LL BE MY TURN TO GO "HAH!"
YOU'LL PROBABLY BE UP AGAINST THEIR NUMBER ONE, KO YONG HA!
DON'T YOU LOSE!
...
DO YOU KNOW, KURATA...
...THAT KO YONG HA IS NOW IN THE MIDDLE OF FIVE MATCHES FOR A KOREAN TITLE CALLED THE "GUKSU"?
HE'S THE CHAL-LENGER TO THE TITLE.
WHEN YOU SAY, "DON'T YOU LOSE!" I CAN'T JUST SAY, "OH, OKAY." HE'S NOT THAT KIND OF OPPONENT.
I KNOW! I'VE DONE MY RESEARCH!
THAT'S WHY I'M TELLING YOU, TOYA...

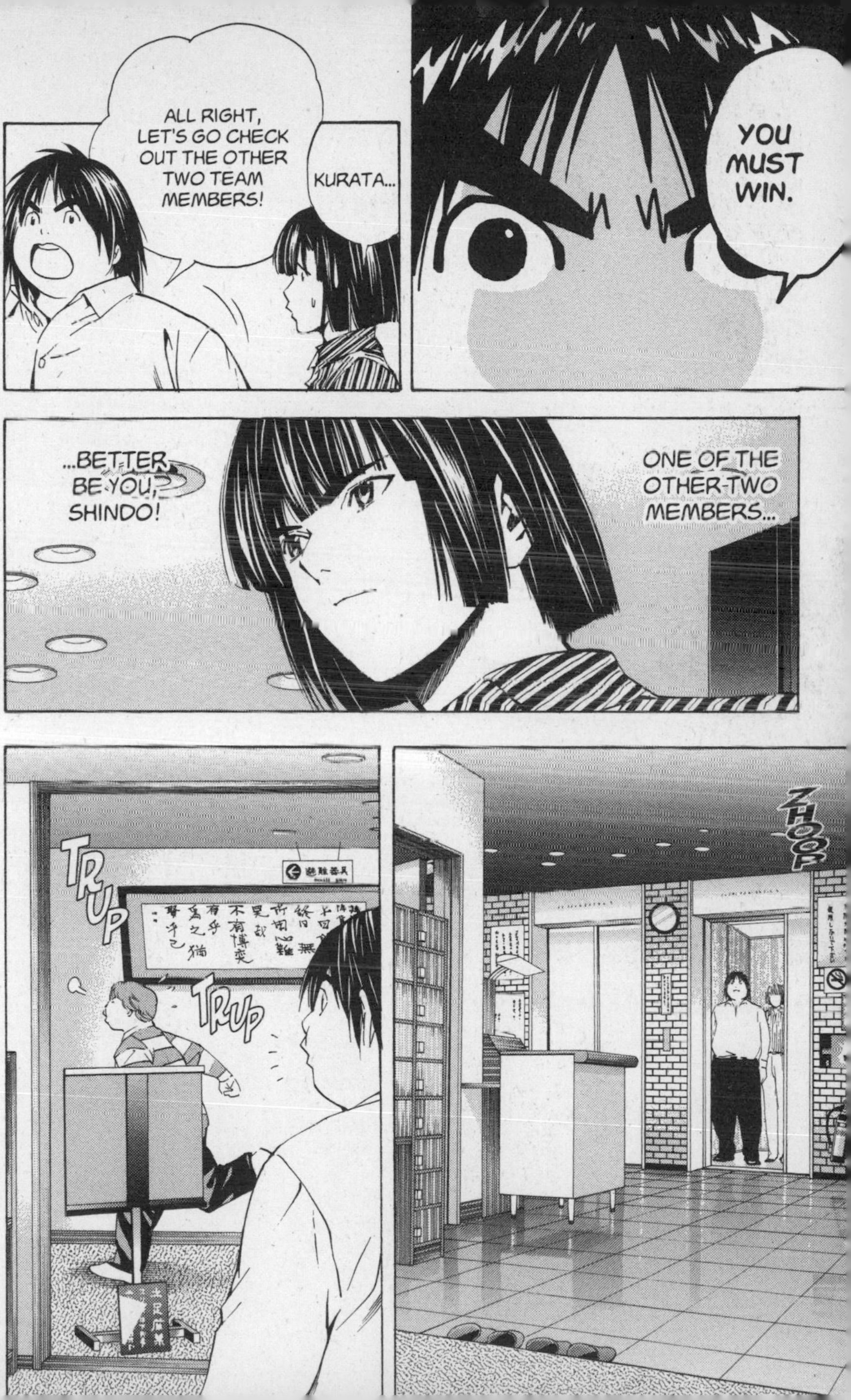
YOU MUST WIN.
ALL RIGHT, LET'S GO CHECK OUT THE OTHER TWO TEAM MEMBERS!
KURATA...
ONE OF THE OTHER-TWO MEMBERS...
...BETTER BE YOU, SHINDO!
ZHOOP
TRUP
TRUP

READ THIS WAY

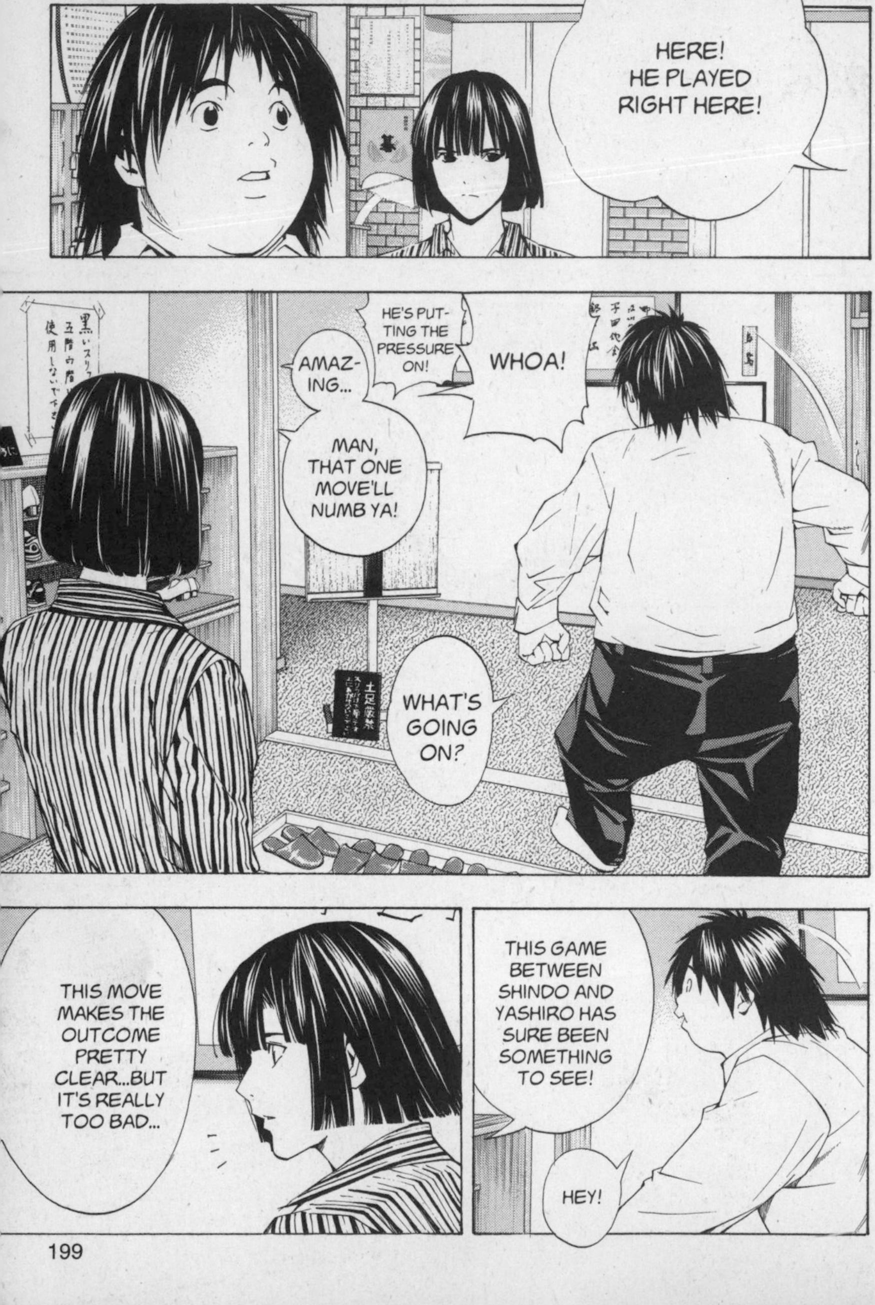
HERE! HE PLAYED RIGHT HERE!
WHOA!
HE'S PUTTING THE PRESSURE ON!
AMAZING...
MAN, THAT ONE MOVE'LL NUMB YA!
WHAT'S GOING ON?
THIS GAME BETWEEN SHINDO AND YASHIRO HAS SURE BEEN SOMETHING TO SEE!
HEY!
THIS MOVE MAKES THE OUTCOME PRETTY CLEAR...BUT IT'S REALLY TOO BAD...

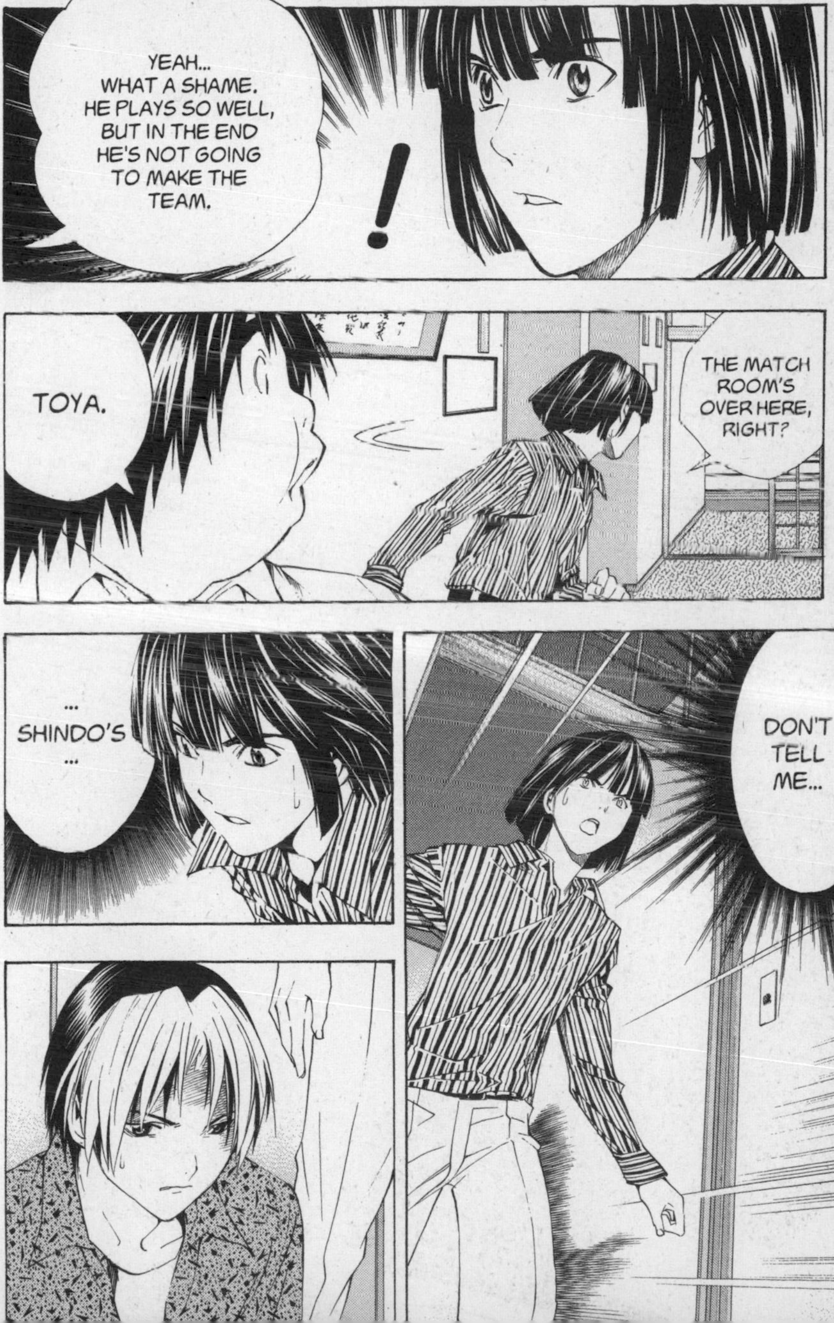
YEAH... WHAT A SHAME. HE PLAYS SO WELL, BUT IN THE END HE'S NOT GOING TO MAKE THE TEAM.
!
THE MATCH ROOM'S OVER HERE, RIGHT?
TOYA.
DON'T TELL ME...
... SHINDO'S ...

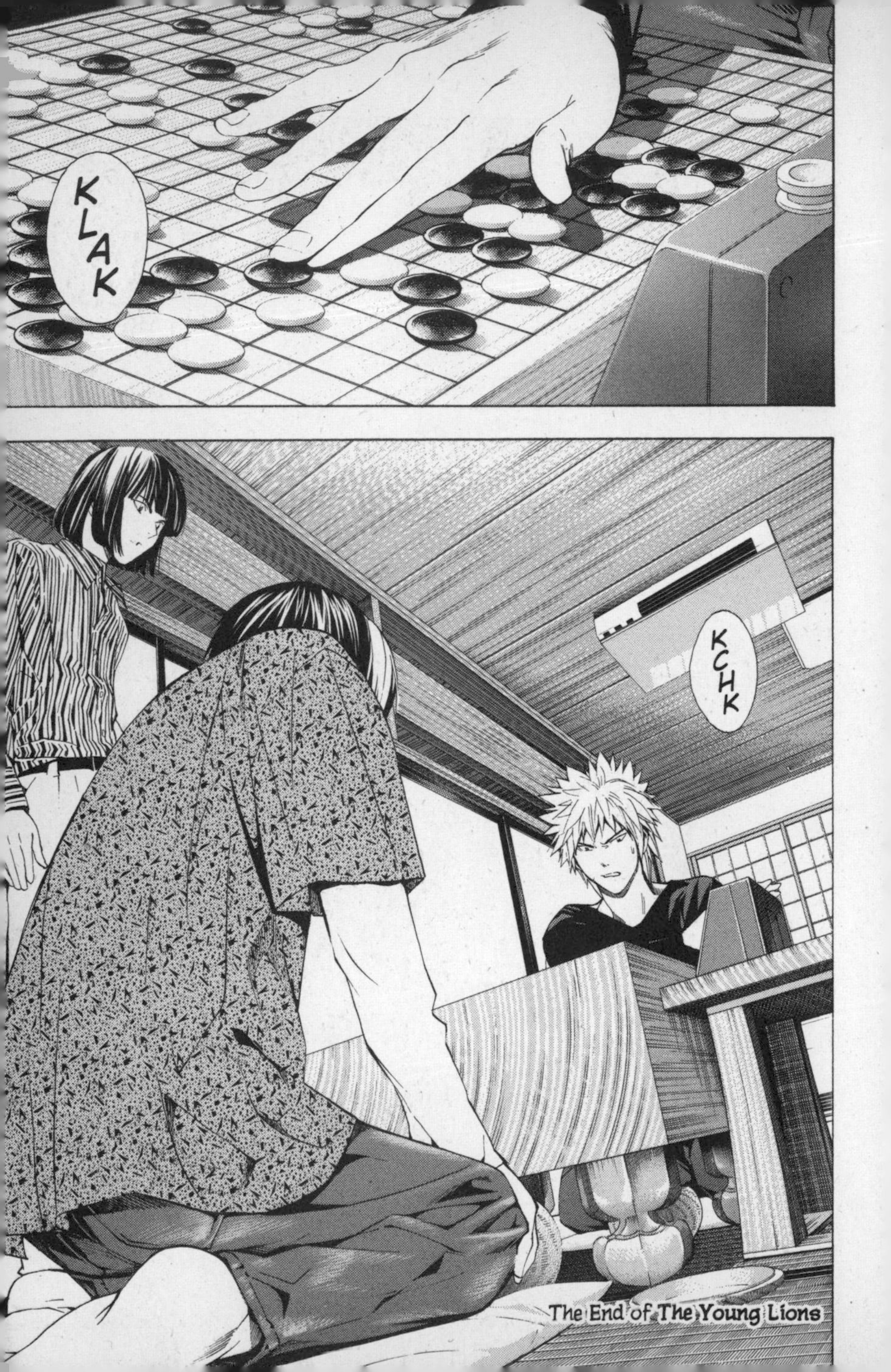
KLAK
KCHK
The End of The Young Lions

Next Volume Preview

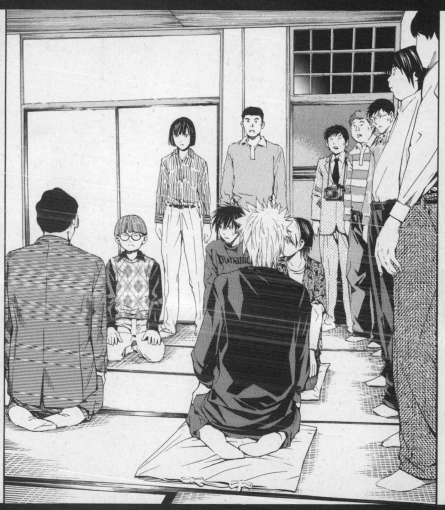

Only three people will be chosen to represent Japan in the Hokuto Cup, and Akira has already nabbed a spot. Attempting to qualify for one of the other two places, Hikaru has played a decidedly unconventional game with Yashiro. Other pro players watching the action can hardly believe what they've seen, but it's their observations that lead to a surprise final skirmish to determine just who will be on Japan's team!

COMING NOVEMBER 2010

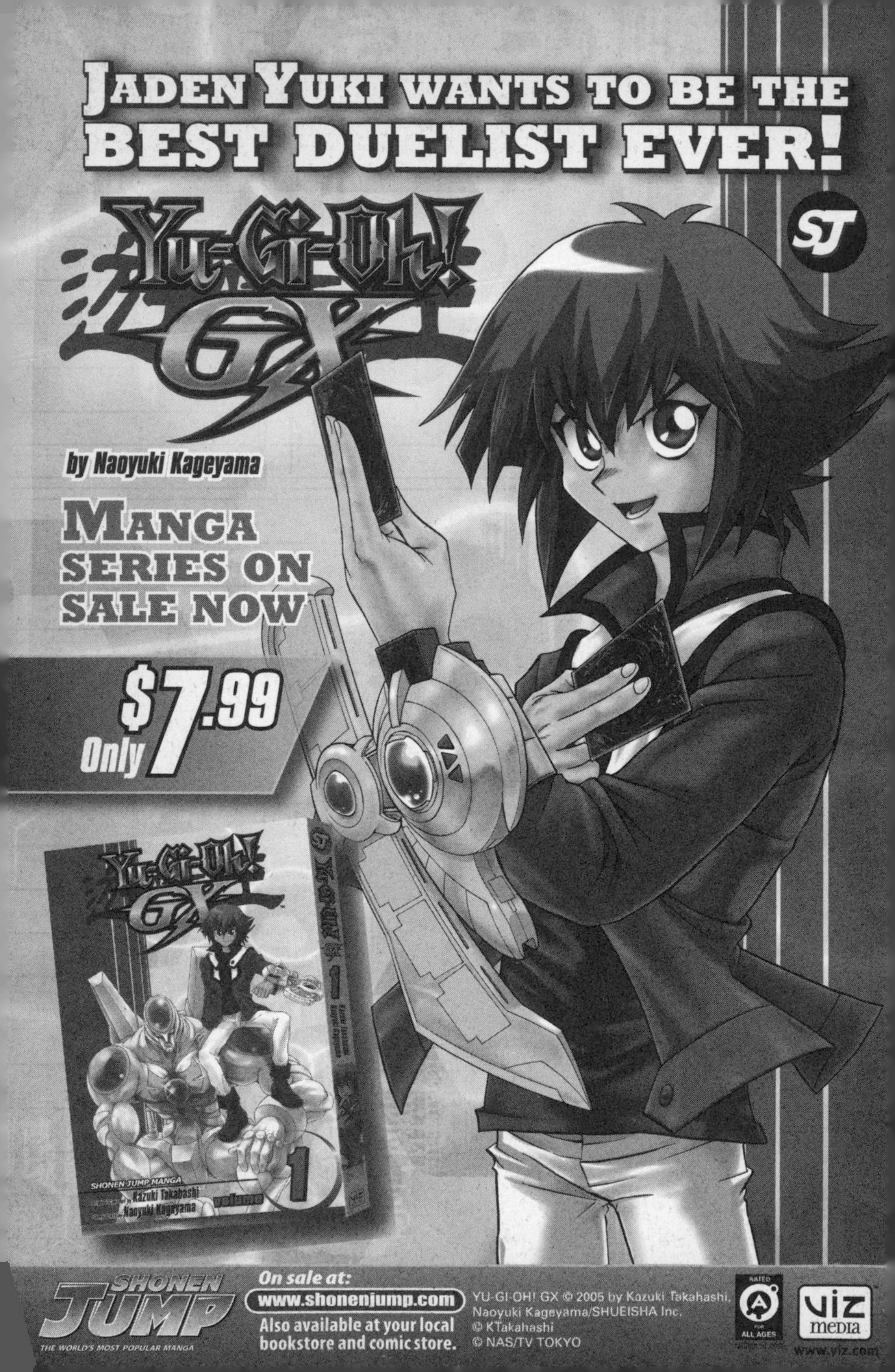
JADEN YUKI WANTS TO BE THE BEST DUELIST EVER!
SJ
YU-GI-OH! GX
by Naoyuki Kageyama
MANGA SERIES ON SALE NOW
Only $7.99
SHONEN JUMP MANGA
Kazuki Takahashi
Naoyuki Kageyama
SHONEN JUMP
THE WORLD'S MOST POPULAR MANGA
On sale at:
www.shonenjump.com
Also available at your local bookstore and comic store.
YU-GI-OH! GX © 2005 by Kazuki Takahashi, Naoyuki Kageyama/SHUEISHA Inc.
© KTakahashi
© NAS/TV TOKYO
RATED A FOR ALL AGES
VIZ media
www.viz.com

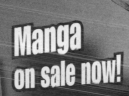

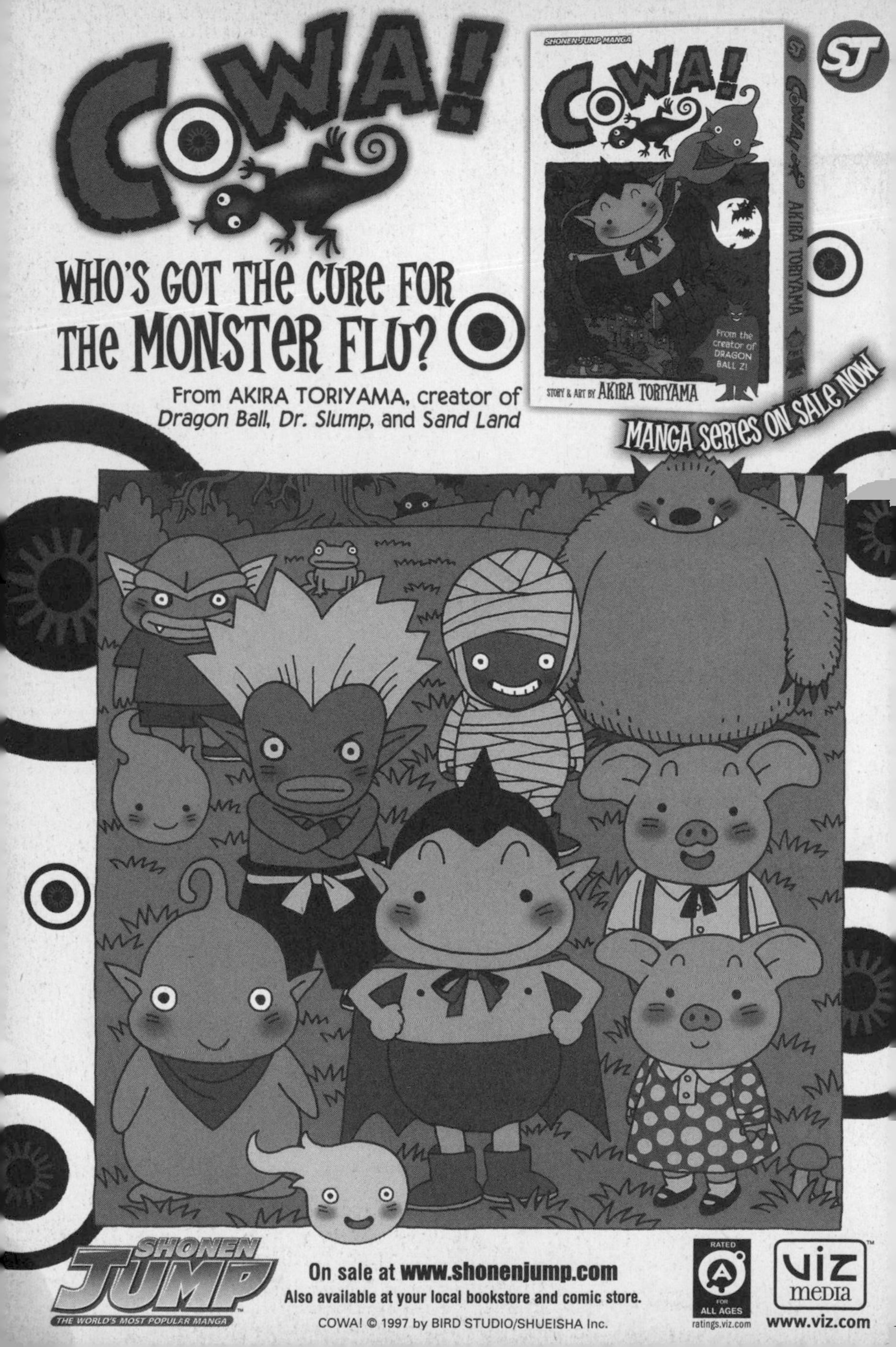
COWA!
WHO'S GOT THE CURE FOR THE MONSTER FLU?
From AKIRA TORIYAMA, creator of Dragon Ball, Dr. Slump, and Sand Land
SHONEN JUMP MANGA
COWA!
From the creator of DRAGON BALL Z!
STORY & ART BY AKIRA TORIYAMA
COWA! AKIRA TORIYAMA
SJ
MANGA SERIES ON SALE NOW
SHONEN JUMP
THE WORLD'S MOST POPULAR MANGA
On sale at www.shonenjump.com
Also available at your local bookstore and comic store.
COWA! © 1997 by BIRD STUDIO/SHUEISHA Inc.
RATED A FOR ALL AGES
ratings.viz.com
VIZ media
www.viz.com

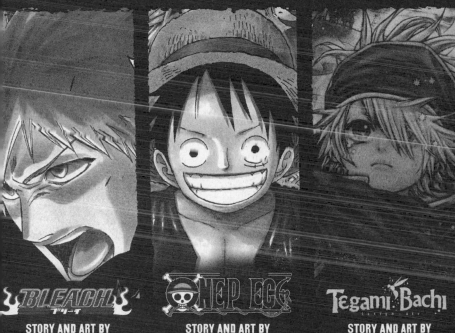

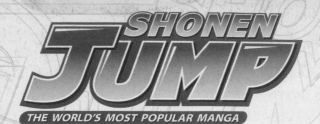
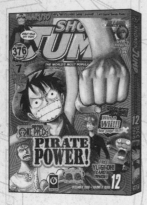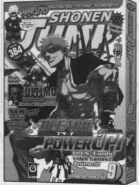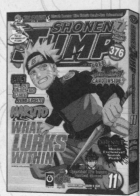

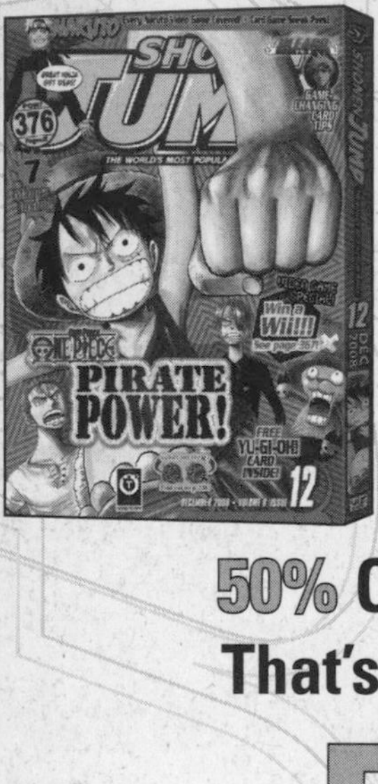

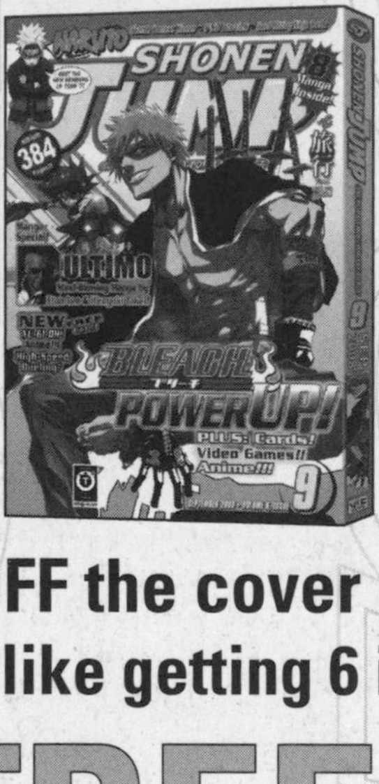

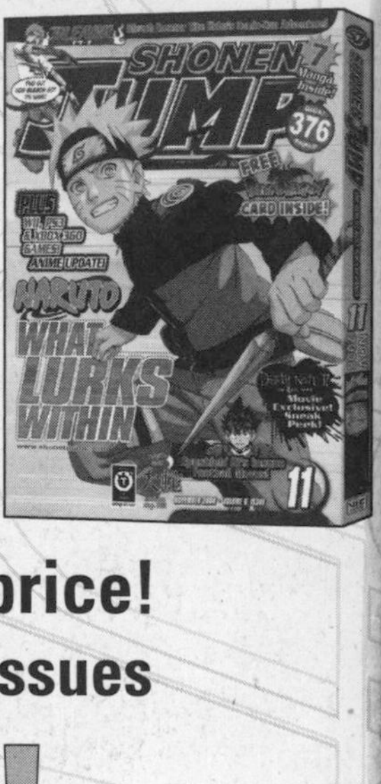

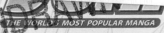

SA~~
TH~~
IT'S~~ **FREE!**

THE WORLD'S MOST POPULAR MANGA

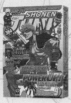

OVER **350+** PAGES PER ISSUE

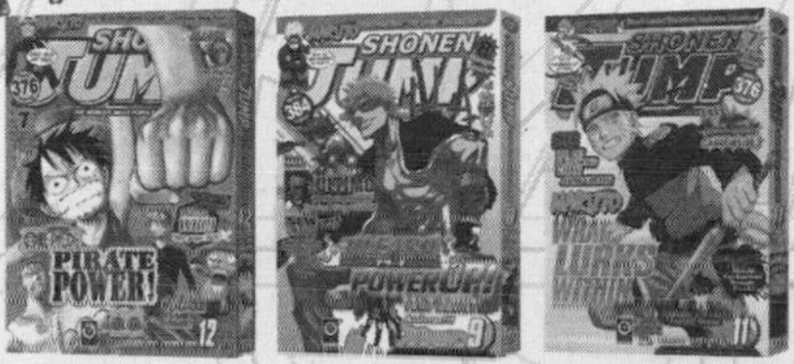

This monthly magazine contains 7 of the coolest manga available in the U.S., PLUS anime news, and info about video & card games, toys AND more!

❏ **I want 12 HUGE issues of SHONEN JUMP for only $29.95*!**

NAME

ADDRESS

CITY/STATE/ZIP

EMAIL ADDRESS   DATE OF BIRTH

❏ YES, send me via email information, advertising, offers, and promotions related
to VIZ Media, SHONEN JUMP, and/or their business partners.

❏ **CHECK ENCLOSED** (payable to SHONEN JUMP)   ❏ **BILL ME LATER**

CREDIT CARD: ❏ **Visa** ❏ **Mastercard**

ACCOUNT NUMBER   EXP. DATE

SIGNATURE

CLIP&MAIL TO:
SHONEN JUMP Subscriptions Service Dept.
P.O. Box 515
Mount Morris, IL 61054-0515

P9GNC1

* Canada price: $41.95 USD, including GST, HST, and QST. US/CAN orders only. Allow 6-8 weeks for delivery.
ONE PIECE © 1997 by Eiichiro Oda/SHUEISHA Inc. BLEACH © 2001 by Tite Kubo/SHUEISHA Inc.
NARUTO © 1999 by Masashi Kishimoto/SHUEISHA Inc.

RATED
TEEN
ratings.viz.com

VIZ
media
www.viz.com